Fodor's *THIRD New EDITION*

Maine, Vermont, New Hampshire

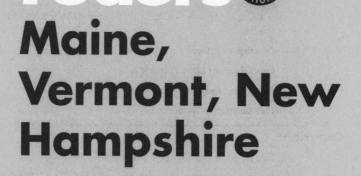

"When it comes to information on regional history, what to see and do, and shopping, these guides are exhaustive."

—*USAir Magazine*

"Usable, sophisticated restaurant coverage, with an emphasis on good value."

—Andy Birsh, *Gourmet Magazine* columnist

"Valuable because of their comprehensiveness."

—*Minneapolis Star-Tribune*

"Fodor's always delivers high quality...thoughtfully presented...thorough."

—*Houston Post*

"An excellent choice for those who want everything under one cover."

—*Washington Post*

Reprinted from *Fodor's New England*

Fodor's Travel Publications, Inc.
New York • Toronto • London • Sydney • Auckland

Fodor's Maine, Vermont, New Hampshire

Editor: Anastasia R. Mills

Contributors: Steven K. Amsterdam, Rob Andrews, Mary Frakes, Tara Hamilton, David Laskin, Hilary Nangle, Tracy Patruno, William G. Scheller, Linda K. Schmidt, Michelle Seaton, M.T. Schwartzman, Dinah Spritzer

Creative Director: Fabrizio La Rocca

Cartographer: David Lindroth

Cover Photograph: Peter Guttman

Text Design: Between the Covers

Copyright

Special Sales

Fodor's Travel Publications are available at special discounts for bulk purchases for sales promotions or premiums. Special editions, including personalized covers, excerpts of existing guides, and corporate imprints, can be created in large quantities for special needs. For more information, contact your local bookseller or write to Special Markets, Fodor's Travel Publications, 201 East 50th Street, New York, NY 10022. Inquiries from Canada should be directed to your local Canadian bookseller or sent to Random House of Canada, Ltd., Marketing Department, 1265 Aerowood Drive, Mississauga, Ontario L4W 1B9. Inquiries from the United Kingdom should be sent to Fodor's Travel Publications, 20 Vauxhall Bridge Road, London, England SW1V 2SA.

MANUFACTURED IN THE UNITED STATES OF AMERICA

10 9 8 7 6 5 4 3 2 1

CONTENTS

ON THE ROAD WITH FODOR'S

A GOOD TRAVEL GUIDE is like a wonderful traveling companion. It's charming, it's brimming with sound recommendations and solid ideas, it pulls no punches in describing lodging and dining establishments, and it's consistently full of fascinating facts that make you view what you've traveled to see in a rich new light. In the creation of *Maine, Vermont, New Hampshire,* we at Fodor's have gone to great lengths to provide you with the very best of all possible traveling companions—and to make your trip the best of all possible vacations.

About Our Writers

The information in these pages is a collaboration of a number of extraordinary writers.

Our Maine updater, **Hilary Nangle,** is the features editor of *the Times Record,* a daily newspaper in Brunswick. She also does freelance travel and ski writing, and formerly specialized in media relations for travel and ski accounts—so she knows this business inside and out.

Tara Hamilton left Fodor's employment in the Big Apple for the fresh air and Green Mountains of Central Vermont. When not producing coffeetable books, she teaches children about the environment and leads outdoor trips. After the bustle of Manhattan, she's enjoying life in the country's least populated state, where she plans to live happily ever after.

An associate editor at *Yankee* magazine, where she covers food and New England history, **Michelle Seaton** updated the New Hampshire chapter.

After many Maine summers, editor **Anastasia Mills** developed her tolerance for swimming in cold water. Although she has sampled the pleasures of 46 states, Mills is determined never to venture too far from her native New England: She believes that a year without making snow angels and crunching on brilliantly colored leaves is a year spent in purgatory.

What's New

A New Design

If this is not the first Fodor's guide you've purchased, you'll immediately notice our new look. More readable and easier-to-use than ever? We think so—and we hope you do, too.

Let Us Do Your Booking

Our writers have scoured Maine, Vermont, and New Hampshire to come up with an extensive and well-balanced list of the best B&Bs, inns, resorts, and hotels, both small and large, new and old. But you don't have to beat the bushes to come up with a reservation. Now we've teamed up with an established hotel-booking service to make it easy for you to secure a room at the property of your choice. It's fast, it's free, and confirmation is guaranteed. If your first choice is booked, the operators can line up your second right away. Just call 800/FODORS–1 or 800/363–6771 (0800/89–1030 when in Great Britain; 0014/800–12–8271 when in Australia; 1800/55–9101 when in Ireland).

Travel Updates

In addition, just before your trip, you may want to order a Fodor's Worldview Travel Update. From local publications all over Maine, Vermont, and New Hampshire, the lively, cosmopolitan editors at Worldview gather information on concerts, plays, opera, dance performances, gallery and museum shows, sports competitions, and other special events that coincide with your visit. See the order blank at the back of this book, call 800/799–9609, or fax 800/799–9619.

And in Maine, Vermont, and New Hampshire

MAINE➤ A new professional opera company, the **Portland Opera Repertory Theatre,** was expected to debut in the summer of 1995 under the direction of Bruce Hangen, former conductor and musical director of the Portland Symphony Orchestra. Productions will be held at the newly renovated **State Theater** in Portland.

The first part of the Sunday River ski resort's new **Bethel Station** development should open late in 1995. It will serve as the train station for Sunday River's Silver Bullet Ski Express train to Portland and also have a 140-room hotel, a movie theater, and retail shops. Also look for growth at the ski resort: **Sunday River** traditionally leads the state in new terrain and lifts each year. **Sugarloaf,** too, is expected to grow rapidly now that Vermont's S-K-I has majority ownership. A new high-speed quad chairlift was put in for 1995, and future plans call for new trails and lifts.

VERMONT➤ Trains are in Vermont's news. **Amtrak** discontinued its *Montrealer* service in 1995 due to low ridership—leaving the state with no passenger rail service—so Vermont subsidized the new *Vermonter,* which still skirts the state's eastern border before slicing over toward Burlington, but commences in Hartford, CT (instead of Washington, D.C.) and terminates in St. Alban's, VT (instead of Montreal). Meanwhile, the state has proposed an alternative route that would run through Vermont's western flanks and link New York City with Rutland and Burlington—resulting in easy access to the slopes. Additionally, Sugarbush Resort's new ownership—which made a windfall by pushing train service from Boston up to the doorstep of their Sunday River, ME resort—has begun a **tourist train** that runs three times daily in warm weather months between Middlebury and Burlington.

NEW HAMPSHIRE➤ Sections of the 250-mile-long **New Hampshire Heritage Trail** have opened, including a 75-mile stretch along the Merrimack River from the Massachusetts border through Nashua and Manchester to Concord, as well as a section in Franconia Notch. The trail may be used for walking, jogging, biking, and cross-country skiing, and connects areas of historic and scenic interest. Eventually it will extend to Canada.

How to Use This Book

Organization
Up front is the **Gold Guide,** comprised of two sections on gold paper that are chock-full of information about traveling within your destination and traveling in general. Both are in alphabetical order by topic. **Important Contacts A to Z** gives addresses

and telephone numbers of organizations and companies that offer destination-related services and detailed information or publications. Here's where you'll find information about how to get to Maine, Vermont, and New Hampshire from wherever you are. **Smart Travel Tips A to Z,** the Gold Guide's second section, gives specific tips on how to get the most out of your travels, as well as information on how to accomplish what you need to in Maine, Vermont, and New Hampshire.

Stars
Stars in the margin denote highly recommended sights, attractions, hotels, and restaurants.

Snowflakes
A snowflake ❄ next to a review marks lodging recommended specifically for skiers.

Restaurant and Hotel Criteria and Price Categories
Restaurants and lodging places are chosen with a view to giving you the cream of the crop in each location and in each price range.

In all restaurant price charts, costs are per person, excluding drinks, tip, and tax. In hotel price charts, rates are for standard double rooms, excluding city and state sales taxes.

Hotel Facilities
Note that in general you incur charges when you use many hotel facilities. We wanted to let you know what facilities a hotel has to offer, but we don't always specify whether or not there's a charge, so when planning a vacation that entails a stay of several days, it's wise to ask what's included in the rate.

Hotel Meal Plans
Assume that hotels operate on the **European Plan** (EP, with no meals) unless we note that they use the **American Plan** (AP, with all meals), the **Modified American Plan** (MAP, with breakfast and dinner daily), or the **Continental Plan** (CP, with a Continental breakfast daily).

Dress Code in Restaurants
Look for an overview in the Packing for Maine, Vermont, and New Hampshire section of Smart Travel Tips A to Z in the Gold Guide pages at the front of this book. In general, we note dress code only

when men are required to wear a jacket or a jacket and tie.

Credit Cards

The following abbreviations are used: **AE,** American Express; **D,** Discover; **DC,** Diners Club; **MC,** MasterCard; and **V,** Visa.

Please Write to Us

Everyone who has contributed to *Maine, Vermont, New Hampshire* has worked hard to make the text accurate. All prices and opening times are based on information supplied to us at press time, and the publisher cannot accept responsibility for any errors that may have occurred. The passage of time will bring changes, so it's always a good idea to call ahead and confirm information when it matters—particularly if you're making a detour to visit specific sights or attractions. When making reservations at a hotel or inn, be sure to mention if you have a disability or are traveling with children, if you prefer a private bath or a certain type of bed, or if you have specific dietary needs or any other concerns.

Were the restaurants we recommended as described? Did our hotel picks exceed your expectations? Did you find a museum we recommended a waste of time? We would love your feedback, positive and negative. If you have complaints, we'll look into them and revise our entries when the facts warrant it. If you've happened upon a special place that we haven't included, we'll pass the information along to the writers so they can check it out. So please send us a letter or postcard (we're at 201 East 50th Street, New York, New York 10022). We'll look forward to hearing from you. And in the meantime, have a wonderful trip!

Karen Cure
Editorial Director

Maine, Vermont, and New Hampshire

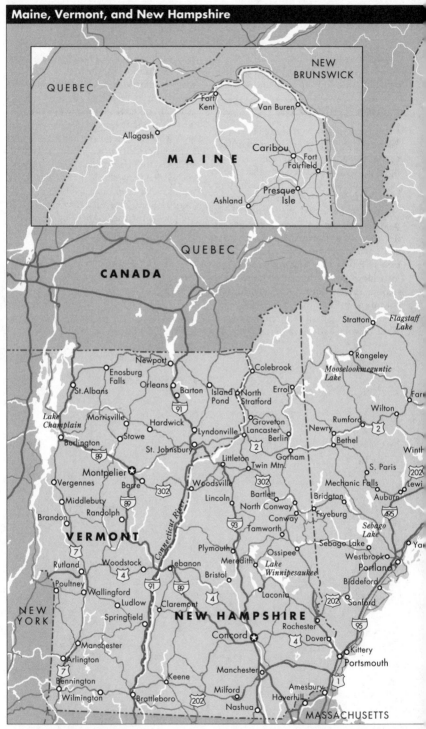

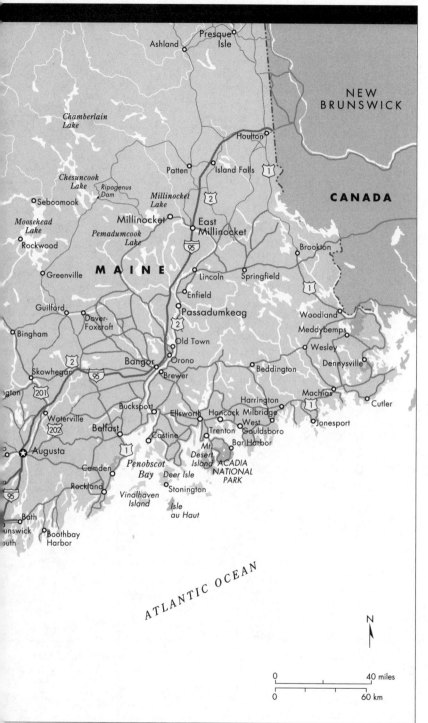

Ashland   Presque
Isle

NEW
BRUNSWICK

Chamberlain
Lake

Houlton

CANADA

Chesuncook
Lake
Ripogenus
Dam

Patten   Island Falls

Millinocket
Lake

Seboomook

Millinocket   East
Millinocket

Brookton

Mooshead
Lake

Pemadumcook
Lake

95

Rockwood

MAINE

Lincoln   Springfield

Greenville

Enfield

Guilford

Passadumkeag

Woodland

Dover-
Foxcroft

2

Meddybemps

Bingham

Old Town

Wesley

Skowhegan

2

Orono

Beddington

Dennysville

95

Bangor

Machias

201

Brewer

Harrington

Cutler

Bucksport

Ellsworth   Hancock Milbridge

1

Waterville

West
Gauldsboro

Jonesport

202

Belfast

Trenton

Castine

Augusta

Bar Harbor

1

Camden

Penobscot
Bay

Mt
Desert
Island

ACADIA
NATIONAL
PARK

95

Rockland

Deer Isle

Vinalhaven
Island

Stonington

Bath

Isle
au Haut

unswick

Boothbay
Harbor

uth

ATLANTIC OCEAN

N

0   40 miles

0   60 km

The United States

THE GOLD GUIDE / IMPORTANT CONTACTS

IMPORTANT CONTACTS A TO Z

An Alphabetical Listing of Publications, Organizations, and Companies That Will Help You Before, During, and After Your Trip

No single travel resource can give you every detail about every topic that might interest or concern you at the various stages of your journey—when you're planning your trip, while you're on the road, and after you get back home. The following organizations, books, and brochures will supplement the information in *Maine, Vermont, New Hampshire*. For related information, including both basic tips on visiting the area and background information on many of the topics below, study Smart Travel Tips A to Z, the section that follows Important Contacts A to Z.

A

AIR TRAVEL

The largest airport in New England is Boston's **Logan International Airport**. Additional New England airports served by major carriers include those in Manchester, New Hampshire; Portland and Bangor, Maine; and Burlington, Vermont. Flying time to Boston is 1 hour from New York, 2 hours and 15 minutes from Chicago, 6 hours from Los Angeles, and 4 hours from Dallas.

CARRIERS

Carriers serving New England include **American** (☎ 800/433–7300), **Continental** (☎ 800/525–0280), **Delta** (800/221–1212), **Northwest** (☎ 800/225–2525), **TWA** (☎ 800/221–2000), **United** (☎ 800/722–5243), and **USAir** (☎ 800/428–4322).

FROM THE U.K.➢ Four airlines fly direct to Boston. **British Airways** (☎ 0181/897–4000) and **American Airlines** (☎ 0345/789–789) depart from Heathrow. **Northwest** (☎ 01293/561–000) and **Virgin Atlantic** (☎ 012393/747–747) fly from Gatwick. Northwest also flies from Glasgow. Flight time is approximately eight hours.

LOW-COST CARRIERS➢ For inexpensive, no-frills flights, contact **Midwest Express** (☎ 800/452–2022), based in Milwaukee, which serves 45 U.S. cities in the Midwest and on both coasts, including Boston.

COMPLAINTS

To register complaints about charter and scheduled airlines, contact the U.S. Department of Transportation's **Office of Consumer Affairs** (400 7th St. NW, Washington, DC 20590, ☎ 202/366–2220 or 800/322–7873).

CONSOLIDATORS

Established consolidators selling to the public

include **Euram Tours** (1522 K St. NW, Suite 430, Washington DC, 20005, ☎ 800/848–6789) and **TFI Tours International** (34 W. 32nd St., New York, NY 10001, ☎ 212/736–1140 or 800/745–8000).

PUBLICATIONS

For general information about charter carriers, ask for the Office of Consumer Affairs' brochure **"Plane Talk: Public Charter Flights."** The Department of Transportation also publishes a 58-page booklet, **"Fly Rights"** ($1.75; Consumer Information Center, Dept. 133-B, Pueblo, CO 81009).

For other tips and hints, consult the Consumers Union's monthly **"Consumer Reports Travel Letter"** ($39 a year; Box 53629, Boulder CO 80322, ☎ 800/234–1970) and the newsletter **"Travel Smart"** ($37 a year; 40 Beechdale Rd., Dobbs Ferry, NY 10522, ☎ 800/327–3633); *The Official Frequent Flyer Guidebook,* by Randy Petersen ($14.99 plus $3 shipping; 4715-C Town Center Dr., Colorado Springs, CO 80916, ☎ 719/597–8899 or 800/487–8893); *Airfare Secrets Exposed,* by Sharon Tyler and Matthew Wonder (Universal Information

Publishing; available for $16.95 plus $3.75 shipping from Sandcastle Publishing, Box 3070-A, South Pasadena, CA 91031, ☎ 213/255–3616 or 800/655 0053); and *202 Tips Even the Best Business Travelers May Not Know,* by Christopher McGinnis ($10 plus $3.00 shipping from Irwin Professional Publishing, 1333 Burr Ridge Pkwy. Burr Ridge, IL 60521, ☎ 708/789–4000 or 800/634–3966).

B

BETTER BUSINESS BUREAU

For other local contacts, consult the **Council of Better Business Bureaus** (4200 Wilson Blvd., Arlington, VA 22203, ☎ 703/276–0100).

BUS TRAVEL

Greyhound Lines (☎ 800/231–2222) provides bus service to major cities and towns in northern New England. **Concord Trailways** (☎ 800/639–3317) connects Boston with Portland, Bangor, and coastal Maine.

C

CAR RENTAL

Major car-rental companies represented in New England include **Alamo** (☎ 800/327–9633, 0800/272–2000 in the U.K.), **Avis** (☎ 800/331–1212, 800/879–2847 in Canada), **Budget** (☎ 800/527–0700, 0800/181–181 in the U.K.), **Hertz** (☎ 800/654–3131, 800/263–0600 in Canada, 0181/679–1799 in the

U.K.), and **National** (☎ 800/227–7368, 0181/950–5050 in the U.K., where it is known as Europcar). Rates in Boston begin at $23 a day and $143 a week for an economy car with unlimited mileage.

CHILDREN AND TRAVEL

DISCOUNT PASS

The **American Lung Association** (☎ 800/458–6472) introduced the "Children's Fun Pass" in 1993; the pass costs $15 annually and gives a child free admission to more than 80 of New England's top attractions with the purchase of an adult admission. Proceeds support the association's many programs aimed at helping children grow up smoke-free.

FLYING

Look into **"Flying With Baby"** ($5.95 plus $1 shipping; Third Street Press, Box 261250, Littleton, CO 80126, ☎ 303/595–5959), cowritten by a flight attendant. **"Kids and Teens in Flight,"** free from the U.S. Department of Transportation's Office of Consumer Affairs, offers tips for children flying alone. Every two years the February issue of **Family Travel Times** (*see* Know-How, *below*), published 10 times a year by Travel With Your Children (TWYCH, 45 W. 18th St., New York, NY 10011, ☎ 212/206–0688; annual subscription $55), covers destinations, types of vacations, and modes of travel.

KNOW-HOW

The *Family Travel Guides* catalog ($1 postage; ☎ 510/527–5849) lists about 200 books and articles on family travel. Also check *Take Your Baby and Go! A Guide for Traveling with Babies, Toddlers and Young Children,* by Sheri Andrews, Judy Bordeaux, and Vivian Vasquez ($5.95 plus $1.50 shipping; Bear Creek Publications, 2507 Minor Ave., Seattle, WA 98102, ☎ 206/322–7604 or 800/326–6566). *The 100 Best Family Resorts in North America,* by Jane Wilford with Janet Tice ($12.95), and the two-volume *50 Great Family Vacations in North America* ($18.95 per volume), both from Globe Pequot Press (plus $3 shipping; Box 833, 6 Business Park Rd., Old Saybrook, CT 06475, ☎ 203/395–0440 or 800/243–0495, 800/962–0973 in CT) help plan your trip with children, from toddlers to teens. Travel With Your Children (*see above*) also publishes *Skiing with Children* ($29).

LOCAL INFORMATION

Consult the lively by-parents for-parents *Where Should We Take the Kids? Northeast* ($17.00; Fodor's Travel Publications, ☎ 800/533–6478 and in bookstores).

TOUR OPERATORS

Contact **Grandtravel** (6900 Wisconsin Ave., Suite 706, Chevy Chase, MD 20815, ☎ 301/986–0790 or 800/247–

THE GOLD GUIDE / IMPORTANT CONTACTS

7651), which has tours for people traveling with grandchildren ages 7 to 17; or **Rascals in Paradise** (650 5th St., Suite 505, San Francisco, CA 94107, ☎ 415/978–9800 or 800/872–7225).

If you're outdoorsy, look into Audubon Society family summer camps and **Ecology Workshops** (613 Riversville Rd., Greenwich, CT 06831, ☎ 203/869–2017).

CUSTOMS

CANADIANS

Contact **Revenue Canada** (2265 St. Laurent Blvd. S, Ottawa, Ontario, K1G 4K3, ☎ 613/993–0534) for a copy of the free brochure **"I Declare/Je Déclare"** and for details on duties that exceed the standard duty-free limit.

U.K. CITIZENS

HM Customs and Excise (Dorset House, Stamford St., London SE1 9NG, ☎ 0171/202–4227) can answer questions about U.K. customs regulations and publishes **"A Guide for Travellers,"** detailing standard procedures and import rules.

D

FOR TRAVELERS WITH DISABILITIES

COMPLAINTS

To register complaints under the provisions of the Americans With Disabilities Act, contact the U.S. Department of Justice's **Public Access Section** (Box 66738, Washington, DC 20035, ☎ 202/514–

0301, TTY 202/514–0383, FAX 202/307–1198).

ORGANIZATIONS

FOR TRAVELERS WITH HEARING IMPAIRMENTS> Contact the **American Academy of Otolaryngology** (1 Prince St., Alexandria, VA 22314, ☎ 703/836–4444, FAX 703/683–5100, TTY 703/519–1585).

FOR TRAVELERS WITH MOBILITY PROBLEMS> Contact the **Information Center for Individuals with Disabilities** (Fort Point Pl., 27–43 Wormwood St., Boston, MA 02210, ☎ 617/727–5540, 800/462–5015 in MA, TTY 617/345–9743); **Mobility International USA** (Box 10767, Eugene, OR 97440, ☎ and TTY 503/343–1284; FAX 503/343–6812), the U.S. branch of an international organization based in Belgium (*see below*) that has affiliates in 30 countries; **MossRehab Hospital Travel Information Service** (1200 W. Tabor Rd., Philadelphia, PA 19141, ☎ 215/456–9603, TTY 215/456–9602); the **Society for the Advancement of Travel for the Handicapped** (347 5th Ave., Suite 610, New York, NY 10016, ☎ 212/447–7284, FAX 212/725–8253); the **Travel Industry and Disabled Exchange** (TIDE, 5435 Donna Ave., Tarzana, CA 91356, ☎ 818/344–3640, FAX 818/344–0078); and **Travelin' Talk** (Box 3534, Clarksville, TN 37043, ☎ 615/552–6670, FAX 615/552–1182).

FOR TRAVELERS WITH VISION IMPAIRMENTS> Contact the **American Council of the Blind** (1155 15th St. NW, Suite 720, Washington, DC 20005, ☎ 202/467–5081, FAX 202/467–5085) or the **American Foundation for the Blind** (15 W. 16th St., New York, NY 10011, ☎ 212/620–2000, TTY 212/620–2158).

IN THE U.K.

Contact the **Royal Association for Disability and Rehabilitation** (RADAR, 12 City Forum, 250 City Rd., London EC1V 8AF, ☎ 0171/250–3222) or **Mobility International** (Rue de Manchester 25, B1070 Brussels, Belgium, ☎ 00–322–410–6297), an international clearinghouse of travel information for people with disabilities.

PUBLICATIONS

Several free publications are available from the U.S. Information Center (Box 100, Pueblo, CO 81009, ☎ 719/948–3334): **"New Horizons for the Air Traveler with a Disability"** (address to Dept. 355A), describing legally mandated changes; the pocket-size **"Fly Smart"** (Dept. 575B), good on flight safety; and the Airport Operators Council's worldwide **Access Travel: Airports** (Dept. 575A).

Fodor's *Great American Vacations for Travelers with Disabilities* ($18; available in bookstores, or call 800/533–6478) details accessible attractions, restaurants, and hotels in U.S. destinations. The 500-page **Travelin' Talk Directory** ($35; Box 3534, Clarksville, TN 37043, ☎ 615/552–6670) lists people and organizations who help travelers with disabilities. For specialist travel agents worldwide, consult the **Directory of Travel Agencies for the Disabled** ($19.95 plus $2 shipping; Twin Peaks Press, Box 129, Vancouver, WA 98666, ☎ 206/694–2462 or 800/ 637–2256). The Sierra Club publishes **Easy Access to National Parks** ($16 plus $3 shipping; 730 Polk St., San Francisco, CA 94109, ☎ 415/776– 2211 or 800/935– 1056).

The New Hampshire office of Vacation Travel publishes the "New Hampshire Guide Book," which includes accessibility ratings for hotels, restaurants, and attractions.

TRAVEL AGENCIES AND TOUR OPERATORS

The Americans with Disabilities Act requires that travel firms serve the needs of all travelers. However, some agencies and operators specialize in making group and individual arrangements for travelers with disabilities, among them **Access Adventures** (206 Chestnut Ridge Rd., Rochester, NY 14624, ☎ 716/889–9096), run by a former physical-rehab counselor. In addition, many general-interest operators and agencies (*see* Tour Operators, *below*) can also arrange vacations

for travelers with disabilities.

FOR TRAVELERS WITH MOBILITY IMPAIRMENTS➤ A number of operators specialize in working with travelers with mobility impairments: **Hinsdale Travel Service** (201 E. Ogden Ave., Suite 100, Hinsdale, IL 60521, ☎ 708/ 325–1335 or 800/303– 5521), a travel agency that will give you access to the services of wheelchair traveler Janice Perkins; and **Wheelchair Journeys** (16979 Redmond Way, Redmond, WA 98052, ☎ 206/ 885–2210), which can handle arrangements worldwide.

FOR TRAVELERS WITH DEVELOPMENTAL DISABILITIES➤ Contact the nonprofit **New Directions** (5276 Hollister Ave., Suite 207, Santa Barbara, CA 93111, ☎ 805/967–2841), for travelers with developmental disabilities and their families, as well as the general-interest operations *above*.

Options include **Entertainment Travel Editions** (fee $28–$53, depending on destination; Box 1068, Trumbull, CT 06611, ☎ 800/445– 4137), **Great American Traveler** ($49.95 annually; Box 27965, Salt

Lake City, UT 84127, ☎ 800/548–2812), **Moment's Notice Discount Travel Club** ($25 annually, single or family; 163 Amsterdam Ave., Suite 137, New York, NY 10023, ☎ 212/486–0500), **Privilege Card** ($74.95 annually; 3391 Peachtree Rd. NE, Suite 110, Atlanta GA 30326, ☎ 404/262–0222 or 800/236–9732), **Travelers Advantage** ($49 annually, single or family; CUC Travel Service, 49 Music Sq. W, Nashville, TN 37203, ☎ 800/548–1116 or 800/ 648–4037), and **Worldwide Discount Travel Club** ($50 annually for family, $40 single; 1674 Meridian Ave., Miami Beach, FL 33139, ☎ 305/534–2082).

ORGANIZATION

The **International Gay Travel Association** (Box 4974, Key West, FL 33041, ☎ 800/ 448–8550), a consortium of 800 businesses, can supply names of travel agents and tour operators.

PUBLICATIONS

The premiere international travel magazine for gays and lesbians is **Our World** ($35 for 10 issues; 1104 N. Nova Rd., Suite 251, Daytona Beach, FL 32117, ☎ 904/441–5367). The 16-page monthly "Out & About" ($49 for 10 issues; ☎ 212/ 645–6922 or 800/ 929–2268), covers gay-friendly resorts, hotels, cruise lines, and airlines.

TOUR OPERATORS

Cruises and resort vacations for gays are handled by **R.S.V.P. Travel Productions** (2800 University Ave. SE, Minneapolis, MN 55414, ☎ 800/328–RSVP); **Toto Tours** (1326 W. Albion Suite 3W, Chicago, IL 60626, ☎ 312/274–8686 or 800/565–1241) has group tours worldwide.

TRAVEL AGENCIES

The largest agencies serving gay travelers are **Advance Travel** (10700 Northwest Freeway, Suite #160, Houston, TX 77092, ☎ 713/682–2002 or 800/695–0880), **Islanders/Kennedy Travel** (183 W. 10th St., New York, NY 10014, ☎ 212/242–3222 or 800/988–1181), **Now Voyager** (4406 18th St., San Francisco, CA 94114, ☎ 415/626–1169 or 800/255–6951), and **Yellowbrick Road** (1500 W. Balmoral Ave., Chicago, IL 60640, ☎ 312/561–1800 or 800/642–2488). **Skylink Women's Travel** (746 Ashland Ave., Santa Monica, CA 90405, ☎ 310/452–0506 or 800/225–5759) works with lesbians.

H
HEALTH ISSUES

For members, the **International Association for Medical Assistance to Travellers** (IAMAT, 417 Center St., Lewiston, NY 14092, ☎ 716/754–4883; 40 Regal Rd., Guelph, Ontario N1K 1B5, ☎ 519/836–0102; 1287 St. Clair Ave., Toronto, Ontario M6E

1B8, ☎ 416/652–0137; 57 Voirets, 1212 Grand-Lancy, Geneva, Switzerland; membership free) publishes a worldwide directory of English-speaking physicians meeting IAMAT standards.

I
INSURANCE

Travel insurance covering baggage, health, and trip cancellations or interruptions are available from **Access America** (Box 90315, Richmond, VA 23286, ☎ 804/285–3300 or 800/284–8300), **Carefree Travel Insurance** (Box 9366, 100 Garden City Plaza, Garden City, NY 11530, ☎ 516/294–0220 or 800/323–3149), **Near** (Box 1339, Calumet City, IL 60409, ☎ 708/868–6700 or 800/654–6700), **Tele-Trip** (Mutual of Omaha Plaza, Box 31716, Omaha, NE 68131, ☎ 800/228–9792), **Travel Insured International** (Box 280568, East Hartford, CT 06128-0568, ☎ 203/528–7663 or 800/243–3174), and **Travel Guard International** (1145 Clark St., Stevens Point, WI 54481, ☎ 715/345–0505 or 800/826–1300).

IN THE U.K.

The **Association of British Insurers** (51 Gresham St., London EC2V 7HQ, ☎ 0171/600–3333; 30 Gordon St., Glasgow G1 3PU, ☎ 0141/226–3905; Scottish Provident Bldg., Donegall Sq. W, Belfast BT1 6JE, ☎ 01232/249176; and other locations) gives

advice by phone and publishes the free pamphlet **"Holiday Insurance,"** which sets out typical policy provisions and costs.

L
LODGING
APARTMENT AND VILLA RENTALS

Among the companies to contact are **Hometours International** (Box 11503, Knoxville, TN 37939, ☎ 615/588–8722 or 800/367–4668), and **Vacation Home Rentals Worldwide** (235 Kensington Ave., Norwood, NJ 07648, ☎ 201/767–9393 or 800/633–3284). Members of the travel club **Hideaways International** ($99 annually; 767 Islington St., Portsmouth, NH 03801, ☎ 603/430–4433 or 800/843–4433) receive two annual guides plus quarterly newsletters, and arrange rentals among themselves.

HOME EXCHANGE

Principal clearinghouses include **Intervac International** ($65 annually; Box 590504, San Francisco, CA 94159, ☎ 415/435–3497), which has three annual directories; and **Loan-a-Home** ($35–$45 annually; 2 Park La., Apt. 6E, Mount Vernon, NY 10552-3443, ☎ 914/664–7640), which specializes in long-term exchanges.

M
MONEY MATTERS
ATMS

For specific **Cirrus** locations in the United

States and Canada, call 800/424–7787. For U.S. **Plus** locations, call 800/843–7587 and enter the area code and first three digits of the number you're calling from (or of the calling area where you want an ATM).

WIRING FUNDS

Funds can be wired via **American Express MoneyGram** (☎ 800/926–9400 from the U.S. and Canada for locations and information) or **Western Union** (☎ 800/325–6000 for agent locations or to send using MasterCard or Visa, 800/321–2923 in Canada).

P

PASSPORTS AND VISAS

U.K. CITIZENS

For fees, documentation requirements, and to get an emergency passport, call the **London passport office** (☎ 0171/271–3000). For visa information, call the **U.S. Embassy Visa Information Line** (☎ 0891/200–290; calls cost 48p per minute or 36p per minute cheap rate) or write the **U.S. Embassy Visa Branch** (5 Upper Grosvenor St., London W1A 2JB). If you live in Northern Ireland, write the **U.S. Consulate General** (Queen's House, 4 Queen St., Belfast BTI 6EQ).

PHOTO HELP

The **Kodak Information Center** (☎ 800/242–2424) answers consumer questions about film and photography.

R

RAIL TRAVEL

Taking the place of **Amtrak**'s (☎ 800/872–7245) *Montrealer,* the *Vermonter* runs from Hartford, CT to St. Albans, VT, skirting Vermont's eastern border before slicing over to Burlington.

The **Massachusetts Bay Transportation Authority** (☎ 617/722–5000) connects Boston with outlying areas on the north and south shores of the state. Canada's **VIA Rail** (☎ 514/871–1331 in Montreal, or contact a travel agent) crosses Maine, providing its only rail service, en route between Montréal and Halifax, stopping at Jackman, Greenville, Brownville Junction, Mattawamkeag, Danforth, and Vanceboro.

S

SENIOR CITIZENS

EDUCATIONAL TRAVEL

The nonprofit **Elderhostel** (75 Federal St., 3rd Floor, Boston, MA 02110, ☎ 617/426–7788), for people 60 and older, has offered inexpensive study programs since 1975. The nearly 2,000 courses cover everything from marine science to Greek myths and cowboy poetry. Fees for programs in the United States and Canada, which usually last one week, run about $300, not including transportation.

ORGANIZATIONS

Contact the **American Association of Retired Persons** (AARP, 601 E St., NW, Washington, DC 20049, ☎ 202/434–2277; $8 per person or couple annually). Its Purchase Privilege Program gets members discounts on lodging, car rentals, and sightseeing, and the AARP Motoring Plan furnishes domestic trip-routing information and emergency road-service aid for an annual fee of $39.95 per person or couple ($59.95 for a premium version).

For other discounts on lodgings, car rentals, and other travel products, along with magazines and newsletters, contact the **National Council of Senior Citizens** (membership $12 annually; 1331 F St. NW, Washington, DC 20004, ☎ 202/347–8800) and **Mature Outlook** (subscription $9.95 annually; 6001 N. Clark St., Chicago, IL 60660, ☎ 312/465–6466 or 800/336–6330).

PUBLICATIONS

The 50+ Traveler's Guidebook: Where to Go, Where to Stay, What to Do, by Anita Williams and Merrimac Dillon ($12.95; St. Martin's Press, 175 5th Ave., New York, NY 10010, ☎ 212/674–5151 or 800/288–2131), offers many useful tips. **"The Mature Traveler"** ($29.95; Box 50400, Reno, NV 89513, ☎ 702/786–7419), a monthly newsletter, covers travel deals.

SHOPPING

Send an SASE to the **Vermont Antiques**

THE GOLD GUIDE / IMPORTANT CONTACTS

Dealers Association (c/o Murial McKirryher, 55 Allen St., Rutland, VT 05701) or the **Maine Antique Dealers Association** (c/o Jane Carr, 105 Mighty St., Gorham, ME 04038) for copies of their annual directories.

The **New Hampshire Department of Agriculture** (Box 2042, Concord, NH 03302, ☎ 603/271–3551) publishes lists of maple-syrup producers and farmers' markets in the state.

SPORTS

BIKING

Free information on biking trails is available from the Maine Publicity Bureau and the Vermont Travel Division; other sources include **Maine Sport** (Rte. 1, Rockport 04856, ☎ 207/236–8797 or 800/722–0826) and **Vermont Bicycle Touring** (Box 711, Bristol 05443, ☎ 802/453–4811).

FISHING

Freshwater lake fishing, surf-casting, deep-sea fishing, angling and trout fishing are among the offerings in the area. Contact the **Maine Department of Inland Fisheries and Wildlife** (284 State St., State House Station 41, Augusta, ME 04333, ☎ 207/287–2043); the **New Hampshire Fish and Game Department** (2 Hazen Dr., Concord, NH 03301, ☎ 603/271–3421); or the **Vermont Fish and Wildlife Department** (103 S. Main St., Waterbury, VT 05676, ☎ 802/241–3700).

HIKING

For free information on hiking the Appalachian Trail contact the Appalachian Mountain Club (Box 298, Gorham, NH 03581, ☎ 603/466–2725) and the White Mountains National Forest (Box 638, Laconia, NH 03247, ☎ 603/528–8721). The **Audubon Society of New Hampshire** (3 Silk Rd., Concord, NH 03301, ☎ 603/224–9909) maintains marked trails for hikers in parks throughout the region.

STUDENTS

GROUPS

A major tour operator is **Contiki Holidays** (300 Plaza Alicante, Suite #900, Garden Grove, CA 92640, ☎ 714/740–0808 or 800/466–0610).

HOSTELING

Contact **Hostelling International–American Youth Hostels** (733 15th St., NW, Suite 840, Washington, DC 20005, ☎ 202/783–6161). Membership ($25) gets you access to 5,000 hostels worldwide that charge $7–$20 nightly per person.

I.D. CARDS

For discounts on transportation and admissions, get the **International Student Identity Card** (ISIC) if you're a bona fide student or the **International Youth Card** (IYC) if you're under 26. In the United States, the ISIC and IYC cards cost $16 each and include basic travel accident and illness coverage, plus a toll-free travel hot line.

Apply through the Council on International Educational Exchange (*see below*). Cards are available for $15 each in Canada from **Travel Cuts** (187 College St., Toronto, Ontario M5T 1P7, ☎ 416/979–2406 or 800/667–2887) and in the United Kingdom for £5 each respectively at student unions and student travel companies.

ORGANIZATIONS

A major contact is the **Council on International Educational Exchange** (CIEE, 205 E. 42nd St., 16th Floor, New York, NY 10017, ☎ 212/661–1450) with locations in Boston (729 Boylston St., Boston, MA 02116, ☎ 617/266–1926), Miami (9100 S. Dadeland Blvd., Miami, FL 33156, ☎ 305/670–9261), Los Angeles (10904 Lindbrook Dr., Los Angeles, CA 90024, ☎ 310/208–3551), 43 college towns nationwide, and the United Kingdom (28A Poland St., London W1V 3DB, ☎ 0171/437–7767). Twice a year, it publishes *Student Travels* magazine. The CIEE's Council Travel Service offers domestic air passes for bargain travel within the United States and is the exclusive U.S. agent for several student-discount cards.

Campus Connections (325 Chestnut St., Suite 1101, Philadelphia, PA 19106, ☎ 215/625–8585 or 800/428–3235) specializes in discounted accommodations and airfares for students. The **Educa-**

tional Travel Centre (438 N. Frances St., Madison, WI 53703, ☎ 608/256–5551) offers rail passes and low-cost airline tickets, mostly for flights departing from Chicago.

In Canada, also contact **Travel Cuts** (*see above*).

TOUR OPERATORS

Among the companies selling tours and packages to northern New England, the following have a proven reputation, are nationally known, and have plenty of options to choose from.

GROUP TOURS

For deluxe escorted motor-coach tours of New England, contact **Maupintour** (Box 807, Lawrence KS 66044, ☎ 800/255–4266 or 913/843–1211) and **Tauck Tours** (11 Wilton Rd., Westport, CT 06880, ☎ 800/468–2825 or 203/226–6911). Another operator falling between deluxe and first-class is **Globus** (5301 South Federal Circle, Littleton, CO 80123-2980, ☎ 800/221–0090 or 303/797–2800). In the first-class and tourist range, try **Mayflower Tours** (1225 Warren Ave., Downers Grove, IL 60515, ☎ 708/960–3430 or 800/323–7064), **Collette Tours** (162 Middle St., Pawtucket, RI 02860, ☎ 800/832–4656 or 401/728–3805), and **Domenico Tours** (750 Broadway, Bayonne, NJ 07002, ☎ 800/554–8687 or 201/823–8687). For budget and tourist class programs,

contact **Cosmos** (*see* Globus, *above*).

PACKAGES

Independent vacation packages including airfare, car rental, accommodations and sightseeing are available from **American Airlines Fly AAway Vacations** (☎ 800/321–2121), **Delta Dream Vacations** (800/872–7786), and **United Airlines Vacation Planning Center** (☎ 800/328–6877). For packages to Boston, try **SuperCities** (239 Main St., Cambridge, MA 02142, ☎ 800/333–1234).

THEME TRIPS

ADVENTURE➤ **All Adventure Travel** (5589 Arapahoe #208, Boulder, CO 80303, ☎ 800/537–4025) books camping, canoe, sailing, and hiking trips.

BICYCLING➤ Contact **Backroads** (1516 5th St., Suite A550, Berkeley, CA 94710, ☎ 510/527–1555 or 800/462–2848), or for those on a more limited budget, **Cycle America** (Box 485, Cannon Falls, MN 55009, ☎ 800/245–3263).

FALL FOLIAGE➤ All of the group tour operators mentioned above have fall foliage itineraries.

HIKING➤ Look into **Hiking Holidays** (Box 750 Bristol, VT 05443, ☎ 802/453–4816), **Hike Inn to Inn** (RR 3, Box 3115, Brandon, VT 05733, ☎ 802/247–3300), and **New England Hiking Holidays** (Box 1648, North Conway, NH 03860, ☎ 800/869–0949) for

backcountry hiking and stays at inns with character. Also try **Country Walkers** (Box 180S, Waterbury, VT 05676, ☎ 802/244–1387).

HORSEBACK RIDING➤ Try **FITS Equestrian** (685 Lateen Rd., Solvang, CA 93463, ☎ 805/688–9494 or 800/666–3487).

INN-HOPPING➤ **Winding Roads Tours** (249 Ball Pond Rd., New Fairfield, CT 06812, ☎ 203/746–4998 or 800/240–4363) has small group tours throughout New England for fans of charming and historic inns. **DestINNations New England** (Box 1173, Osterville, MA 02655, ☎ 800-333-4667) arranges personalized touring itineraries.

SKIING➤ **Backroads** (*see* Adventure, *above*) has cross-country adventure tours in several New England states.

WHALE-WATCHING➤ **Oceanic Society Expeditions** (Fort Mason Center, Bldg. E, San Francisco, CA 04123, ☎ 415/441–1106 or 800/326–7491) cruises the New England coastline searching (usually successfully) for whales.

YACHT CHARTERS➤ For crewed or bareboat sailing off the New England Coast, try **Lynn Jachney Charters** (Box 302, Marblehead, MA 01945, ☎ 617/639–0787 or 800/223–2050), **Nicholson Yacht Charters** (432 Columbia St., Cambridge, MA 02141, ☎ 617/225–0555 or 800/662–6066), **Ocean Voyages**

THE GOLD GUIDE / IMPORTANT CONTACTS

THE GOLD GUIDE / IMPORTANT CONTACTS

(1709 Bridgeway, Sausalito, CA 94965, ☎ 415/332–4281), and **Russell Yacht Charters** (404 Hulls Hwy., Suite 175. Southport, CT 06490, ☎ 203/255–2783 or 800/635–8895).

ORGANIZATIONS

The **National Tour Association** (546 E. Main St., Lexington, KY 40508, ☎ 606/226–4444 or 800/682–8886) and **United States Tour Operators Association** (USTOA, 211 E. 51st St., Suite 12B, New York, NY 10022, ☎ 212/750–7371) can provide lists of member operators and information on booking tours.

PUBLICATIONS

Consult the brochure **"Worldwide Tour & Vacation Package Finder"** from the National Tour Association (*see above*) and the Better Business Bureau's **"Tips on Travel Packages"** (publication No. 24-195, $2; 4200 Wilson Blvd., Arlington, VA 22203).

TRAVEL AGENCIES

For names of reputable agencies in your area, contact the **American**

Society of Travel Agents (1101 King St., Suite 200, Alexandria, VA 22314, ☎ 703/739–2782).

V

VISITOR

INFORMATION

Contact the following for information in their respective areas.

Maine Publicity Bureau, 325-B Water St., Box 2300, Hallowell, ME 04347, ☎ 207/623–0363 or 800/533–9595.

Maine Innkeepers Association, 305 Commercial St., Portland, ME 04101, ☎ 207/773–7670.

Maine Bureau of Parks and Recreation, State House Station 22, Augusta, ME 04033, ☎ 207/287–3821.

New Hampshire Office of Travel and Tourism Development, Box 856, Concord, NH 03302, ☎ 603/271–2343 or, for a recorded message about seasonal events, 800/258–3608.

New Hampshire Division of Parks and Recreation, Box 856, Concord, NH 03302, ☎ 603/271–3254.

Vermont Travel Division, 134 State St., Montpelier, VT 05602, ☎ 802/828–3236 or, for a brochure, ☎ 800/837–6668.

Vermont Chamber of Commerce, Department of Travel and Tourism, Box 37, Montpelier, VT 05601, ☎ 802/223–3443.

Vermont Department of Forests, Parks, and Recreation, 103 S. Main St., 10 South, Waterbury, VT 05671, ☎ 802/241–3655.

In the U.K., also contact the **United States Travel and Tourism Administration** (Box 1EN, London W1A 1EN, ☎ 0171/495-4466). For a free USA pack, write the USTTA at Box 170, Ashford, Kent TN24 0ZX). Enclose stamps worth £1.50.

W

WEATHER

For current weather and forecasts, plus the local time and helpful travel tips, call the **Weather Channel Connection** (☎ 900/932–8437; 95¢ per minute) from a touch-tone phone.

SMART TRAVEL TIPS A TO Z

Basic Information on Traveling in Maine, Vermont, and New Hampshire and Savvy Tips to Make Your Trip a Breeze

The more you travel, the more you know about how to make trips run like clockwork. To help make your travels hassle-free, Fodor's editors have rounded up dozens of tips from our contributors and travel experts all over the world, as well as basic information on visiting Maine, Vermont, and New Hampshire. For names of organizations to contact and publications that can give you more information, *see* Important Contacts A to Z, *above*.

A
AIR TRAVEL

If time is an issue, **always look for nonstop flights,** which require no change of planes and make no stops. If possible, **avoid connecting flights,** which stop at least once and can involve a change of planes, although the flight number remains the same; if the first leg is late, the second waits.

CUTTING COSTS

The Sunday travel section of most newspapers is a good source for deals.

MAJOR AIRLINES➤ The least-expensive airfares from the major airlines are priced for round-trip travel and are subject to restrictions. You must usually **book in advance and buy the ticket within 24 hours** to get cheaper fares, and you may have to **stay over a Saturday night** or possibly at least seven and no more than 30 days). The lowest fare is subject to availability, and only a small percentage of the plane's total seats are sold at that price. It's good to **call a number of airlines—and when you are quoted a good price, book it on the spot**—the same fare on the same flight may not be available the next day. Airlines generally allow you to change your return date for a $25 to $50 fee, but most low-fare tickets are nonrefundable. However, if you don't use it, you can apply the cost toward the purchase price of a new ticket, again for a small charge.

CONSOLIDATORS➤ Consolidators, who buy tickets at reduced rates from scheduled airlines, sell them at prices below the lowest available price from the airlines directly—usually without advance restrictions. Sometimes you can even get your money back if you need to return the ticket. Carefully read the fine print detailing penalties for changes and cancellations. If you doubt the reliability of a consolidator, confirm your reservation with the airline.

ALOFT

AIRLINE FOOD➤ If you hate airline food, **ask for special meals when booking.** These can be vegetarian, low cholesterol, or kosher, for example; commonly prepared to order in smaller quantities than standard catered fare, they can be tastier.

SMOKING➤ Smoking is banned on all flights within the U.S. of less than six hours' duration.

C
CAMERAS, CAMCORDERS, AND COMPUTERS

LAPTOPS

Before you depart, **check your portable computer's battery,** because you may be asked at security to turn on the computer to prove that it is what it appears to be. At the airport, you may prefer to **request a manual inspection,** although security X-rays do not harm hard-disk or floppy-disk storage.

PHOTOGRAPHY

If your camera is new or if you haven't used it for a while, **shoot and develop a few rolls of film** before you leave. Always **store film in a cool, dry place**—never in the car's glove compartment or on the shelf under the rear window.

Every pass through an X-ray machine increases film's chance of clouding. To protect it, carry it in a clear plastic bag and **ask for hand inspection at security.** Such requests are virtually always honored at U.S. airports.

VIDEO

Before your trip, **test your camcorder, invest in a skylight filter to protect the lens, and charge the batteries.** (Airport security personnel may ask you to turn on the camcorder to prove that it's what it appears to be).

Videotape is not damaged by X-rays, but it may be harmed by the magnetic field of a walk-through metal detector, so **ask that videotapes be hand-checked.**

CHILDREN AND TRAVEL

In northern New England, there's no shortage of things to do with children. Major museums have children's sections, and **there are children's museums in cities large and small.** Children love the roadside attractions found in many tourist areas, and **miniature golf courses are easy to come by.** Attractions such as **beaches and boat rides, parks and planetariums, lighthouses and llama treks are fun for youngsters as are special events, such as crafts fairs and food festivals.**

BABY-SITTING

For recommended local sitters, **check with your hotel desk.**

DINING

As for restaurants, you don't have to stick with fast food. Asking around will turn up family-oriented restaurants that specialize in pizza or pasta and come equipped with Trivial Pursuit cards, pull toys, fish tanks, and other families traveling with children—sure-fire entertainment for the interval between ordering and eating. A New England–based restaurant chain known for its legendary ice cream desserts, Friendly's is particularly family-friendly: In some, you'll find crayons on the tables and a rack of children's books not far from the stack of booster seats. Like many restaurants in the region, **Friendly's has a children's menu and an array of special deals for families.**

DRIVING

If you are renting a car, **arrange for a car seat when you reserve.** Sometimes they're free.

FLYING

On domestic flights, children under 2 not occupying a seat travel free, and older children currently travel on the "lowest applicable" adult fare.

BAGGAGE➤ In general, the adult baggage allowance applies for children paying half or more of the adult fare.

SAFETY SEATS➤ According to the FAA, it's a good idea to **use safety seats aloft.** Airline policy varies. U.S. carriers allow FAA-approved models, but airlines usually require that you buy a ticket, even if your child would otherwise ride free, because the seats must be strapped into regular passenger seats.

FACILITIES➤ When making your reservation, **ask for children's meals or freestanding bassinets** if you need them; the latter are available only to those with seats at the bulkhead, where there's enough legroom. If you don't need bassinets, **think twice before requesting bulkhead seats**—the only storage for inflight necessities is in the inconveniently distant overhead bins.

LODGING

Most hotels allow children under a certain age to stay in their parents' room at no extra charge, while others charge them as extra adults; be sure to **ask about the cut-off age.** Chain hotels and motels welcome children, and northern New England has many family-oriented resorts with lively children's programs. You'll also find family farms that accept guests and that are lots of fun for children; the Vermont Travel Division (*see* Visitor Information, *above*) publishes a directory. Rental houses and apartments abound, particularly around ski areas; off-season, these can be economical as well as comfortable touring bases. Some country inns, especially those with a quiet, romantic atmosphere and those furnished with antiques, are less enthusiastic about small fries.

CUSTOMS
AND DUTIES

BACK HOME

IN CANADA➤ Once per calendar year, when you've been out of Canada for at least seven days, you may bring in C$300 worth of goods duty-free. If you've been away less than seven days but more than 48 hours, the duty-free exemption drops to C$100 but can be claimed any number of times (as can a C$20 duty-free exemption for absences of 24 hours or more). You cannot combine the yearly and 48-hour exemptions, use the C$300 exemption only partially (to save the balance for a later trip), or pool exemptions with family members. Goods claimed under the C$300 exemption may follow you by mail; those claimed under the lesser exemptions must accompany you.

Alcohol and tobacco products may be included in the yearly and 48-hour exemptions but not in the 24-hour exemption. If you meet the age requirements of the province through which you reenter Canada, you may bring in, duty-free, 1.14 liters (40 imperial ounces) of wine or liquor *or* 24 12-ounce cans or bottles of beer or ale. If you are 16 or older, you may bring in, duty-free,

200 cigarettes, 50 cigars or cigarillos, and 400 tobacco sticks or 400 grams of manufactured tobacco. Alcohol and tobacco must accompany you on your return.

An unlimited number of gifts valued up to C$60 each may be mailed to Canada duty-free. These do not count as part of your exemption. Label the package "Unsolicited Gift— Value under $60." Alcohol and tobacco are excluded.➤

IN THE U.K.➤ From countries outside the EU, including the U.S., you may import duty-free 200 cigarettes, 100 cigarillos, 50 cigars or 250 grams of tobacco; 1 liter of spirits or 2 liters of fortified or sparkling wine; 2 liters of still table wine; 60 milliliters of perfume; 250 milliliters of toilet water; plus £136 worth of other goods, including gifts and souvenirs.

D
FOR TRAVELERS
WITH DISABILITIES

In Kennebunkport, like in many of Maine's coastal towns south of Portland, travelers with mobility problems will have to cope with crowds as well as with narrow, uneven steps, and sporadic curb cuts. L.L. Bean's outlet in Freeport is fully accessible, and Acadia National Park has some 50 accessible miles of carriage roads that are closed to motor vehicles. In New Hampshire, many of Franconia Notch's

natural attractions are accessible.

When discussing accessibility with an operator or reservationist, **ask hard questions.** Are there any stairs, inside *or* out? Are there grab bars next to the toilet *and* in the shower/tub? How wide is the doorway to the room? To the bathroom? For the most extensive facilities, meeting the latest legal specifications, **opt for newer facilities,** which more often have been designed with access in mind. Older properties or ships must usually be retrofitted and may offer more limited facilities as a result. Be sure to **discuss your needs before booking.**

DISCOUNT CLUBS

Travel clubs offer members unsold space on airplanes, cruise ships, and package tours at as much as 50% below regular prices. Membership may include a regular bulletin or access to a toll-free hot line giving details of available trips departing from three or four days to several months in the future. Most also offer 50% discounts off hotel rack rates. Before booking with a club, **make sure the hotel or other supplier isn't offering a better deal.**

DRIVING

Because Maine, Vermont, and New Hampshire form a relatively compact region with an effective network of interstate highways and other good roads linking the many cities, towns, and recreational and shopping areas that attract visitors, **a car is the most convenient means of travel.** Yet driving is not without its frustrations; traffic can be heavy on coastal routes and beach-access highways on weekends and in midsummer. Each state makes available, free on request, an official state map that has directories, mileage, and other useful information in addition to routings. The speed limit in much of New England is 65 miles per hour (55 in more populated areas).

I
INSURANCE

Travel insurance can protect your investment, replace your luggage and its contents, or provide for medical coverage should you fall ill during your trip. Most tour operators, travel agents, and insurance agents sell specialized health-and-accident, flight, trip-cancellation, and luggage insurance as well as comprehensive policies with some or all of these features. Before you make any purchase, **review your existing health and homeowner policies** to find out whether they cover expenses incurred while traveling.

BAGGAGE

Airline liability for your baggage is limited to $1,250 per person on domestic flights. On international flights, the airlines' liability is $9.07 per pound or $20 per kilogram for checked baggage (roughly $640 per 70-pound bag) and $400 per passenger for unchecked baggage. However, this excludes valuable items such as jewelry and cameras that are listed in your ticket's fine print. You can buy additional insurance from the airline at check-in, but first **see if your homeowner's policy covers lost luggage.**

FLIGHT

You should **think twice before buying flight insurance.** Often purchased as a last-minute impulse at the airport, it pays a lump sum when a plane crashes, either to a beneficiary if the insured dies or sometimes to a surviving passenger who loses eyesight or a limb. Supplementing the airlines' coverage described in the limits-of-liability paragraphs on your ticket, it's expensive and basically unnecessary. Charging an airline ticket to a major credit card often automatically entitles you to coverage and may also embrace travel by bus, train, and ship.

HEALTH

FOR U.K. TRAVELERS➤ According to the Association of British Insurers, a trade association representing 450 insurance companies, it's wise to **buy extra medical coverage when you visit the United States.** You can buy an annual travel-insurance policy valid for most vacations during the year in which it's purchased. If you go this route, make sure you will be covered if you have a preexisting medical condition or are pregnant.

TRIP

Without insurance, you will lose all or most of your money if you must cancel your trip due to illness or any other reason. Especially if your airline ticket, cruise, or package tour is nonrefundable and cannot be changed, it's essential that you **buy trip-cancellation-and-interruption insurance.** When considering how much coverage you need, look for a policy that will cover the cost of your trip plus the nondiscounted price of a one-way airline ticket should you need to return home early. Read the fine print carefully, especially sections defining "family member" and "preexisting medical conditions." Also **consider default or bankruptcy insurance,** which protects you against a supplier's failure to deliver. However, such policies often do not cover default by a travel agency, tour operator, airline, or cruise line if you bought your tour and the coverage directly from the firm in question.

L
LODGING

Hotel and motel chains provide standard rooms and amenities in major cities and at or near traditional vacation destinations. At small inns, where each room is different and amenities vary in number and quality, **price isn't always a reliable indicator;** fortunately, when you call to make reservations, most hosts will be happy to give all manner of details about their properties, down to the color scheme of the handmade quilts—so ask all your questions before you book. Don't expect telephone, TV, or honor bar in your room; you might even have to share a bathroom. Most inns offer breakfast—hence the name bed-and-breakfast—yet this formula varies, too; at one B&B you may be served muffins and coffee, at another a multicourse feast with fresh flowers on the table. Many inns prohibit smoking, which is a fire hazard in older buildings, and some are wary of children. Almost all say "no" to pets.

APARTMENT AND VILLA RENTALS

If you want a home base that's roomy enough for a family and comes with cooking facilities, **consider a furnished rental.** It's generally cost-wise, too, although not always—some rentals are luxury properties (economical only when your party is large). Home-exchange directories do list rentals—often second homes owned by prospective house swappers—and some services search for a house or apartment for you (even a castle if that's your fancy) and handle the paperwork. Some send an illustrated catalogue and others send photographs of specific properties, sometimes at a charge; up-front registration fees may apply.

HOME EXCHANGE

If you would like to find a house, an apartment, or other vacation property to exchange for your own while on vacation, **become a member of a home-exchange organization,** which will send you its annual directories listing available exchanges and will include your own listing in at least one of them. Arrangements for the actual exchange are made by the two parties involved in it, not by the organization.

M
MONEY
AND EXPENSES

ATMS

Chances are that you can **use your bank card at ATMs** to withdraw money from an account and get cash advances on a credit-card account if your card has been programmed with a personal identification number, or PIN. Before leaving home, **check on frequency limits** for withdrawals and cash advances.

On cash advances you are charged interest from the day you receive the money from ATMs as well as from tellers. Transaction fees for ATM withdrawals outside your home turf may be higher than for withdrawals at home.

TRAVELER'S CHECKS

Whether or not to buy traveler's checks depends on where you are headed; **take cash to rural areas and small towns, traveler's checks to cities.** The most widely recognized are American Express, Citicorp, Thomas Cook, and Visa, which are sold by major commercial banks for 1% to 3% of the checks' face value—it pays to **shop around.** Both American Express and Thomas Cook issue checks that can be counter-signed and used by you or your traveling companion. You can cash them in banks without paying a fee (which can be as much as 20%) and use them as readily as cash in many hotels, restaurants, and shops. Record the numbers of the checks, cross them off as you spend them, and keep this information separate from your checks.

WIRING MONEY

You don't have to be a cardholder to send or receive funds through MoneyGram[SM] from American Express. Just go to a MoneyGram agent, located in retail and convenience stores and in American Express Travel Offices. Pay up to $1,000 with cash or a credit card, anything over that in cash. The money can be picked up within 10 minutes. There's no limit, and the recipient need only present photo identification. The cost, which includes a free long-distance phone call, runs from 3% to 10%, depending on the amount sent, the destination, and how you pay.

You can also send money using Western Union. Money sent

from the United States or Canada will be available for pickup at agent locations in 100 countries within 15 minutes. Once the money is in the system, it can be picked up at any one of 25,000 locations. Fees range from 4% to 10%, depending on the amount you send.

P

PACKAGES
AND TOURS

A package or tour can make your vacation less expensive and more convenient. Firms that sell tours and packages purchase airline seats, hotel rooms, and rental cars in bulk and pass some of the savings on to you. In addition, the best operators have local representatives to help you out at your destination.

A GOOD DEAL?

The more your package or tour includes, the better you can predict the ultimate cost of your vacation. Make sure you know exactly what is included, and **beware of hidden costs.** Are taxes, tips, and service charges included? Transfers and baggage handling? Entertainment and excursions? These can add up.

Most packages and tours are rated deluxe, first-class superior, first class, tourist, and budget. The key difference is usually accommodations. If the package or tour you are considering is priced lower than in your wildest dreams, **be skeptical.** Also, **make sure your travel agent knows the hotels** and other services. Ask about your hotel's location, room size, beds, and whether it has a pool, room service, or programs for children, if you care about these. Has your agent been there or sent others you can contact?

BUYER BEWARE

Each year consumers are stranded or lose their money when operators go out of business—even very large ones with excellent reputations. If you can't afford a loss, take the time to **check out the operator**—find out how long the company has been in business, and ask several agents about its reputation. Next, **don't book unless the firm has a consumer-protection program.** Members of the United States Tour Operators Association and the National Tour Association are required to set aside funds exclusively to cover your payments and travel arrangements in case of default. Nonmember operators may instead carry insurance; look for the details in the operator's brochure—and the name of an underwriter with a solid reputation. Note: When it comes to tour operators, **don't trust escrow accounts.** Although there are laws governing those of charter-flight operators, no governmental body prevents tour operators from raiding the till.

Next, **contact your local Better Business Bureau and the attorney general's office** in both your own state and the operator's; have any complaints been filed? Last, **pay with a major credit card.** Then you can cancel payment, provided that you can document your complaint. Always **consider trip-cancellation insurance** (*see* Insurance, *above*).

BIG VS. SMALL➤ An operator that handles several hundred thousand travelers annually can use its purchasing power to give you a good price. Its high volume may also indicate financial stability. But some small companies provide more personalized service; because they tend to specialize, they may also be experts on an area.

USING AN AGENT

Travel agents are an excellent resource. In fact, large operators accept bookings only through travel agents. But it's good to **collect brochures from several agencies,** because some agents' suggestions may be skewed by promotional relationships with tour and package firms that reward them for volume sales. If you have a special interest, **find an agent with expertise in that area;** the American Society of Travel Agents can give you leads in the United States. (Don't rely solely on your agent, though; agents may be unaware of small niche operators, and some special-interest travel companies only sell direct).

SINGLE TRAVELERS

Prices are usually quoted per person, based on two sharing a room. If traveling solo, you may be required to pay the full double occupancy rate. Some operators eliminate this surcharge if you agree to be matched up with a roommate of the same sex, even if one is not found by departure time.

PACKING FOR MAINE, VERMONT, NEW HAMPSHIRE

The principal rule on weather in New England is that there are no rules. A cold, foggy morning can and often does become a bright, 60-degree afternoon. A summer breeze can suddenly turn chilly, and rain often appears with little warning. Thus, the best advice on how to dress is to **layer your clothing** so that you can peel off or add garments as needed for comfort. Showers are frequent, so **pack a raincoat and umbrella.** Even in summer you should bring long pants, a sweater or two, and a waterproof windbreaker, for **evenings are often chilly** and the sea spray can make things cool on a whale-watch or deep-sea fishing trip. If you'll be walking in the woods, bring heavy boots and expect to encounter mud. November and early December are hunting season in much of New England; those who venture into the woods then should wear bright orange clothing. Winter requires heavy clothing, gloves, a hat, warm socks, and waterproof shoes or boots.

Casual sportswear—walking shoes and jeans—will take you almost everywhere, but swimsuits and bare feet will not: Shirts and shoes are required attire at even the most casual venues. Dress in restaurants is generally casual, except at some of the distinguished restaurants of Maine coast towns such as Kennebunkport and a number of inns in all three states.

In summer, bring a hat and sunscreen. Remember also to **pack insect repellent**—and use it! Recent outbreaks of Lyme disease all over the East Coast make it imperative (even in urban areas) that you protect yourself from ticks from early spring through the summer.

Bring an extra pair of eyeglasses or contact lenses in your carry-on luggage, and if you have a health problem, **pack enough medication** to last the trip. In case your bags go astray, **don't put prescription drugs or valuables in luggage to be checked.**

LUGGAGE

REGULATIONS➤ Free airline baggage allowances depend on the airline, the route, and the class of your ticket; ask in advance. In general, on domestic flights you are entitled to check two bags—neither exceeding 62 inches, or 158 centimeters (length + width + height), or weighing more than 70 pounds (32 kilograms). A third piece may be brought aboard; its total dimensions are generally limited to less than 45 inches (114 centimeters), so it will fit easily under the seat in front of you or in the overhead compartment. In the United States, the Federal Aviation Administration gives airlines broad latitude to limit carry-on allowances and tailor them to different aircraft and operational conditions. Charges for excess, oversize, or overweight pieces vary.

SAFEGUARDING YOUR LUGGAGE➤ Before leaving home, **itemize your bags' contents** and their worth, and label them with your name, address, and phone number. (If you use your home address, cover it so that potential thieves can't see it.) Inside your bag, **pack a copy of your itinerary.** At check-in, **make sure that your bag is correctly tagged** with the airport's three-letter destination code. If your bags arrive damaged or not at all, file a written report with the airline before leaving the airport.

AIRLINE LIABILITY➤ In the event of loss, damage, or theft on domestic flights, airlines' liability is $2,000 per passenger, excluding the valuable items such as jewelry and cameras that are listed in your ticket's fine print. Excess-valuation insurance can be bought directly from the airline at check-in. Your homeowner's policy may fill the gap, or you can purchase insurance from firms that specialize in these policies (*see* Insurance, *above*).

PASSPORTS AND VISAS

U.K. CITIZENS

Citizens of the United Kingdom need a valid passport to enter the United States. Applications for new and renewal passports are available from main post offices and at passport offices in Belfast, Glasgow, Liverpool, London, Newport, and Peterborough. You may apply in person at all passport offices, or by mail to all except the London office. Children under 16 may travel on an accompanying parent's passport. All passports are valid for 10 years. Allow a month for processing.

If you are staying fewer than 90 days and traveling on a vacation, with a return or onward ticket, you will probably not need a visa. However, you will need to fill out the Visa Waiver Form, 1-94W, supplied by the airline.

While traveling, **keep one photocopy of your passport's data page** separate from your wallet and leave another copy with someone at home. If you lose your passport, promptly call the nearest embassy or consulate, and the local police; having the data page can speed replacement.

R
RENTING A CAR

CUTTING COSTS

To get the best deal, **book through a travel agent and shop around.** When pricing cars, **ask where the rental lot is located.** Some off-airport locations offer lower rates—even though their lots are only minutes away from the terminal via complimentary shuttle. You may also want to **price local car-rental companies,** whose rates may be lower still, although service and maintenance standards may not be up to those of a national firm. Also **ask your travel agent about a company's customer-service record.** How has it responded to late plane arrivals and vehicle mishaps? Are there often lines at the rental counter, and, if you're traveling during a holiday period, does a confirmed reservation guarantee you a car?

INSURANCE

When you drive a rented car, you are generally responsible for any damage or personal injury that you cause as well as damage to the vehicle. Before you rent, **see what coverage you already have** by means of your personal auto-insurance policy and credit cards. For about $14 a day, rental companies sell insurance, known as a collision damage waiver (CDW), that eliminates your liability for damage to the car; it's always optional and should never be automatically added to your bill.

SURCHARGES

Before picking up the car in one city and leaving it in another, **ask about drop-off charges** or one-way service fees, which can be substantial. Note, too, that some rental agencies charge extra if you return the car before the time specified on your contract. To avoid a hefty refueling fee, **fill the tank just before you turn in the car.**

FOR U.K. CITIZENS

In the United States you must be 21 to rent a car; rates may be higher for those under 25. Extra costs cover child seats, compulsory for children under 5 (about $3 per day), and additional drivers (around $1.50 per day). To pick up your reserved car you will need the reservation voucher, a passport, a U.K. driver's license, and a travel policy covering each driver.

S
SENIOR-CITIZEN DISCOUNTS

To qualify for age-related discounts, **mention your senior-citizen status up front** when booking hotel reservations, not when checking out, and before you're seated in restaurants, not when paying your bill. Note that discounts may be limited to certain menus, days, or hours. When renting a car, **ask about promotional car-rental discounts**—they can net lower costs than your senior-citizen discount.

W
WHEN TO GO

Maine, Vermont, and New Hampshire are largely year-round

destinations. While summer is a favored time all over New England, fall is balmy and idyllically colorful, and winter's snow makes for great skiing. The only times vacationers might want to stay away are during mud season in April and black-fly season in the last two weeks of May. Note that **many smaller museums and attractions are open only from Memorial Day to mid-October,** at other times by appointment only.

Summer is the time of outdoor music festivals (*see* Festivals and Seasonal Events *in* Chapter 1). Reservations for these popular events should be made months in advance. Memorial Day is the start of the migration to the beaches and the mountains, and summer begins in earnest on July 4.

Fall is the most colorful season in New England, a time when many inns and hotels are booked months in advance by foliage-viewing visitors. The first scarlet and gold colors emerge in mid-September in northern areas; "peak" color occurs at different times from year to year. Generally, it is best to **visit the northern reaches in early October and then move southward as the month progresses.**

All leaves are off the trees by Halloween, and **hotel rates fall as the leaves do,** dropping significantly until ski season begins.

Winter is the time for downhill and cross-country skiing. New England's major ski resorts, having seen dark days in years when snowfall was meager, now have snowmaking equipment.

In spring, despite mud season, maple sugaring goes on in Maine, New Hampshire, and Vermont, and the fragrant scent of lilacs is never far behind.

CLIMATE

What follows are average daily maximum and minimum temperatures for two major cities in New England. Expect New Hampshire's weather to be much the same as Vermont's.

Climate in Maine, Vermont, and New Hampshire

PORTLAND, ME

Jan.	31F	– 1C	May	61F	16C	Sept.	68F	20C
	16	– 9		47	8		52	11
Feb.	32F	0C	June	72F	22C	Oct.	58F	14C
	16	– 9		54	15		43	6
Mar.	40F	4C	July	76F	24C	Nov.	45F	7C
	27	– 3		61	16		32	0
Apr.	50F	10C	Aug.	74F	23C	Dec.	34F	1C
	36	2		59	15		22	– 6

BURLINGTON, VT

Jan.	29F	– 2C	May	67F	19C	Sept.	74F	23C
	11	–12		45	7		50	10
Feb.	31F	– 1C	June	77F	25C	Oct.	59F	15C
	11	–12		56	13		40	4
Mar.	40F	4C	July	83F	28C	Nov.	45F	7C
	22	– 6		59	15		31	– 1
Apr.	54F	12C	Aug.	79F	26C	Dec.	31F	– 1C
	34	1		58	14		16	– 9

THE GOLD GUIDE / SMART TRAVEL TIPS

1 Destination: Maine, Vermont, and New Hampshire

DEEP ROOTS IN STONY SOIL

BACK IN THE 1940S, photographer Paul Strand took two pictures that capture the essence of northern New England. One photograph, "Susan Thompson, Cape Split Maine," shows a late-middle-aged woman standing perfectly still at the entrance to her barn. She stands, as if pausing in her work, with her worn hands resting at her sides and her wistful, rather tired eyes just averted from the camera. Susan Thompson has the composure of a person who has lived long and hard in a single place.

The second picture, "Side Porch, New England," is a stark, almost abstract composition. Broad, rough-sawn, white painted boards frame the porch. A ladder-back chair with a cane seat (unoccupied) stands on the cracked, weathered boards of the porch floor. A broom and a wire rug-beater hang from nails on the wall. The scene is one of poverty, but not of neglect. The broom has obviously swept the porch clean that very morning, and, though the house has not been painted in years, one imagines that the rugs inside receive regular and thorough beatings.

Susan Thompson is gone, and so, most likely, is the old farmhouse with the clean-swept side porch. But even today, you don't have to travel far off the interstates that knife through Maine, Vermont, and New Hampshire before you run across people and houses and landscapes that are hauntingly similar to those Paul Strand photographed 50 years ago. The serenity, the austere beauty, the reverence for humble objects, the unassuming pride in place, the deep connection between man and landscape—all of these remain very much alive in northern New England.

In northern New England, the people and the land (and in Maine, the sea) seem bound by a marriage that has withstood many hardships. The relationship derives its character in part from the harsh climate. Spring withholds its flowers until mid-May, winter blows through in November, and a summer sunny spell is interrupted by rain-storms before it's had time to settle in properly. (There's a saying that there are two seasons in the north country—winter and July.)

There is a heritage here of self-reliance: the hardship of scratching out a living in small farms; the loneliness of sailing onto the cold northern waters to fish. In some places, isolation and hardship breed suspicion and meanness of spirit; in northern New England, they have engendered patience, endurance, a shrewd sardonic humor, and bottomless loyalty.

People sink deep roots in the thin, stony soil. They forgive the climate its cruelty. The north has a way of taking hold of the body and the spirit, as if weaving a kind of spell. It's not just the residents who are susceptible; summer visitors who have endured years of humid, overcast Julys and fog-shrouded Augusts keep coming back.

Distinct as they are in landscape, geology, and feeling, Maine, Vermont, and New Hampshire are linked by their northerness. There is something pure and fine and mystical about the North, just as there is something lush and soft and voluptuous about the South. You can feel the spirit of the North in the very light. The sun seems to burn more sharply and cleanly in the north country: It scours the rocks on the Maine coast, fills Vermont valleys with powdered gold in September, and turns the new snow of January into sapphires and diamonds.

Even more evocative than the light are the sounds of the North: the mournful, five-note whistle of the white-throated sparrow piercing the stillness of a June morning; the slap of lake water against a sandy shore; or the more insistent murmur of the sea reaching into a cove.

The explosions of warfare have not sounded in northern New England since the War of 1812, but throughout the 19th century the explosions of the industrial revolution ripped through the rural quiet in parts of these three states, particularly in southern New Hampshire. But eventually the noise of this revolution subsided. For the first half of the 20th century, the history of northern New England was primarily a history of decline. Mills and quarries were closed. Farms were abandoned. Fishing villages dwindled to a handful of old folks. Fields were overgrown by maple and spruce.

It was only when Americans began to have the time, money, and inclination to travel that the region had a resurgence. Motor courts popped up along Maine's coastal Route 1 during the 1950s. Ski chalets peeked above the pines in Vermont and New Hampshire. Artists, teachers, and urban professionals snatched up the old farmhouses, and hippies set up communes in southern Vermont.

In the 1970s and '80s gentrification began to alter the towns and villages of the North. Second homes and condominiums went up in record numbers on the shores of Lake Winnepesaukee, alongside Maine's Casco and Linekin bays, and throughout the green countryside of southern Vermont.

Gentrification looks lovely compared with some of the other changes that have overtaken northern New England in the past couple of decades. Strip development has swallowed long stretches of Vermont's Route 4, especially around Rutland; and a good deal of southern New Hampshire has a distinctly suburban cast. Factory-outlet fever has reached epidemic proportions in Maine and New Hampshire. It used to be that tourists came to northern New England to buy a jug of maple syrup or a little pillow stuffed with balsam needles—now it's a pair of Bass shoes or Calvin Klein jeans.

Equally distressing are the crowds that have brought urban headaches into the heart of the northern wilderness. An endless caravan of leaf peepers crawls along the Kancamagus Highway in late September. The lift lines at Mount Snow or Bromley can be long enough to make you want to trade skiing for shopping at Manchester's boutiques and outlets. I have found few vacation experiences more depressing than slogging up the long, increasingly steep trail of Vermont's Camel's Hump mountain only to find the summit mobbed with fellow hikers. "Do we seat ourselves, or should we wait for the maitre d'?" one hiker remarked as he surveyed the scores of picnickers who had beat him to the top.

BUT EVEN IN THE MIDST of the changes and crowding of the present, the eternal images, tastes, and experiences of the North endure. The steam of boiling maple sap still rises from sugarhouses all over the Green and White mountains every March. In May, lilacs bloom in fragrant, extravagant mounds beside seemingly every old farmhouse in the North. Loons flapping through the dawn mist rising off a lake, a scarlet-maple branch blazing beside a white church, cows grazing on a lush, green hillside—these images have become cliches, but they are nonetheless stirring and satisfying.

Whenever I feel the first chill of autumn in the air, whenever I see a flock of geese winging north, whenever I come upon a stand of spruce and white pine rising at the end of a freshly mown hay field, I feel the tug of northern New England. The drive north from my home outside New York City is long and dull, and, on the way up, there always comes a moment of doubt: Will it be worth the time and money? Will it have changed? Will it rain or fog the entire time?

Then I see the first ramshackle house with a side porch, the first rough pasture strewn with stones and humps of grass, the first kind wistful face, and I know it will be all right.

— *David Laskin*

David Laskin penned the Maine chapter of this book; he has also written for The New York Times *and* Travel and Leisure.

WHAT'S WHERE

Maine

Due to overdevelopment, Maine's southernmost coastal towns won't give you the rugged, "downeast" experience, but the Kennebunks will: classic townscapes, rocky shorelines punctuated by sandy beaches, quaint downtown districts. Nevertheless, purists hold that the Maine coast begins at Penobscot Bay. Acadia National Park is Maine's principal tourist attraction; and in Freeport, a bewildering assortment of outlets has sprung up around the famous outfitter L.L. Bean. The vast north woods is a destination for outdoors enthusiasts.

Vermont

Southern Vermont has farms, freshly starched New England towns, quiet back roads, bustling ski resorts, and strip-mall sprawl. Central Vermont's trademarks include marble quarries and large dairy herds and pastures that create the quilted patchwork of the Champlain Valley. The heart of the area is the Green Mountains, and the surrounding wilderness of the Green Mountain National Forest. Both the state's largest city (Burlington) and the nation's smallest state capital (Montpelier) are in northern Vermont, as are some of the most rural and remote areas of New England. Much of the state's logging, dairy farming, and skiing take place here. With Montréal only an hour from the border, the Canadian influence is strong, and Canadian accents and currency common.

New Hampshire

Portsmouth, the star of New Hampshire's coastline, has great shopping and restaurants and one of the best historic districts in the nation; Exeter is New Hampshire's enclave of Revolutionary War history. The lakes region, rich with historic landmarks, also has good restaurants, golf courses, hiking trails, and antiquing. People come to the White Mountains to hike and climb, to photograph the dramatic vistas and the vibrant foliage, and to ski. Western and central New Hampshire comprise the unspoiled heart of the state: This region has managed to keep the water slides and the outlet malls at bay. This area offers Lake Sunapee and Mt. Monadnock,

the second-most-climbed mountain in the world. It is also an informal artists' colony.

PLEASURES & PASTIMES

Beaches

Long, wide beaches edge the New England coast from southern Maine to southern Connecticut; the most popular are in the Kennebunk area of Maine and the coastal region of New Hampshire. Many are maintained by state and local governments and have lifeguards on duty; they may have picnic facilities, rest rooms, changing facilities, and concession stands. Depending on the locale, you may need a parking sticker to use the lot. The waters are at their warmest in August, though they're cold even at the height of summer along much of the Maine coast. Inland, there are small lake beaches, most notably in New Hampshire and Vermont.

Biking

Biking is popular in the New Hampshire lakes region. Biking in Maine is especially scenic in and around Kennebunkport, Camden, and Deer Isle; the carriage paths in Acadia National Park are ideal.

Boating and Sailing

In most lakeside and coastal resorts, sailboats and powerboats can be rented at a local marina. Maine's Penobscot Bay is a famous sailing area. Lakes in New Hampshire and Vermont are splendid for all kinds of boating.

Dining

Seafood is king throughout New England. Clams, quahogs, lobster, and scrod are prepared here in an infinite number of ways, some fancy and expensive, others simple and moderately priced. One of the best ways to enjoy seafood is in the rough—off paper plates on a picnic table at a clam boil or clambake—or at one of the many shacklike eating places along the coast, where you can smell the salt air.

At inland resorts and inns, traditional fare dominates the menu. Among the quintessentially New England dishes are

Indian pudding, clam chowder, fried clams, and cranberry anything. You can also find multicultural variations on themes, such as Portuguese *chouriço* (a spicy red sausage that transforms a clamboil into something heavenly) and the mincemeat pie made with pork in the tradition of the French Canadians who populate the northern regions.

Fishing

Anglers will find sport aplenty throughout the region—surf-casting along the shore, deep-sea fishing in the Atlantic on party and charter boats, fishing for trout in rivers, and angling for bass, landlocked salmon, and other fish in freshwater lakes. Sporting goods stores and bait-and-tackle shops are reliable sources for licenses—necessary in fresh waters—and for leads to the nearest hot spots.

Hiking

Probably the most famous trails are the 255-mile Long Trail, which runs north–south through the center of Vermont, and the Maine-to-Georgia Appalachian Trail, which runs through New England on both private and public land. You'll find good hiking in many state parks throughout the region.

National and State Parks and Forests

National and state parks offer a broad range of visitor facilities, including campgrounds, picnic grounds, hiking trails, boating, ranger programs, and more. State forests are usually somewhat less developed. For more information on any of these, contact the state tourism offices or parks departments (*see* Visitor Information *in* the Gold Guide, *above*).

MAINE➤ Acadia National Park, which preserves fine stretches of shoreline and high mountains, covers much of Mount Desert Island and more than half of Isle au Haut and Schoodic Point on the mainland. Camping is permitted at designated campgrounds; hiking, biking, carriage rides, and boat cruises are the most popular activities. Isle au Haut, accessible by mailboat, is the least crowded section; the Park Loop Road on Mount Desert is the busiest.

White Mountain National Forest has camping areas in rugged mountain locations, hiking trails, and picnic areas.

Baxter State Park comprises more than 200,000 acres of wilderness surrounding Katahdin, Maine's highest mountain. Campgrounds are at sites near the park's dirt road and in remote backcountry sections; reservations are strongly recommended. Hiking and moose-watching are major activities. The Allagash Wilderness Waterway is a 92-mile corridor of lakes and rivers surrounded by vast commercial forest property. Canoeing the Allagash is a highly demanding activity that requires advance planning and the ability to handle white water. Guides are recommended for novice canoeists.

VERMONT➤ The 275,000-acre Green Mountain National Forest extends south from the center of the state to the Massachusetts border. Hikers treasure the miles of trails; canoeists work its white waters; and campers and anglers find plenty to keep them happy. Among the most popular spots are the Falls of Lana and Silver Lake near Middlebury; Hapgood Pond between Manchester and Peru; and Chittenden Brook near Rochester.

The 43 parks owned and maintained by the state contain numerous recreational areas that may include hiking trails, campsites, swimming, boating facilities, nature trails (some have an on-site naturalist), and fishing. The official state map details the facilities available at each.

NEW HAMPSHIRE➤ The White Mountain National Forest covers 770,000 acres of northern New Hampshire. New Hampshire parklands vary widely, even within a region. Major recreation parks are at Franconia Notch, Crawford Notch, and Mt. Sunapee. Rhododendron State Park (Monadnock) has a singular collection of wild rhododendrons; Mt. Washington Park (White Mountains) is on top of the highest mountain in the northeast. In addition, 23 state recreation areas provide vacation facilities that include camping, picnicking, hiking, boating, fishing, swimming, bike trails, winter sports, and food services.

Shopping

Antiques, crafts, maple syrup and sugar, fresh produce, and the greatly varied offerings of the factory outlets lure shoppers to New England's outlet stores, flea markets, shopping malls, bazaars, yard sales, country stores, and farmers' markets. Vermont sales tax is 5%; Maine is 6%. New Hampshire has no sales tax.

ANTIQUES➤ People sometimes joke that New Hampshire's two cash crops are fudge and antiques. Particularly in the Monadnock region, dealers abound in barns and home stores that are strung along back roads. Best antiquing concentrations are in North Conway; along Route 119, from Fitzwilliam to Hinsdale; Route 101, from Marlborough to Wilton; and the towns of Hopkinton, Hollis, and Amherst.

In Maine, antiques shops are clustered in Searsport and scattered around the outskirts of villages, in farmhouses, and in barns; yard sales abound in summer.

Timber Rail Village in Quechee, Vermont, bills itself as an antiques mall with inventory from 225 dealers. A small-scale working railroad will take the kids for a ride while Mom and Dad browse. The Antiques Center at Hartland, one of the best known in Vermont, displays the wares of 50 dealers. Head east on Route 15 at its junction with Route 108 for a pleasant antiques-store-dotted drive through the towns of Johnson and Morrisville, looping back toward Stowe.

CRAFTS➤ In Vermont, Burlington produces many fine crafts, and Putney and its environs are home to scores of artisans whose baskets, pottery, quilts, etc. are for sale. North Conway, New Hampshire is a shopper's mecca. On Deer Isle in Maine, Haystack Mountain School of Crafts attracts internationally renowned glassblowers, potters, sculptors, jewelers, blacksmiths, printmakers, and weavers to its summer institute. Local newspapers and the bulletin boards of country stores carry notices of flea markets, shows, and sales.

OUTLET STORES➤ In Maine the outlet area runs along the coast, in Kittery, Freeport, Kennebunkport, Wells, and Ellsworth. In New Hampshire the largest outlet concentration is in North Conway. Manchester is Vermont's outlet mecca.

PRODUCE➤ Opportunities abound for obtaining fresh farm produce from the source; some farms allow you to pick your own strawberries, raspberries, and blueberries, and there are maple-syrup producers who demonstrate the process to visitors. Maple syrup is available in different grades;

light amber is the most refined; many Vermonters prefer grade C, the richest in flavor and the one most often used in cooking. A sugarhouse can be the most or the least expensive place to shop, depending on how tourist-oriented it is. Small grocery stores are often a good source of less-expensive syrup.

Skiing

For close to 100 years the softly rounded peaks of New England have attracted people who want to ski. In the beginning you had to climb a mountain in order to realize the experience of skiing down it. Then came the lifts; the first rope tow in the United States was installed at Suicide Six in Woodstock, Vermont. T-bars and chairlifts soon followed, and gondolas and tram cars enclosed and protected skiers from the elements on long rides to mountaintops. Today's high-speed chairlifts move skiers up the mountain in half the time of the older lifts.

Ski lifts made the sport widely accessible, and the continuing development of technology for manufacturing and treating snow when nature fell short has made skiing less dependent on weather conditions. The costs of these facilities—and those of safety features and insurance—are borne by the skier in the price of the lift ticket.

LIFT TICKETS➤ A good bet is that the bigger and more famous the resort, the higher the lift ticket price. Although lift tickets come in many configurations, most people make the mistake of listing the single-day, weekend-holiday adult lift pass as the "guidepost." It is always the highest price; astute skiers look for off-site purchase locations, senior discounts, and junior pricing; and package rates, multiple days, stretch weekends (a weekend that usually includes a Monday or Friday), frequent-skier programs, season-ticket plans, and other promotions to save their skiing dollars.

On the positive side of things, skiing remains one of the more inexpensive sports, even at resorts that demand top-of-the-line rates. Divide six hours of skiing time into $45 (for a high-end full-day lift ticket), and the price is $7.50 per hour.

LODGING➤ Lodging is among the most important considerations for skiers who plan more than a day trip. While some of the ski areas described in this book are small and draw only day trippers, most offer a variety of accommodations—lodges, condominiums, hotels, motels, inns, bed-and-breakfasts—close to or at a short distance from the action. Because of the general state of the New England economy, some prices have dropped a bit to lure skiers back to the hills. There might be a pleasant surprise or two awaiting your pocketbook.

For a longer vacation, you should request and study the resort area's accommodations brochure. For stays of three days or more, a package rate may offer the best deal. Packages vary in composition, price, and availability throughout the season; their components may include a room, meals, lift tickets, ski lessons, rental equipment, transfers to the mountain, parties, races, and use of a sports center, tips, and taxes.

EQUIPMENT RENTAL➤ Rental equipment is available at all ski areas, at ski shops around resorts, and even in cities far from ski areas. Shop personnel will advise customers on the appropriate equipment for an individual's size and ability and on how to operate the equipment. Good skiers should ask to "demo" or test premium equipment.

First-time skiers may find that the best way to start is a one-day outing as close to home as possible. On arrival at the ski area, go to the base lodge and ask at an information desk about special arrangements for beginners. Packages usually include basic equipment (rental skis with bindings, ski boots, ski poles), a lesson lasting one hour or more, and a lift ticket that may be valid only on the beginners' slopes.

TRAIL RATING➤ Ski areas have devised standards for rating and marking trails and slopes that offer fairly accurate guides. Trails are rated Easier (green circle), More Difficult (blue square), Most Difficult (black diamond), and Expert (double diamond). Keep in mind that trail difficulty is measured relative to other trails *at the same ski area*, not to those of an area down the road, in another state, or in another part of the country; a black-diamond trail at one area may rate only a blue square at a neighboring area. Yet the trail-marking system throughout New England is remarkably consistent and reliable.

LESSONS➤ Within the United States, the Professional Ski Instructors of America (PSIA) have devised a progressive teaching system that is used with relatively little variation at most ski schools. This allows skiers to take lessons at ski schools in different ski areas and still improve. Class lessons usually last 1½–2 hours and are limited in size to 10 participants. Some ski areas have specific workshops such as "Centered Skiing" (Sugarbush, VT) and "Perfect Turn" (Sunday River, ME).

Most ski schools have adopted the PSIA teaching system for children, and many also use SKIwee, which awards progress cards and applies other standardized teaching approaches. Classes for children are normally formed according to age and ability. Many ski schools offer half-day or full-day sessions in which the children ski together with an instructor and eat together.

CHILD CARE➤ Nurseries can be found at virtually all ski areas, and often accept children ages 6 weeks to 6 years. Parents must usually supply formula and diapers for infants; some youngsters may want to bring their own toys. Reservations are advisable. Although skiing may be offered for children at age 3, this activity is geared more to play than to serious learning.

FURTHER READING

New England has been home to some of America's classic authors, among them Herman Melville, Edith Wharton, Mark Twain, Robert Frost, and Emily Dickinson. Henry David Thoreau wrote about New England in *Cape Cod, The Maine Woods,* and his masterpiece, *Walden.* The longtime editor of *Yankee* magazine, Judson Hale, examines with humor the culture, language, legends, and weather of the six states in *Inside New England.*

Among books written about the Maine islands are Philip Conkling's *Islands in Time,* Bill Caldwell's *Islands of Maine,* and Charlotte Fardelmann's *Islands Down East.* Kenneth Roberts set a series of historical novels, beginning with *Arundel,* in the coastal Kennebunk region during the Revolutionary War. Ruth Moore's *Candalmas Bay, Speak to the Winds,* and *The*

Weir; and Elisabeth Ogilvie's "Tide Trilogy" books capture both the romanticism and hardships of coastal life. Carolyn Chute's 1985 bestseller, *The Beans of Egypt, Maine,* offers a fictional glimpse of the hardships of contemporary rural life. After a limited theatrical release in 1994, the movie version of the book, starring Martha Plimpton, is in video stores with the title, *Forbidden Choices.*

Vermont: An Explorers Guide, by Christina Tree and Peter Jennison, relates virtually every back road, event, attraction, town, and recreational opportunity in Vermont. Charles Morrissey's *Vermont: A History* delivers just what the title promises. *Without a Farmhouse Near,* by Deborah Rawson, describes the impact of change on small Vermont communities. *Real Vermonters Don't Milk Goats,* by Frank Bryan and Bill Mares, looks at the lighter side of life in the Green Mountain state. Both books and movies, *Peyton Place* and *Ethan Frome* have links to Vermont.

Visitors to New Hampshire may enjoy: *The White Mountains: Their Legends, Landscape, and Poetry,* by Starr King and *The Great Stone Face and Other Tales of the White Mountains,* by Nathaniel Hawthorne. New Hampshire was also blessed with the poet Robert Frost, whose first books, *A Boy's Way* and *North of Boston,* are set here. It's commonly accepted that the Grover's Corners of Thornton Wilder's *Our Town* is the real-life Peterborough; Willa Cather wrote part of *Death Comes for the Archbishop* while residing in Peterborough. The 1981 movie, *On Golden Pond,* was partially filmed on Squam Lake.

Also published by Fodor's, *New England's Best Bed & Breakfasts* has more than 300 reviews; *Exploring Boston & New England* is illustrated with photos and full-color fold-out maps; *National Parks and Seashores of the East* covers many New England destinations; *Halliday's New England Food Explorer* will guide you to the region's best farms, diners, roadside stands, and sophisticated eateries; *Where Should We Take the Kids? The Northeast* provides ideas on what to do with the little ones while in New England.

FODOR'S CHOICE

Sights

★ **Sunrise from the top of Cadillac Mountain on Mt. Desert Island, ME; sunset over Moosehead Lake from the Lily Bay Road in Greenville, ME.** From the summit of Cadillac Mountain you have a 360° view of the ocean, islands, jagged coastline, woods, and lakes; Lily Bay Road passes through Greenville, the largest town on Moosehead Lake, as well as outposts with populations of "not many."

★ **Yacht-filled Camden Harbor, ME, from the summit of Mt. Battie.** Mt. Battie may not be very tall, but it has a lovely vista over Camden Harbor, which has the nation's largest fleet of windjammers.

★ **The view from Appalachian Gap on Route 17, VT.** Views from the top and on the way down this panoramic mountain pass toward the quiet town of Bristol are a just reward for the challenging drive.

★ **Early October on the Kancamagus Highway between Lincoln and Conway, NH.** This 34-mile trek with classic White Mountains vistas erupts into fiery color each fall.

Ski Resorts

★ **Saddleback, ME, for scenic wilderness views.** A down-home, laid-back atmosphere prevails at Saddleback, where the quiet and the absence of crowds, even on busy weekends, draw return visitors.

★ **Sugarloaf, ME, for the East's only above-treeline skiing.** With a vertical of 2,820 feet, Sugarloaf is taller than any other New England ski peak except Killington.

★ **Smugglers' Notch, VT, for learning to ski.** Smugglers' third mountain, Morse (1,150-foot vertical), specializes in beginner trails.

★ **Jay Peak, VT, for the international ambience.** Because of its proximity to Québec, Jay Peak, which boasts the most natural snow of any ski area in the East, attracts Montréalers.

★ **Mad River Glen, VT, for challenging terrain.** Rugged individualists come here for less-polished terrain: The apt area motto is "Ski It If You Can."

★ **Sugarbush, VT, for an overall great place to ski.** Sugarbush has formidable steeps, beginner runs, and intermediate cruisers; there's a with-it attitude, but everyone feels comfortable.

★ **Waterville Valley, NH, for vacation packages.** The bulk of the 53 trails are intermediate, but no one will be bored.

Country Inns and Bed-and-Breakfasts

★ **Bufflehead Cove, Kennebunkport, ME.** On the Kennebunk River at the end of a winding dirt road, this friendly bed-and-breakfast with dollhouse-pretty guest rooms affords the quiet of country fields and apple trees only five minutes from Dock Square. $$$–$$$$

★ **Inn at Sunrise Point, Camden/Lincolnville Beach, ME.** For luxury and location, you can't beat this elegant B&B perched on the water's edge, with magnificent views over Penobscot Bay. $$$$

★ **Vermont Marble Inn, Fair Haven (Rutland), VT.** Anything less than the classical music, crystal chandelier, and candlelight in the dining room would scarcely do justice to the wonderful food; antiques furnish rooms named for authors. $$$

★ **West Mountain Inn, Arlington, VT.** This former farmhouse of the 1840s has a llama ranch on the property and sits on 150 acres that provide glorious views. $$$

★ **Snowvillage Inn, Snowville, NH.** Innkeepers of this 18-room abode take guests on gourmet-picnic hikes; cuisine is dueling Continental: The Austrian chef has a French assistant. $$–$$$

Places to Eat

★ **Hurricane, Ogunquit, ME.** Don't let its weather-beaten exterior deter you—this small, seafood bar-and-grill offers first-rate cooking and spectacular views of the crashing surf. $$–$$$

★ **Jessica's, Rockland, ME.** The Swiss chef at this European bistro in a Victorian home whips up delicious creations such as veal Zurich, paella, and pork Portofino. $$

★ **Georgio's, Waitsfield, VT.** This restaurant with a warm Mediterranean feel in the Tucker Hill Lodge, serves dishes like stone-seared scallops, and fondue, pasta, and pizza. $$–$$$

★ **Inn at Montpelier, Montpelier, VT.** This spacious inn with elegant guest rooms

and a wide wraparound Colonial Revival porch has an outstanding restaurant. $$–$$$

★ **The Balsams Grand Resort Hotel, Dixville Notch, NH.** In summer the buffet lunch is heaped upon a 100-foot-long table; stunning dinners might include chilled strawberry soup spiked with Grand Marnier and poached fillet of salmon with caviar sauce. $$$$

GREAT ITINERARY

Kancamagus Trail

This circuit takes in some of the most spectacular parts of the White and Green mountains, along with the upper Connecticut River Valley. In this area the antiques hunting is exemplary and the traffic is often nonexistent. The scenery evokes the spirit of Currier & Ives.

Duration: Three to six days

The Main Route:

ONE TO THREE DAYS➢ From the New Hampshire coast, head northwest to Wolfeboro, perhaps detouring to explore around Lake Winnipesaukee. Take Route 16 north to Conway, then follow Route 112 west along the scenic Kancamagus Pass through the White Mountains to the Vermont border.

ONE TO TWO DAYS➢ Head south on Route 10 along the Connecticut River, past scenic Hanover, New Hampshire, home of Dartmouth College. At White River Junction, cross into Vermont. You may want to follow Route 4 through the lovely town of Woodstock to Killington, then travel along Route 100 and I–89 to complete the loop back to White River Junction. Otherwise, simply proceed south along I–91, with stops at such pleasant Vermont towns as Putney and Brattleboro.

ONE TO TWO DAYS➢ Take Route 119 east to Rhododendron State Park in Fitzwilliam, New Hampshire. Nearby is Mt. Monadnock, the most-climbed mountain in the United States; in Jaffrey take the trail to the top. Dawdle along back roads to visit the preserved villages of Harrisville, Dublin, and Hancock, then continue east along Route 101 to return to the coast.

10

Maine, Vermont, and New Hampshire Ski Areas

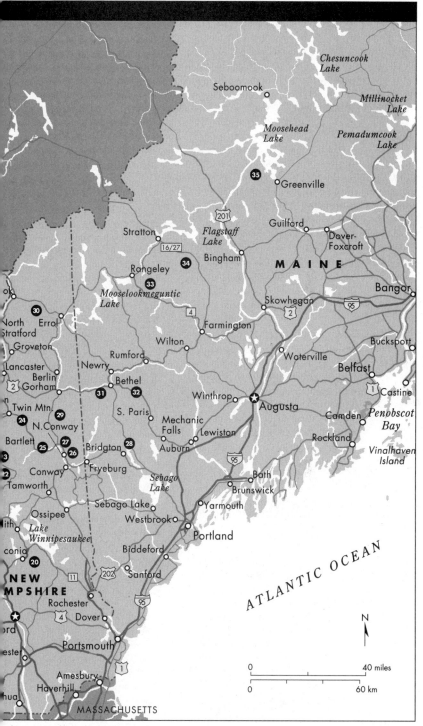

FESTIVALS AND SEASONAL EVENTS

WINTER

JAN.➤ Stowe's (VT) **Winter Carnival** heats up around mid-month; it's among the country's oldest such celebrations. Brookfield (VT) holds its **Ice Harvest Festival,** one of New England's largest.

FEB.➤ The **Brattleboro Winter Carnival** (VT), held weekends throughout the month, features jazz concerts and an ice fishing derby. The **Mad River Valley Winter Carnival** (VT) is a week of winter festivities including dogsled races and a masquerade ball.

FEB.➤ Burlington's **Vermont Mozart Festival** showcases the Winter Chamber Music Series.

SPRING

MAR.➤ Maine's Moosehead Lake has a renowned **Ice-Fishing Derby,** and Rangeley's (ME) **New England Sled Dog Races** attract more than 100 teams from throughout the Northeast and Canada. Stratton Mountain (VT) hosts the **US Open Snowboarding Championships.**

MAR.–APR.➤ This is a boon time for **maple-sugaring festivals and events:** the sugarhouses of Maine, Vermont, and New Hampshire demonstrate procedures from maple-tree tapping to sap boiling. Many offer tastings of various grades of syrup, sugar-on-snow, traditional unsweetened doughnuts, and pickles.

APR.➤ You can gorge on sea grub at Boothbay Harbor's (ME) **Fishermen's Festival** the third weekend of the month.

MAY➤ You know all those holsteins you see grazing in fields alongside Vermont's windy roads? Well, the Enosburg Falls **Vermont Dairy Festival** is just the place to celebrate the delicious fruits (or cheeses, rather) of their labor.

MAY➤ If you're a sheep fancier, stop by the **New Hampshire Sheep and Wool Festival** in New Boston, where shearing, carding, and spinning are demonstrated.

SUMMER

JUNE➤ In Vermont, you can listen to jazz at Burlington's **Discover Jazz Festival** or folk at Warren's **Ben & Jerry's One World One Heart Festival,** held at Sugarbush.

JUNE➤ The spring thaw calls for a number of boating celebrations, including the **Vermont Canoe and Kayak Festival** at Waterbury State Park and the **Boothbay Harbor Windjammer Days,** which starts the high season for Maine's boating set.

JUNE➤ Young ones are the stars of Somersworth's (NH) **International Children's Festival,** where games, activities, and crafts keep everybody busy.

JULY➤ **Fourth of July** parties and parades kick off concerts, family entertainment, an art show, a parade, and fireworks in Bath (ME). Exeter (NH) celebrates with 18th-century Revolutionary War battle reenactments, period crafts and antiques, and a visit from George Washington himself at the American Independence Museum.

JULY➤ Two of New England's better music festivals include the **Marlboro Music Festival** of classical music, held at Marlboro College (VT), and the **Bar Harbor Festival** (ME), which hosts classical, jazz, and popular music concerts into August.

JULY➤ Shoppers can rummage through major **antiques fairs** in Wolfeboro (NH) and Dorset (VT).

JULY➤ The **Great Schooner Race** (ME), which runs from Penobscot Bay to Rockland, features replicas and relics of the age of sail.

JULY➤ One of the region's most popular **country fairs** is held in Bangor (ME).

AUG.➤ Stowe (VT) hosts a popular **Antique and Classic Car Rally.**

AUG.➤ Popular arts, crafts, and antiques festivals are held at **Haystack Mountain** (VT), at the **Southern Vermont Crafts Fair** in Manchester (VT), at the **Maine Antiques**

Festival in Union, and at the **Fair of the League of New Hampshire Craftsmen** at Mt. Sunapee State Park in Newbury—the nation's oldest crafts fair.

AUG.➤ Foodies should bring their appetites to Maine's **Lobster Festival** in Rockland and **Blueberry Festival** in Rangeley Lake.

AUTUMN

SEPT.➤ Summer's close is met with dozens of Labor Day fairs including the **Vermont State Fair** in Rutland, with agricultural exhibits and entertainment; the **International Seaplane Fly-In Weekend,** which sets Moosehead Lake (ME) buzzing; and Burlington's (VT) **Champlain Valley Exposition,** which has all the features of a large county fair.

SEPT.➤ Foot stomping and guitar strumming are the activities of choice at several musical events: the **National Traditional Old-**Time Fiddler's Contest in Barre (VT), the **Bluegrass Festival** in Brunswick (ME), and the **Rockport Folk Festival** (ME). In Stratton (VT), artists and performers gather for the **Stratton Arts Festival.**

SEPT.➤ Agricultural fairs not to be missed are **the Common Ground Country Fair** in Windsor (ME), an organic farmer's delight, and the **Deerfield Fair** (NH), one of New England's oldest.

SEPT.➤ Autumn is ushered in at the **Northeast Kingdom Fall Foliage Festival** (NH), a week-long affair hosted by the six small towns of Walden, Cabot, Plainfield, Peacham, Barnet, and Groton.

SEPT.➤ Fish lovers show up in schools to attend the **Annual Seafood Festival** in Hampton Beach (NH), where you can sample the seafood specialties of more than 50 local restaurants, dance to live bands, and watch fireworks explode over the ocean.

OCT.➤ In Maine, the **Fryeburg Fair** features agricultural exhibits, harness racing, an iron-skillet-throwing contest, and a pig scramble.

NOV.➤ In Vermont there are two major events in this otherwise quiet month: The **EarthPeace International Film Festival** presents films dealing with environmental, human rights, and political issues for a week in Burlington, and the **Bradford Wild Game Supper** draws thousands to taste a variety of large and small game animals and birds.

DEC.➤ In Arlington (VT), the **St. Lucia Pageant** is a "Festival of Lights" that celebrates the winter solstice.

LATE DEC.➤ Historic Strawbery Banke (NH) has a **Christmas Stroll,** with carolers, through nine historic homes decorated for the season.

DEC.31➤ The final day of the year is observed with festivals, entertainment, and food in Burlington (VT) during **First Night Celebrations.**

2 Maine

Due to overdevelopment, Maine's southernmost coastal towns won't give you the rugged, "downeast" experience, but the Kennebunks will: classic townscapes, rocky shorelines, sandy beaches, and quaint downtown districts. Purists hold that the Maine coast begins at Penobscot Bay. Acadia National Park is Maine's principal tourist attraction, and in Freeport a bewildering assortment of outlets has sprung up around the famous outfitter L. L. Bean. The vast north woods is a destination for outdoors enthusiasts.

By David
Laskin, with an
introduction by
William G.
Scheller

Updated by
Hilary Nangle

IF ANY TWO INDIVIDUALS can be associated directly with the disparate images evoked by the very mention of the state of Maine, they are George Bush and Carolyn Chute.

Former president George Bush is the most famous summer resident of Kennebunkport, where he and his family vacation in his grandfather's rambling seaside mansion. Having so recently had a summer White House on the Maine coast reminds Americans that this craggy, wildly irregular stretch of shoreline has long enjoyed an aristocratic cachet: Here Nelson Rockefeller was born in the millionaires' enclave at Bar Harbor; here the Brahmin historian Samuel Eliot Morison sailed the cold waters of Frenchman Bay. In those times, anyone living on the coast of Maine who wasn't rich, famous, or powerful was almost certainly an old-stock yeoman, probably someone with a lobster boat.

Carolyn Chute is the novelist who wrote *The Beans of Egypt, Maine*. Chute's fictional Egypt and its inhabitants are a reminder that Appalachia stretches far to the north of the Cumberland Gap and that not far inland from the famous rockbound coast there are places where rusting house trailers are far more common than white Federalist sea captains' mansions.

In fact, neither stereotype (and both have strong foundations in fact) makes a serious dent in the task of defining or explaining Maine. Reality in most of the state resembles neither a cross between a Ralph Lauren ad and a Winslow Homer painting nor a milieu in which modern history dates from the day they began renting videos at the gas station.

Maine is by far the largest state in New England. At its extremes it measures 300 miles north to south and 200 miles across; all five other New England states could fit within its perimeters. There is an expansiveness to Maine, a sense of real distance between places that hardly exists elsewhere in the region, and along with the sheer size and spread of the place there is a tremendous variety of terrain. One speaks of "coastal" Maine and "inland" Maine, as though the state could be summed up under the twin emblems of lobsters and pine trees. Yet the state's topography and character are a good deal more complicated.

Even the coast is several places in one. South of the rapidly gentrifying city of Portland, such resort towns as Ogunquit, Kennebunkport, and Old Orchard Beach (sometimes called the Québec Riviera because of its popularity with French Canadians) predominate along a reasonably smooth shoreline. Development has been considerable; north of Portland and Casco Bay, secondary roads turn south off Route 1 onto so many oddly chiseled peninsulas that it's possible to drive for days without retracing your route and to conclude that motels, discount outlets, and fried-clam stands are taking over the domain of presidents and lobstermen. Freeport is an entity unto itself, a place where a bewildering assortment of off-price, name-brand outlets has sprung up around the famous outfitter L. L. Bean (no relation to the Egypt clan).

Inland Maine likewise defies characterization. For one thing, a good part of it is virtually uninhabited. This is the land Henry David Thoreau wrote about in *The Maine Woods* nearly 150 years ago; aside from having been logged over several times, much of it hasn't changed since Thoreau and his Native American guides passed through. Ownership of vast portions of northern Maine by forest-products corporations has

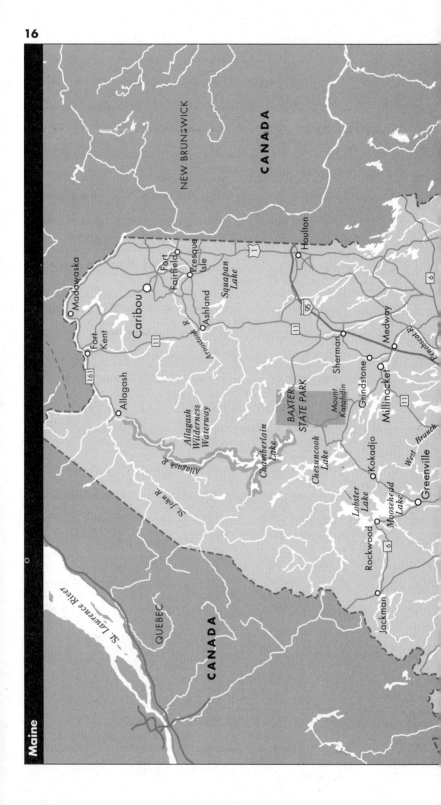

N

40 miles
60 km

Passamaquoddy Bay

Campobello Island

Grand Manan Island

1

1

9

Passadumkeag

Old Town

Bangor

Dead R.

R.

Hancock

West Gouldsboro

Ellsworth

Frenchman Bay

Bar Harbor

ACADIA NA'L PARK

Mt. Desert Island

Castine

Islesboro

Deer Isle

Stonington

Penobscot Bay

Isle au Haut

1

Belfast

Camden

Rockland

Waterville

Augusta

Damariscotta

Newcastle

Muscongus Bay

Newport

95

Kennebec R.

Farmington

201

Bath

Boothbay Harbor

Georgetown

Freeport

Phippsburg

Casco Bay

ATLANTIC OCEAN

Lewiston

Auburn

Brunswick

Androscoggin R.

495

Portland

Biddeford

Kennebunkport

Rangeley

Rangeley Lake

Mooselookmeguntic Lake

17

Bethel

26

WHITE MOUNTAIN NAT'L FOREST

Lovell

Sebago Lake

25

1

95

Kennebunk

Ogunquit

202

Kittery

Portsmouth

NEW HAMPSHIRE

121

kept out subdivision and development; many of the roads here are private, open to travel only by permit. The north woods' day of reckoning may be coming, however, for the paper companies plan to sell off millions of acres in a forested belt that reaches all the way to the Adirondacks in New York State. In the 1990s state governments and environmental organizations are working to preserve as much as possible of the great silent expanses of pine.

Logging the north created the culture of the mill towns, the Rumfords, Skowhegans, Millinockets, and Bangors that lay at the end of the old river drives. The logs arrive by truck today, but Maine's harvested wilderness still feeds the mills and the nation's hunger for paper.

Our hunger for potatoes has given rise to an entirely different Maine culture, in one of the most isolated agricultural regions of the country. Northeastern Aroostook County is where the Maine potatoes come from, and this place, too, is changing. In what was once called the Potato Empire, farmers are as pressed between high costs and low prices as any of their counterparts in the Midwest; add to the bleak economic picture a growing national preference for Idaho baking potatoes rather than the traditional small, round Maine boiling potatoes, and Aroostook's troubles are compounded.

The visitor seeking an untouched fishing village with locals gathered around a pot-bellied stove in the general store may be sadly disappointed; that innocent age has passed in all but the most remote of villages. Tourism has supplanted fishing, logging, and potato farming as Maine's number one industry, and most areas are well equipped to receive the annual onslaught of visitors. But whether you are stepping outside a motel room for an evening walk or watching a boat rock at its anchor, you can sense the infinity of the natural world. Wilderness is always nearby, growing to the edges of the most urbanized spots.

NORTH FROM KITTERY

Maine's southernmost coastal towns won't give you the rugged, wind-bitten "downeast" experience, but they offer all the amenities, they are easily reached from the south, and most have the sand beaches that all but vanish beyond Portland.

Kittery, which lacks a large sand beach, hosts a complex of factory outlets. North of Kittery the Maine coast has long stretches of hard-packed white-sand beach, closely crowded by nearly unbroken ranks of beach cottages, motels, and oceanfront restaurants. The summer colonies of York Beach, Ogunquit, and Wells Beach have the crowds and the ticky-tacky shorefront overdevelopment. Farther inland, York's historic district is on the National Register.

More than any other region south of Portland, the Kennebunks—and especially Kennebunkport—offer the complete Maine coast experience: classic townscapes where perfectly proportioned white-clapboard houses rise from manicured lawns and gardens; rocky shorelines punctuated by sandy beaches, beach motels, and cottages; quaint downtown districts packed with gift shops, ice-cream stands, and tourists; harbors where lobster boats bob alongside yachts; lobster pounds and well-appointed dining rooms. The range of accommodations includes rambling Victorian-era hotels, beachside family motels, and inns.

Exploring

Numbers in the margin correspond to points of interest on the Southern Maine Coast map.

❶ Begin at **Kittery,** just across the New Hampshire border, off I–95 on Route 1. Kittery will be of most interest to shoppers headed for its factory outlet stores—all 115 of them. Here along a several-mile stretch of Route 1 you can find just about anything you want, from hardware to underwear. And when you've had it with shopping (or if you want to skip the shopping all together, for that matter), head east on Haley Road, at the northern end of "outlet row," straight for the water. At the end of Haley Road, along Route 103, lies the hidden Kittery most tourists miss. This winding stretch includes some history: **Ft. Foster** (1872), an active military installation until 1949, and **Ft. McClary** (1690), manned during five wars. Along the way there are also hiking and biking trails, and, best of all, great views of the water.

❷ Beyond Kittery, Route 1 heads north to **the Yorks,** and a right onto Route 1A (York Street) leads to the **York Village Historic District,** where a number of 18th- and 19th-century buildings have been restored and maintained by the Old York Historical Society. Most of the buildings are clustered along York Street and Lindsay Road, and you can buy an admission ticket for all the buildings at the **Jefferds Tavern** (Rte. 1A and Lindsay Rd.), a restored late-18th-century inn. Other historic buildings open to the public include the **Old York Gaol** (1720), once the King's Prison for the Province of Maine, which has dungeons, cells, and jailer's quarters; and the **Elizabeth Perkins House** (1731), with Victorian-era furniture that reflects the style of its last occupants, the prominent Perkins family. The historical society offers tours with guides in period costumes, crafts workshops, and special programs in summer. ☎ 207/363–4974. ☛ *$6 adults, $2.50 children 6–16, $16 family.* ☉ *Mid-June–Sept., Tues.–Sat. 10–5, Sun. 1–5.*

Complete your tour of the Yorks by driving down Nubble Road (turn right off Rte. 1A) to the end of Cape Neddick, where you can park and gaze out at the **Nubble Light** (1879), which sits on a tiny island just offshore. The keeper's house is a tidy Victorian cottage with pretty gingerbread woodwork and a red roof.

Shore Road to Ogunquit passes the 100-foot Bald Head Cliff, which allows a view up and down the coast; on a stormy day the surf can be quite wild here. Shore Road will take you right into **Ogunquit,** a coastal village that became a resort in the 1880s and gained fame as an artists' colony. Today visitors enjoy exploring the town's art galleries, including the Ogunquit Art Association Gallery on Route 1 and the Barn Gallery on Bourne Lane, where the works of many local and regional artists are displayed.

On Shore Road, the **Ogunquit Museum of American Art,** a low-lying concrete building overlooking the ocean and set amid a 3-acre sculpture garden, shows works by Henry Strater, Marsden Hartley, William Bailey, Gaston Lachaise, Walt Kuhn, and Reginald Marsh. The huge windows of the sculpture court command a view of cliffs and ocean. *Shore Rd.,* ☎ *207/646–4909.* ☛ *$3 adults, $2 seniors and students, children under 12 free.* ☉ *July–Sept., Mon.–Sat. 10:30–5, Sun. 2–5.*

Perkins Cove, a neck of land connected to the mainland by Oarweed Road and a pedestrian drawbridge, is a half-mile from the art museum. "Quaint" is the only word for this jumble of sea-beaten fish houses transformed by the tide of tourism to shops and restaurants. When you've

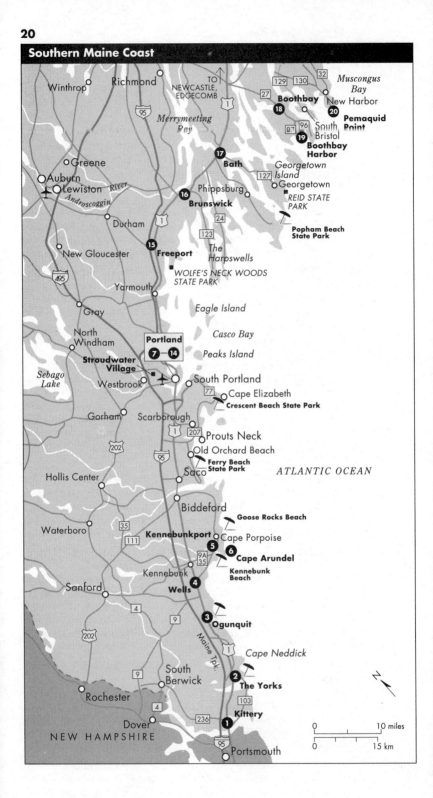

Southern Maine Coast

had your fill of browsing and jostling the crowds at Perkins Cove, stroll out along the Marginal Way, a mile-long footpath that hugs the shore of a rocky promontory known as Israel's Head.

 Follow Route 1 north to **Wells,** a family-oriented beach community consisting of several densely populated summer communities along 7 miles of shore. The 1,600-acre Wells Reserve at Laudholm Farm consists of meadows, orchards, fields, salt marshes, and an extensive trail network, as well as two estuaries and 9 miles of seashore. The visitor center features an introductory slide show and five rooms of exhibits. *Laudholm Farm Rd.,* ☎ *207/646–1555.* ☛ *Free. Parking: $5.* ☉ *Grounds daily 8–5; visitor center May–Oct., Mon.–Sat. 10–4, Sun. noon–4; Nov.–Apr., weekdays only.*

Five miles north of Wells, Route 1 becomes Main Street in Kennebunk. For a sense of the area's history and architecture, begin here at the **Brick Store Museum.** The cornerstone of this block-long preservation of early 19th-century commercial buildings is William Lord's Brick Store, built as a dry-goods store in 1825 in the Federal style, with an open-work balustrade across the roof line, granite lintels over the windows, and paired chimneys. Walking tours of Kennebunk's National Historic Register District depart from the museum on Friday at 1 and on Wednesday at 10, June through October. *117 Main St.,* ☎ *207/985–4802.* ☛ *$3 adults, $1 children 6–16.* ☉ *Tues.–Sat. 10–4:30. Closed Sat. in winter.*

❺ While heading for **Kennebunkport** on Summer Street (Rte. 35), keep an eye out for the **Wedding Cake House** about a mile along on the left. The legend behind this confection in fancy wood fretwork is that its sea-captain builder was forced to set sail in the middle of his wedding, and the house was his bride's consolation for the lack of a wedding cake. The home, built in 1826, is not open to the public but there is a gallery and studio in the attached carriage house.

Route 35 merges with Route 9 and takes you right into Kennebunkport's **Dock Square,** the busy town center, which is lined with shops and galleries and draws crowds in the summer. Parking is tight in Kennebunkport in peak season. Possibilities include the municipal lot next to the Congregational Church ($2/hour, May–Oct.), the Consolidated School on School Street (free, June 25–Labor Day), and, except on Sunday mornings, St. Martha's Church (free year-round) on North Street.

When you stroll the square, walk onto the drawbridge to admire the tidal Kennebunk River. Then turn around and head up Spring Street two blocks to Maine Street and the very grand **Nott House,** known also as White Columns, an imposing Greek Revival mansion with Doric columns that rise the height of the house. The Nott House is the gathering place for village walking tours on Wednesdays and Fridays in July and August. *Maine St.,* ☎ *207/967–2751.* ☛ *$3 adults, $1 children 12 and under.* ☉ *June–late Oct., Wed.–Sat. 1–4.*

Return to your car for a leisurely drive on Ocean Avenue, which follows the Kennebunk River to the sea and then winds around the peninsula of **Cape Arundel.** Parson's Way, a small and tranquil stretch of rocky shoreline, is open to all. As you round Cape Arundel, look to the right for the entrance to George Bush's summer home at Walker's Point.

The **Seashore Trolley Museum,** on Log Cabin Road about 3 miles from Dock Square, shows a century of streetcars (1872–1972) and includes trolleys from major metropolitan areas and world capitals—

Boston to Budapest, New York to Nagasaki, and San Francisco to Sydney, Australia—all beautifully restored. Best of all, you can take a trolley ride for nearly four miles over the tracks of the former Atlantic Shoreline trolley line, with a stop along the way at the museum restoration shop, where trolleys are transformed from junk into gems. *Log Cabin Rd., ☎ 207/967–2800.* ☛ *$6 adults, $5 senior citizens, $4 children 6–16. ☉ May–mid-Oct., daily 10 5:30; reduced hrs in spring and fall.*

What to See and Do with Children

Maine Aquarium. Live sharks, seals, penguins, a petting zoo, a tidal pool, snack bar, and gift shop make a busy stop on a rainy day. *Rte. 1, Saco, ☎ 207/284–4511.* ☛ *$6.50 adults, $5.50 senior citizens, $4.50 children 5–12, $2.50 children 2–4. ☉ Daily 9–5.*

Wells Auto Museum. A must for motor fanatics as well as youngsters, the museum has 70 vintage cars, antique coin games, and a restored Model T you can ride in. *Rte. 1, ☎ 207/646–9064.* ☛ *$3.50 adults, $2 children 6–12. ☉ Mid-June–Sept., daily 10–5; Memorial Day–Columbus Day, weekends 10–5.*

Off the Beaten Path

Old Orchard Beach, a 3-mile strip of sand beach with an amusement park reminiscent of Coney Island, is only a few miles north of Biddeford on Route 9. Despite the summertime crowds and fried-food odors, the carnival atmosphere can be infectious. **Palace Playland** (☎ 207/934–2001) on Old Orchard Street has an array of rides and booths, including a 1906 carousel and a Ferris wheel with dizzying ocean views. There is no free parking anywhere in town. ☉ *June–Labor Day.*

Shopping

Several factory outlet stores along Route 1 in Kittery and Wells offer clothing, shoes, glassware, and other products from top-of-the-line manufacturers. As an outgrowth of its long-established art community, Ogunquit has numerous galleries, many on Shore Road. Perkins Cove in Ogunquit and Dock Square in Kennebunkport have seasonal gift shops, boutiques, and galleries.

Antiques

J. J. Keating (Rte. 1, Kennebunk, ☎ 207/985–2097) deals in antiques, reproductions, and auctions. **Kenneth & Ida Manko** (Seabreeze Dr., Wells, ☎ 207/646–2595) shows folk art, rustic furniture, paintings, and a large selection of 19th-century weather vanes. (From Route 1 head east on Eldridge Road for a half-mile, then turn left on Seabreeze Drive.) **Old Fort Inn and Antiques** (Old Fort Ave., Kennebunkport, ☎ 207/967–5353) stocks a small but choice selection of primitives, china, and country furniture in a converted barn adjoining an inn. **R. Jorgensen** (Rte. 1, Wells, ☎ 207/646–9444) features an eclectic selection of 18th- and 19th-century formal and country period antiques from the British Isles, Europe, and the United States.

Books

Douglas N. Harding Rare Books (Rte. 1, Wells, ☎ 207/646–8785) has a huge stock of old books, maps, and prints. **Kennebunk Book Port** (10 Dock Sq., Kennebunkport, ☎ 207/967–3815 or 800/382–2710), housed in a rum warehouse built in 1775, has a wide selection of titles and specializes in local and maritime subjects.

Crafts

Marlow's Artisans Gallery (39 Main St., Kennebunk, ☎ 207/985–2931) carries a large and eclectic collection of crafts. **The Wedding Cake Studio** (104 Summer St., Kennebunkport, ☎ 207/985–2818) offers faux finishes, trompe l'oeil, decorative painting, hand-painted clothing, and original artwork.

Women's Clothing

Chadwick's (10 Main St., Kennebunk, ☎ 207/985–7042) carries a selection of women's casual clothing. The **Shoe String** (Rte. 1, Ogunquit, ☎ 207/646–3533) has a range of shoes and handbags, from the sporty (including athletic wear) to the dressy.

Sports and the Outdoors

Biking

Cape-Able Bike Shop (Townhouse Corners, Kennebunkport, ☎ 207/967–4382) has bicycles for rent and free maps of the area; rates are $8–$25.

Bird-Watching

Biddeford Pool East Sanctuary (Rte. 9, Biddeford) is a nature preserve where shorebirds congregate. **Rachel Carson National Wildlife Refuge** (Rte. 9, Wells) is a mile-long loop through a salt marsh bordering the Little River and a white-pine forest.

Boat Trips

Finestkind (Perkins Cove, Ogunquit, ☎ 207/646–5227) has cruises to Nubble Lighthouse, cocktail cruises, lobstering trips, and sailing cruises. **Chick's Marina** (75 Ocean Ave., Kennebunkport, ☎ 207/967–2782) offers sightseeing and fishing cruises for up to six people.

Canoeing

The **Maine Audubon Society** (☎ 207/781–2330 or 207/883–5100 mid-June–Labor Day) offers daily guided canoe trips and canoe rentals in **Scarborough Marsh** (Rte. 9, Scarborough), the largest salt marsh in Maine. Programs at Maine Audubon's Falmouth headquarters include nature walks and a discovery room for children. Call ahead for information.

Deep-Sea Fishing

Cape Arundel Cruises (Performance Marine, Rte. 9, Kennebunkport, ☎ 207/967–5595) has half-day and full-day trips on its deepwater fishing boat. *Elizabeth II* (Performance Marine, Kennebunkport, ☎ 207/967–5595) carries passengers on 1½-hour narrated cruises down the Kennebunk River and out to Cape Porpoise. The *Nautilus,* run by the same outfit, goes on whale-watching cruises from May through October daily at 10 AM. *Ugly Anne* (Perkins Cove, ☎ 207/646–7202) offers half- and full-day trips.

Whale-Watching

Indian (Ocean Ave., Kennebunkport, ☎ 207/967–5912) offers half-day trips. *See also* Deep-Sea Fishing, *above.*

Beaches

Maine's sand beaches tend to be rather hard-packed and built up with beach cottages and motels. Yet the water is clean (and cold), the surf usually gentle, and the crowds manageable except on the hottest summer weekends.

Kennebunk Beach. Gooch's Beach, Middle Beach, and Kennebunk Beach (also called Mother's Beach) are the three areas of Kennebunk Beach. Beach Road with its cottages and old Victorian boardinghouses runs right behind them. For parking permits (fee charged in summer), go to the Kennebunk Town Office (1 Summer St., ☎ 207/985–2102). Gooch's and Middle beaches attract lots of teenagers; Mother's Beach, which has a small playground and tidal puddles for splashing, is popular with moms and kids.

Kennebunkport. Goose Rocks, a few minutes' drive north of town, is the largest beach in the Kennebunk area and the favorite of families with small children. For a parking permit (fee charged), go to the Kennebunkport Town Office (Elm St., ☎ 207/967–4244; ☉ Weekdays 8–4:30) or the police department (Rte. 9, ☎ 207/967–2454; ☉ 24 hrs).

Ogunquit. The 3 miles of sand beach have snack bars, boardwalk, rest rooms, and changing areas at the Beach Street entrance. The less crowded section to the north is accessible by footbridge and has rest rooms, all-day paid parking, and trolley service. The ocean beach, backed by the Ogunquit River, is ideal for children because it is sheltered and waveless. There is a parking fee.

York. York's Long Sands Beach has free parking and Route 1A running right behind it; the smaller Short Sands beach has meter parking. Both beaches have commercial development.

Dining and Lodging

Kennebunk

DINING

$$ The Impastable Dream. If it's pasta you crave, head to this cozy restaurant set in an old Cape Cod cottage on Main Street. Tables are small and close together and the decor is simple, but the food is reasonably priced, plentiful, and very good. ✗ *17 Main St., ☎ 207/985–6039. No reservations. D, MC, V. Closed Sun.*

Kennebunkport

DINING

$$$–$$$$ White Barn Inn. The rustic but elegant dining room of this inn serves regional New England cuisine. The fixed price menu changes weekly and may include steamed Maine lobster nestled on fresh fettuccine with carrots and ginger in a Thai-inspired honey and sherry vinegar sauce or grilled veal chop with baby carrots, wild rice cakes, sorrel, and lemon grass scented with curry sauce; or roasted breast of free-range chicken with aromatic vegetables Brunoise, fried herbs, olive oil, mashed potatoes, and a thyme-infused consommé. ✗ *Beach St., ☎ 207/967–2321. Reservations advised. Jacket required. AE, MC, V.*

$$$–$$$$ Windows on the Water. This restaurant overlooks Dock Square and the working harbor of Kennebunkport. Try the California lobster ravioli or the gorgonzola-stuffed mignon. The "A Night on the Town" special, a five-course dinner for two, including wine, tax, and gratuity, for $74, is a good value if you have a healthy appetite. ✗ *Chase Hill Rd., ☎ 207/967–3313. Reservations required. AE, D, DC, MC, V.*

DINING AND LODGING

$$$–$$$$ Cape Arundel Inn. Were it not for the rocky shore beyond the picture
★ windows, the pillared porch with wicker chairs, and the cozy parlor (with fireplace and backgammon boards) that you pass through en route to the dining room, you might well think you were dining at a major Boston restaurant. The lobster bisque is creamy, with just a bit of cognac. Entrées include marlin with sorrel butter; coho salmon with mushrooms, white wine, and lemon; rack of lamb; and pecan chicken with peaches and crème fraîche. The inn has 14 guest rooms, seven in the Victorian-era converted summer "cottage" and six in a motel facility adjoining.

There's also a carriage-house apartment. ⊡ *Ocean Ave., 04046,* ☎ *207/ 967–2125. Restaurant (reservations advised; no lunch). AE, MC, V. Closed mid-Oct.–mid-May.*

LODGING

$$$$ Captain Lord Mansion. A long and distinguished history, a three-story elliptical staircase, and a cupola with widow's walk make this something more than the standard bed-and-breakfast. The rooms, named for clipper ships, are mostly large and stately—11 have a fireplace—though the style relaxes as one ascends from the ground-floor rooms (damask and mahogany) to the country-style third-floor accommodations (pine furniture and leafy views). ⊡ *Pleasant and Green Sts., Box 800, 04046,* ☎ *207/967–3141,* FAX *207/967–3172. 16 rooms with bath. D, MC, V.*

$$$$ Inn at Harbor Head. The 100-year-old shingled farmhouse on the harbor at Cape Porpoise has become a tiny bed-and-breakfast full of antiques, paintings, and heirlooms. The Harbor Suite upstairs has murals and a fireplace; the Greenery downstairs boasts a whirlpool tub and a garden view. The Summer suite and the Garden room have the best water views. The grounds are bright with flower beds. ⊡ *41 Pier Rd., 04046,* ☎ *207/967–5564. 3 rooms with bath, 2 suites. Dock. MC, V.*

$$$$ Old Fort Inn. This inn at the crest of a hill on a quiet road off Ocean Avenue has a secluded, countryish feel and the welcome sense of being just a touch above the Kennebunkport action. The front half of the former barn is an antiques shop (specializing in Early American pieces); the rest of the barn is the reception area and parlor decorated with grandfather clocks, antique tools, and funny old canes. Guest rooms are in a long, low fieldstone-and-stucco carriage house. Rooms are not large, but the decor is witty and creative: There are quilts on the four-poster beds; wreaths, primitive portraits, and framed antique bodices hang on the walls; the loveseats are richly upholstered. Superior rooms and suites have whirlpools. ⊡ *Old Fort Ave., Box M, 04046,* ☎ *207/967– 5353,* FAX *207/967–4547. 14 rooms with bath, 2 suites. Air-conditioning, minibars, pool, tennis courts. Buffet breakfast included. AE, D, MC, V. Closed mid-Dec.–mid-Apr.*

$$$–$$$$ Bufflehead Cove. Situated on the Kennebunk River at the end of a wind-
★ ing dirt road, the friendly gray-shingle bed-and-breakfast affords the quiet of country fields and apple trees only five minutes from Dock Square. The guest rooms in the main house are dollhouse-pretty, with white wicker and flowers painted on the walls. The Hideaway Suite, with a two-sided gas fireplace, king-size bed, and large whirlpool tub, overlooks the river, while the Garden Studio offers the most privacy. ⊡ *Gornitz La., Box 499, 04046,* ☎ *207/967–3879. 3 rooms with bath, 3 suites. Dock. AE, D, MC, V. Closed midweek Jan.–Mar.*

$$$–$$$$ Captain Jefferds Inn. The three-story white-clapboard sea captain's mansion with black shutters, built in 1804, has been restored and filled with the innkeeper's collections of majolica, American art pottery, and Sienese pottery. Most rooms are done in Laura Ashley fabrics and wallpapers, and many have been furnished with a wide variety of antiques and collections from all over the world. A hearty breakfast is included. ⊡ *Pearl St., Box 691, 04046,* ☎ *207/967–2311. 13 rooms with bath; 4 suites in carriage house, 2 with kitchenettes. Croquet. MC, V. Closed Dec.–Apr.*

$$$–$$$$ Maine Stay Inn and Cottages. Located on a quiet residential street, a short walk from Dock Square, the Maine Stay offers rooms and suites with private baths in the square-block Italianate-style main house as well as cottages with kitchens and fireplaces. Children are welcome here and there's even a play area for them. Cottage guests can choose to have their breakfast delivered to them. ☎ *34 Maine St., Box 500A, 04046,* ☎ *207/967–2117 or 800/950–2117,* FAX *207/967–8757. 4 rooms with baths, 2 suites, 11 cottages. Croquet. AE, D, MC, V.*

$$$–$$$$ **The Seaside.** The modern motel units, all with sliding glass doors opening onto private decks or patios, half of them with ocean views, are appropriate for families; so are the cottages, which have from one to four bedrooms. The four bedrooms in the inn, furnished with antiques, are more suitable for adults. ☎ *Gooch's Beach, 04046,* ☎ *207/ 967–4461. 26 rooms with bath, 10 cottages. Beach, playground, laundry. CP for inn and motel guests. MC, V. Inn rooms closed Labor Day–June; cottages closed Nov.–Apr.*

Kittery

DINING

$–$$ **Warren's Lobster House.** A local institution, this waterfront restaurant offers reasonably priced boiled lobster, first-rate scrod, and a huge salad bar. You can dine outdoors overlooking the water in season. ✕ *Rte. 1,* ☎ *207/439–1630. Reservations advised. AE, MC, V.*

LODGING

$–$$ **Deep Water Landing.** This comfortable, turn-of-the-century New Englander welcomes guests to the three rooms on its third floor. Fruit trees and flower beds border the lawns, and the breakfast room offers water views. ☎ *92 Whipple Rd., 03904,* ☎ *207/439–0824. 3 rooms with shared bath. Full breakfast included. No credit cards.*

Ogunquit

DINING

$$$–$$$$ **Arrows.** Elegant simplicity is the hallmark of this 18th-century farm-
★ house, 2 miles up a back road. The menu changes daily, offering such entrées as fillet of beef glistening in red and yellow sauces, grilled salmon and radicchio with marinated fennel and baked polenta, and Chinese-style duck glazed with molasses. Appetizers (Maine crabmeat mousse or lobster risotto) and desserts (strawberry shortcake with Chantilly cream or steamed chocolate pudding) are also beautifully executed and presented. ✕ *Berwick Rd.,* ☎ *207/361–1100. Reservations advised. MC, V. Closed Mon. and Thanksgiving–May.*

$$$–$$$$ **Hurricane.** Don't let its weather-beaten exterior deter you—this small,
★ comfortable seafood bar-and-grill offers first-rate cooking and spectacular views of the crashing surf. Start with lobster chowder, napoleon of smoked salmon, grilled chicken satay, or the house salad (assorted greens with pistachio nuts and roasted shallots). Entrées include fresh lobster-stuffed pasta shells, baked salmon and brie baklava, and shrimp scampi served over fresh pasta. Be sure to save room for the classic crème brûlée. ✕ *Perkins Cove,* ☎ *207/646–6348. AE, D, DC, MC, V.*

$$ **Ogunquit Lobster Pound.** Select your lobster live, then dine under the trees or in the rustic dining room of the log cabin. The menu includes steamed clams, steak, and chicken; and there is a special children's menu. ✕ *Rte. 1,* ☎ *207/646–2516. No reservations. AE, MC, V. Closed late Oct.–mid-May.*

LODGING

$$–$$$ **The Colonial: A Resort by the Sea.** This complex of accommodations in the middle of Ogunquit includes a large white Victorian inn, modern motel units, and efficiency apartments. Inn rooms have flowered wallpaper, Colonial reproduction furniture, and white ruffle curtains. Efficiencies are popular with families. One-third of the rooms have water views. ☎ *Shore Rd., Box 895, 03907,* ☎ *207/646–5191. 80 units, 44*

with bath; 36 suites. Restaurant, pool, hot tub, shuffleboard, playground, laundry. AE, D, MC, V. Closed Nov.–Apr.

$–$$$ Seafair Inn. A century-old white-clapboard house set back behind shrubs and lawn in the center of town, the Seafair has a homey atmosphere and proximity to the beach. Rooms are furnished with odds and ends of country furniture; breakfast is served on an enclosed sun porch. ▨ *14 Shore Rd., Box 1221, 03907, ☎ 207/646–2181. 18 units, 14 with bath; 4 efficiency suites. CP. MC, V. Closed Nov.–Mar.*

Prouts Neck
LODGING

$$$$ Black Point Inn. At the neck of the peninsula that juts into the ocean
★ at Prouts Neck, 12 miles south of Portland, stands one of the great old-time resorts of Maine. The sun porch has wicker and plants, the music room—in the English country-house style—has wing chairs, fresh flowers, Chinese prints, and a grand piano. In the guest rooms are mahogany bedsteads, Martha Washington bedspreads, and white-ruffle Priscilla curtains. Older guests prefer the main inn; families choose from the four cottages. The extensive grounds offer beaches, hiking, a bird sanctuary, and sports. The dining room, done in beautiful floral-pattern wallpaper and water-stained pine paneling, has a menu strong in seafood. ▨ *510 Black Point Rd., Scarborough 04074, ☎ 207/883–4126 or 800/258–0003; ℻ 207/883–9976. 80 rooms with bath, 6 suites. Restaurant, bar, indoor and outdoor pools, hot tub, croquet, volleyball, boating, bicycles, golf, tennis courts. AE, MC, V. Closed Dec.–Apr.*

Wells
DINING

$$–$$$ The Grey Gull. This charming Victorian inn offers views of the open sea and rocks on which seals like to sun themselves. In the evening, try any of the excellent seafood dishes, chicken breast rolled in walnuts and baked with maple syrup, Yankee pot roast, or soft-shell crabs almondine. Breakfast is popular here in the summer: Blueberry pancakes, ham-and-cheese strata, or eggs McGull served on crabcakes with hollandaise sauce are good choices. ✕ *321 Webhannet Dr., at Moody Point, ☎ 207/646–7501. Reservations advised. AE, MC, V.*

$$ Billy's Chowder House. As the crowded parking lot suggests, this simple restaurant in a salt marsh is popular with locals and tourists alike. For a generous lobster roll or haddock sandwich (not to mention chowders), Billy's is hard to beat. ✕ *Mile Rd., ☎ 207/646–7558. AE, MC, V. Closed 1 month in winter.*

The Yorks
DINING

$$–$$$ Cape Neddick Inn. This restaurant and art gallery has an airy ambience, with tables set well apart, lots of windows, and art everywhere. The New American menu has offered lobster macadamia tart (shelled lobster sautéed with shallots, macadamia nuts, sherry, and cream and served in pastry), breaded pork tenderloin, and such appetizers as spicy sesame chicken dumplings and gravlax with Russian pepper vodka. Duckling flamed in brandy is always on the menu. ✕ *Rte. 1, Cape Neddick, ☎ 207/363–2899. Reservations advised. AE, MC, V. No lunch. Closed Mon. and Tues. Columbus Day–May 31.*

$$–$$$ York Harbor Inn. The dining room of this inn has country charm and
★ great ocean views. In the past, Frank Jones, king of New England ale-makers, patronized the inn; nowadays you might spot local resident and poet May Sarton enjoying a meal here. For dinner, start with Maine crab cakes, a classic Caesar salad, or a creamy seafood chowder, and then try the lobster-stuffed chicken breast with Boursin sauce

or the angel hair pasta with shrimp and scallops. Just save room for the crème caramel or any of the other wonderful desserts. ✕ *Rte. 1A (Box 573), York Harbor 03911,* ☎ *207/363–5119 or 800/343–3869. Reservations advised. AE, DC, MC, V. No lunch off-season.*

DINING AND LODGING

$$–$$$$ **Dockside Guest Quarters and Restaurant.** On an 8-acre private island in the middle of York Harbor, the Dockside promises water views, seclusion, and quiet. Rooms in the Maine House, the oldest structure on the site, are furnished with Early American antiques, marine artifacts, and nautical paintings and prints. Four modern cottages tucked among the trees have less character but bigger windows on the water, and many have kitchenettes. Entrées in the esteemed dining room may include scallop-stuffed shrimp Casino, broiled salmon, steak au poivre with brandied mushroom sauce, and roast stuffed duckling. There's also a children's menu. ⊞ *York Harbor off Rte. 103, Box 205, York 03909,* ☎ *207/363–2868,* ℻ *207/363–1977. 22 rooms, 20 with bath; 5 suites. Restaurant (*☎ *207/363–2722; reservations advised on weekends; closed Mon; $$), dock, boating, badminton, croquet, bicycles. MC, V. Closed late Oct.–Apr.*

The Arts

Music
Hamilton House (Vaughan's La., S. Berwick, ☎ 603/436–3205), the Georgian home featured in Sarah Orne Jewett's *The Tory Lover,* presents "Sundays in the Garden," a series of free summer concerts in July and August. Concerts begin at 3; the grounds are open noon until 5 for picnicking.

Theater
Ogunquit Playhouse (Rte. 1, ☎ 207/646–5511), one of America's oldest summer theaters, mounts plays and musicals from late June to Labor Day.

North from Kittery Essentials

Getting Around
BY CAR
Route 1 from Kittery is the shopper's route north, while other roads hug the coastline. Interstate 95 should be faster for travelers headed for specific towns. The exit numbers can be confusing: As you go north from Portsmouth, Exits 1–3 lead to Kittery and Exit 4 leads to the Yorks. After the tollbooth in York, the Maine Turnpike begins, and the numbers start over again, with Exit 2 for Wells and Ogunquit and Exit 3 (and Route 35) for Kennebunk and Kennebunkport. Route 9 goes from Kennebunkport to Cape Porpoise and Goose Rocks.

BY TROLLEY
A trolley circulates among the Yorks from June to Labor Day. Eight trolleys serve the major tourist areas and beaches of Ogunquit, including four that connect with Wells from mid-May through mid-October. The trolley from Dock Square in Kennebunkport to Kennebunk Beach runs from late June to Labor Day. ☛ *$1–$3 depending on destination; $1 children 5–12.*

Important Addresses and Numbers
EMERGENCIES
Maine State Police (Gray, ☎ 207/793–4500 or 800/482–0730). **Kennebunk Walk-in Clinic** (Rte. 1 N, ☎ 207/985–6027). **Southern Maine**

Medical Center (1 Medical Center Dr., Biddeford, ☎ 207/283–7000; emergency room, 207/283–7100).

VISITOR INFORMATION
Off-season, most chambers are open weekdays 9–5; the hours below are for summer only.

Kennebunk-Kennebunkport Chamber of Commerce (173 Port Rd., ☎ 207/967–0857; ⊘ Mon.–Thurs. 9–6, Fri. 9–8, Sat. 10–6, Sun. 11–4). **Kittery-Eliot Chamber of Commerce** (191 State Rd., Kittery, ☎ 207/439–7545; ⊘ Weekdays 10–5). **Maine Publicity Bureau** (Rte. 1 and I–95, ☎ 207/439–1319; ⊘ Daily 9–5; extended hours in summer). **Ogunquit Chamber of Commerce** (Box 2289, Ogunquit, ☎ 207/646–2939 or 207/646–5533, mid-May–mid-Oct.; ⊘ Daily 9–5, later Fri. and Sat.). **Wells Chamber of Commerce** (Box 356, Wells 04090, ☎ 207/646–2451; ⊘ Daily 9–5, Fri. and Sat. until 6). The **Yorks Chamber of Commerce** (Box 417, York, ☎ 207/363–4422; ⊘ Daily 9–6; extended hours on weekends).

PORTLAND TO PEMAQUID POINT

Maine's largest city, small enough to be seen in a day or two, Portland is undergoing a cultural and economic renaissance. New hotels and a bright new performing arts center have joined the neighborhoods of historic homes; the Old Port Exchange, perhaps the finest urban renovation project on the East Coast, balances modern commercial enterprise with a salty waterfront character in an area bustling with restaurants, shops, and galleries. The piers of Commercial Street abound with opportunities for water tours of the harbor and excursions to the Calendar Islands.

Freeport, north of Portland, is a town made famous by the L. L. Bean store, whose success led to the opening of scores of other clothing stores and outlets. Brunswick is best known for Bowdoin College. Bath has been a shipbuilding center since 1607, and the Maine Maritime Museum preserves its history.

The Boothbays—the coastal areas of Boothbay Harbor, East Boothbay, Linekin Neck, Southport Island, and the inland town of Boothbay—attract hordes of vacationing families and flotillas of pleasure craft. The Pemaquid peninsula juts into the Atlantic south of Damariscotta and just east of the Boothbays, and near Pemaquid Beach one can view the objects unearthed at the Colonial Pemaquid Restoration.

Exploring

Numbers in the margin correspond to points of interest on the Southern Maine Coast and Portland maps.

➐ Congress Street, **Portland**'s main street, runs the length of the peninsular city from the Western Promenade in the southwest to the Eastern Promenade in the northeast, passing through the small downtown area. A few blocks southeast of downtown, the bustling Old Port Exchange sprawls along the waterfront.

➑ One of the notable homes on Congress Street is the **Neal Dow Memorial,** a brick mansion built in 1829 in the late Federal style by General Neal Dow, a zealous abolitionist and prohibitionist. The library has fine ornamental ironwork, and the furnishings include the family china, silver, and portraits. Don't miss the grandfather clocks and the

Portland

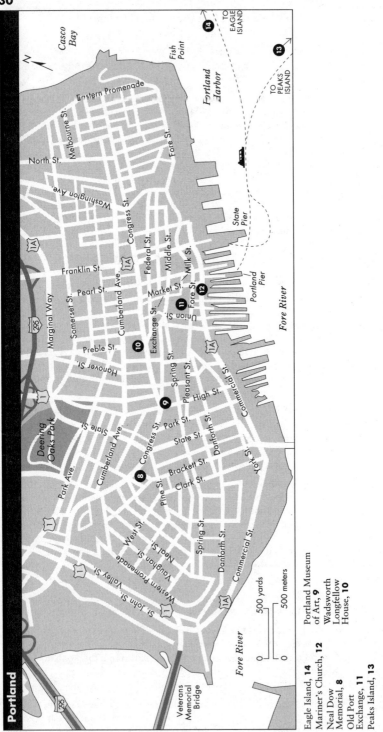

Casco Bay

Fish Point

Eastern Promenade

Portland Harbor

N

TO EAGLE ISLAND

14

TO PEAKS ISLAND

13

North St.

Melbourne St.

Washington Ave.

Congress St.

Fore St.

State Pier

Franklin St.

Federal St.

Middle St.

Milk St.

11A

11A

Pearl St.

Market St.

Fore St.

12

Marginal Way

Cumberland Ave.

Exchange St.

Union St.

11

Portland Pier

Somerset St.

295

Preble St.

10

Fore River

Hanover St.

Spring St.

11A

Deering Oaks Park

State St.

Pleasant St.

High St.

Commercial St.

11

9

Park St.

Congress St.

Pine St.

State St.

Danforth St.

Park Ave.

Cumberland Ave.

1

8

Brackett St.

Clark St.

York St.

West St.

Neal St.

Vaughan St.

Spring St.

Danforth St.

11

St. John St.

Valley St.

Western Promenade

Commercial St.

11

11A

Fore River

Veterans Memorial Bridge

295

0   500 yards

0   500 meters

original deed granted by James II. *714 Congress St.,* ☎ *207/773–7773.* ☛ *Free.* ☾ *Tours weekdays 11–4.*

❾ On Congress Square, the distinguished **Portland Museum of Art** has a strong collection of seascapes and landscapes by such masters as Winslow Homer, John Marin, Andrew Wyeth, and Marsden Hartley. Homer's *Pulling the Dory* and *Weatherbeaten,* two quintessential Maine coast images, are here. The Joan Whitney Payson Collection includes works by Monet, Picasso, and Renoir. The strikingly modern Charles Shipman Payson building was designed by Harry N. Cobb, an associate of I. M. Pei, in 1983. *7 Congress Sq.,* ☎ *207/775–6148 or 207/773–2787.* ☛ *$6 adults, $5 senior citizens and students, $1 children 6–12, free Thurs. evenings 5–9.* ☾ *Tues.–Sat. 10–5 (Thurs. until 9), Sun. noon–5. Call for winter hrs.*

❿ Walk east on Congress Street to the **Wadsworth Longfellow House** of 1785, the boyhood home of the poet and the first brick house in Portland. The late-Colonial-style structure sits well back from the street and has a small portico over its entrance and four chimneys surmounting the hip roof. Most of the furnishings are original to the house. *485 Congress St.,* ☎ *207/879–0427.* ☛ *$4 adults, $1 children under 12.* ☾ *June–Oct., Tues.–Sun. 10–4.*

⓫ You can walk from downtown to the **Old Port Exchange,** or you can drive and park your car either at the city garage on Fore Street (between Exchange and Union streets) or opposite the U.S. Customs House at the corner of Fore and Pearl streets. Like the Customs House, the brick buildings and warehouses of the Old Port Exchange were built following the Great Fire of 1866 and were intended to last for ages. When the city's economy slumped in the middle of the present century, however, the Old Port declined and seemed slated for demolition. Then artists and craftspeople began opening shops here in the late 1960s, and in time restaurants, chic boutiques, bookstores, and gift shops followed.

The Old Port is best explored on foot. Allow a couple of hours to wander at leisure on Market, Exchange, Middle, and Fore streets. The **⓬ Mariner's Church** (376 Fore St.) has a fine facade of granite columns, and the Elias Thomas Block on Commercial Street demonstrates the graceful use of bricks in commercial architecture. Inevitably the salty smell of the sea will draw you to one of the wharves off Commercial Street; Custom House Wharf retains some of the older, rougher waterfront atmosphere.

The brightly painted ferries of **Casco Bay Lines** (☎ 207/774–7871) are the lifeline to the Calendar Islands of Casco Bay, which number about 136, depending on the tides and how one defines an island.

⓭ **Peaks Island,** nearest Portland, is the most developed, and some residents commute to work in Portland. Yet you can still commune with the wind and the sea on Peaks, explore an old fort, and ramble along the alternately rocky and sandy shore.

⓮ The 17-acre **Eagle Island,** owned by the State of Maine and open to the public for day trips in summer, was the home of Admiral Robert E. Peary, the American explorer of the North Pole. Peary built a stone-and-wood house on the island as a summer retreat in 1904, then made it his permanent residence. The house remains as it was when Peary was here with his stuffed Arctic birds and the quartz he brought home and set into the fieldstone fireplace. The *Kristy K.,* departing from Long Wharf, makes a four-hour narrated tour. *Long Wharf,* ☎ *207/774–*

6498. ☛ *Excursion tour: $15 adults, $12 senior citizens, $9 children 5–12.* ☉ *Departures mid-June–Labor Day, daily 10 AM.*

⑮ **Freeport,** on Route 1, 15 miles northeast of Portland, has charming back streets lined with old clapboard houses and even a small harbor on the Harraseeket River, but the overwhelming majority of visitors come to shop, and L. L. Bean is the store that put Freeport on the map. Founded in 1912 as a small mail order merchandiser of products for hunters, guides, and fisherfolk, L. L. Bean now attracts some 3.5 million shoppers a year to its giant store in the heart of Freeport's shopping district on Route 1. Here you can still find the original hunting boots, along with cotton, wool, and silk sweaters; camping and ski equipment; comforters; and hundreds of other items for the home, car, boat, or campsite. Across the street from the main store, a Bean factory outlet has seconds and discontinued merchandise at discount prices. *Rte. 1, Freeport,* ☎ *800/341–4341.* ☉ *24 hrs.*

All around L. L. Bean, like seedlings under a mighty spruce, some 70 outlets have sprouted, offering designer clothes, shoes, housewares, and toys at discount prices (*see* Shopping, *below*).

⑯ It's 9 miles northeast on Route 1 from Freeport to **Brunswick.** Follow the signs to the Brunswick business district, Pleasant Street, and—at the end of Pleasant Street—Maine Street, which claims to be the widest (198 feet across) in the state. Friday from May through October sees a fine farmer's market on the town mall, between Maine Street and Park Row.

Maine Street takes you to the 110-acre campus of **Bowdoin College,** an enclave of distinguished architecture, gardens, and grassy quadrangles in the middle of town. Campus tours (☎ 207/725–3000) depart every day but Sunday from Chamberlain Hall, the admissions office. Among the historic buildings are Massachusetts Hall, a stout, sober, hip-roofed brick structure that dates from 1802 and that once housed the entire college. Hubbard Hall, an imposing 1902 neo-Gothic building is home to Maine's only gargoyle. In addition, it houses the **Peary-MacMillan Arctic Museum.** The museum contains photographs, navigational instruments, and artifacts from the first successful expedition to the North Pole, in 1909, by two of Bowdoin's most famous alumni, Admiral Robert E. Peary and Donald B. MacMillan. ☎ *207/725–3416.* ☛ *Free.* ☉ *Tues.–Sat. 10–5, Sun. 2–5.*

Don't miss the **Bowdoin College Museum of Art,** a splendid limestone, brick, and granite structure in a Renaissance Revival style, with three galleries upstairs, and four more downstairs, radiating from a rotunda. Designed in 1894 by Charles F. McKim, the building stands on a rise, its facade adorned with classical statues and the entrance set off by a triumphal arch. The collections encompass Assyrian and Classical art and that of the Dutch, Italian, French, and Flemish old masters; a superb gathering of Colonial and Federal paintings, notably the Gilbert Stuart portraits of Madison and Jefferson; and a Winslow Homer Gallery of engravings, etchings, and memorabilia (open summer only). The museum's collection also includes 19th- and 20th-century American painting and sculpture, with works by Mary Cassatt, Andrew Wyeth, John Sloan, Rockwell Kent, Jim Dine, and Robert Rauschenberg. *Walker Art Bldg.,* ☎ *207/725–3275.* ☛ *Free.* ☉ *Tues.–Sat. 10–5, Sun. 2–5.*

Before going on to Bath, drive down Route 123 or Route 24 to the peninsulas and islands known collectively as the **Harpswells.** The numerous small coves along Harpswell Neck shelter the boats of local lobstermen, and summer cottages are tucked away amid the birch and spruce trees.

17 **Bath,** 7 miles east of Brunswick on Route 1, has been a shipbuilding center since 1607. Today the Bath Iron Works turns out guided-missile frigates for the U.S. Navy and merchant container ships.

The **Maine Maritime Museum and Shipyard** in Bath (take the Bath Business District exit from Route 1, turn right on Washington Street, and follow the signs) has ship models, journals, photographs, and other artifacts to stir the nautical dreams of old salts and young. The 142-foot Grand Banks fishing schooner *Sherman Zwicker,* one of the last of its kind, is on display when in port. You can watch apprentice boatbuilders wield their tools on classic Maine boats at the restored Percy & Small Shipyard and Apprentice Shop. The outdoor shipyard is open May–November; during these months visitors may take scenic tours of the Kennebec River on the *Summertime.* During off-season, the Maritime History Building has indoor exhibits, videos, and activities. *243 Washington St.,* ☎ *207/443–1316.* ☛ *$6.50 adults, $5.85 senior citizens, $4 children 6–17.* ⊙ *Daily 9:30–5.*

From Bath it's 10 miles northeast on Route 1 to Wiscasset, where the huge rotting hulls of the schooners *Hester* and *Luther Little* rest, testaments to the town's once-busy harbor. Those who appreciate both music and antiques will enjoy a visit to the **Musical Wonder House** to see and hear the vast collection of antique music boxes from around the world. *18 High St.,* ☎ *207/882–7163.* ☛ *1-hr presentation on main floor: $10 adults, $7.50 children under 12 and senior citizens; 3-hr tour of entire house: $30 or $50 for 2 people.* ⊙ *May 15–Oct. 15, daily 10–6. Last tour usually 4 PM; call ahead for 3-hr tours.*

TIME OUT **Treats** (Main St., ☎ 207/882–6192) is a good spot to pick up a gourmet snack, a cappuccino or espresso, or picnic fixings. Take your treat down to the waterfront park or across the street to the Hidden Garden, a small park made in an old foundation.

18 Across the river, drive south on Route 27 to reach the **Boothbay Railway Village,** about a mile north of **Boothbay,** where you can ride 1½ miles on a narrow-gauge steam train through a re-creation of a turn-of-the-century New England village. Among the 24 village buildings is a museum with more than 50 antique automobiles and trucks. *Rte. 27, Boothbay,* ☎ *207/633–4727.* ☛ *$6 adults, $3 children 2–12.* ⊙ *Weekends Memorial Day–mid-Oct., 9:30–5; 9:30–5 daily June 10–Columbus Day; special Halloween schedule; closed Columbus Day–Memorial Day.*

19 Continue south on Route 27 into Boothbay Harbor, bear right on Oak Street, and follow it to the waterfront parking lots. **Boothbay Harbor** is a town to wander through: Commercial Street, Wharf Street, the By-Way, and Townsend Avenue are lined with shops, galleries, and ice-cream parlors. Excursion boats (*see* Sports and the Outdoors, *below*) leave from the piers off Commercial Street.

Having explored Boothbay Harbor, return to Route 27 and head north again to Route 1. Proceed north to Business Route 1, and follow it through Damariscotta, an appealing shipbuilding town on the Damariscotta River. Bear right on the Bristol Road (Rte. 129/130), and when the highway splits, stay on Route 130, which leads to Bristol and **20** terminates at **Pemaquid Point.**

About 5 miles south of Bristol you'll come to New Harbor, where a right turn will take you to Pemaquid Beach and the **Colonial Pemaquid Restoration.** Here, on a small peninsula jutting into the Pemaquid River, English mariners established a fishing and trading settlement in the early 17th century. The excavations at **Ft. William Henry,** begun in the mid-1960s, have turned up thousands of artifacts from the Colonial settlement, including the remains of an old customs house, tavern, jail, forge, and homes, and from even earlier Native American settlements. The State of Maine operates a museum displaying many of the artifacts. *Rte. 130, Pemaquid Point,* ☎ *207/677–2423.* ☛ *$1.50 adults, 50¢ children 6–12.* ⊙ *Memorial Day–Labor Day, daily 9:30–5.*

Route 130 terminates at the **Pemaquid Point Light,** which looks as though it sprouted from the ragged, tilted chunk of granite that it commands. The former lighthouse-keeper's cottage is now the **Fishermen's Museum,** with photographs, models, and artifacts that explore commercial fishing in Maine. Here, too, is the Pemaquid Art Gallery, which mounts changing exhibitions from July 1 through Labor Day. *Rte. 130,* ☎ *207/ 677–2494.* ☛ *Donation requested.* ⊙ *Memorial Day–Columbus Day, Mon.–Sat. 10–5, Sun. 11–5.*

What to See and Do with Children

Boothbay Railway Village, Boothbay
Children's Museum of Maine. Touching is okay at this museum where little ones can pretend they are lobstermen, shopkeepers, or computer experts. Camera Obscura, a new permanent exhibit on the third floor, charges a separate admission fee ($2). *142 Free St., Portland,* ☎ *207/ 828–1234.* ☛ *$4 adults and children over 1.* ⊙ *Mon., Wed., Thurs. 10–5, Fri. 10–8, Tues. and Sun. noon–5.*
Maine Coast Railroad. Travel from Wiscasset to Newcastle in restored 1930s coaches. *Rte. 1, Wiscasset,* ☎ *207/882–8000.* ☛ *$10 adults, $5 children ages 5–12, under 5 free when not occupying a separate seat, $25 family (2 adults, 4 children).*

Off the Beaten Path

Stroudwater Village, 3 miles west of Portland, was spared the devastation of the fire of 1866 and thus contains some of the best examples of 18th- and early 19th-century architecture in the region. Here are the remains of mills, canals, and historic homes, including the Tate House, built in 1755 with paneling from England. It overlooks the old mast yard where George Tate, Mast Agent to the King, prepared tall pines for the ships of the Royal Navy. The furnishings date to the late 18th century. *Tate House, 1270 Westbrook St.,* ☎ *207/774–9781.* ☛ *$3 adults, $1 children.* ⊙ *July–Sept. 15, Tues.–Sat. 10–4, Sun. 1–4.*

Shopping

The best shopping in Portland is at the Old Port Exchange, where many shops are concentrated along Fore and Exchange streets. Freeport's name is almost synonymous with shopping: **L. L. Bean** and the 70 factory outlets that opened during the 1980s are here. Outlet stores are in the Fashion Outlet Mall (2 Depot St.) and the Freeport Crossing (200 Lower Main St.), and many others crowd Main Street and Bow Street. The *Freeport Visitors Guide* (Freeport Merchants Association, Box 452, Freeport 04032, ☎ 207/865–1212) has a complete listing. Boothbay Harbor, and Commercial Street in particular, is chockablock with gift shops, T-shirt shops, and other seasonal emporia catering to visitors.

Antiques
F. O. Bailey Antiquarians (141 Middle St., Portland, ☎ 207/774–1479), Portland's largest retail showroom, features antique and reproduction furniture and jewelry, paintings, rugs, and china. **Harrington House Museum Store** (45 Main St., Freeport, ☎ 207/865–0477) is a restored 19th-century merchant's home owned by the Freeport Historical Society; all the period reproductions that furnish the rooms are for sale. In addition, you can buy books, rugs, jewelry, crafts, Shaker items, toys, and kitchen utensils. **Maine Trading Post** (80 Commercial St., Boothbay Harbor, ☎ 207/633–2760) sells antiques and fine reproductions that include rolltop desks able to accommodate personal computers, as well as gifts and decorative accessories.

Books and Maps
Carlson and Turner (241 Congress St., Portland, ☎ 207/773–4200) is an antiquarian book dealer with an estimated 75,000 titles. **DeLorme's Map Store** (Rte. 1, Freeport, ☎ 207/865–4171) carries an exceptional selection of maps and atlases of Maine, New England, and the rest of the world; nautical charts; and travel books. **Maine Coast Book Shop** (Main St., Damariscotta, ☎ 207/563–3207) carries a good selection of books and magazines and often hosts author signings. **Raffles Cafe Bookstore** (555 Congress St., Portland, ☎ 207/761–3930) presents an impressive selection of fiction and nonfiction, plus the best selection of periodicals north of Boston. Coffee and a light lunch are served, and there are frequent readings and literary gatherings.

Clothing
House of Logan (Townsend Ave., Boothbay Harbor, ☎ 207/633–2293) has specialty clothing for men and women, plus children's clothes next door at the Village Store. **Joseph's** (410 Fore St., ☎ 207/773–1274) has elegant tailored designer clothing for men and women.

Crafts
Edgecomb Potters (Rte. 27, Edgecomb, ☎ 207/882–6802) sells glazed porcelain pottery and other crafts. **Sheepscot River Pottery** (Rte. 1, Edgecomb, ☎ 207/882–9410) has original hand-painted pottery as well as a large collection of American-made crafts including jewelry, kitchenware, furniture, and home accessories.

Galleries
Abacus (44 Exchange St., Portland, ☎ 207/772–4880) has unusual gift items in glass, wood, and textiles, plus fine modern jewelry. **Franciska Needham Gallery,** (Water St., Damariscotta 207/563–1227) has contemporary paintings and sculpture by Maine and New York artists. The **Gil Whitman Gallery** (Rte. 1, N. Edgecomb, ☎ 207/882–7705) exhibits the work of bronze sculptor Gil Whitman in a barn gallery and an outdoor sculpture garden, where giant metal flowers bloom amidst the real thing. The studio and workshop areas also are open to visitors. The **Pine Tree Shop & Bayview Gallery** (75 Market St., Portland, ☎ 207/773–3007 or 800/244–3007) has original art and prints by prominent Maine painters. **Stein Glass Gallery** (20 Milk St., Portland, ☎ 207/772–9072) specializes in contemporary glass, both decorative and utilitarian. The **Wiscasset Bay Gallery** (Water St., Wiscasset, ☎ 207/882–7682) emphasizes 19th- and 20th-century American and European artists.

Sports and the Outdoors

Boat Trips

BOOTHBAY HARBOR

Appledore (☎ 207/633–6598), a 66-foot windjammer, departs from Pier 6 at 9:30, noon, 3, and 6 for voyages to the outer islands. **Argo Cruises** (☎ 207/633–2500) runs the *Islander* for morning cruises, Bath Hellgate cruises, whale watching, and the popular Cabbage Island Clambake; the *Islander II* for 1½-hour trips to Seal Rocks; the *Miss Boothbay*, a licensed lobster boat, for lobster-trap hauling trips. Biweekly evening cruises feature R&B or reggae. Departures are from Pier 6. **Balmy Day Cruises** (☎ 207/633–2284 or 800/298–2284) has day trips to Monhegan Island and tours of the harbor and nearby lighthouses. *Bay Lady* (☎ 207/633–6990), a 31-foot Friendship sloop, offers sailing trips of under 2 hours from Pier 8. **Cap'n Fish's Boat Trips** (☎ 207/633–3244) offers sightseeing cruises throughout the region, including puffin cruises, lobster-hauling and whale-watching rides, trips to Damariscove Harbor, Pemaquid Point, and up the Kennebec River to Bath, departing from Pier 1. *Eastward* (☎ 207/633–4780) is a Friendship sloop with six-passenger capacity that departs from Ocean Point Road in East Boothbay for full- or half-day sailing trips. Itineraries vary with passengers' desires and the weather.

FREEPORT

Atlantic Seal Cruises (S. Freeport, ☎ 207/865–6112) has daily trips to Eagle Island, where you can tour Admiral Peary's museum home, and evening seal and osprey watches on the *Atlantic Seal.*

PORTLAND

For tours of the harbor, Casco Bay, and the nearby islands, try **Bay View Cruises** (Fisherman's Wharf, ☎ 207/761–0496), **The Buccaneer** (Long Wharf, ☎ 207/799–8188), **Casco Bay Lines** (Maine State Pier, ☎ 207/774–7871), **Eagle Tours** (Long Wharf, ☎ 207/774–6498), or **Old Port Mariner Fleet** (Long Wharf, ☎ 207/775–0727).

Deep-Sea Fishing

Half- and full-day fishing charter boats are operated out of Portland by *Devils Den* (DeMillo's Marina, ☎ 207/761–4466). Operating out of Boothbay Harbor, **Cap'n Fish's Deep Sea Fishing** (☎ 207/633–3244) schedules full- and half-day trips, departing from Pier 1, and **Lucky Star Charters** (☎ 207/633–4624) runs full- and half-day private charters for up to six people, with departures from Pier 8.

Nature Walks

Wolfe's Neck Woods State Park has self-guided trails along Casco Bay, the Harraseeket River, and a fringe salt marsh, as well as walks led by naturalists. Picnic tables and grills are available, but there's no camping. Follow Bow Street opposite L. L. Bean off Route 1. *Wolfe's Neck Rd.,* ☎ 207/865–4465. ☞ *Memorial Day–Labor Day: $2 adults ($1 off-season), 50¢ children 5–11.*

Sea Kayaking

H2Outfitters (Orr's Island, ☎ 207/833–5257) offers instruction, rentals, and half-day through multi-day trips. **Maine Island Kayak Co.** (70 Luther St., Peak's Island, ☎ 800/796–2373) provides instruction, expeditions, and tours all along the Maine coast.

Beaches

Crescent Beach State Park (Rte. 77, Cape Elizabeth, ☎ 207/767–3625; ☞ Late Apr.–mid-Oct.: $2.50 adults [$1 off-season], 50¢ children 5–

11), about 8 miles from Portland, has a sand beach, picnic tables, seasonal snack bar, and bathhouse. **Ferry Beach State Park** (follow signs off Rte. 9 in Saco, ☎ 207/283–0067; ☛ Late Apr.–mid-Oct.: $2 adults, 50¢ children 5–11), near Old Orchard Beach, has picnic facilities with grills and extensive nature trails. **Popham Beach State Park** (Phippsburg, ☎ 207/389–1335; ☛ $2 adults [$1 Nov.–Apr.], 50¢ children 5–11), at the end of Route 209, south of Bath, has a good sand beach, a marsh area, and picnic tables. **Reid State Park** (☎ 207/371–2303; ☛ Late Apr.–mid-Oct.: , $2.50 adults, 50¢ children 5–11), on Georgetown Island, off Route 127, has 1½ miles of sand on three beaches. Facilities include bathhouses, picnic tables, fireplaces, and snack bar. Parking lots fill by 11 AM on summer Sundays and holidays.

Dining and Lodging

Many of Portland's best restaurants are in the Old Port Exchange district.

Bath

DINING

$$ Kristina's Restaurant & Bakery. This frame house-turned-restaurant, with a front deck built around a huge maple tree, turns out some of the finest pies, pastries, and cakes on the coast. A satisfying dinner menu features new American cuisine, including fresh seafood and grilled meats. All meals can be packed to go. ✗ *160 Centre St., ☎ 207/442–8577. D, MC, V. No dinner Sun. Call ahead in winter.*

LODGING

$$$ Fairhaven Inn. This cedar-shingle house built in 1790 is set on 27 acres of pine woods and meadows sloping down to the Kennebec River. Guest rooms are furnished with handmade quilts and mahogany pineapple four-poster beds. The home-cooked breakfast offers such treats as peach soup, blintzes, and apple upside-down French toast. ▥ *R.R. 2, Box 85, N. Bath, 04530, ☎ 207/443–4391. 7 rooms, 5 with bath. Hiking, cross-country skiing. Full breakfast included. AE, MC, V.*

Boothbay

LODGING

$$–$$$ Kenniston Hill Inn. The oldest inn in Boothbay (circa 1786), this classic center-chimney colonial with its white clapboards and columned porch offers comfortably old-fashioned accommodations on 4 acres of land only minutes from Boothbay Harbor. Four guest rooms have fireplaces, some have four-poster beds, rocking chairs, and gilt mirrors. ▥ *Rte. 27, Box 125, 04537, ☎ 207/633–2159. 10 rooms with bath. Full breakfast included. MC, V.*

Boothbay Harbor

DINING

$$–$$$ Black Orchid. The classic Italian fare includes fettuccine Alfredo with fresh lobster and mushrooms, and *petit filet à la diabolo* (fillets of Angus steak with marsala sauce). The upstairs and downstairs dining rooms sport a Roman-trattoria ambience, with frilly leaves and fruit hanging from the rafters and little else in the way of decor. In the summer there is a raw bar outdoors. ✗ *5 By-Way, ☎ 207/633–6659. AE, MC, V. No lunch. Closed Nov.–Apr.*

$$ Andrew's Harborside. The seafood menu is typical of the area—lobster, fried clams and oysters, haddock with seafood stuffing—but the harbor view makes it memorable. Lunch features lobster and crab rolls; children's and seniors' menus are available. You can dine outdoors on a harborside screened porch during the summer. ✗ *8 Bridge St., ☎ 207/*

633–4074. *Dinner reservations accepted for 5 or more. MC, V. Closed mid-Oct.–mid-May.*

LODGING

$$$–$$$$ **Fisherman's Wharf Inn.** All rooms overlook the water at this Colonial-style motel built 200 feet out over the harbor. The large dining room has floor-to-ceiling windows, and several day-trip cruises leave from this location. 🖼 *42 Commercial St., 04538, 📞 and FAX 207/633–5090 ext. 602 or 800/628–6872. 54 rooms with bath. Restaurant. AE, D, DC, MC, V. Closed late Oct.–mid-May.*

$$$ **Anchor Watch.** This country Colonial on the water overlooks the outer harbor and lies within easy walking distance of town. Guest rooms are decorated with quilts and stenciling and are named for the Monhegan ferries that ran in the 1920s. Breakfast includes apple puff pancake, muffins, fruit, omelets, blueberry blintzes, and more. 🖼 *3 Eames Rd., 04538, 📞 207/633–7565. 4 rooms with bath. Pier. Full breakfast included. MC, V. Closed Jan.*

$$ **The Pines.** Families seeking a secluded setting with lots of room for little ones to run will be interested in this motel on a hillside a mile from town. Rooms have sliding glass doors opening onto private decks, two double beds, and small refrigerators. 🖼 *Sunset Rd., Box 693, 04538, 📞 207/633–4555. 29 rooms with bath. Pool, tennis, playground. D, MC, V. Closed mid-Oct.–early May.*

Brunswick

DINING

$–$$ **The Great Impasta.** This small, storefront restaurant is a great spot for lunch, tea, or dinner. Try the seafood lasagna, or match your favorite pasta and sauce to create your own dish. ✕ *42 Maine St., 📞 207/729–5858. No reservations. AE, D, DC, MC, V.*

DINING AND LODGING

$$$–$$$$ **Captain Daniel Stone Inn.** This Federal inn overlooks the Androscoggin River. While no two rooms are furnished identically, all offer executive-style comforts and many have whirlpool baths and pullout sofas in addition to queen-size beds. A guest parlor, 24-hour breakfast room, and excellent service in the Narcissa Stone Restaurant make this an upscale escape from college-town funk. 🖼 *10 Water St., 04011, 📞 and FAX 207/725–9898. 32 rooms with bath. CP. Restaurant (no lunch Sat.). AE, DC, MC, V.*

Freeport

DINING

$–$$ **Freeport Cafe.** This small restaurant south of Freeport's shopping district serves creative homemade food, including soups, salads, sandwiches, and dinner entrées. Breakfast is available all day. ✕ *Rte. 1, 📞 207/865–3106. MC, V.*

$ **Harraseeket Lunch & Lobster Co.** This no-frills, bare-bones, genuine lobster pound and fried-seafood place is located beside the town landing in South Freeport. Seafood baskets and lobster dinners are what it's all about; there are picnic tables outside and a dining room inside. ✕ *Main St., S. Freeport, 📞 207/865–4888. No reservations. No credit cards. ⊙ May 1–Oct. 15.*

DINING AND LODGING

$$$$ **Harraseeket Inn.** This gracious Greek Revival home of 1850, just two blocks from the biggest retailing explosion ever to hit Maine, includes a three-story addition that looks like an old New England inn—white clapboard with green shutters—but is in fact a steel and concrete structure with elevators, whirlpools, and modern fireplaces. Despite these modern appointments, the Harraseeket gives its visitors a country-inn experience, with afternoon tea served in the mahogany drawing room. Guest rooms (vintage 1989) have reproductions of Federal canopy beds and bright, coordinated fabrics. The formal, no-smoking dining room upstairs, serving New England–influenced Continental cuisine, is a simply decorated, light and airy space with picture windows facing the inn's garden courtyard. The Broad Arrow Tavern downstairs appears to have been furnished by L. L. Bean, with fly rods, snowshoes, moose heads, and other hunting-lodge trappings; the hearty fare includes ribs, burgers, and charbroiled skewered shrimp and scallops. ⌶ *162 Main St., 04032,* ☎ *207/865–9377 or 800/342–6423,* FAX *207/865–1684. 48 rooms, 6 suites. Restaurant (reservations advised; collar shirt at dinner), bar, croquet. AE, D, DC, MC, V.*

Georgetown
DINING

$$$–$$$$ **The Osprey.** Located in a marina on the way to Reid State Park, this gourmet restaurant may be reached both by land and sea. The appetizers alone are worth the stop: homemade garlic and Sicilian sausages; artichoke strudel with three cheeses; and warm braised duck salad with Oriental vegetables in rice paper. Entrées might include such classics as saltimbocca or such originals as salmon en papillote with julienne leeks, carrots, and fresh herbs. The wine list is excellent. The glassed-in porch offers water views and breezes. ✕ *6 mi down Rte. 127, turn left at restaurant sign on Robinhood Rd.,* ☎ *207/371–2530. Reservations advised. MC, V. Call ahead for off-season hrs.*

Newcastle
LODGING

$$$$ **Newcastle Inn.** The white-clapboard house, vintage mid-19th century,
★ has a romantic living room with a fireplace, loveseat, plenty of books, and river views. It also has a sun porch with white wicker furniture and ice-cream parlor chairs. The "Stencil Room," a favorite common room, has a hand-decorated hardwood floor. Guest rooms have been carefully appointed with unique beds—an old spool bed, wrought-iron beds, a brass-pewter bed, a sleigh bed, and several canopy beds—and rabbits are everywhere: stuffed, wooden, ceramic. Breakfast is a gourmet affair that might include scrambled eggs with caviar in puff pastry, ricotta cheese pie, or frittata. The five-course dinner served nightly brings people back again and again. ⌶ *River Rd., 04553,* ☎ *207/563–5685 or 800/832–8669. 15 rooms with bath. 2 dining rooms, pub. Full breakfast included; MAP available. MC, V.*

Peaks Island
LODGING

$$ **Keller's B&B.** This turn-of-the-century home provides rustic accommodations with deck views of Casco Bay and the Portland skyline. The beach is only steps away from your room. Guests select breakfast from a menu. ⌶ *20 Island Ave.,* ☎ *207/766–2441. 4 rooms with bath. Full breakfast included. No credit cards.*

Pemaquid Point
DINING AND LODGING

$$$–$$$$ **Bradley Inn.** Within walking distance of the Pemaquid Point lighthouse, beach, and fort, the 1900 Bradley Inn began as a rooming house for summer rusticators and alternated between abandonment and operation as a B&B until its complete renovation in the early 1990s. Rooms are comfortable and uncluttered; ask for one of the cathedral-ceiling, waterside rooms on the third floor, which deliver breathtaking views of the sun setting over the water. The Ship's Restaurant has a frequently

rotating menu, including a variety of fresh seafood dishes; there's light entertainment in the pub on weekends. ☎ *Rte. 130, HC 61, Box 361, New Harbor 04554,* ☎ *207/677–2105,* ℻ *207/677–3367. 12 rooms with bath, 1 cottage, 1 carriage house. Restaurant, pub, croquet, bicycles. CP. AE, D, MC, V. Closed Jan.–Mar.*

Portland

DINING

$$$–$$$$ ★ **Back Bay Grill.** Mellow jazz, a 28-foot mural, an impressive wine list, and good food make this simple, elegant restaurant a popular spot. Appetizers such as black-pepper raviolis of red swiss chard, pancetta, and Fontina cheese in chicken broth are followed by grilled chicken, halibut, oysters, salmon, trout, veal chops, or steak. Don't miss the desserts—the crème brûlée is legendary. ✗ *65 Portland St.,* ☎ *207/772–8833. Reservations advised. AE, D, DC, MC, V. Closed Sun.*

$$–$$$ ★ **Cafe Always.** White linen tablecloths, candles, and Victorian-style murals by local artists set the mood for innovative cuisine. Begin with Pemaquid Point oysters seasoned with pink peppercorns and champagne, or grilled duck, before choosing from vegetarian dishes, pasta, or more substantial entrées, such as grilled tuna with a fiery Japanese sauce or leg of lamb with goat cheese and sweet peppers. ✗ *7 Middle St.,* ☎ *207/774–9399. Reservations advised. MC, V. Closed Sun., Mon.*

$$–$$$ **Seamen's Club.** Built just after Portland's Great Fire of 1866, and an actual sailors' club in the 1940s, this restaurant has become an Old Port Exchange landmark, with its Gothic windows and carved medallions. Seafood is an understandable favorite—moist, blackened tuna, salmon, and swordfish prepared differently each day and lobster fettuccine are among the highlights. ✗ *375 Fore St.,* ☎ *207/772–7311. Reservations advised. AE, DC, MC, V.*

$$–$$$ ★ **Street and Co.** You enter through the kitchen, with all its wonderful aromas, and dine amid dried herbs and shelves of staples on one of a dozen copper-topped tables (so your waiter can place a skillet of steaming seafood directly in front of you). A second dining room for walk-ins was added in 1994. Begin with lobster bisque or grilled eggplant—vegetarian dishes are the only alternatives to fish. Choose from an array of superb entrées, ranging from calamari, clams, or shrimp served over linguine, to blackened, broiled, pan-seared, or grilled seafood. The desserts are top-notch. ✗ *33 Wharf St.,* ☎ *207/775–0887. Reservations advised. AE, MC, V. No lunch.*

$$ **Katahdin.** Somehow, the painted tables, flea-market decor, mismatched dinnerware, and log pile bar work together here. The cuisine, large portions of home-cooked New England fare, is equally unpretentious and fun: Try the chicken potpie, fried trout, crab cakes, or the nightly Blue Plate special—and save room for the fruit cobbler. ✗ *106 High St.,* ☎ *207/774–1740. No reservations. MC, V.*

LODGING

$$$$ **Pomegranate Inn.** Clever touches such as faux marbling on the moldings and mustard-colored rag-rolling in the hallways give this bed-and-breakfast a bright, postmodern air. Most guest rooms are spacious and bright, accented with original paintings on floral and tropical motifs; the location on a quiet street in the city's Victorian Western Promenade district ensures serenity. Telephones and televisions make this a good choice for businesspeople. ☎ *49 Neal St., 04102,* ☎ *207/772–1006 or 800/356–0408. 7 rooms with bath, 1 suite. Full breakfast included. AE, D, MC, V.*

$$$–$$$$ ★ **Portland Regency Hotel.** The only major hotel in the center of the Old Port Exchange, the Regency building was Portland's armory in the late 19th century and is now the city's most luxurious, most distinctive hotel.

The bright, plush, airy rooms have four-poster beds, tall standing mirrors, floral curtains, and loveseats. The health club, the best in the city, offers massage and has an aerobics studio, free weights, Nautilus equipment, a large whirlpool, sauna, and steam room. ☎ *20 Milk St., 04101, ☎ 207/774–4200 or 800/727–3436, FAX 207/775–2150. 95 rooms with bath, 8 suites. Restaurant, health club, nightclub, banquet and convention rooms. AE, D, DC, MC, V.*

$$–$$$ **Eastland Plaza.** Although it's a bit dowdy, this 1927 hotel has a prime location in Portland's up-and-coming arts district. Rooms in the tower section (added in 1961) have floor-to-ceiling windows; higher floors have harbor views. The small health room offers Universal gym equipment, rowing machines, stationary bikes, and a sauna. ☎ *157 High St., 04101, ☎ 207/775–5411 or 800/777–6246, FAX 207/775–2872. 204 rooms with bath. 2 restaurants, 2 bars, exercise room with sauna, banquet and convention rooms. AE, D, DC, MC, V.*

The Arts

Chocolate Church Arts Center (804 Washington St., ☎ 207/442–8455) offers changing exhibits by Maine artists in a variety of mediums, including textiles, photography, painting, and sculpture. The center also hosts folk, jazz, and classical concerts; theater productions; and performances for children, including puppet shows and Portland Symphony Orchestra Kinderkonzerts. Sign up for classes and workshops in visual and performing arts. **Portland Performing Arts Center** (25A Forest Ave., Portland, ☎ 207/774–0465) hosts music, dance, and theater performances. **Round Top Center for the Arts** (Business Rte. 1, Damariscotta, ☎ 207/563–1507) has exhibits, concerts, shows, and classes. The **State Theatre** (609 Congress St., ☎ 207/879–1112) has come along way from its days as Portland's porn-film house—it's now one of the star attractions in Portland's up-and-coming arts district. Among the numerous events hosted here are film premieres and concerts by nationally known artists.

Music

Bowdoin Summer Music Festival (Bowdoin College, Brunswick, ☎ 207/725–3322 for information or ☎ 207/725–3895 for tickets) is a six-week concert series featuring performances by students, faculty, and prestigious guest artists. **Carousel Music Theater** ("The Meadows," Boothbay Harbor, ☎ 207/633–5297) mounts musical revues from Memorial Day to Columbus Day. **Cumberland County Civic Center** (1 Civic Center Sq., Portland, ☎ 207/775–3458) hosts concerts, sporting events, and family shows in a 9,000-seat auditorium. **Portland Symphony Orchestra** (30 Myrtle St., Portland, ☎ 207/773–8191) gives concerts October through August.

Theater

Mad Horse Theatre Company (955 Forest Ave., Portland, ☎ 207/797–3338) performs contemporary and original works. **Maine State Music Theater** (Pickard Theater, Bowdoin College, Brunswick, ☎ 207/725–8769) stages musicals from mid-June through August. **Portland Stage Company** (25A Forest Ave., Portland, ☎ 207/774–0465), a producer of national reputation, mounts six productions, from October through May, at the Portland Performing Arts Center. **Theater Project of Brunswick** (14 School St., Brunswick, ☎ 207/729–8584) performs from late June through August.

Nightlife

Portland's hot nightspot, **Brian Boru** (57 Center St., Portland, ☎ 207/780–1506) is a traditional Irish pub serving up hearty fare and entertainment. For dancing, head to **Granny Killam's** (55 Market St., Portland, ☎ 207/761–2787). **Gritty McDuff's—Portland's Original Brew Pub** (396 Fore St., Portland, ☎ 207/772–2739) serves fine ales, brewed on the premises, along with British pub fare and local seafood dishes. **Khalidi's Creative Seafoods** (36 Market St., Portland, ☎ 207/871–1881) has a good selection of Maine microbrewery beers on draft. **Three Dollar Dewey's** (446 Fore St., Portland, ☎ 207/772–3310), long a popular night spot, is an English-style ale house. **Top of the East** (Sonesta Hotel, 157 High St., Portland, ☎ 207/775–5411) has a view of the city and live entertainment—jazz, piano, and comedy. **McSeagull's Gulf Dock** (Boothbay Harbor, ☎ 207/633–4041) draws young singles with live music and a loud bar scene.

Portland to Pemaquid Point Essentials

Getting Around

BY BUS

Greater Portland's **Metro** (☎ 207/774–0351) runs seven bus routes in Portland, South Portland, and Westbrook. The fare is $1 for adults, 50¢ for senior citizens and people with disabilities, and children (under 5 free); exact change ($1 bills accepted) is required. Buses run from 5:30 AM to 11:45 PM.

BY CAR

The Congress Street exit from I–295 takes you into the heart of Portland. Numerous city parking lots have hourly rates of 50¢ to 85¢; the Gateway Garage on High Street, off Congress, is a convenient place to leave your car while exploring downtown. North of Portland, I–95 takes you to Exit 20 and Route 1, Freeport's Main Street, which continues on to Brunswick and Bath. East of Wiscasset you can take Route 27 south to the Boothbays, where Route 96 is a good choice for further exploration.

Important Addresses and Numbers

EMERGENCIES

Maine Medical Center (22 Bramhall St., Portland, ☎ 207/871–0111). **Mid Coast Hospital** (1356 Washington St., Bath, ☎ 207/443–5524; 58 Baribeau Dr., Brunswick, ☎ 207/729–0181). **St. Andrews Hospital** (3 St. Andrews Ln., Boothbay Harbor, ☎ 207/633–2121).

VISITOR INFORMATION

Off-season, most information offices are open weekdays 9–5; the hours below are for summer only.

Boothbay Harbor Region Chamber of Commerce (Box 356, Boothbay Harbor, ☎ 207/633–2353; ☉ Weekdays 9–5, Sat. 11–4, Sun. noon–4). **Chamber of Commerce of the Bath Brunswick Region** (45 Front St., Bath, ☎ 207/443–9751, and 59 Pleasant St., Brunswick, ☎ 207/725–8797; ☉ Weekdays 8:30–5). **Convention and Visitors Bureau of Greater Portland** (305 Commercial St., ☎ 207/772–5800; ☉ Weekdays 8–6 and weekends 10–6 from June 1 to Columbus Day; weekdays 8–5 and weekends 10–3 from Columbus Day to June 1). **Freeport Merchants Association** (Box 452, Freeport, ☎ 207/865–1212; ☉ Weekdays 9–5). **Greater Portland Chamber of Commerce** (145 Middle St., Portland, ☎ 207/772–2811; ☉ Weekdays 8–5). **Maine Publicity Bureau, the Maine Information Center** (Rte. 1 [Exit 17 off I–95], Yarmouth, ☎ 207/846–0833).

PENOBSCOT BAY

Purists hold that the Maine coast begins at Penobscot Bay, where the vistas over the water are wider and bluer, the shore a jumble of broken granite boulders, cobblestones, and gravel punctuated by small sand beaches, and the water numbingly cold. Port Clyde in the southwest and Stonington in the southeast are the outer limits of Maine's largest bay, 35 miles apart across the bay waters but separated by a drive of almost 100 miles on scenic but slow two-lane highways.

Rockland, the largest town on the bay, is Maine's major lobster distribution center and the port of departure for several bay islands. The Camden Hills, looming green over Camden's fashionable waterfront, turn bluer and fainter as one moves on to Castine, the elegant small town across the bay. In between Camden and Castine is the Mayberryesque town of Belfast and the flea-market mecca of Searsport. Because both communities are less glitzy than other bay towns, they offer value dining and lodging. Deer Isle is connected to the mainland by a slender, high-arching bridge, but Isle au Haut, accessible from Deer Isle's fishing town of Stonington, can be reached by passenger ferry only: More than half of this steep, wooded island is wilderness, the most remote section of Acadia National Park.

Exploring

Numbers in the margin correspond to points of interest on the Penobscot Bay map.

From Pemaquid Point at the western extremity of Muscongus Bay to Port Clyde at its eastern extent, it's less than 15 miles across the water, but it's 50 miles for the motorist, who must return north to Route 1 to reach the far shore.

Travelers on Route 1 can make an easy detour south through Tenants Harbor and Port Clyde before reaching Rockland. Turn onto Route 131S at Thomaston, 5 miles west of Rockland, and follow the winding road past waterside fields, spruce woods, ramshackle barns, and

❶ trim houses. **Tenants Harbor,** 7 miles from Thomaston, is a quintessential Maine fishing town, its harbor dominated by lobster boats, its shores rocky and slippery, its center a scattering of clapboard houses, a church, a general store. The fictional Dunnet Landing of Sarah Orne Jewett's classic book, *The Country of the Pointed Firs*, is based on this region.

Route 131 ends at Port Clyde, a fishing village that is the point of departure for the *Laura B.* (☎ 207/372–8848 for schedules), the mail-

❷ boat that serves Monhegan Island. Tiny, remote **Monhegan Island,** with its high cliffs, fronting the open sea was known to Basque, Portuguese, and Breton fishermen well before Columbus "discovered" America. About a century ago Monhegan was discovered again by some of America's finest painters, including Rockwell Kent, Robert Henri, and Edward Hopper, who sailed out to paint the savage cliffs, the meadows, the wild ocean views, and the shacks of fisherfolk. Tourists followed, and today Monhegan is overrun with visitors in summer.

❸ Returning north to Route 1, you have less than 5 miles to go to **Rockland** on Penobscot Bay. This large fishing port is the commercial hub of the coast, with working boats moored alongside a growing flotilla of cruise schooners. Although Rockland retains its working-class flavor, the recent expansion of the Farnsworth Museum, combined with new boutiques, restaurants, and bed-and-breakfasts is making Rockland a good

Penobscot Bay

Unity Pond

Dixmont

Unity

Winterport

1A

1A

Monroe

Frankfort

Alamoosook Lake

Branch Pond

Brooks

Bucksport

Orland

Swan Lake

Prospect

Verona

1

Ellsworth

Freedom

Swanville

1

175

199

199

15

172

Searsport ❼

MOOSE POINT STATE PARK

Morrill

166A   166

175

❻ Belfast

Castine ❽

Blue Hill ❾

Bayside

Pripet

Liberty

3

1

❺ Northport

Holbrook I. Sanctuary

15

Brooksville

Searsmont

❶❷ Islesboro

Little Deer Isle

Sargentville

175

Brooklin

Hope

Lincolnville

Dark Harbor

Eggemoggin Reach

CAMDEN HILLS STATE PARK

Mt. Battie

Penobscot Bay

❿ Deer Isle

Union

17

❹ Camden

15

West Rockport

Rockport

North Haven Island

⓫ Stonington

Rockland ❸

1

Thomaston

Owls Head

Vinalhaven Island

131

73

ACADIA NATIONAL PARK

⓭ Isle au Haut

Spruce Head

❶ Tenants Harbor

131

Muscongus Bay

Port Clyde

Metinic Island

Seal Island

Matinicus Island

N

Monhegan Island ❷

ATLANTIC OCEAN

Penobscot River

Ducktrap River

0   10 miles

0   15 km

stop for coastal travelers. This also is the point of departure for popular day trips to Vinal Haven, North Haven, and Matinicus islands.

The outer harbor is bisected by a nearly mile-long granite breakwater, which begins on Samoset Road and ends with a lighthouse that was built in 1888. Next to the breakwater, on the Rockland–Rockport town line, is the **Samoset Resort** (Warrenton St., Rockport, ☎ 207/594–2511 or, outside ME, 800/341–1650), a sprawling oceanside resort providing an 18-hole golf course, indoor and outdoor swimming pools, tennis, racquetball, restaurant, and fitness center.

In downtown Rockland is the **William A. Farnsworth Library and Art Museum.** Here are oil and watercolor landscapes of the coastal areas you have just seen, among them N. C. Wyeth's *Eight Bells* and Andrew Wyeth's *Her Room.* Jamie Wyeth is also represented in the collections, as are Winslow Homer, Rockwell Kent, and the sculptor Louise Nevelson. Next door, and part of the museum's holdings, is the Farnsworth Homestead, a handsome Greek Revival dwelling furnished in the Victorian style. Also operated by the museum is the **Olson House** in Cushing, approximately 14 miles away, which was made famous by Andrew Wyeth's painting, *Christina's World. 352 Main St.,* ☎ *207/596–6457. ☛ Museum and homestead: $5 adults, $2 senior citizens, $1 children 8–18. Olson House: $3 adults, $1 children 8–18. ☉ Mon.–Sat. 10–5, Sun. 1–5. Museum closed Mon. Oct.–May. Olson House open Wed.–Sun. 11–4. Closed Oct.–May.*

④ From Rockland it's 8 miles north on Route 1 to **Camden,** "Where the mountains meet the sea"—an apt description, as you will discover when you step out of your car and look up from the harbor. Camden is famous not only for geography but for the nation's largest fleet of windjammers—relics and replicas from the age of sail. At just about any hour during the warmer months you're likely to see at least one windjammer tied up in the harbor, and windjammer cruises are a superb way to explore the ports and islands of Penobscot Bay.

TIME OUT **Ayer's Fish Market** (43 Main St.) has the best fish chowder in town; take a cup to the pleasant park at the head of the harbor when you're ready for a break from the shops on Bay View and Main streets.

The entrance to the 5,500-acre **Camden Hills State Park** (☎ 207/236–3109) is 2 miles north of Camden on Route 1. If you're accustomed to the Rockies or the Alps, you may not be impressed with heights of not much more than 1,000 feet, yet the Camden Hills are landmarks for miles along the low, rolling reaches of the Maine coast. The park contains 20 miles of trails, including the easy Nature Trail up Mount Battie. The 112-site camping area, open mid-May through mid-October, has flush toilets and hot showers. ☛ *Trails and auto road up Mount Battie: $2 adults, 50¢ children 5–11.*

⑤ The lovely community of Bayside, a section of **Northport** that is off Route 1 on the way to Belfast, is dotted with 150-year-old Queen Anne cottages that have freshly painted porches and exquisite architectural details. Some of these homes line the main one-car thoroughfare of George Street; others are clustered on bluffs with water views around town greens complete with flagpoles and swings; yet others are on the shore.

⑥ Back on Route 1, the next town north is **Belfast,** which has a lively waterfront and a charming Main Street. Architectural buffs will want to do the 1-mile self-guided walking tour of period sea captain's homes, reminders of the town's heyday in the 1800s: Belfast was once home to more sea captains than any other port in the world. Belfast also offers trains rides along the water and through fall foliage; a bay excursion on a former Mississippi riverboat; sailing; and kayaking. Belfast also has an active artistic community, and is included in the book, *The 100 Best Small Art Towns in America.*

❼ Seven miles north on Route 1, **Searsport**—Maine's second-largest deepwater port (after Portland)—claims to be the antiques capital of Maine. The town's stretch of Route 1 hosts a seasonal weekend flea market in addition to its antiques shops.

Searsport preserves a rich nautical history at the **Penobscot Marine Museum,** where eight historic and two modern buildings document the region's seafaring way of life. Included are display photos of 284 sea captains, artifacts of the whaling industry (lots of scrimshaw), hundreds of paintings and models of famous ships, navigational instruments, and treasures collected by seafarers. *Church St.,* ☎ *207/548–2529.* ☛ *$5 adults, $3.50 senior citizens, $1.50 children 7–15.* ⊙ *June–mid-Oct., Mon.–Sat. 10–5, Sun. noon–5.*

❽ Historic **Castine,** over which the French, the British, the Dutch, and the Americans fought from the 17th century to the War of 1812, has two museums and the ruins of a British fort, but the finest aspect of Castine is the town itself: the lively, welcoming town landing, the serene Federal and Greek Revival houses, and the town common. Castine invites strolling, and you would do well to start at the town landing, where you can park your car, and walk up Main Street past the two inns and on toward the white Trinitarian Federated Church with its tapering spire.

Turn right on Court Street and walk to the town common, which is ringed by a collection of white-clapboard buildings that includes the Ives House (once the summer home of the poet Robert Lowell), the Abbott School, and the Unitarian Church, capped by a whimsical belfry that suggests a gazebo.

❾ From Castine, take Route 166 north to Route 199 and follow the signs to **Blue Hill.** Castine may have the edge over Blue Hill in charm, for its Main Street is not a major thoroughfare and it claims a more dramatic perch over its harbor, yet Blue Hill is certainly appealing and boasts a better selection of shops and galleries. Blue Hill is renowned for its pottery, and two good shops are right in town.

❿ The scenic Route 15 south from Blue Hill passes through Brooksville and on to the graceful suspension bridge that crosses Eggemoggin Reach to **Deer Isle.** The turnout and picnic area at Caterpillar Hill, 1 mile south of the junction of routes 15 and 175, commands a fabulous view of Penobscot Bay, the hundreds of dark green islands, and the Camden Hills across the bay, which from this perspective look like a range of mountains dwarfed and faded by an immense distance—yet they are less than 25 miles away.

⓫ Route 15 continues the length of Deer Isle—a sparsely settled landscape of thick woods opening to tidal coves, shingled houses with lobster traps stacked in the yards, and dirt roads that lead to summer cottages—to **Stonington,** an emphatically ungentrified community that tolerates summer visitors but makes no effort to cater to them. Main Street has gift shops and galleries, but this is a working port town, and the principal activity is at the waterfront, where fishing boats arrive with the day's catch. The high, sloped island that rises beyond the archipelago of Merchants Row is Isle au Haut (accessible by mailboat from Stonington), which contains sections of Acadia National Park.

Island Excursions

⑫ **Islesboro,** reached by car-and-passenger ferry (Maine State Ferry Service, ☎ 207/734–6935 or 800/491–4883) from Lincolnville Beach, on Route 1 north of Camden, has been a retreat of wealthy, very private families for more than a century. The long, narrow, mostly wooded island has no real town to speak of; there are scatterings of mansions as well as humbler homes at Dark Harbor (where celebrity couples Kirstie Alley and Parker Stevenson and John Travolta and Kelly Preston live) and at Pripet near the north end. Since the amenities on Islesboro are quite spread out, you don't want to come on foot. If you plan to spend the night here, you should make a reservation well in advance (*see* Islesboro *in* Dining and Lodging, *below*).

TIME OUT **Dark Harbor Shop** (Main Rd., ☎ 207/734–8878; ⊘ Memorial Day–Labor Day) on Islesboro is an old-fashioned ice cream parlor where tourists, locals, and summer folk gather for sandwiches, newspapers, gossip, and gifts.

⑬ **Isle au Haut** thrusts its steeply ridged back out of the sea 7 miles south of Stonington. Accessible only by passenger mailboat (☎ 207/367–5193), the island is worth visiting for the ferry ride alone, a half-hour cruise amid the tiny, pink-shore islands of Merchants Row, where you may see terns, guillemots, and harbor seals. More than half the island is part of Acadia National Park; 17½ miles of trails extend through quiet spruce and birch woods, along cobble beaches and seaside cliffs, and over the spine of the central mountain ridge. From late June to mid-September, the mailboat docks at Duck Harbor within the park. The small campground here, with five Adirondack-type lean-tos (⊘ Mid-May–mid-Oct.), fills up quickly; reservations are essential, and they can be made only after April 1 by writing to Acadia National Park (Box 177, Bar Harbor 04609).

What to See and Do with Children

Belfast & Moosehead Lake Railroad, one of the oldest railroads in the country, has two narrated scenic rail trips in Waldo County. A diesel train leaves from Belfast's waterfront and runs along an inland river. The other railhead is in Unity, 35 miles inland, where a steam locomotive passes over Unity Pond and alongside working farmlands and small villages. A staged train robbery is fun for children, as is the pre-ride demonstration of turning the engine around at Unity station. Both locations have dining facilities and offer seating in first-class, coach, or open-air cars, which are the most fun in good weather. There are special fall foliage tours that are longer than the usual 1½ hour excursions, and there's a discount if you ride both the railroad and Belfast's riverboat, **Voyager.** *One Depot Square, Unity ME. 04988,* ☎ *207/948–5500 or 800/392–5500.* ☛ *$14 adults, $7 children 3–16.* ⊘ *May–Oct. Call for schedule information and directions.*

Owls Head Transportation Museum, 2 miles south of Rockland on Route 73, displays antique aircraft, cars, and engines and stages weekend air shows. *Rte. 73, Owls Head,* ☎ *207/594–4418.* ☛ *$6 adults, $3 children 6–12, $12 family (2 adults and all children under 18).* ⊘ *May–Oct., daily 10–5; Nov.–Apr., weekdays 10–4, weekends 10–3.*

Off the Beaten Path

Haystack Mountain School of Crafts, on Deer Isle, attracts internationally renowned glassblowers, potters, sculptors, jewelers, blacksmiths, printmakers, and weavers to its summer institute. You can attend evening lectures or visit the studios of artisans at work (by appointment only). *South of Deer Isle Village on Rte. 15, turn left at Gulf gas station and follow signs for 6 mi,* ☎ *207/348–2306.* ✒ *Free.* ☉ *June–Sept.*

Shopping

The most promising shopping areas are Main and Bay View streets in Camden, Main Street in Blue Hill, and Main Street in Stonington. Antiques shops are clustered in Searsport and scattered around the outskirts of villages, in farmhouses and barns; yard sales abound in summertime.

Antiques

Old Cove Antiques (Rte. 15, Sargentville, ☎ 207/359–2031) has folk art, quilts, hooked rugs, and folk carvings. **Old Deer Isle Parish House Antiques** (Rte. 15, Deer Isle Village, ☎ 207/348–9964) is a place for poking around in the jumbles of old kitchenware, glassware, books, and linen. Billing itself the antiques capital of Maine, Searsport hosts a massive weekend **flea market** on Route 1 during the summer months. Indoor shops, most of them in old houses and barns, are also on Route 1, in Lincolnville Beach as well as in Searsport. Shops are open daily during the summer months, by chance or by appointment from mid-October through the end of May.

Art Galleries

Blue Heron Gallery & Studio (Church St., Deer Isle Village, ☎ 207/348–6051) features the work of the Haystack Mountain School of Crafts faculty. **Deer Isle Artists Association** (Rte. 15, Deer Isle Village, no ☎) has group exhibits of prints, drawings, and sculpture from mid-June through Labor Day. **J. S. Ames Fine Art** (68 Main St., Belfast, ☎ 207/338–1558) carries contemporary art in all media. **Leighton Gallery** (Parker Point Rd., Blue Hill, ☎ 207/374–5001) shows oil paintings, lithographs, watercolors, and other contemporary art in the gallery, and sculpture in its garden. **Maine's Massachusetts House Galleries** (Rte. 1, Lincolnville, ☎ 207/789–5705) offers a broad selection of regional art, including bronzes, carvings, sculptures, and landscapes and seascapes in pencil, oil, and watercolor. The **Pine Tree Shop & Bayview Gallery** (33 Bay View St., Camden, ☎ 207/236–4534) specializes in original art, prints, and posters—almost all with Maine themes.

Books

The **Owl and Turtle Bookshop** (8 Bay View St., Camden, ☎ 207/236–4769) sells a thoughtfully chosen selection of books, CDs, cassettes, and cards, including Maine-published works. The two-story shop has special rooms devoted to marine books and children's books. The **Personal Bookstore** (78 Main St, Thomaston, ☎ 207/354–8058 or 800/391–8058) is a booklover's treasure. Maine authors frequently do book-signings; browsers will find some autographed copies on the shelves. **Reading Corner** (408 Main St., Rockland, ☎ 207/596–6651) carries an extensive inventory of cookbooks, children's books, Maine titles, best-sellers, and one of the area's best newspaper and magazine selections.

Crafts and Pottery

Chris Murray Waterfowl Carver (Upper Main St., Castine, ☎ 207/326–9033) sells award-winning wildfowl carvings and offers carving instruction. **Handworks Gallery** (Main St., Blue Hill, ☎ 207/374–5613) carries unusual crafts, jewelry, and clothing. **North Country Textiles** (Main St., Blue Hill, ☎ 207/374–2715) specializes in fine woven shawls, placemats, throws, baby blankets, and pillows in subtle patterns and color schemes. **Rackliffe Pottery** (Rte. 172, Blue Hill, ☎ 207/374–2297) is famous for its vivid blue pottery, including plates, tea and coffee sets, pitchers, casseroles, and canisters. **Rowantrees Pottery** (Union St., Blue Hill, ☎ 207/374–5535) has an extensive selection of styles and patterns in dinnerware, tea sets, vases, and decorative items.

Furniture

The **Windsor Chairmakers** (Rte. 1, Lincolnville, ☎ 207/789–5188 or 800/789–5188) sells custom-made, handcrafted beds, chests, china cabinets, dining tables, highboys—and, of course, chairs.

Gourmet Supplies

The Good Table (72 Main St., Belfast, ☎ 207/338–4880) carries an imaginative array of gifts and gourmet items. **Heather Harland** (37 Bay View St., Camden, ☎ 207/236–9661) is a two-story cornucopia of cookbooks, imported pottery and cookware, designer linens, and unusual condiments. **The Store** (435 Main St., Rockland, ☎ 207/594–9246) features top-of-the-line cookware, table accessories, and an outstanding card selection.

Skiing

Camden Snowbowl

Box 1209, Camden 04843
☎ *207/236–3438*

DOWNHILL

No other ski area can boast a view over island-studded Penobscot Bay like Camden Snowbowl. The Currier & Ives setting includes the 950-foot-vertical mountain adjacent to a small lake that is cleared for ice skating. Also on premises is a 400-foot toboggan run that shoots sledders out onto the lake. There is a small lodge with cafeteria, a ski school, and ski and toboggan rentals. Camden Snowbowl has 11 trails accessed by one double chair and two T-bars. It also has night skiing.

CROSS-COUNTRY

There are 16 kilometers (10 miles) of cross-country skiing trails at the **Camden Hills State Park** SM (☎ 207/236–9849), and 20 kilometers (12½ miles) at the **Tanglewood 4-H Camp** in Lincolnville (☎ 207/789–5868), about 5 miles away.

Other Sports

Boat Trips

Windjammers create a stir whenever they sail into Camden harbor, and a voyage around the bay on one of them, whether for an afternoon or a week, is unforgettable. The season for the excursions is June through September. Excursion boats, too, provide a great opportunity for getting afloat on the waters of Penobscot Bay.

The 150-passenger *Voyageur* (☎ 800/392–5500) leaves Belfast twice daily in season for 1½-hour narrated tours of the bay. Sightings of seals and cormorants are common; dolphins show up more rarely. This former Mississippi riverboat has both open and enclosed decks and food-

and-beverage service. Sailing schedules coordinate with that of the Belfast & Moosehead Lake Railroad; a discount applies if you employ both.

CAMDEN

Angelique (Yankee Packet Co., Box 736, ☎ 207/236–8873 or 800/282–9989) makes three- and six-day trips. *Appledore* (0 Lily Pond Dr., ☎ 207/236–8353 or 800/233–7437) has two-hour day sails as well as private charters. *Betselma* (35 Pearl St., ☎ 207/236–4446) offers two two-hour excursions and eight one-hour trips from Camden's Public Landing every day between June and October. No reservations needed. **Maine Windjammer Cruises** (Box 617, ☎ 207/236–2938 or 800/736–7981) has three two-masted schooners making two-, four-, and six-day trips along the coast and to the islands. *Roseway* (Box 696, ☎ 207/236–4449 or 800/255–4449) takes three-, four-, and six-day cruises.

ROCKLAND

North End Shipyard Schooners (Box 482, ☎ 800/648–4544) operates three- and six-day cruises on the schooners *American Eagle, Isaac H. Evans,* and *Heritage.* The **Vessels of Windjammer Wharf** (Box 1050, ☎ 207/236–3520 or 800/999–7352) organizes three- and six-day cruises on the *Pauline,* a 12-passenger motor yacht, and the *Stephen Taber,* a windjammer.

ROCKPORT

Timberwind (Box 247, ☎ 207/236–0801 or 800/759–9250) is a 100-foot windjammer that sails out of Rockport harbor on three- and six-day trips.

STONINGTON

Palmer Day IV (☎ 207/367–2207) departs Stonington Harbor each day at 2 between July 1 and Labor Day for a two-hour excursion. Each Thursday morning, a special four-hour cruise stops at North Haven and Vinalhaven Islands.

Biking

Maine Sport (Rte. 1, Rockport, ☎ 207/236–8797) rents bikes, camping and fishing gear, canoes, kayaks, cross-country skis, ice skates, and skis.

Deep-Sea Fishing

The 42-foot *Henrietta* (☎ 207/594–5411) departs the Rockland Landings Marina (end of Sea St.) at 7:30 daily, returning at 5, from late May through September, weather permitting. Bait and tackle are provided, alcohol is prohibited, reservations are essential.

Flightseeing

Ace Aviation (Belfast Municipal Airport, Belfast, ☎ 207/338–2970) takes up to three people, at approximately $25 per 15 minutes, for panoramic views of the jagged coastline, lighthouses, and islands. Planes are available for charter.

Water Sports

Eggemoggin Reach is a famous cruising ground for yachts, as are the coves and inlets around Deer Isle and the Penobscot Bay waters between Castine and Camden. **Bay Island Yacht Charters** (Box 639, Camden, ☎ 207/236–2776 or 800/421–2492) offers bareboat and charters, daysailer rentals, and sailing lessons. **Belfast Kayak Tours** (RR 1, Box 715, Freedom, ☎ 207/382–6204) guides paddlers of all levels by the hour in sturdy double kayaks. **Chance Along** (140 High St., Belfast, ☎ 207/338–6003 or in Maine 800/286–6696) offers sailing instructions and outings, sailboat rentals and bareboat charters, and boat repairs and storage. **Indian Island Kayak Co.** (16 Mountain St., Camden, ☎

207/236–4088) gives one- and multi-day kayaking tours. **Maine Sport** (Rte. 1, Rockport, ☎ 207/236–8797), the best sports outfitter north of Freeport, rents sailboards and organizes whitewater-rafting and sea-kayaking expeditions, starting at the store. The **Phoenix Centre** (Rte. 175, Blue Hill Falls, ☎ 207/374–2113) gives sea-kayaking tours of Blue Hill Bay and Eggemoggin Reach.

State Parks

Holbrook Island Sanctuary (on Penobscot Bay in Brooksville, ☎ 207/ 326–4012) has a gravelly beach with a splendid view; hiking trails through meadow and forest; no camping facilities. **Moose Point State Park** (Rte. 1, between Belfast and Searsport, ☎ 207/548–2882) is ideal for hikes and picnics overlooking Penobscot Bay; no camping facilities.

Dining and Lodging

The Camden-Rockport area has the greatest variety of restaurants, bed-and-breakfasts, and inns in the region.

Belfast

DINING

$–$$ 90 Main. This family-run restaurant with an outdoor patio in the back is helmed by young chef and owner Sheila Costello. Using Pemaquid oysters, Maine blueberries, organic vegetables grown on a nearby farm, and other fresh, local ingredients, Costello creates flavorful dishes that delight all the senses. Choose from a chalkboard full of specials that always includes a macrobiotic option, or start with the smoked seafood and paté sampler or the spinach salad topped with sautéed chicken, sweet peppers, hazelnuts and a warmed raspberry vinaigrette. Entreés include ribeye steak and seafood linguine fra diablo. ✕ *90 Main St.,* ☎ *207/338–1106. Reservations accepted for 5 or more. AE, MC, V.*

$ Weathervane. Because this small northeastern chain has cut out the middleman—buying directly from fishers and self-distributing their goods—an average meal of very fresh raw, grilled, fried, broiled, or sautéed seafood costs under $10. Shellfish such as littleneck clams and the ubiquitous Maine lobster, tender rings of calamari, and fish from smelt to swordfish are available in combination platters. There are also token non-seafood items like sirloin and chicken tenders. This location has outdoor waterfront seating. ✕ *Main St.,* ☎ *207/338–1774. No reservations. MC, V.*

LODGING

$$ The Inn on Primrose Hill. Built in 1812 and once the home of a navy admiral, this 14-room inn near the waterfront is the most elegant in town. The inn's Ionic columns belie its original Federal architecture. The two acres that surround it have formal gardens, a terrace with wrought-iron furniture, and both horseshoes and a boccie court; a porch swing is an agreeable addition. Owners Pat and Linus Heinz have taken great care to keep and restore authentic details like ornate Waterford chandeliers, a mahogany dining set, and black marble fireplace. There are several spacious public rooms including double parlors, a library with a large-screen cable TV, and a sunny conservatory with wicker and plump, upholstered furniture. Guest rooms are large and have partial bay views. ▦ *100 High St.,* ☎ *207/338–6982. 2 rooms, 1 with private bath, 1 with shared bath. Boccie, horseshoes. Full breakfast included. No credit cards.*

$–$$ Thomas Pitcher House. Easygoing hosts Fran and Ron Kresge run a cheerful bed and breakfast that's one block from Belfast's Main Street.

Bright common areas include a small library, a formal dining room with Chippendale furnishings, and a parlor with a marble fireplace and Victorian touches. Upstairs, carefully decorated guest rooms have supremely comfortable beds and floral, paisley, and/or striped accents. Ron is a master breakfast chef—beg for his ham and cheese soufflé. ⌂ *5 Franklin St., ☎ 207/338–6454. 4 rooms with bath. Full breakfast included. No credit cards. No children under 12.*

Blue Hill

DINING

$$–$$$ **The Firepond.** Reopened in 1994 after a two-year hiatus, the Firepond
★   attracts customers from all over the region. The upstairs dining room has the air of an English country gentleman's library, with built-in bookshelves, antiques, and Oriental carpets; a new street-level dining area increases the seating capacity to 120. The kitchen delivers old favorites like lobster Firepond—with three cheeses, served over pasta—and new veal, pork, and scallop specialties. ✗ *Main St., ☎ 207/374–9970. Reservations advised. AE, MC, V. Closed Jan.–Apr.*

$$ **Jonathan's.** The downstairs room has captain's chairs, linen tablecloths, and local art; in the post-and-beam upstairs, there's wood everywhere, plus candles with hurricane globes and high-back chairs. The menu may include chicken breast in a fennel sauce with peppers, garlic, rosemary, and shallots; shrimp *scorpio* (served on linguine with a touch of ouzo and feta cheese); pan-seared medallions of venison with sweet-potato pancakes; and several fresh-fish entrées. The wine list has 200 selections from French and California vineyards as well as from the Bartlett Maine Estate Winery in Gouldshore. ✗ *Main St., ☎ 207/374–5226. Reservations advised in summer. MC, V.*

LODGING

$$$$ **John Peters Inn.** The John Peters is unsurpassed for the privacy of its
★   location and the good taste in the decor of its guest rooms. The living room has two fireplaces, books and games, a baby grand piano, and Empire furniture. Oriental rugs are everywhere. Huge breakfasts in the light and airy dining rooms include the famous lobster omelet, served complete with lobster-claw shells as decoration. The Surry Room, one of the best rooms, has a king-size bed, a fireplace, curly-maple chest, gilt mirror, and six windows. The large rooms in the carriage house, a stone's throw down the hill from the inn, have dining areas, cherry floors and woodwork, wicker and brass accents, and a modern feel. ⌂ *Peters Point, Box 916, 04614, ☎ 207/374–2116. 7 rooms with bath and 1 suite in inn; 6 rooms with bath in carriage house. Pool, pond, boating. Full breakfast included. MC, V. Closed Nov.–Apr.*

Camden

DINING

$$ **Waterfront Restaurant.** A ringside seat on Camden Harbor can be had here; the best view is from the outdoor deck, open in warm weather. The fare is primarily seafood: boiled lobster, scallops, bouillabaisse, steamed mussels, Cajun barbecued shrimp. Lunchtime highlights include Tex-Mex dishes, lobster and crabmeat salads, and tuna niçoise. ✗ *Bay View St., ☎ 207/236–3747. No reservations. AE, MC, V.*

$–$$ **Cappy's Chowder House.** Lobster traps, a moose head, and a barbershop pole decorate the bar in this lively but cozy eatery; the Crow's Nest dining room upstairs is quieter and has a harbor view. Simple fare is the rule here: burgers, sandwiches, seafood, and, of course, chowder. A bakery downstairs sells breads, cookies, and filled croissants to go. ✗ *1 Main St., ☎ 207/236–2254. No reservations. MC, V.*

DINING AND LODGING

$$$$ **Whitehall Inn.** Camden's best-known inn, just north of town on Route
★ 1, is an 1843 white-clapboard, wide-porch ship-captain's home with
a turn-of-the-century wing. Just off the comfortable main lobby with
its faded Oriental rugs, the Millay Room preserves memorabilia of the
poet Edna St. Vincent Millay, who grew up in the area. Rooms are
sparsely furnished, with dark-wood bedsteads, white bedspreads, and
clawfoot bathtubs. Some rooms have ocean views. The dining room,
serving traditional and creative American cuisine, is open to the public. Dinner entrées include Eastern salmon in puff pastry, swordfish grilled
with roast red pepper sauce, and lamb tenderloin. ☎ *52 High St. (Rte.
1), Box 558, 04843, ☎ 207/236–3391 or 800/789–6565, FAX 207/236–
4427. 44 rooms with bath. Restaurant (reservations advised; no lunch),
shuffleboard, golf privileges, tennis courts. MAP. AE, MC, V. Closed
mid-Oct.–late May.*

LODGING

$$$$ **Norumbega.** This stone castle, built in 1886 amid Camden's elegant
★ clapboard houses, was obviously the fulfillment of a fantasy. The public rooms have gleaming parquet floors, oak and mahogany paneling,
richly carved wood mantels over four fireplaces on the first floor alone,
gilt mirrors, and Empire furnishings. At the back of the house, several
decks and balconies overlook the garden, the gazebo, and the bay. The
view improves as you ascend; the penthouse suite has a small deck,
private bar, and a skylight in the bedroom. On arrival, guests are wel-
comed with complimentary aperitifs. ☎ *61 High St., 04843, ☎ 207/
236–4646, FAX 207/236–0824. 12 rooms with bath. Full breakfast included. AE, MC, V.*

$$$–$$$$ **Blackberry Inn.** This Victorian painted lady furnishes nine rooms dec-
orated in the minimalist Victorian style and a carriage-house suite, com-
plete with kitchen, which is ideal for traveling families. Also in the
carriage house, two renovated garden rooms have fireplaces, whirlpool
tubs, and separate entrances. ☎ *82 Elm St., 04843, ☎ 207/346–
6060, FAX 207/236–4117. 7 rooms with bath, 2 rooms share shower,
1 suite with kitchen. Full breakfast included. MC, V.*

$$$–$$$$ **Windward House.** A choice bed-and-breakfast, this Greek Revival
house of 1854, at the edge of downtown, has rooms furnished with
fishnet lace canopy beds, cherry highboys, curly-maple bedsteads, and
clawfoot mahogany dressers. Guests are welcome to use any of three
sitting rooms, including the Wicker Room with its glass-top white wicker
table where morning coffee is served. Breakfasts may include quiche,
apple puff pancakes, peaches-and-cream French toast, or soufflés. A
pleasant, private deck in back overlooks extensive English cutting gar-
dens. ☎ *6 High St., 04843, ☎ 207/236–9656. 7 rooms with bath, 1
suite. Full breakfast included. AE, MC, V.*

Castine

DINING AND LODGING

$$$$ **The Pentagoet.** The rambling, pale-yellow Pentagoet, a block from Cas-
tine's waterfront, has been a favorite stopping place for more than a
century. The porch wraps around three sides of the inn and has two
charming "courting swings." Decor in guest rooms includes hooked
rugs, a mix of Victorian antiques, and floral wallpapers. Dinner in the
deep-rose-and-cream formal dining room is an elaborate affair; entrées
always include lobster creatively prepared, plus two other selections,
such as grilled salmon with Dijon sauce, or pork loin braised in apple
cider. Complimentary hors d'oeuvres are served evenings in the li-
brary-cum-music room, where there is often live chamber music. Inn
guests can choose from a hearty breakfast or a lighter breakfast buf-

fet. ☎ *Main St., 04421,* ☎ *207/326–8616 or 800/845–1701. 16 rooms with bath. Restaurant (reservations required; no lunch). MAP. MC, V. Closed Nov.–late May.*

$$–$$$$ **The Castine Inn.** Light, airy rooms, upholstered easy chairs, and fine
★ prints and paintings are typical of the guest-room furnishings here. One room has a pineapple four-poster bed. The third floor has the best views: the harbor over the handsome formal gardens on one side, the village on the other. The dining room, decorated with a wraparound mural of Castine and its harbor, is open to the public for breakfast and dinner; the menu includes traditional New England fare—Maine lobster, crabmeat cakes with mustard sauce, roast leg of lamb, and chicken-and-leek potpie—plus such creative entrées as sweetbreads with hazelnut butter and roast duck with peach chutney. In the snug, English-style pub off the lobby are small tables, a fireplace, and antique spirit jars over the mantel. ☎ *Main St., Box 41, 04421,* ☎ *207/326–4365,* ☎ *207/326–4570. 17 rooms with bath, 3 suites. Restaurant, pub. Full breakfast included. MC, V. Closed Nov.–mid-Apr.*

Deer Isle

DINING AND LODGING

$$$$ **Pilgrim's Inn.** The bright red, four-story, gambrel-roof house dating from
★ about 1793 overlooks a mill pond and harbor in Deer Isle Village. The library has wing chairs and Oriental rugs; a downstairs taproom has a huge brick fireplace, pine furniture, braided rugs, and parson's benches. A generous array of hors d'oeuvres is served in the taproom and common room before dinner each evening. Guest rooms, each with its own character, sport English fabrics and select antiques. The dining room is in the attached barn, an open space both rustic and elegant, with farm implements, French oil lamps, and tiny windows. The five-course, single-entrée menu changes nightly; it might include rack of lamb or fresh local seafood, scallop bisque, asparagus and smoked salmon, and poached pear tart for dessert. ☎ *Rte. 15A, Deer Isle 04627,* ☎ *207/348–6615. 13 rooms, 8 with bath, 1 seaside cottage. Restaurant (reservations required; no lunch), bicycles. Full breakfast included; MAP available. No credit cards. Closed mid-Oct.–mid-May.*

$$–$$$ **Goose Cove Lodge.** The heavily wooded property at the end of a back road has 2,500 feet of ocean frontage, two sandy beaches, a long sandbar that leads to the Barred Island nature preserve, and nature trails. Some cottages and suites are in secluded woodlands, some on the shore, some attached, some with a single large room, others with one or two bedrooms. All but two units have fireplaces. The restaurant's prix-fixe four-course repast (always superb and always including at least one vegetarian entrée) is preceded by complimentary hors d'oeuvres. Friday nights, there's a lobster feast on the inn's private beach. ☎ *Box 40, Sunset 04683,* ☎ *207/348–2508,* ☎ *207/348–2624. 11 cottages, 10 suites. Restaurant (reservations required; no lunch), volleyball, boating. MC, V. MAP. Closed mid-Oct.–mid-May. One wk minimum stay in July and Aug.*

LODGING

$–$$ **Captain's Quarters Inn & Motel.** Accommodations, as plain and unadorned as Stonington itself, are in the middle of town, a two-minute walk from the Isle au Haut mailboat. You have your choice of motel-type rooms and suites or efficiencies, and you can take your breakfast muffins and coffee to the sunny deck overlooking the water. ☎ *Main St., Box 83, Stonington 04681,* ☎ *207/367–2420 or 800/942–2420. 13 units, 11 with bath. AE, D, MC, V.*

Isle au Haut

LODGING

$$$–$$$$ **The Keeper's House.** This converted lighthouse-keeper's house, set on a rock ledge surrounded by thick spruce forest, has its own special flavor. There is no electricity, but every guest receives a flashlight at registration; guests dine by candlelight on seafood or chicken and read in the evening by kerosene lantern. Trails link the historic inn with Acadia National Park's Isle au Haut trail network, and you can walk to the village—a collection of simple houses, a church, a tiny school, and a general store. The innkeepers are happy to pack lunches for anyone who wants to spend the day exploring the island. The five guest rooms are spacious, airy, and simply decorated with painted wood furniture and local crafts. A separate cottage, the Oil House, has no indoor plumbing. Access to the island is via the daily (except Sunday and holidays) mailboat from Stonington—a scenic, 40-minute trip. ⌂ *Box 26, 04645,* ☎ *207/367–2261. 5 rooms share bath, 1 cottage. Dock, bicycles. AP, BYOB. No credit cards. No Sun. or holiday check-in. Closed Nov.–Apr.*

Islesboro

LODGING

$$$$ **Dark Harbor House.** The yellow-clapboard, neo-Georgian summer "cottage" of 1896 has a stately portico and a dramatic hilltop setting on the island of Islesboro. An elegant double staircase curves from the ground floor to the bedrooms, which are spacious, some with balconies, five with fireplaces, two with four-poster beds. The dining room, open to the public for dinner by reservation, emphasizes seafood. ⌂ *Main Rd., Box 185, 04848,* ☎ *207/734–6669. 10 rooms with bath. Restaurant. MC, V. Closed mid-Oct.–mid-May.*

Lincolnville Beach

DINING

$–$$ **Chez Michel.** This unassuming restaurant, serving up a fine rabbit pâté, mussels marinière, steak au poivre, and poached salmon, might easily be on the Riviera instead of Lincolnville Beach. Chef Michel Hetuin creates bouillabaisse as deftly as he whips up New England fisherman chowder, and he welcomes special requests. ✗ *Rte. 1,* ☎ *207/789–5600. Reservations accepted for 6 or more. D, MC, V. Closed Nov.–mid-Apr.*

LODGING

$$$$ **Inn at Sunrise Point.** For luxury and location, you can't beat this ele-
★ gant B&B perched on the water's edge, with magnificent views over Penobscot Bay. Travel-writer Jerry Levitin built his dream getaway here. Three rooms in the main house and four cottages are simply, but tastefully decorated. Each room has a television and VCR, fireplace, terrycloth robes, and telephone. The cottages also have whirlpool tubs and private decks. A full breakfast is served in the solarium; guests take high tea in the paneled library with stone fireplace. ⌂ *Box 1344, Camden 04843,* ☎ *207/236–7716 or 800/435–6378. 7 rooms with bath.*

Rockland

DINING

$$ **Jessica's.** Perched on a hill at the extreme southern end of Rockland,
★ Jessica's occupies four cozy dining rooms in a tastefully renovated Victorian home. Billed as a European bistro, this restaurant lives up to its Continental label with creative entrées that include veal Zurich, paella, and pork Portofino; other specialties of the Swiss chef are focaccia with a selection of toppings and a half-dozen pastas and risottos. ✗ *2 S. Main St. (Rte. 73),* ☎ *207/596–0770. Reservations advised. D, MC, V. Closed Tues. in winter.*

LODGING

$$$–$$$$ **Limerock Inn.** The onetime commercial-fishing town of Rockland is coming back to life as one that caters to tourists. You can walk to the Farnsworth and the Shore Village museums from this magnificent Queen Anne–style Victorian, located on a quiet residential street. Meticulously decorated rooms include Island Cottage, with a whirlpool tub and doors that opens onto a private deck overlooking the backyard garden, and Grand Manan, which has a fireplace, whirlpool tub, and a four-poster king-size bed. ☎ *98 Limerock St., 94841, ☎ 207/594–2257 or 800/546–3762. 8 rooms with bath, 2 can be suites. Croquet, bicycles, boating. MC, V. Full breakfast included.*

Stockton Springs

LODGING

$–$$ **Hichborn Inn.** A Victorian Italianate on the National Register for Historic Places, this inn was originally the home of N.G. Hichborn, a prolific shipbuilder and politician and a cousin of Paul Revere. Small and romantic, the Hichborn is just north of Searsport, off Route 1, in a quiet neighborhood one door down from a classic white-steepled New England church. Public areas include a music room with a piano; a cheery sunporch with tables for two set for breakfast; and a dark and cozy parlor with maroon walls, a fireplace, and a tray of brandy, sherry, and cordials for self-service. Of the three guest rooms, one has a brass bed, one a sleigh bed, and the other an ornate, Victorian carved-walnut bed. Finishing touches include marble top dressers and robes. Your hosts, Nancy and Bruce Suppes, might serve fruit soup and Belgian waffles for breakfast. Eight friendly, protective ghosts have been spotted here over the years. ☎ *Church St. (Box 115), ☎ 207/567–4183. 2 rooms with bath, 1 room shares bath. No credit cards accepted. No Children. Full breakfast included.*

Tenants Harbor

DINING AND LODGING

$$–$$$ **East Wind Inn & Meeting House.** On Route 131, 10 miles off Route 1, and set on a knob of land overlooking the harbor and the islands, the East Wind offers simple hospitality, a wraparound porch, and unadorned but comfortable guest rooms, each furnished with an iron bedstead, flowered wallpaper, and heritage bedspread. The dinner menu features seafood supreme, prime rib, boiled lobster, and baked stuffed haddock. ☎ *Rte. 131, Box 149, 04860, ☎ 207/372–6366, FAX 207/372–6320. 23 rooms, 9 with bath; 3 suites. Restaurant (reservations advised; no lunch). Full breakfast included. AE, MC, V. Closed Feb.*

The Arts

Music

Bay Chamber Concerts (Rockport Opera House, Rockport, ☎ 207/236–2823) offers chamber music every Thursday night and some Friday nights during July and August; concerts are given once a month September through May. **Kneisel Hall Chamber Music Festival** (Kneisel Hall, Rte. 15, Blue Hill, ☎ 207/374–2811) has concerts on Sunday and Friday in summer.

Theater

The Belfast Maskers (Railroad Theater, Box 1017, Belfast, ☎ 207/338–9668) deserve their strong regional reputation. This group, which has received celebrity support from the likes of Ali McGraw and Liv Ullmann, presents both modern and classic works year-round.

Camden Civic Theatre (Camden Opera House, ☎ 207/236–7595), a community theater, specializes in musicals June through August. **Cold Comfort Productions** (Box 259, Castine, no ☎), a community theater, mounts plays in July and August.

Nightlife

Dennett's Wharf (Sea St., Castine, ☎ 207/326–9045) draws a crowd every lunchtime for a terrific view, and every evening for drinking and dancing. It's open from May through October. **Left Bank Bakery and Cafe** (Rte. 172, Blue Hill, ☎ 207/374–2201) rates a gold star for bringing top-notch musical talent from all over the country to sleepy Blue Hill. **Peter Ott's Tavern** (16 Bay View St., Camden, ☎ 207/236–4032) is a steakhouse with a lively bar scene. **Sea Dog Tavern & Brewery** (43 Mechanic St., Camden, ☎ 207/236–6863) is a popular brew pub offering locally made lagers and ales in a retrofitted woolen mill.

Penobscot Bay Essentials

Getting Around

BY CAR

Route 1 follows the west coast of Penobscot Bay, linking Rockland, Rockport, Camden, Belfast, and Searsport. On the east side of the bay, Route 175 (south from Route 1) takes you to Route 166A (for Castine) and Route 15 (for Blue Hill, Deer Isle, and Stonington). A car is essential for exploring the bay area.

Important Addresses and Numbers

EMERGENCIES

Blue Hill Memorial Hospital (Water St., Blue Hill, ☎ 207/374–2836). **Island Medical Center** (Airport Rd., Stonington, ☎ 207/367–2311). **Penobscot Bay Medical Center** (Rte. 1, Rockport, ☎ 207/596–8000). **Waldo County General Hospital** (56 Northport Ave., Belfast, ☎ 207/338–2500).

VISITOR INFORMATION

Belfast Area Chamber of Commerce (Box 58, Belfast 04915, ☎ 207/338–5900; Information booth: 31 Front St., ☉ Daily 10–6, May–Oct.). **Blue Hill Chamber of Commerce** (Box 520, Blue Hill 04614, no ☎). **Castine Town Office** (Emerson Hall, Court St., Castine 04421, ☎ 207/326–4502). **Deer Isle–Stonington Chamber of Commerce** (Box 459, Stonington 04681, ☎ 207/348–6124). **Rockland–Thomaston Area Chamber of Commerce** (Harbor Park, Box 508, Rockland 04841, ☎ 207/596–0376; ☉ Daily 8–5 in summer, weekdays 9–4 in winter). **Rockport-Camden-Lincolnville Chamber of Commerce** (Public Landing, Box 919, Camden 04843, ☎ 207/236–4404; ☉ Weekdays 9–5, Sat. 10–5, Sun. noon–4 in summer; weekdays 9–5, Sat. 10–4 in winter). **Searsport Chamber of Commerce** (East Main St., Searsport 04974, ☎ 207/548–6510).

ACADIA

East of Penobscot Bay, Acadia is the informal name for the area that includes Mount Desert Island (pronounced dessert) and its surroundings: Blue Hill Bay; Frenchman Bay; and Ellsworth, Hancock, and other mainland towns. Mount Desert, 13 miles across, is Maine's largest island, and it harbors most of Acadia National Park, Maine's principal tourist attraction with more than 4 million visitors a year. The 40,000 acres of woods and mountains, lake and shore, footpaths, carriage roads, and hiking trails that make up the park extend as well to other islands and some of the mainland. Outside the park, on Mount Desert's east shore, Bar Harbor has become a busy tourist town. An upper-class resort town of the 19th century, Bar Harbor serves park visitors with a variety of inns, motels, and restaurants.

Exploring

Numbers in the margin correspond to points of interest on the Acadia map.

① Coastal Route 1 passes through Ellsworth, where Route 3 turns south to Mount Desert Island and takes you into the busy town of **Bar Harbor.** Most of Bar Harbor's grand mansions were destroyed in a mammoth fire that devastated the island in 1947, but many of the surviving estates have been converted to attractive inns and restaurants. Motels abound, yet the town retains the beauty of a commanding location on Frenchman Bay. Shops, restaurants, and hotels are clustered along Main, Mt. Desert, and Cottage streets.

Bar Harbor Historical Society Museum, on the lower level of the Jesup Memorial Library, displays photographs of Bar Harbor from the days when it catered to the very rich. Other exhibits document the great fire of 1947. *34 Mt. Desert St., ☎ 207/288–4245. ☛ Free. ☉ Mid-June–mid-Oct., Mon.–Sat. 1–4 or by appointment.*

② The **Hulls Cove** approach to Acadia National Park is four miles northwest of Bar Harbor on Route 3. Even though it is often clogged with traffic in summer, the Park Loop Road provides the best introduction to Acadia National Park. At the start of the loop at Hulls Cove, the visitor center shows a free 15-minute orientation film. Also available at the center are books, maps of the hiking trails and carriage roads in the park, the schedule for naturalist-led tours, and cassettes for drive-it-yourself park tours.

③ Follow the road to the small ticket booth, where you pay the $5-per-vehicle entrance fee. Take the next left to the parking area for **Sand Beach,** a small stretch of pink sand backed by the mountains of Acadia and the odd lump of rock known as The Beehive. The **Ocean Trail,** which parallels the Park Loop Road from Sand Beach to the Otter Point parking area, is a popular and easily accessible walk with some of the most spectacular scenery in Maine: huge slabs of pink granite heaped at the ocean's edge, ocean views unobstructed to the horizon, and **Thunder Hole,** a natural seaside cave into which the ocean rushes and roars.

④ Those who want a mountaintop experience without the effort of hiking can drive to the summit of **Cadillac Mountain,** at 1,532 feet the highest point along the eastern seaboard. From the smooth, bald summit you have a 360-degree view of the ocean, islands, jagged coastline, and the woods and lakes of Acadia and its surroundings.

⑤ On completing the 27-mile Park Loop Road, you can continue your auto tour of the island by heading west on Route 233 for the villages on Somes Sound, a true fjord—the only one on the East Coast—which almost bisects Mount Desert Island. **Somesville,** the oldest settlement on the island (1621), is a carefully preserved New England village of white-clapboard houses and churches, neat green lawns, and bits of blue water visible behind them.

⑥ Route 102 south from Somesville takes you to **Southwest Harbor,** which combines the rough, salty character of a working port with the refinements of a summer resort community. From the town's Main Street (Rte. 102), turn left onto Clark Point Road to reach the harbor.

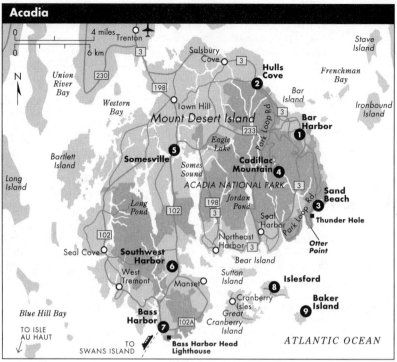

Acadia

TIME OUT At the end of Clark Point Road in Southwest Harbor, **Beal's Lobster Pier** serves lobsters, clams, and crab rolls in season at dockside picnic tables.

Those who want to tour more of the island can continue south on Route 102, following Route 102A where the road forks, and passing through the communities of Manset and Seawall. The Bass Harbor Head lighthouse, which clings to a cliff at the eastern entrance to Blue Hill Bay, **7** was built in 1858. The tiny lobstering village of **Bass Harbor** has cottages for rent, inns, a restaurant, a gift shop, and the Maine State Ferry Service's car-and-passenger ferry to Swans Island. ☎ *207/244–3254, 5 daily runs June–Nov., fewer trips rest of yr.*

Island Excursions

Off the southeast shore of Mount Desert Island at the entrance to Somes Sound, the five **Cranberry Isles**—Great Cranberry, Islesford (or Little Cranberry), Baker Island, Sutton Island, and Bear Island—escape the hubbub that engulfs Acadia National Park in summer. Great Cranberry and Islesford are served by the **Beal & Bunker passenger ferry** (☎ 207/244–3575) from Northeast Harbor, and by **Cranberry Cove Boating Company** (☎ 207/244–5882) from Southwest Harbor. Baker Island is reached by the summer cruise boats of the **Islesford Ferry Company** (☎ 207/276–3717) from Northeast Harbor; Sutton and Bear islands are privately owned.

8 **Islesford** comes closest to having a village: a collection of houses, a church, a fishermen's co-op, a market, and a post office near the ferry dock. The **Islesford Historical Museum,** run by Acadia National Park, has displays of tools, documents relating to the island's history, and books and manuscripts of the writer Rachel Field (1894–1942), who summered on Sutton Island. The simple **Islesford Dock Restaurant** (☎ 207/244–7446), overlooking the island's harbor, serves lunch and dinner mid-June to mid-September. *Islesford Historical Museum,* ☎ *207/288–3338.* ☛ *Free.* ☉ *Mid-June–Labor Day, Tues.–Sat. 10:30–noon, 12:30–4:30.*

⑨ The 123-acre **Baker Island,** the most remote of the group, looks almost black from a distance because of its thick spruce forest. The Islesford Ferry cruise boat from Northeast Harbor offers a 4½-hour narrated tour, during which you are likely to see ospreys nesting on a sea stack off Sutton Island, harbor seals basking on ledges, and cormorants flying low over the water. Because Baker Island has no natural harbor, the tour boat ties up off-shore, and you take a fishing dory to get to shore.

What to See and Do with Children

Acadia Zoo has pastures, streams, and woods that shelter about 40 species of wild and domestic animals, including reindeer, wolves, monkeys, and a moose. A barn has been converted to a rain-forest habitat for monkeys, birds, reptiles, and other Amazon creatures. *Rte. 3, Trenton,* ☎ *207/667–3244.* ☛ *$5 adults, $4 senior citizens and children 3–12.* ☉ *May–Nov., daily 9:30–dusk.*

Mount Desert Oceanarium has exhibits in three locations on the fishing and sea life of the Gulf of Maine, as well as hands-on exhibits such as a "touch tank." *Clark Point Rd., Southwest Harbor,* ☎ *207/244–7330; Rte. 3, Thomas Bay, Bar Harbor,* ☎ *207/288–5005; Lobster Hatchery at 1 Harbor Pl., Bar Harbor,* ☎ *207/288–2334. Call for admission fees (combination tickets available for all 3 sites).* ☉ *Mid-May–mid-Oct., Mon.–Sat. 9–5; hatchery open evenings July–Aug.*

Off the Beaten Path

Bartlett Maine Estate Winery offers tours, tastings, and gift packs. Wines are produced from locally grown apples, pears, blueberries, and other fruit. *Rte. 1, Gouldsboro, north of Bar Harbor (via Ellsworth),* ☎ *207/546–2408.* ☉ *June–mid-Oct., Tues.–Sat. 10–5, Sun. noon–5.*

Jackson Laboratory, a center for research in mammalian genetics, studies cancer, diabetes, heart disease, AIDS, muscular dystrophy, and other diseases. *Rte. 3, 3½ mi south of Bar Harbor,* ☎ *207/288–3371.* ☛ *Free audiovisual presentations, mid-June–mid-Sept., Tues. and Thurs. at 3.*

Shopping

Bar Harbor in summer is prime territory for browsing for gifts, T-shirts, and novelty items; for bargains, head for the outlets that line Route 3 in Ellsworth, which have good discounts on shoes, sportswear, cookware, and more.

Antiques
E. and L. Higgins (Bernard Rd., Bernard, ☎ 207/244–3983) has a good stock of wicker, along with pine and oak country furniture. **Marianne Clark Fine Antiques** (Main St., Southwest Harbor, ☎ 207/244–9247) has an eclectic array of formal and country furniture, American paintings, and accessories from the 18th and 19th centuries.

Books
Port in a Storm Bookstore (Main St., Somesville, ☎ 207/244–4114) is a book lover's nirvana on a rainy day (or even a sunny one) on Mount Desert Island.

Crafts
Acadia Shops (5 branches: inside the park at Cadillac Mountain summit; Thunder Hole on Ocean Dr.; Jordan Pond House on Park Loop Rd.; and 45 and 85 Main St., Bar Harbor) sell crafts and Maine foods and books. **Island Artisans** (99 Main St., Bar Harbor, ☎ 207/288–4214) is a crafts cooperative. **The Lone Moose–Fine Crafts** (78 West St., Bar Harbor, ☎ 207/288–4229) has ship models, art glass, and works in clay, pottery, wood, and fiberglass. The **Eclipse Gallery** (12 Mt. Desert St., Bar Harbor, ☎ 207/288–9048) represents the work of nearly 200 contemporary American artisans, carrying handblown glass, jewelry, and ceramics.

Sports and the Outdoors
Biking, Jogging, and Cross-Country Skiing
The network of carriage roads that wind through the woods and fields of Acadia National Park is ideal for biking and jogging when the ground is dry and for cross-country skiing in winter. The Hulls Cove Visitor Center has a carriage-road map.

Bikes can be rented at **Acadia Bike & Canoe** (48 Cottage St., Bar Harbor, ☎ 207/288–9605), **Bar Harbor Bicycle Shop** (141 Cottage St., ☎ 207/288–3886), and **Southwest Cycle** (Main St., Southwest Harbor, ☎ 207/244–5856).

Boat Trips
BAR HARBOR
Acadian Whale Watcher (Golden Anchor Pier, West St., ☎ 207/288–9794 or 800/421–3307) runs 3½-hour whale-watching cruises June–mid-October. ***Chippewa*** (Bar Harbor Inn Pier, ☎ 207/288–4585 or 207/288–2373) is a 65-foot classic motor vessel that cruises past islands and lighthouses three times a day (including sunset) in summer. **Frenchman Bay Company** (Harbor Place, ☎ 207/288–3322 or 800/508–1499) operates the windjammer *Bay Lady,* the nature/sightseeing cruise vessel *Acadian,* and the 300-passenger *Whale Watcher* in summer. ***Natalie Todd*** (Bar Harbor Inn Pier, ☎ 207/288–4585 or 207/288–2373) offers two-hour cruises on a three-masted windjammer mid-May–mid-October.

BASS HARBOR
Bass Harbor Cruises (Bass Harbor Ferry Dock, ☎ 207/244–5365) operates two-hour nature cruises (with an Acadia naturalist) twice daily in summer.

NORTHEAST HARBOR
Blackjack (Town Dock, ☎ 207/276–5043 or 207/288–3056), a 33-foot Friendship sloop, makes four trips daily, mid-June–mid-October.

Camping
The two campgrounds in Acadia National Park—**Blackwoods** (Rte. 3, ☎ 800/365–2267), open year-round, and **Seawall** (Rte. 102A, ☎ 207/244–3600), open late May to late September—fill up quickly during the summer season, even though they have a total of 530 campsites. Space at Seawall is allocated on a first-come, first-served basis, starting at 8 AM. Between mid-May and mid-October, reserve a Blackwoods site within eight weeks of a scheduled visit. No reservations are required off-season. Off Mount Desert Island, but convenient to it, the campground at **Lamoine State Park** (Rte. 84, Lamoine, ☎ 207/667–4778) is open mid-May–mid-October; the 55-acre park has a splendid front-row seat on Frenchman Bay.

Canoeing and Sea Kayaking

For canoe rentals and guided kayak tours, try **Acadia Bike & Canoe,** above, or **National Park Canoe Rentals** (137 Cottage St., Bar Harbor, ☎ 207/288–0342, or Pretty Marsh Rd., Somesville, at the head of Long Pond, ☎ 207/244–5854).

Carriage Rides

Wildwood Stables (Park Loop Rd., near Jordan Pond House, ☎ 207/ 276–3622) gives romantic tours in traditional horse-drawn carriages on the 51-mile network of carriage roads designed and built by philanthropist John D. Rockefeller, Jr. There are three two-hour trips and three one-hour trips daily, including a "tea-and-popover ride" that stops at Jordan Pond House (*see* Dining and Lodging, *below*) and a sunset ride to the summit of Day Mountain.

Hiking

Acadia National Park maintains nearly 200 miles of foot and carriage paths, ranging from easy strolls along flatlands to rigorous climbs that involve ladders and handholds on rock faces. Among the more rewarding hikes 'are the Precipice Trail to Champlain Mountain, the Great Head Loop, the Gorham Mountain Trail, and the path around Eagle Lake. The Hulls Cove Visitor Center has trail guides and maps.

Sailing and Boating

Harbor Boat Rentals (Harbor Pl., 1 West St., ☎ 207/288–3757) has 13- and 17-foot Boston whalers and other powerboats. **Manset Yacht Service** (Shore Rd., ☎ 207/244–4040) rents sailboats.

Dining and Lodging

Bar Harbor has the greatest concentration of accommodations on Mount Desert Island. Much of this lodging has been converted from elaborate 19th-century summer cottages. A number of fine restaurants are also tucked away in these old homes and inns. Dress is casual unless noted otherwise.

Bar Harbor

DINING

$$$ **The Porcupine Grill.** Named for a cluster of islets in Frenchman Bay, this two-story restaurant has earned culinary fame for its cornbread-stuffed pork chops, crabmeat terrine made with local goat cheese, salmon with citrus relish, fresh pastas, and a Caesar salad tossed with Reggiano Parmesan and fried shrimp. Soft green walls, antique furnishings, and Villeroy & Boch porcelain create an ambience that complements the cuisine. ✕ *123 Cottage St., ☎ 207/288–3884. Reservations advised. AE, MC, V. No lunch. Closed Mon.–Thurs. Jan.–June.*

$$–$$$ **George's.** Candles, flowers, and linens grace the tables in four small
★ dining rooms in an old house. The menu shows a distinct Mediterranean influence in the phyllo-wrapped lobster; the lamb and wild game entrées are superb. Couples tend to linger in the romantic setting. ✕ *7 Stephen's La., ☎ 207/288–4505. Reservations advised. AE, D, DC, MC, V. No lunch. Closed late Oct.–mid-June.*

$$ **Jordan Pond House.** Oversize popovers (with homemade strawberry jam) and tea are a century-old tradition at this rustic restaurant in the park, where in fine weather you can sit on the terrace or the lawn and admire the views of Jordan Pond and the mountains. Teatime is 2:30 to 5:30. The dinner menu offers lobster stew, seafood thermidor, and fisherman's stew. ✕ *Park Loop Rd., ☎ 207/276–3316. Reserve a day ahead in summer. AE, D, MC, V. Closed late Oct.–May.*

LODGING

$$$$ Holbrook House. Built in 1876 as a summer home and originally known as Ashley Cottage, the lemon-yellow Holbrook House stands right on Mt. Desert Street, the main access route through Bar Harbor. The downstairs public rooms include a lovely, formal sitting room with bright, summery chintz on chairs and framing windows and a Duncan Phyfe sofa upholstered in white silk damask. The guest rooms and two separate cottages are all furnished with lovingly handled family pieces in the same refined taste as the public rooms. ⊞ *74 Mt. Desert St., 04609,* ☎ *207/288–4970 or 800/695–1120. 10 rooms with bath in inn, 2 cottage suites. Croquet. Full breakfast and afternoon refreshments included. MC, V. Closed late-Oct.–May.*

$$$$ Inn at Canoe Point. Seclusion and privacy are bywords of this snug, 100-★ year-old Tudor-style house on the water at Hulls Cove, 2 miles from Bar Harbor and ¼ mile from Acadia National Park's Hulls Cove Visitor Center. The Master Suite, a large room with a fireplace, is a favorite for its size and for its French doors, which open onto a waterside deck. The inn's large living room has huge windows on the water, a granite fireplace, and a waterfront deck where a full breakfast is served on summer mornings. ⊞ *Box 216, Rte. 3, 04609,* ☎ *207/288–9511. 3 rooms with bath, 2 suites. Full breakfast included. No credit cards.*

$$$–$$$$ Cleftstone Manor. Attention, lovers of Victoriana! This inn was made in high Victorian heaven expressly for you. Ignore the fact that it is set amid sterile motels just off Route 3, the road along which traffic roars into Bar Harbor. Inside this rambling brown house, a deeply plush mahogany-and-lace world awaits. The parlor is cool and richly furnished with red velvet and brocade-trim sofas with white doilies, grandfather and mantel clocks, and oil paintings hanging on powder-blue walls. Guest rooms are similarly ornate, and five rooms have fireplaces. ⊞ *Rte. 3, Eden St., 04609,* ☎ *207/288–4951 or 800/962–9762. 14 rooms with bath, 2 suites. Full breakfast and afternoon and evening refreshments included. D, MC, V. Closed Nov.–late Apr.*

$$–$$$ Wonder View Inn. Although the rooms here are standard motel accommodations, with two double beds and nondescript furniture, this establishment is distinguished by its extensive grounds, an imposing view of Frenchman Bay, and a convenient location opposite the Bluenose Ferry Terminal. The woods muffle the sounds of traffic on Route 3. The gazebo-shaped dining room—the Rinehart Dining Pavilion—has picture windows overlooking the bay and is open to the public for breakfast and dinner. ⊞ *Rte. 3, Box 25, 04609,* ☎ *207/288–3358 or 800/ 341–1553,* ℻ *207/288–2005. 80 rooms with bath. Dining room, pool. AE, D, MC, V. Closed late Oct.–mid-May.*

Hancock

DINING AND LODGING

$$$–$$$$ Le Domaine. This inn, on 100 acres 9 miles east of Ellsworth, has seven ★ rooms done in French country style, with chintz and wicker, simple desks, and window seats; five of them have balconies or porches over the gardens. The elegant but not intimidating dining room has polished wood floors, copper pots hanging from the mantel, and silver, crystal, and linen on the tables; a screened-in dining area overlooks the gardens in back. Owner Nicole Purslow, trained at Cordon Bleu in her native France, prepares such specialties as *lapin pruneaux* (rabbit in a rich brown sauce), sweetbreads with lemon and capers, and coquilles St. Jacques. ⊞ *Rte. 1, Box 496, 04640,* ☎ *207/422–3395, 207/422–3916, or 800/554– 8498;* ℻ *207/422–2316. 7 rooms with bath. Restaurant (reservations advised; no lunch; $$$), badminton, hiking, boating, fishing. AE, D, MC, V. MAP. Closed Nov.–mid-May.*

Northeast Harbor

DINING AND LODGING

$$$–$$$$ **Asticou Inn.** This grand turn-of-the-century inn at the head of exclusive Northeast Harbor serves a loyal clientele. Guest rooms in the main building have a country feel, with bright fabrics, white lace curtains, and white painted furniture. The more modern cottages scattered around the grounds afford greater privacy; among them, the decks and picture windows make the Topsider Cottages particularly attractive. Also part of the inn is the Victorian-style Cranberry Lodge, across the street. At night, guests trade Topsiders and polo shirts for jackets and ties to dine in the stately formal dining room, which is open to the public by reservation. A typical menu includes swordfish with orange mustard glaze, lobster, shrimp scampi, and chicken in a lemon cream and mushroom sauce. ⛏ *Rte. 3, 04662,* ☎ *207/276–3344 or 800/258– 3373,* 𝖥𝖠𝖷 *207/276–3373. 27 rooms with bath, 23 suites, 6 cottages. Restaurant (reservations required; no lunch), pool, tennis courts. MAP in summer. MC, V. Inn and restaurant closed mid-Sept.–mid-June; cottages, lodge closed Jan.–Apr.*

Southwest Harbor

DINING AND LODGING

$$$$ **Claremont Hotel.** Built in 1884 and operated continuously as an inn, the Claremont calls up memories of long, leisurely vacations of days gone by. The yellow-clapboard structure commands a view of Somes Sound, croquet is played on the lawn, and cocktails and lunch are served at the Boat House in midsummer. The highlight of the summer season is the annual Claremont Croquet Classic, held at the hotel the first week in August. The main hotel received a complete updating in 1994, but traditionalists will be hard pressed to notice any changes: A historic preservationist oversaw the rewiring and replumbing. There are also two guest houses on the property and 12 cottages, some with water views. The large, elegant dining room, open to the public for breakfast and dinner, is awash in light streaming through the picture windows. The menu changes weekly and always includes fresh fish and at least one vegetarian entrée. ⛏ *Off Clark Point Rd., Box 137, 04679,* ☎ *207/244–5036 or 800/244–5036,* 𝖥𝖠𝖷 *207/244–3512. 24 rooms with bath, 12 cottages, 2 guest houses. Restaurant (reservations required; jacket required for dinner; no lunch; $$), croquet, dock, boating, bicycles, tennis court. MAP. No credit cards. Hotel and restaurant closed mid-Oct.–mid-June. Cottages closed Nov.–late May.*

LODGING

$$–$$$ **The Island House.** This sweet B&B on the quiet side of the island has simply decorated bedrooms in the main house as well as a carriage house suite, complete with sleeping loft and kitchenette. Rate includes full breakfast. *Box 1006, 04679,* ☎ *207/244–5180. 4 rooms share 3 baths, 1 suite. No credit cards.*

The Arts

Music

Arcady Music Festival (☎ 207/288–3151) schedules concerts (primarily classical) at a number of locations around Mount Desert Island, as well as at selected off-island sites, from mid-July through August. **Bar Harbor Festival** (59 Cottage St., Bar Harbor, ☎ 207/288–5744) programs recitals, jazz, chamber music, string orchestra, and pops concerts by up-and-coming young professionals from mid-July to mid-August. **Pierre Monteux School for Conductors and Orchestra Musicians**

(Rte. 1, Hancock, ☎ 207/422–3931) presents public concerts by faculty and students during the term (late June–late July). Symphonic concerts are Sundays at 5 and chamber-music concerts are Wednesday at 8—all held in the Pierre Monteux Memorial Hall.

Theater
Acadia Repertory Company (Masonic Hall, Rte. 102, Somesville, ☎ 207/244–7260) mounts plays in July and August.

Nightlife

Acadia has relatively little nighttime activity. A lively boating crowd frequents the lounge at the **Moorings Restaurant** (Shore Rd. Manset, ☎ 207/244–7070), which is accessible by boat and car, and stays open until after midnight from mid-May through October.

Acadia Essentials

Getting Around
BY CAR

North of Bar Harbor, the scenic 27-mile Park Loop Road takes leave of Route 3 to circle the eastern quarter of Mount Desert Island, with one-way traffic from Sieur de Monts Spring to Seal Harbor and two-way traffic between Seal Harbor and Hulls Cove. Route 102, which serves the western half of Mount Desert, is reached from Route 3 just after it crosses onto the island or from Route 233 west from Bar Harbor. All of these island roads pass in, out, and through the precincts of Acadia National Park.

Guided Tours
Acadia Taxi and Tours (☎ 207/288–4020) conducts half-day historic and scenic tours of the area.

National Park Tours (☎ 207/288–3327) operates a 2½-hour bus tour of Acadia National Park, narrated by a local naturalist. The bus departs twice daily, May–October, across from Testa's Restaurant at Bayside Landing on Main Street in Bar Harbor.

Acadia Air (☎ 207/667–5534), on Route 3 in Trenton, between Ellsworth and Bar Harbor at Hancock County Airport, offers aircraft rentals and seven different aerial sightseeing itineraries, from spring through fall.

Important Addresses and Numbers
EMERGENCIES

Mount Desert Island Hospital (10 Wayman La., Bar Harbor, ☎ 207/288–5081). **Maine Coast Memorial Hospital** (50 Union St., Ellsworth, ☎ 207/667–5311). **Southwest Harbor Medical Center** (Herrick Rd., Southwest Harbor, ☎ 207/244–5513).

VISITOR INFORMATION

Acadia National Park (Box 177, Bar Harbor 04609, ☎ 207/288–3338; the Hulls Cove Visitor Center, off Rte. 3, at start of Park Loop Rd., is ☉ Daily 8–4:30, May–June and Sept.–Oct.; until 6 PM July and Aug.). **Bar Harbor Chamber of Commerce** (93 Cottage St., Box 158, Bar Harbor 04609, ☎ 207/288–3393, 207/288–5103, or 800/288–5103; ☉ Weekdays 8–5 in summer, weekdays 8–4:30 in winter). There's also an information office in **Bluenose Ferry Terminal** (Rte. 3, Eden St.; ☉ Daily 8 AM–11 PM July–early Oct.; daily 9–5 mid-May–July and early Oct.–mid-Oct.).

WESTERN LAKES AND MOUNTAINS

Less than 20 miles northwest of Portland and the coast, the lakes and mountains of western Maine begin their stretch north along the New Hampshire border to Québec. In winter this is ski country; in summer the woods and waters draw vacationers to recreation or seclusion in areas less densely populated than much of Maine's coast.

The Sebago–Long Lake region has antiques stores and lake cruises on a 42-mile waterway. Kezar Lake, tucked away in a fold of the White Mountains, has long been a hideaway of the wealthy. Bethel, in the Androscoggin River valley, is a classic New England town, its town common lined with historic homes. The far more rural Rangeley Lake area brings long stretches of pine, beech, spruce, and sky—and stylish inns and bed-and-breakfasts with easy access to golf, boating, fishing, and hiking.

Exploring

Numbers in the margin correspond to points of interest on the Western Maine map.

❶ A tour of the lakes begins at **Sebago Lake,** west of Route 302, fewer than 20 miles northwest of Portland. At the north end of the lake, the **Songo Lock** (☎ 207/693–6231), which permits the passage of watercraft from Sebago Lake to Long Lake, is the one surviving lock of the Cumberland and Oxford Canal. Built of wood and masonry, the original lock dates from 1830 and was expanded in 1911; today it sees heavy traffic during the summer months.

The 1,300-acre **Sebago Lake State Park** on the north shore of Sebago Lake provides opportunities for swimming, picnicking, camping, boating, and fishing (salmon and togue). ☎ *207/693–6613 June 20–Labor Day; other times, 207/693–6231.*

Route 302 continues north to Naples, where the Naples Causeway has rental craft for fishing or cruising on Long Lake. You can also see the **Naples Historical Society Museum,** which includes a jailhouse, a bandstand, a Dodge 1938 fire truck, a coach, and information about the Cumberland and Oxford Canal and the Sebago–Long Lake steamboats. *Village Green, Rte. 302,* ☎ *207/693–6364.* ☛ *Free.* ☉ *July–Aug.; call for hrs.*

Continue on to rather drab Bridgton, near Highland Lake, which has antiques shops in and around the town. You might also visit the **Bridgton Historical Society Museum,** housed in a former fire station built in 1902; it displays artifacts of the area's history and materials on the local narrow-gauge railroad. *Gibbs Ave.,* ☎ *207/647–2765.* ☛ *Free.* ☉ *June–Aug., Mon.–Sat. 1–4.*

The most scenic route to Bethel, 30 miles to the north, follows Route 302 west from Bridgton, across Moose Pond to Knight's Hill Road, turning north to Lovell and Route 5, which will take you on to Bethel. It's a drive that lets you admire the jagged crests of the White Mountains outlined against the sky to the west and the lush, rolling hills that **❷** alternate with brooding forests at roadside. At **Center Lovell** you can barely glimpse the secluded Kezar Lake to the west, the retreat of wealthy and very private people; Sabattus Mountain, which rises behind Center Lovell, has a public hiking trail and stupendous views of the Presidential range from the summit.

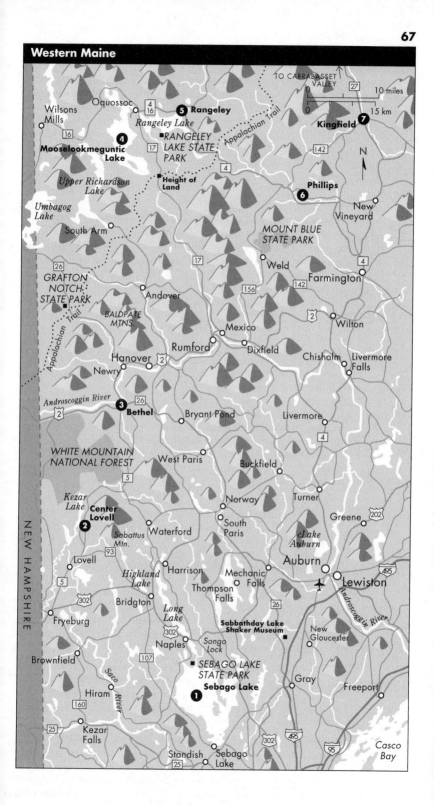

❸ Bethel is pure New England, a town with white-clapboard houses and white-steeple churches and a mountain vista at the end of every street. In the winter this is ski country, and Bethel serves the Sunday River ski area. A stroll of Bethel should begin at the **Moses Mason House and Museum,** a Federal home of 1813. On the town common, across from the sprawling Bethel Inn and Country Club, the Mason Museum has nine period rooms and a front hall and stairway wall decorated with murals by Rufus Porter. You can also pick up materials for a walking tour of Bethel Hill Village, most of which is on the National Register of Historic Places. *14 Broad St.,* ☏ *207/824–2908.* ☛ *$2 adults, $1 children under 12.* ⊙ *July–Labor Day, Tues.–Sun. 1–4; day after Labor Day–June, by appointment.*

The **Major Gideon Hastings House** nearby on Broad Street has a columned front portico typical of the Greek Revival style. Around the common, on Church Street, stands the severe white **West Parish Congregational Church** (1847), with its unadorned triangular pediment and steeple supported on open columns. Beyond the church is the campus of **Gould Academy,** a preparatory school chartered in 1835; the dominant style of the school buildings is Georgian, and the tall brick main campus building is surmounted by a white cupola. Main Street will take you from the common past the Town Hall-Cole Block, built in 1891, to the shops.

The routes north from Bethel to the Rangeley district are all scenic, particularly in the autumn when the maples are aflame. On Route 26 it's about 12 miles to **Grafton Notch State Park,** where you can hike to stunning gorges and waterfalls and into the Baldpate Mountains. En route to the park, in the town of Newry, make a short detour to the **Artist's Bridge** (turn off of Rte. 26 onto Sunday River Rd. and drive about 3 mi), the most painted and photographed of Maine's eight covered bridges. Route 26 continues on to Errol, New Hampshire, where Route 16 will return you east around the north shore of Mooselookmeguntic Lake, through Oquossoc, and into Rangeley.

A more direct—if marginally less scenic—tour follows Route 2 north and east from Bethel to the twin towns of Rumford and Mexico, where Route 17 continues north to Oquossoc, about an hour's drive. When you've gone about 20 minutes beyond Rumford, the signs of civilization all but vanish and you pass through what seems like untouched territory; in fact, the lumber companies have long since tackled the virgin forests, and sporting camps and cottages are tucked away here and there. The high point of this route is **Height of Land,** about 30 miles north of Rumford, with its unforgettable views of range after range of mountains and the huge, island-studded blue mass of Mooselookmeguntic Lake directly below. Turnouts on both sides of the highway allow you to pull over for a long look.

❹ Route 4 ends at Haines Landing on **Mooselookmeguntic Lake,** 7 miles west of Rangeley. Here you can stand at 1,400 feet above sea level and face the same magnificent scenery you admired at 2,400 feet from Height of Land on Route 17. Boat and canoe rentals are available at Mooselookmeguntic House.

❺ Rangeley, north of Rangeley Lake on Route 4/16, has lured fisherfolk, hunters, and winter-sports enthusiasts for a century to its more than 40 lakes and ponds and 450 square miles of woodlands. Rangeley has a rough, wilderness feel to it—indeed some of its best parts, including the choice lodgings, are tucked away in the woods, around the lake, and along the golf course.

On the south shore of Rangeley Lake, **Rangeley Lake State Park** (☏ 207/864–3858) offers superb lakeside scenery, swimming, picnic tables, a boat ramp, showers, and camping sites set well apart in a spruce and fir grove.

❻ In **Phillips,** 20 miles southeast of Rangeley on Route 4, the Sandy River & Rangeley Lakes Railroad, a restored narrow-gauge railroad, has a mile of track through the woods, where you can board a century-old train drawn by a replica of the Sandy River No. 4 locomotive. ☏ *207/639–3352.* ☛ *$3 adults, $1.50 children 6–12.* ☺ *May–Oct., 1st and 3rd Sun. each month; rides at 11, 1, and 3.*

❼ Just west of Phillips on Route 4, Route 142 takes you northeast to **Kingfield,** prime ski country in the heart of the western mountains. In the shadows of Mt. Abraham and Sugarloaf Mountain, Kingfield has everything a "real" New England town should have: a general store, historic inns, and a white-clapboard church. The **Stanley Museum** houses a collection of original Stanley Steamer cars built by the Stanley twins, Kingfield's most famous natives. *School St.,* ☏ *207/265–2729.* ☛ *$2 adults, $1 children.* ☺ *Tues.–Sun. 1–4; Closed Apr. and Nov.*

What to See and Do with Children

Songo River Queen II, a 92-foot stern-wheeler, takes passengers on hour-long cruises on Long Lake and longer voyages down the Songo River and through Songo Lock. *Rte. 302, Naples Causeway,* ☏ *207/693–6861.* ☛ *Songo River ride: $9 adults, $6 children; Long Lake cruise: $6 adults, $4 children.* ☺ *July–Labor Day, 5 trips daily; June and Sept., weekends.*

Off the Beaten Path

Sabbathday Lake Shaker Museum on Route 26, 20 miles north of Portland, is the last active Shaker community in the United States (established in the late 18th century). Members continue to farm crops and herbs, and visitors are shown the meetinghouse of 1794—a paradigm of Shaker design—and the ministry shop with 14 rooms of Shaker furniture, folk art, tools, farm implements, and crafts of the 18th to early 20th centuries. On Sunday, the Shaker day of prayer, the community is closed to visitors. *Rte. 26, New Gloucester,* ☏ *207/ 926–4597.* ☛ *Tour: $4 adults, $2 children 6–12; extended tour, $5.50 adults, $2.75 children.* ☺ *Memorial Day–Columbus Day, Mon.–Sat. 10–4:30.*

Shopping

Antiques

The Lyons' Den (Rte. 2, Hanover, near Bethel, ☏ 207/364–8634), a great barn of a place, carries glass, china, tools, prints, rugs, handwrought iron, and some furniture.

Crafts

Bonnema Potters (146 Lower Main St., Bethel, ☏ 207/824–2821) features colorful modern designs in plates, lamps, tiles, and vases. **Cry of the Loon Shop Fine Gifts and Crafts Art Gallery** (Rte. 302, S. Casco, ☏ 207/655–5060) has crafts, gifts, gourmet foods, and two galleries.

Skiing

Saddleback Ski and Summer Lake Preserve
Box 490, Rangeley 04970
☎ *207/864–5671; snow conditions, 207/864–3380; reservations, 207/864–5364*

A down-home, laid-back atmosphere prevails at Saddleback, where the quiet and the absence of crowds, even on busy weekends, draw return visitors—many of them families. The base area has the feeling of a small community for the guests at trailside homes and condominiums. With recent expansion and plans for more, Saddleback is becoming a major resort.

DOWNHILL
The expert terrain is short and concentrated at the top of the mountain; an upper lift makes the trails easily accessible. The middle of the mountain is mainly intermediate, with a few meandering easy trails; the beginner or novice slopes are toward the bottom. Two double chairlifts and three T-bars carry skiers to the 40 trails on the 1,830 feet of vertical.

CROSS-COUNTRY
Forty kilometers (25 miles) of groomed cross-country trails spread out from the base area and circle Saddleback Lake and several ponds and rivers.

OTHER ACTIVITIES
More than 100 miles of maintained snowmobile trails in the Rangeley Region, along with ice skating, sledding, and tobogganing, are available in winter.

CHILD CARE
The nursery takes children ages 6 weeks through 8 years. There are ski classes and programs for children of different levels and ages, through the teen years.

Shawnee Peak
Box 734, Rte. 302, Bridgton 04009
☎ *207/647–8444*

On the New Hampshire border, Shawnee Peak (formerly Pleasant Mountain) draws many skiers from the North Conway, New Hampshire, region 18 miles away and from Portland, 45 miles distant. In 1994, new management set goals to maintain its popularity with families while upgrading facilities.

DOWNHILL
Recent lighting installations have opened more trails for night skiing off the 1,300-foot vertical; this resort has perhaps the most night-skiing terrain in New England. Most trails are pleasant cruisers for intermediates, with some beginner slopes and a few pitches suitable for advanced skiers. One triple and three double chairlifts service the 30 ski runs.

CHILD CARE
The area's nursery takes children from 6 months through 6 years. The SKIwee program is for children 4–6; those 7–12 also have a program. Children under 8 ski free when accompanied by a parent. The Youth Ski League has instruction for aspiring racers.

Ski Mt. Abram
Rte. 26, Box 120, Locke Mills 04255
☎ *207/875–5003*

This complete resort has a friendly, rustic Maine feeling and is known for its snow grooming, home-style cooking, and family atmosphere. Skiers here prefer its low-key, friendly attitude and wallet-friendly rates compared to the much bigger Sunday River, nearby; new owners are bringing old-fashioned Ski Mt. Abrams up to date. Many skiers choose to stay in reasonably priced condominiums on the mountain road.

DOWNHILL

The mountain reaches just over 1,000 vertical feet, the majority of its terrain intermediate, with fall-line steep runs and two areas for beginning and novice skiers. The area has two double chairlifts and three T-bars. In addition to learn-to-ski classes, there are regular improvement clinics for all ability levels and age groups. New management has a five-year plan, which includes 100% snowmaking coverage, a new chairlift to the top, and a new base facility. Already in place are a children's terrain garden, a half-pipe for snowboarders, a snowboard park, two expert trails, and expanded snowmaking.

OTHER ACTIVITIES

There is an ice skating rink at the mountain's base.

CHILD CARE

The Ski Mt. Abram's Day Care Center takes children from 6 months through 6 years. The ski school offers class lessons on weekends and during vacation weeks to children 3–6 who are enrolled in the nursery. For juniors 6–16 there are individual classes plus a series of 10 two-hour lessons on weekends.

Sugarloaf/USA
Kingfield 04947
☎ *207/237–2000; snow conditions, 207/237–2000*

The 1980s saw Sugarloaf emerge as a major ski resort, with two sizable hotels, a condominium complex, and a village cluster of shops, restaurants, and meeting facilities. Sugarloaf/USA likes to refer to itself as the "Snowplace of the East" because of the abundance of natural snow it usually receives, plus its ability to manufacture 20 tons of snow per minute (via an $11 million infusion into its snowmaking plant since 1986). In 1994, S-K-I Inc. acquired partial ownership of Sugarloaf, giving it the capital it needed to upgrade snowmaking even further, add new lifts, and expand terrain.

DOWNHILL

With a vertical of 2,820 feet, Sugarloaf is taller than any other New England ski peak, except Killington, Vermont. The advanced terrain begins with the steep snowfields on top, wide open and treeless. Coming down the face of the mountain, there are black-diamond runs everywhere, often blending into easier terrain. A substantial number of intermediate trails can be found down the front face, and a couple more come off the summit. Easier runs are predominantly toward the bottom, with a few long, winding runs that twist and turn from higher elevations. A new high-speed quad added for the 1994–95 ski season greatly improved skier access to the resort's 98 trails. Other lifts are Maine's only gondola, two quads, one triple, eight double chairlifts, and 2 T-bars. Snowboarders will find a snowboard park and a half-pipe.

CROSS-COUNTRY

The Sugarloaf Ski Touring Center has 85 kilometers (53 miles) of cross-country trails that loop and wind through the valley. Trails connect to the resort.

The Sugarloaf Sports and Fitness Club (☎ 207/237–6946) has an indoor pool, six indoor and outdoor hot tubs, racquetball courts, full fitness and spa facilities, and a beauty salon. Use of club facilities is included in all lodging packages.

CHILD CARE
A nursery takes children from 6 weeks through 6 years. Once they reach 3, children are allowed to try ski equipment for free. A night nursery is open on Wednesday and Saturday, 6–10 PM, by reservation. Instruction is provided on a half-day or full-day basis for ages 4–14. Nightly activities are free.

Sunday River
Box 450, Bethel 04217
☎ *207/824–3000; snow conditions, 207/824–6400; reservations, 800/543–2754*

In the 1980s, Sunday River was a sleepy little ski area with minimal facilities. Today it is among the best managed, forward-looking ski areas in the East; in fact, expansion could be the resort's middle name. A ski train operates between Portland and Bethel in season. Jordan Bowl, the resort's seventh mountain peak, added 100 new acres of terrain for the 1994 season, increasing the resort's size by nearly 20%. Sunday River also is home to the Maine Handicapped Skiing program, which provides lessons and services for skiers with disabilities.

Spread throughout the valley are three base areas, a condominium hotel, trailside condominiums, town houses, and a ski dorm that provide the essentials.

DOWNHILL
White Heat has gained fame as the steepest, longest, widest lift-served trail in the East; but skiers of all abilities will find plenty of suitable terrain, from a 5-kilometer (3-mile) beginner run to newly cut glades. The area has 101 trails, the majority in the intermediate range. Expert and advanced runs are grouped from the peaks, and most beginner slopes are near the base of the area. Trails spreading down from seven peaks have a total vertical descent of 2,300 feet and are served by seven quads, five triples, and two double chairlifts.

OTHER ACTIVITIES
Within the housing complexes are indoor pools, outdoor heated pools, saunas, and hot tubs. Sunday River also has a snowboard park for snowboarders.

CHILD CARE
Sunday River operates two licensed day-care centers for children ages 6 weeks through 6 years. Coaching for children ages 3 to 18 is available in the new Children's Center at the South Ridge base area.

Other Sports

Canoeing
The Saco River (near Fryeburg) is a gentle stretch from Swan's Falls to East Brownfield (19 miles). Another scenic route runs from East Brownfield to Hiram (14 miles). Rangeley and Mooselookmeguntic lakes are good for scenic canoeing.

For canoe rentals, try **Canal Bridge Canoes** (Rte. 302, Fryeburg Village, ☎ 207/935–2605), **Mooselookmeguntic House** (Haines Landing,

Oquossoc, ☎ 207/864–2962), **Rangeley Region Sport Shop** (Main St., Rangeley, ☎ 207/864–5615), or **Saco River Canoe and Kayak** (Rte. 5, Fryeburg, ☎ 207/935–2369).

Camping
See National and State Parks and Forests, *below*. The Maine Campground Owners Association (655 Main St., Lewiston 04240, ☎ 207/782–5874) has a statewide listing of private campgrounds.

Dog-Sledding
T.A.D. Dog Sled Services (Rte. 27, Carrabassett Valley, ☎ 207/246–4461) offers short 1½-mile rides near Sugarloaf/USA. Sleds accommodate up to two adults and two children. **Mahoosuc Guide Service** (Bear River Rd., Newry, ☎ 207/824–2073) furnishes day and multiday, fully-outfitted dog-sledding expeditions on the Maine/New Hampshire border.

Fishing
Freshwater fishing for brook trout and salmon is at its best in May, June, and September; the Rangeley area is especially popular with fly-fishermen. Nonresident freshwater anglers over the age of 12 must have a fishing license. The **Department of Inland Fisheries and Wildlife** (284 State St., Augusta 04333, ☎ 207/287–2871) can provide further information.

GUIDES
Try **Clayton (Cy) Eastlack** (Mountain View Cottages, Oquossoc, ☎ 207/864–3416) or **Grey Ghost Guide Service** (Box 24, Oquossoc, ☎ 207/864–5314).

Recreation Areas
In summer, **Sugarloaf/USA** has an 18-hole golf course and six tennis courts; **Sunday River** has two tennis courts, a volleyball court, and a mountain bike park with lift-accessed trails. For contact information, *see* Skiing, *above*.

Snowmobiling
This is a popular mode of winter transportation in the Rangeley area, with trails linking lakes and towns to wilderness camps. **Maine Snowmobile Association** (Box 77, Augusta 04330) has information on Maine's nearly 8,000-mile Interconnecting Trail System.

Water Sports
Sebago, Long, Rangeley, and Mooselookmeguntic lakes are the most popular areas for sailing and motorboating. For rentals, try **Long Lake Marina** (Rte. 302, Naples, ☎ 207/693–3159), **Mountain View Cottages** (Rte. 17, Oquossoc, ☎ 207/864–3416), **Naples Marina** (Rtes. 302 and 114, Naples, ☎ 207/ 693–6254; motorboats only), or **Sunny Breeze Sports** (Rte. 302, Naples, ☎ 207/693–3867).

National and State Parks and Forests

Grafton Notch State Park (☎ 207/824–2912), on Route 26, 14 miles north of Bethel on the New Hampshire border, offers unsurpassed mountain scenery, picnic areas, gorges to explore, swimming holes, and camping. You can take an easy nature walk to Mother Walker Falls or Moose Cave and see the spectacular Screw Auger Falls; or you can hike to the summit of Old Speck Mountain, the state's third-highest peak. If you have the stamina and the equipment, you can pick up the Appalachian Trail here, hike over Saddleback Mountain, and continue on to Katahdin. The **Maine Appalachian Trail Club** (Box 283, Augusta 04330) publishes a map and trail guide.

Rangeley Lake State Park (☎ 207/864–3858) has 50 campsites on the south shore of the lake (*see* Exploring the Western Lakes and Mountains, *above*).

Sebago Lake State Park (June 20–Labor Day, ☎ 207/693–6613; other times, 207/693–6231) has 250 campsites on the lake's north shore (*see* Exploring the Western Lakes and Mountains, *above*).

White Mountain National Forest straddles New Hampshire and Maine. Although the highest peaks are on the New Hampshire side, the Maine section has magnificent rugged terrain, camping and picnic areas, and hiking opportunities from hour-long nature loops to a 5½-hour scramble up Speckled Mountain—with open vistas at the summit. *Evans Notch Visitation Center, 18 Mayville Rd., Bethel 04217, ☎ 207/824–2134. ☉ Weekdays 8–4:30.*

Dining and Lodging

Bethel has the largest concentration of inns and bed-and-breakfasts; its Chamber of Commerce (☎ 207/824–3585) has a central reservations service. Condominium lodging at Shawnee Peak is available through the Bridgton Group (☎ 207/647–2591).

Bethel

DINING

$$ Mother's Restaurant. This gingerbread house furnished with wood stoves and bookshelves is a cozy place to enjoy the likes of Maine crab cakes, broiled trout, and a variety of pastas. There's outside dining in summer. ✕ *Upper Main St., ☎ 207/824–2589. Reservations accepted for large groups. MC, V. Closed Wed. in summer.*

DINING AND LODGING

$$–$$$ Bethel Inn and Country Club. Bethel's grandest accommodation, once
★   a rambling country inn on the town common, is now a full-service resort providing golf, a health club, and conference facilities. Although not very large, guest rooms in the main inn, sparsely furnished with Colonial reproductions and George Washington bedspreads, are the most desirable: The choice rooms have fireplaces and face the mountains over the golf course. All 40 two-bedroom condos on the fairway face the mountains; they are clean, even a bit sterile. The health club's facilities are extensive. A formal dining room, done in lemon yellow with pewter accents, serves elaborate dinners of roast duck, prime rib, lobster, scampi, and swordfish. ▣ *Village Common, Box 49, 04217, ☎ 207/824–2175 or 800/654–0125, ℻ 207/824–2233. 57 rooms with bath, 40 condo units. Restaurant, bar, pool, health club, golf, cross-country skiing, tennis, conference center. MAP available. AE, D, DC, MC, V.*

$$–$$$ Sudbury Inn. The classic white-clapboard inn on Main Street offers good value, basic comfort, and a convenient location. Guest rooms are clean and nicely decorated. The lobby's redbrick fireplace and pressed-tin ceiling are warm and welcoming and the dining room (upholstered booths and square wood tables) has a country charm; the dinner menu runs to prime rib, sirloin au poivre, broiled haddock, and lasagna. The pub, with a large-screen TV, is a popular hangout. A huge country breakfast includes omelets, eggs Benedict, pancakes, and homemade granola. ▣ *151 Main St., Box 369, 04217, ☎ 207/824–2174 or 800/395–7837, ℻ 207/824–2329. 18 rooms with bath, 5 suites, 1 apartment. Restaurant, pub. Full breakfast included. MC, V.*

$$–$$$ Summit Hotel and Conference Center. Opened Christmas 1992, the con-
❆   dominium hotel was an instant hit with Sunday River skiers. It has 230

slope-side units, most with kitchenettes. An 800-seat ballroom and conference facilities give a great excuse to combine business and skiing for groups of 10–400. ☒ *Bethel 04217,* ☎ *207/824–3000 or 800/543–2754,* ℻ *207/824–2111. 230 units with bath. Restaurant, pool, health club, tennis, child care. AE, D, MC, V.*

$ **Sunday River Inn.** On the Sunday River ski-area access road, this mod-
❄ ern chalet has private rooms for families and dorm rooms (bring your sleeping bag) for groups and students, all within easy access of the slopes. Hearty meals are served buffet-style, and the comfy living room is dominated by a stone hearth. The inn operates a ski touring center. ☒ *Sunday River Rd., RFD 2 (Box 1688), Bethel 04217,* ☎ *207/824–2410,* ℻ *207/824–3181. 12 rooms, 5 dorms, 1 apartment chalet with 4 rooms. Sauna, cross-country skiing. MAP. Closed Apr.–Thanksgiving. AE, MC, V.*

Bridgton

DINING

$–$$ **Black Horse Tavern.** The 200-year-old Cape Cod cottage contains a country-style restaurant with a shiny bar, horse blankets and stirrups for decor, and an extensive menu of steak and seafood specialties. A predominantly young crowd dines here on pan-blackened swordfish or sirloin, scallop pie, and ribs. Starters include nachos, buffalo wings, and chicken and smoked-sausage gumbo. ✕ *8 Portland St.,* ☎ *207/647–5300. No reservations. D, MC, V.*

LODGING

$$–$$$ **Noble House.** Set on a hill on a quiet tree-lined street overlooking High-
❄ land Lake and the White Mountains, this stately B&B with a wide porch dates from the turn of the century. The parlor is dominated by a grand piano and fireplace; in the dining room beyond, hearty breakfasts (fruit, eggs, blueberry pancakes, waffles, muffins) are served family-style on china and linen. The honeymoon suite, a single large room, has a lake view, a whirlpool bath, and white wicker furniture. ☒ *37 Highland Rd., Box 180, 04009,* ☎ *207/647–3733. 9 rooms, 6 with bath; 2 suites. Croquet, dock, boating. Full breakfast included. AE, MC, V. Closed mid-Oct.–mid-June.*

Carrabasset

DINING AND LODGING

$$–$$$$ **Sugarloaf Inn Resort.** This lodge provides ski-on access to Sugar-
❄ loaf/USA, a complete health club, and rooms that range from king-size on the fourth floor to dorm-style (bunk beds) on the ground floor. A greenhouse section of the Seasons restaurant affords views of the slopes and offers "ski-in" lunches. At breakfast the sunlight pours into the dining room, and at dinner you can watch the snow-grooming machines prepare your favorite run. Adult alpine and Nordic lessons are available. ☒ *R.R. 1 (Box 5000), Kingfield 04947,* ☎ *207/237–2000 or 800/843–5623,* ℻ *207/237–3773. 37 rooms with bath, 5 dorm rooms. Restaurant, health club, meeting rooms. AE, MC, V.*

$$–$$$$ **Sugarloaf Mountain Hotel.** This six-story brick structure at the base of
❄ the lifts on Sugarloaf combines a New England ambience with European-style hotel service. Oak and redwood paneling in the main rooms is enhanced by contemporary furnishings. Valet parking, ski tuning, lockers, and mountain guides are available through the concierge. ☒ *R.R. 1, Box 2299, Carrabassett Valley 04947,* ☎ *207/237–2222 or 800/527–9879,* ℻ *207/237–2874. 90 rooms with bath, 26 suites. Restaurant, pub, 2 hot tubs, massage, sauna, spa. AE, D, DC, MC, V.*

LODGING

$ **Lumberjack Lodge.** Only a half mile from Sugarloaf's access road, this
❄ Tyrolean-style building contains eight efficiency units, each with living
and dining area, kitchenette, full bath, and bedroom, but no phone or
TV. Units sleep up to eight people. A free shuttle to the lifts operates during the peak season. There are restaurants nearby. ⊡ *Rte. 27, 04947,*
☎ *207/237–2141. 8 units. Sauna, recreation room. AE, MC, V.*

Center Lovell

DINING AND LODGING

$$$$ **Quisisana.** Music lovers will think they've found heaven on earth at
this delightful resort on Kezar Lake. After dinner, the staff, students
and graduates of some of the finest music schools in the country, perform at the music hall—everything from Broadway revue to concert
piano. White cottages have pine interiors and cheerful decor. One
night you might have a typical New England dinner of clam chowder,
lobster, and blueberry pie; the next night you might have a choice of
saddle of lamb with a black olive tapenade, confit of red peppers, and
a vegetable garnis or salmon and leek roulade with a roasted red pepper sauce. All baking is done on the premises and all meals and activities are included in the rates (except for a nominal fee for use of the
motor boats). ⊡ *Point Pleasant Rd., 04016,* ☎ *207/925–3500,* ℻ *207/
925–1004 in season. 16 rooms with bath in 2 lodges, 38 cottages. Restaurant, windsurfing, boating, waterskiing, 3 tennis courts. MAP. Closed
Sept.–mid-June.*

Kingfield

LODGING

$$$–$$$$ **Inn on Winter's Hill.** This Georgian Revival mansion, which was de-
❄ signed in 1895, was the first home in Maine to have central heating.
The mansion's four rooms are eclectically furnished, with pressed-tin
ceilings and picture windows overlooking an apple orchard and the
mountains beyond; the renovated barn's 16 rooms are simply and
brightly furnished.The inn has a restaurant renowned for its New En-
gland dinners and its wine tastings. Try the beef Wellington, or duck
with blueberry-apple sauce and the crêpes suzette for dessert. ⊡ *R.R.
1, Box 1272, 04947,* ☎ *207/265–5421 or 800/233–9687,* ℻ *207/265–
5424. 20 rooms with bath. Pool, hot tub, cross-country skiing, tennis.
AE, D, DC, MC, V.*

Naples

DINING

$$$ **Epicurean Inn.** Originally a stagecoach stop, this rambling white Vic-
torian building on the edge of town serves classic French and new Amer-
ican cuisine in its small dining rooms with wood floors and paisley drapes.
Entrées might include maple-pecan duck, shrimp curry, tournedos
with shrimp, and coho salmon. ✗ *Rte. 302,* ☎ *207/693–3839. Reservations advised. AE, D, DC, MC, V. No lunch. Closed Mon. and
(Sept.–June) Tues.*

LODGING

$$$–$$$$ **Inn at Long Lake.** This three-story inn, built in 1900, is far enough off
the main road to ensure quiet, yet it is within walking distance of the
Naples Causeway for boating trips on Long Lake. The rooms, named
after barges, all have television and air-conditioning, and some have
a lake view. ⊡ *Lake House Rd., Box 806, 04055,* ☎ *207/693–6226
or 800/437–0328. 14 rooms with bath; 2 suites. CP. AE, D, MC, V.*

$$–$$$ **Augustus Bove House.** Built as the Hotel Naples in 1850, the brick bed-
and-breakfast at the crossroads of routes 302 and 114 has lake views

from the front rooms and is convenient to water and shops. It has been restored to show off its gracious charm: Each wallpapered room is done in a different color scheme and is furnished with antiques. ⚏ *R.R. 1, Box 501, 04055, ☎ 207/693–6365. 11 rooms, 7 with bath. Full breakfast included. D, MC, V.*

Oquossoc

DINING

$–$$ Oquossoc House. Stuffed bears and bobcats keep you company as you dine on lobster, prime rib, filet mignon, or pork chops. The lunch menu promises chili, fish chowder, and lobster roll. ✕ *Rtes. 17 and 4, ☎ 207/ 864–3881. Reservations required on summer weekends. No credit cards. Closed weekdays Nov.–mid-May.*

Rangeley

DINING AND LODGING

$$$$ Country Club Inn. This retreat, built in the 1920s on the Mingo Springs
❊ Golf Course, enjoys a secluded hilltop location and sweeping lake and mountain views. The inn's baronial living room has a cathedral ceiling, a fieldstone fireplace at each end, and game trophies. Guest rooms downstairs in the main building and in the motel-style wing added in the 1950s are cheerfully if minimally decorated with wood paneling or bright wallpaper. The glassed-in dining room—open to nonguests by reservation only—has linen-draped tables set well apart. The menu includes roast duck, veal, fresh fish, and filet mignon. ⚏ *Box 680, Mingo Loop Rd., 04970, ☎ 207/864–3831. 19 rooms with bath. Restaurant, pool. MAP. AE, MC, V. Closed Apr.–mid-May, mid-Oct.–Dec. 25.*

$–$$ Rangeley Inn and Motor Lodge. From Main Street you see only the mas-
❊ sive, three-story, blue inn building (circa 1907), but behind it the newer motel wing commands Haley Pond, a lawn, and a garden. The traditional lobby and a smaller parlor have 12-foot ceilings, a jumble of rocking and easy chairs, and polished wood. The inn's sizable guest rooms have iron and brass beds and subdued wallpaper; some have clawfoot tubs while others have whirlpool tubs. Motel units contain Queen Anne reproduction furniture and velvet chairs. Gourmet meals are served in the spacious dining room with the Williamsburg brass chandeliers. ⚏ *Main St., Box 160, 04970, ☎ 207/864–3341 or 800/ 666–3687, ⚏ 207/864–3634. 36 rooms with bath, 15 motel units with bath. Restaurant, bar, meeting room. MAP available. AE, D, MC, V.*

LODGING

$$$–$$$$ Hunter Cove on Rangeley Lake. These lakeside cabins, which sleep two
❊ to six people, offer all the comforts of home in a rustic setting. The interiors are unfinished knotty pine and include fully furnished kitchens, screened porches, full baths, and comfortable, if plain, living rooms. Cabin No. 1 has a fieldstone fireplace and all others have wood-burning stoves for backup winter heat. Cabins No. 5 and No. 8 have hot tubs. Summer guests can take advantage of a sand swimming beach, boat rentals, and a nearby golf course. In winter, snowmobile right to your door or ski nearby (cross-country and downhill). ⚏ *Mingo Loop Rd., ☎ 207/864–3383. 8 cabins with bath. AE.*

$–$$ Town & Lake Motel. This complex of efficiencies, motel units, and cot-
❊ tages alongside the highway and on Rangeley Lake is just down the road from the shops and restaurants of downtown Rangeley. Two-bedroom cottages with well-equipped kitchens are farther from the highway, and some face Saddleback. Pets are welcome. ⚏ *Rte. 16, 04970, ☎ 207/864–3755. 16 motel units with bath, 9 cottages. Boating. AE, MC, V.*

Waterford

LODGING

$$$ **The Waterford Inne.** This gold-painted, curry-trimmed house on a hill-
❄ top provides a good home base for trips to local lakes, ski trails, and
antiques shops. The bedrooms, each with its own theme in furnishings,
have lots of nooks and crannies. Nicest are the Nantucket Room, with
whale wallpaper and a harpoon, and the Chesapeake Room, with pri-
vate porch and fireplace. A converted wood shed has five additional
rooms, and though they have slightly less character than the inn rooms,
four have the compensation of sunny decks. ⊡ *Chadbourne Rd., Box
149, 04088,* ☎ *207/583–4037. 9 rooms, 6 with bath; 1 suite. Bad-
minton, ice-skating, cross-country skiing. Full breakfast included. AE.
Closed Apr.*

The Arts

Rangeley Friends of the Arts (Box 333, Rangeley, ☎ 207/864–5364)
sponsors musical theater, fiddlers' contests, rock and jazz, classical, and
other summer fare, mostly at Lakeside Park. **Sebago–Long Lake Re-
gion Chamber Music Festival** (Deertrees Theatre, Harrison, ☎ 207/627–
4939) schedules concerts from mid-July to mid-August.

Nightlife

Both Sugarloaf/USA and the Sunday River area offer plenty of nightlife
during ski season. At Sugarloaf, nightlife is concentrated at the moun-
tain's base village, with frequent entertainment in the base lodge at **Wid-
owmaker's Lounge** (☎ 207/237–6845). Also in the base lodge is
Gepetto's (☎ 207/237–2953), a popular après-ski hangout that serves
American-style food. Get there early to get a seat in the greenhouse,
which overlooks the mountain. Monday night is blues night at the **Bag
& Kettle** (☎ 207/237–2451), which is the best choice for pizza and burg-
ers. There also is a new micro-brewery on the access road, the **Sugar-
loaf Brewing Company** (☎ 207/237–2211). At Sunday River, nightlife
is spread out between the mountain and downtown Bethel. At the moun-
tain, try **Bumps Pub** (☎ 207/824–3000) for après-ski and evening en-
tertainment—Tuesday night is comedy night, ski movies are shown on
Wednesday, and bands play weekends and holidays. **Sunday River
Brewery** (☎ 207/824–4253) on Route 2 has pub fare and live enter-
tainment—usually progressive rock bands—on weekends. The **Sudbury
Inn** (☎ 207/824–2174) also is popular for après-ski and has music that
tends towards the blues. For a quieter evening, head to the piano bar
at the **Bethel Inn** (☎ 207/824–2175).

Western Lakes and Mountains Essentials

Getting Around

BY CAR

A car is essential to a tour of the western lakes and mountains. Of the
variety of routes available, the itinerary in Exploring, *above,* takes Route
302 to Route 26 to Route 2 to Route 17 to Route 4/16 to Route 142.

BY PLANE

Mountain Air Service (Rangeley, ☎ 207/864–5307) provides air access
to remote areas.

Guided Tours

Naples Flying Service (Naples Causeway, ☎ 207/693–6591) offers sight-
seeing flights over the lakes in summer.

Important Addresses and Numbers

EMERGENCIES

Bethel Area Health Center (Railroad St., Bethel, ☎ 207/824–2193).
Rangeley Regional Health Center (Main St., Rangeley, ☎ 207/864–3303).

VISITOR INFORMATION

Off-season, most chambers are open weekdays 9–5; the hours below
are for summer only.

Bethel Area Chamber of Commerce (Box 439, Bethel, 04217, ☎ 207/
824–2282; ☉ Mon.–Sat. 9–5). **Bridgton–Lakes Region Chamber of Commerce** (Box 236, Bridgton, 04009, ☎ 207/647–3472; ☉ Daily 10–4
July and Aug., reduced hrs rest of year). **Rangeley Lakes Region Chamber of Commerce** (Box 317, Rangeley, 04970, ☎ 207/864–5571; ☉
Mon.–Sat. 9–5, Sun. in July and Aug. 10–2).

THE NORTH WOODS

Maine's north woods, a vast area of the north central section of the
state, is best experienced by canoe or raft, hiking trail, or on a fishing
or hunting trip. The driving tour below takes in the three great theaters for these activities—Moosehead Lake, Baxter State Park, and the
Allagash Wilderness Waterway—as well as the summer resort town of
Greenville, dramatically situated Rockwood, and the no-frills outposts that connect them.

Exploring

*Numbers in the margin correspond to points of interest on the North
Woods map.*

❶ **Moosehead Lake,** Maine's largest, offers more in the way of rustic camps,
restaurants, guides, and outfitters than any other northern locale. Its
420 miles of shorefront, three-quarters of which is owned by paper manufacturers, is virtually uninhabited.

❷ **Rockwood,** on the lake's western shore, is a good starting point for a
wilderness trip or a family vacation on the lake. While not offering much
in the way of amenities, Rockwood has the most striking location of
any town on Moosehead: The dark mass of **Mt. Kineo,** a sheer cliff that
rises 760 feet above the lake, looms just across the narrows (you get
an excellent view just north of town on Rte. 6/15). Once a thriving
summer resort, the original Mount Kineo Hotel (built in 1830 and torn
down in the 1940s) was accessed primarily by steamship. An effort to
renovate the remaining buildings in the early 1990s failed. Kineo
makes a pleasant day trip from Rockwood: Rent a boat or take a shuttle operated by **Rockwood Cottages** (☎ 207/534–7725) or **Old Mill Campground** (☎ 207/534–7333) and hike one of the trails to the summit
for a picnic lunch and panoramic views of the region.

From Rockwood, follow Route 6/15 south, with Moosehead Lake on
your left. After about 10 miles you'll come to a bridge with a dam to
the left; this is the **East Outlet of the Kennebec River,** a popular class
II and III whitewater run for canoeists and whitewater rafters that ends
at the Harris Station Dam at Indian Pond, headwaters of the Kennebec.

❸ Farther south on Route 6/15, **Greenville,** the largest town on the lake,
has a smattering of shops, restaurants, and hotels. Turn left at the "T"
intersection in town, following signs for Lily Bay State Park and
Millinocket (the road is called both Lily Bay Road and Greenville
Road). On your left is the **Moosehead Marine Museum** (☎ 207/695–

The North Woods

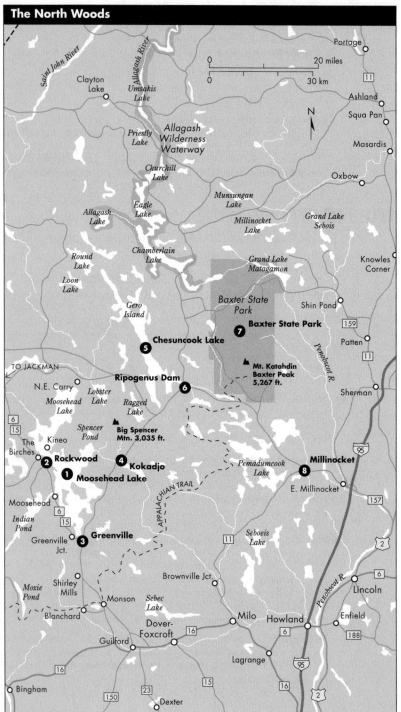

Saint John River

Allagash River

Portage

11

Clayton
Lake

Umsakis
Lake

0   20 miles

0   30 km

Ashland

Squa Pan

Priestly
Lake

Allagash
Wilderness
Waterway

N

Masardis

Churchill
Lake

Munsungan
Lake

Oxbow

Eagle
Lake

Millinocket
Lake

Grand Lake
Sebois

Allagash
Lake

Knowles
Corner

Round
Lake

Chamberlain
Lake

Grand Lake
Matagamon

Loon
Lake

Gero
Island

Baxter State
Park

Shin Pond

⑦ Baxter State Park

159

Patten

TO JACKMAN

⑤ Chesuncook Lake

▲ Mt. Katahdin
Baxter Peak
5,267 ft.

11

N.E. Carry

Ripogenus Dam ⑥

Penobscot R.

Sherman

Moosehead
Lake

Lobster
Lake

Ragged
Lake

6
15

Spencer
Pond

▲ Big Spencer
Mtn. 3,035 ft.

Pemadumcook
Lake

95

The
Birches

Kineo

② Rockwood

④ Kokadjo

⑧ Millinocket

① Moosehead Lake

E. Millinocket

157

Moosehead

6

15

Indian
Pond

Seboeis
Lake

2

Greenville
Jct.

③ Greenville

APPALACHIAN TRAIL

11

Lincoln

Moxie
Pond

Shirley
Mills

Monson

Sebec
Lake

Brownville Jct.

Penobscot R.

6

Blanchard

Dover-
Foxcroft

16

Milo

Howland

Enfield

188

Guilford

6

Bingham

16

150

23

Dexter

15

Lagrange

95

16

2

2716), with exhibits on the local logging industry and the steamship era on Moosehead Lake, plus photographs of the Mount Kineo Hotel. The museum also runs cruises on the restored, 115-foot *Katahdin* (fondly called the *Kate*), a steamer (now diesel) built in 1914 that carried passengers to Kineo until 1942 and then was used in the local logging industry until 1975. It's a good idea to get a full tank of gas before leaving town, as it's almost 90 nearly deserted miles to Millinocket, some of it on well-maintained dirt roads.

Eight miles northeast of Greenville is **Lily Bay State Park** (☎ 207/695–2700), with a wooded, 93-site campground, swimming beach, and two boat-launching ramps.

4 Lily Bay Road continues northeast to the outpost of **Kokadjo,** population "not many," on First Roach Pond. Kokadjo is easily recognizable by the sign: "Keep Maine Green. This is God's country. Why set it on fire and make it look like hell?".

As you leave Kokadjo, bear left at the fork and follow signs to Baxter State Park. Five miles along this road (now a dirt road) brings you to the Bowater/Great Northern Paper Company's Sias Hill checkpoint, where June–November you'll need to sign in and pay a user fee ($8 per car for nonresidents, valid for 24 hours) to travel the next 40 miles of this road. Now you enter the working forest; you're likely to encounter logging trucks (yield right of way), logging equipment, and work in progress. At the bottom of the hill after you pass the checkpoint, look to your right—there's a good chance you'll spot a moose in this boggy area.

5 At the end of the logging road on your left sits **Chesuncook Lake,** with **Chesuncook Village** at its far end, accessible only by boat or seaplane in summer. This tiny wilderness settlement has a church (open in summer), a few houses, a small store, and a spectacularly remote setting (it's home to two sporting camps).

East of Chesuncook Lake is Ripogenus Lake. Bear left at the sign for **6** Pray's Cottages to reach **Ripogenus Dam** and the granite-walled Ripogenus Gorge, the jumping-off point for the famous 12-mile West Branch of the Penobscot River whitewater rafting trip and the most popular jumping-off point for Allagash canoe trips. The **Allagash Wilderness Waterway** is a 92-mile corridor of lakes and rivers that cuts across 170,000 acres of wilderness, beginning at the northwest corner of Baxter and running north to the town of Allagash, 10 miles from the Canadian border (from the Ripogenus area, take Telos Rd. north toward Telos Lake). The Penobscot River drops more than 70 feet per mile through the gorge, giving rafters a hold-on-for-your-life ride.

The best spot to watch the Penobscot rafters is from Pray's Big Eddy Wilderness Campground, overlooking the rock-choked **Crib Works rapid** (a class V rapid); be careful not to tread too close to the edge. To get here, return to the main road, continue northeast, and head left on Telos Road; the campground is about 10 yards after the bridge.

Take the main road (here called the Golden Road for the amount of money it took the Great Northern Paper Company to build it) southeast toward Millinocket. The road soon becomes paved. After you drive over the one-lane Abol Bridge and pass through the Bowater/Great Northern Paper Company's Debsconeag checkpoint, bear left to reach **7** Togue Pond Gatehouse, the southern entrance to **Baxter State Park** (☎ 207/723–5140). A gift from Governor Percival Baxter, the park is the jewel in the crown of northern Maine, a 201,018-acre wilderness area that surrounds **Katahdin,** Maine's highest mountain (5,267 feet at Baxter Peak) and the terminus of the Appalachian Trail. The 50-mile Perimeter Road makes a semicircle around the western side of the park; maximum speed is 20 mph.

❽ From the Togue Pond Gatehouse it's 24 miles to **Millinocket,** home to the **Bowater/Great Northern Paper Company mill,** which produces more than 800,000 tons of paper annually, and the **Ambajejus Boom House,** which displays log drive memorabilia and artifacts. *Accessible by watercraft or snowmobile. Ambajejus Lake, Millinocket, no* ☎ .

Off the Beaten Path

For a worthwhile day trip from Millinocket, take Route 11 west to a trailhead just north of Brownville Junction. Follow the trail to **Katahdin Iron Works,** the site of a once-flourishing mining operation that employed nearly 200 workers in the mid-1800s; a deteriorated kiln, a stone furnace, and a charcoal-storage building are all that remain. The trail continues over fairly rugged terrain into **Gulf Hagas,** the Grand Canyon of the east, with natural chasms, cliffs, a 3-mile gorge, waterfalls, pools, exotic flora, and natural rock formations.

Lumberman's Museum. This museum comprises 10 buildings filled with exhibits depicting the history of logging, including models, dioramas, and equipment. *Shin Pond Rd. (Rte. 159), Patten,* ☎ *207/528–2650.* ☛ *$2.50 adults, $1 children 6–12.* ☾ *Memorial Day–Sept., Tues.–Sat. 9–4, Sun. 11–4.*

Shopping

Crafts
The Corner Shop (Rte. 6/15, Greenville, ☎ 207/695–2142) has a selection of books, gifts, and crafts. **Maine Street Station** has a nice selection of north woods gifts and crafts. **Sunbower Pottery** (Scammon Rd., Greenville, ☎ 207/695–2870) has local art and pottery, specializing in moose mugs.

Sporting Goods
Indian Hill Trading Post (Rte. 6/15, Greenville, ☎ 207/695–2104) stocks just about anything you might possibly need for a north woods vacation, including sporting and camping equipment, canoes, casual clothing, shoes, hunting and fishing licenses; there's even an adjacent grocery store.

Skiing

Big Squaw Mountain Resort
Box D, Greenville 04441
☎ *207/695–2272*

Remote but pretty, Big Squaw Mountain Resort has stumbled along in recent years, with frequent changes in management. It appears to be stabilizing, though, and this should bode well for skiers. It is best to call for up-to-date information before visiting. A hotel at the base of the mountain, integrated into the main base lodge, has a restaurant, bar, and other services.

DOWNHILL
Trails are laid out according to difficulty, with the easy slopes toward the bottom, intermediate trails weaving from midpoint, and steeper runs high up off the 1,750-vertical-foot peak. The 17 trails are served by one triple and one double chairlift and one surface lift.

The nursery takes children from infants through age 6. The ski school
has daily lessons and racing classes for children of all ages and abilities.

Other Sports

Boating

Mt. Kineo Cabins (Rte. 6/15, Rockwood, ☎ 207/534–7744) and
Salmon Run Camps (Rte. 6/15, Rockwood, ☎ 207/534–8880) are
only two of the many lodgings that rent boats and canoes on Moosehead Lake for the trip to Kineo.

MOOSEHEAD LAKE CRUISES

The **Moosehead Marine Museum** (☎ 207/695–2716) offers 2½-hour,
six-hour, and full-day trips, late May through September, on Moosehead Lake aboard the *Katahdin*, a 1914 steamship (now diesel). **Jolly
Roger's Moosehead Cruises** (☎ 207/534–8827 or 207/534–8817)
has scheduled scenic cruises, mid-May through mid-October, aboard
the 48-foot *Socatean* from Rockwood. Reservations are advised for the
1½-hour moonlight cruise, which runs only eight evenings in summer.
Charters are also available.

Camping

Reservations for state park campsites (excluding Baxter State Park) can
be made from January until August 15 through the **Bureau of Parks
and Recreation** (☎ 207/287–3824 or 800/332–1501 in Maine). Make
reservations as far ahead as possible (at least 14 days in advance) because sites go quickly. **Baxter State Park** is open for camping from May
15 to October 15, and it's important that you reserve in advance by
mail (Baxter State Park Authority, 64 Balsam Dr., Millinocket 04462;
phone reservations not accepted) if you plan to camp inside the park.
Reservations can be made beginning January 1, and some sites are fully
booked for midsummer weekends soon after that. The state also maintains primitive backcountry sites that are available without charge on
a first-come, first-served basis.

CAMPING AND FIRE PERMITS

Camping and fire permits are required for many areas outside of state
parks. The **Bureau of Parks and Recreation** (State House Station 22,
Augusta 04333, ☎ 207/287–3821) will tell you if you need a camping permit and where to obtain one; the **Maine Forest Service, Department
of Conservation** (State House Station 22, Augusta 04333, ☎ 207/287–
2791) will direct you to the nearest ranger station, where you can get
a fire permit (Greenville Ranger Station: ☎ 207/695–3721). **North Maine
Woods** (Box 421, Ashland 04732, ☎ 207/435–6213) maintains 500
wilderness campsites on commercial forest land and takes reservations
for 20 of them; early reservations are recommended. **Maine Publicity
Bureau** (325B Water St., Box 2300, Hallowell 04347, ☎ 207/623–0363
or, outside ME, 800/533–9595) publishes a listing of private campsites and cottage rentals. The **Maine Campground Owners Association
(MECOA)** (655 Main St., Lewiston 04240, ☎ 207/782–5874) publishes a helpful annual directory of its members; a dozen are located
in the Katahdin/Moosehead area, and 20 are in the Kennebec and Moose
River Valleys.

Canoeing

The Allagash rapids are ranked class I and class II (very easy and
easy), but that doesn't mean the river is a piece of cake; river conditions vary greatly with the depth and volume of water, and even a class
I rapid can hang your canoe up on a rock, capsize you, or spin you

around in the wink of an eye. On the lakes, strong winds can halt your progress for days. The Allagash should not be undertaken lightly or without advance planning; the complete 92-mile course requires seven to 10 days. The canoeing season along the Allagash is mid-May through October, although it's wise to remember that the black-fly season ends about July 1. The best bet for a novice is to go with a guide; a good outfitter will help plan your route and provide your craft and transportation.

The Mount Everest of Maine canoe trips is the 110-mile route on the St. John River from Baker Lake to Allagash Village, with a swift current all the way and two stretches of class III rapids. Best time to canoe the St. John is between mid-May and mid-June, when the river level is high. The **Bureau of Parks and Recreation** (State House Station 22, Augusta 04333, ☎ 207/287–3821) has a list of outfitters that arrange Allagash trips and also provides information on independent Allagash canoeing and camping.

Those with their own canoe who want to go it alone can take Telos Road north from Ripogenus Dam, putting in at Chamberlain Thoroughfare Bridge at the southern tip of Chamberlain Lake, or at Allagash Lake, Churchill Dam, Bissonnette Bridge, or Umsaskis Bridge.

One popular and easy route follows the Upper West Branch of the Penobscot River from Lobster Lake (just east of Moosehead Lake) to Chesuncook Lake. From Chesuncook Village you can paddle to Ripogenus Dam in a day.

The Aroostook River from Little Munsungan Lake to Fort Fairfield (100 mi) is best run in late spring. More challenging routes include the Passadumkeag River from Grand Falls to Passadumkeag (25 mi with class I–III rapids); the East Branch of the Penobscot River from Matagamon Wilderness Campground to Grindstone (38 mi with class I–III rapids); and the West Branch of the Pleasant River from Katahdin Iron Works to Brownville Junction (10 mi with class II–III rapids).

OUTFITTERS

Most canoe rental operations will arrange transportation, help plan your route, and provide a guide. Transport to wilderness lakes can be arranged through the flying services listed under Getting Around by plane *in* North Woods Essentials, *below.*

Allagash Canoe Trips (Box 713, Greenville 04441, ☎ 207/695–3668) offers guided trips on the Allagash Waterway, plus the Moose, Penobscot, and St. John rivers. **Allagash Wilderness Outfitters/Frost Pond Camps** (Box 620, Greenville 04441, ☎ 207/695–2821) provides equipment, transportation, and information for canoe trips on the Allagash and the Penobscot rivers. **Mahoosuc Guide Service** (Bear River Rd., Newry 04261, ☎ 207/824–2073) offers guided trips on the Penobscot, Allagash, and Moose rivers. **North Country Outfitters** (Box 41, Rockwood 04478, ☎ 207/534–2242 or 207/534–7305) operates a white-water canoeing and kayaking school, rents equipment, and sponsors guided canoe trips on the Allagash Waterway and the Moose, Penobscot, and St. John rivers. **North Woods Ways** (R.R. 2 Box 159-A, Guilford, 04443, ☎ 207/997–3723) organizes wilderness canoeing trips on the Allagash, as well as on the Moose, Penobscot, St. Croix, and St. John rivers. **Willard Jalbert Camps** (6 Winchester St., Presque Isle, 04769, ☎ 207/764–0494) has been sponsoring guided Allagash trips since the late 1800s.

Fishing

Togue, landlocked salmon, and brook and lake trout lure thousands of fisherfolk to the region from ice-out in mid-May through September; the hardiest return between January 1 and March 30 for the ice fishing. For up-to-date information on water levels, call 207/695–3756.

GUIDES

Guides are available through most wilderness camps, sporting goods stores, and canoe outfitters. For assistance in finding a guide, contact **North Maine Woods** (see Visitor Information, in North Woods Essentials, below).

A few well-established guides are **Gilpatrick's Guide Service** (Box 461, Skowhegan 04976, ☏ 207/453–6959), **Maine Guide Fly Shop and Guide Service** (Box 1202, Main St., Greenville 04441, ☏ 207/695–2266), and **Professional Guide Service** (Box 346, Sheridan 04775, ☏ 207/435–8044).

Hiking

Katahdin, in Baxter State Park, draws thousands of hikers every year for the daylong climb to the summit and the stunning views of woods, mountains, and lakes from the hair-raising Knife Edge Trail along its ridge.

Because the crowds at Katahdin can be formidable on clear summer days, those who seek a greater solitude might choose to tackle instead one of the 45 other mountains in the park, all accessible from a 150-mile trail network. South Turner can be climbed in a morning (if you're fit), and it affords a great view of Katahdin across the valley. On the way you'll pass Sandy Stream Pond, where moose are often seen at dusk. The Owl, the Brothers, and Doubletop Mountain are good day hikes.

Pack Trips

Northern Maine Riding Adventures (Box 16, Dover-Foxcroft 04426, ☏ 207/564–3451 or 207/564–2965), owned by Registered Maine Guides Judy Cross-Strehlke and Bob Strehlke, offers one-day, two-day, and week-long pack trips (10 people maximum) through various parts of Piscataquis County. A popular two-day trip explores the White-cap–Barren Mountain Range, near Katahdin Iron Works (see Off the Beaten Path, above).

Rafting

The Kennebec and Dead rivers, and the West Branch of the Penobscot River, offer thrilling white-water rafting (guides strongly recommended). These rivers are dam-controlled also, so trips run rain or shine daily from May through October (day trips and multi-day trips are offered). Most guided raft trips on the Kennebec and Dead rivers leave from The Forks, southwest of Moosehead Lake, on Route 201; Penobscot River trips leave from either Greenville or Millinocket. Many rafting outfitters offer resort facilities in their base towns.

OUTFITTERS

The following outfitters are among the more than two dozen that are licensed to lead trips down the Kennebec and Dead rivers and the West Branch of the Penobscot River: **Crab Apple Whitewater** (Crab Apple Acres Inn, The Forks 04985, ☏ 207/663–2218), **Eastern River Expeditions** (Box 1173, Greenville 04441, ☏ 800/634–7238), **Maine Whitewater, Inc.** (Box 633, Bingham 04920, ☏ 207/672–4814 or 800/345–6246), **Northern Outdoors** (Box 100, The Forks 04985, ☏ 207/663–4466 or 800/765–7238), and **Unicorn Expeditions** (Box T, Brunswick

04011, ☎ 207/725–2255 or 800/UNICORN). For additional information, contact the **Raft Maine Association** (☎ 800/359–2106).

Recreation Area

In summer, Squaw Mountain ski area has two tennis courts, hiking, and lawn games. A recreation program for children functions midweek.

Dining and Lodging

Greenville and Rockwood offer the largest selection of restaurants and accommodations in the region.

Chesuncook Village

LODGING

$$ Chesuncook Lake House. Accessible only by boat or floatplane, Chesuncook Lake House has been an oasis of civilization in otherwise rugged wilderness since 1864. It is listed on the National Register as a historical site. Rooms in the main house include meals. French-born Maggie McBurnie cooks all the meals—solid New England fare with a French touch. She operates the sporting camp with her husband, Bert. In winter, guests can drive to within 3 miles of the inn and come in by snowmobile or cross-country skis. ⊞ *Rte. 76, Box 656, Chesuncook Village, Greenville, 04441,* ☎ *207/745–5330 or 207/695–2821, for Folsom's Air Service. 4 rooms in main house share 2 baths; 3 housekeeping cottages. Boating. No credit cards.* ☯ *Year-round.*

Greenville

DINING

$ Kelly's Landing. This casual, family-oriented restaurant on the Moosehead shorefront has both indoor and outdoor seating, excellent views, and a dock for visiting boaters. The fare includes sandwiches, burgers, lasagna, seafood dinners, and ribs. ✕ *Rte. 6/15, Greenville Junction.,* ☎ *207/695–4438. MC, V.*

$ Road Kill Cafe. The motto here is "Where the food used to speak for itself." It's not for everyone, but if you don't mind a menu with items such as the chicken that didn't make it across the road, bye-bye Bambi burgers, brake and scrape sandwiches, and mooseballs, this fun-loving spot is for you. The staff takes pride in its borderline-rude attitude, but it's all in fun. Tables on the rear deck have a view of the water. ✕ *Rte. 5/16, Greenville Junction,* ☎ *207/695–2230. No credit cards.*

DINING AND LODGING

$$–$$$ Greenville Inn. Built more than a century ago as the retreat of a wealthy
★ lumbering family, this rambling blue/gray-and-white structure stands on a rise over Moosehead Lake, a block from town. The ornate cherry and mahogany paneling, Oriental rugs, and leaded glass create an aura of masculine ease. Two of the sparsely furnished, sunny bedrooms have fireplaces and two have lake views. Two clapboard cottages with decks overlook the lake as do two dining rooms; a third dining room, with dark-wood paneling, has a subdued, gentlemanly air. The menu, revised daily, reflects the owners' Austrian background: shrimp with mustard dill sauce, salmon marinated in olive oil and basil, veal cutlet with mushroom cream sauce; popovers accompany the meal. ⊞ *Norris St., Box 1194, 04441,* ☎ *207/695–2206. 6 rooms, 4 with bath; 1 suite in carriage house; 2 cottages. Restaurant (reservations advised; no lunch). Full breakfast included. D, MC, V. Closed Nov. and Apr.*

LODGING

$$$$ Lodge at Moosehead Lake. This mansion overlooking Moosehead Lake is about as close to luxury as it gets in the north woods. All rooms have whirlpool baths, fireplaces, and hand-carved four-poster beds; most have lake views. The restaurant, where breakfast is served year-round and dinner is served in the off season, has a spectacular view of the lake. ⌂ *Lily Bay Rd. 04441,* ☎ *207/695–4400,* FAX *207/695–2281. 5 rooms with bath. Restaurant, bar, hot tubs. D, MC, V.*

$$ **Chalet Moosehead.** Just 50 yards off Route 6/15, the efficiencies — which have two double beds, a living room with sofabed, and a kitchenette—motel room, and cabin are right on Moosehead Lake and have picture windows to capture the view. The attractive grounds lead to a private beach and dock. ⌂ *Rte. 6/15, Box 327, Greenville Junction 04442,* ☎ *207/695–2950 or 800/290–3645. 8 efficiencies, 7 motel rooms with bath, 1 cabin with bath. Horseshoes, beach, dock, boating. MC, V.*

$–$$ **Sawyer House Bed & Breakfast.** The convenient in-town location across the street from the lake makes it easy to tour Greenville by foot from this comfortable B&B. The two upstairs rooms are on the smallish side, but the first-floor suite (actually just one room) is huge. Guests have use of a family room with television, where a full breakfast also is served. ⌂ *Lakeview St., Box 521, 04441,* ☎ *207/695–2369. 3 rooms with bath. D, MC, V.*

$ **Squaw Mountain Resort.** From the door of the resort you can ski to
❄ the slopes and to cross-country trails. The motel-style units and dorm rooms have picture windows opening onto the woods or the slopes, and Katahdin and Moosehead Lake (6 miles away) can be seen from the lawn. The restaurant serves hearty family meals, and there's usually entertainment on the weekends. ⌂ *Rte. 15, 04441,* ☎ *207/695–2272. 58 rooms with bath. Restaurant, cafeteria, ski school, ski shop, tennis, playground. AE, MC, V.*

Jackman

LODGING

$$$$ **Attean Lake Lodge.** This lodge, about an hour west of Rockwood, has been owned and operated by the Holden family since 1900. The 18 log cabins (sleeping two to six) offer a secluded, island environment. A central lodge—tastefully renovated in 1990—has a library and games. ⌂ *Birch Island, Box 457, 04945,* ☎ *207/668–3792. 18 cabins with bath. Beach, boating, library, recreation room. AP. AE, MC, V. Closed Oct.–May.*

Millinocket

DINING

$–$$ **Scootic Inn and Penobscot Room.** This informal restaurant and lounge offers lunch and dinner daily, with a varied menu of steak, seafood, pizza, and sandwiches. A large-screen TV is usually tuned to sports. ✗ *70 Penobscot Ave.,* ☎ *207/723–4566. Reservations advised for 5 or more. AE, D, MC, V.*

LODGING

$$ **Atrium Inn.** Off Route 157 next to a shopping center, this motor inn has a large central atrium with facilities that make up for its unappealing location and standard motel furnishings. ⌂ *740 Central Ave., 04462,* ☎ *and* FAX *207/723–4555. 60 standard and king rooms, 10 suites. Indoor pool, wading pool, hot tub, health club. CP. AE, D, DC, MC, V.*

Rockwood

DINING AND LODGING

$$ **The Birches Resort.** The family-oriented resort offers the full north-country experience: Moosehead Lake, birch woods, log cabins, and boats for rent. The recently renovated turn-of-the-century main lodge has four guest rooms, a lobby with trout pond, and a living room dominated by

a fieldstone fireplace. Most guests occupy one of the 17 cottages that have wood-burning stoves or fireplaces and sleep from two to 15 people. The dining room overlooking the lake is open to the public for breakfast and dinner; the fare is pasta, seafood, and steak. ⌕ *Off Rte. 6/15, on Moosehead Lake, Box 41, 04478,* ☎ *207/534–7305 or 800/825– 9453,* ℻ *207/534–8835. 4 lodge rooms shared bath; 17 cottages. Dining room, hot tub, sauna, boating, horseback riding. AE, D, MC, V. Dining room closed Nov.–Apr.*

LODGING

$ Rockwood Cottages. These eight white cottages with blue trim, on Moosehead Lake off Route 15 and convenient to the center of Rockwood, are ideal for families. The cottages, which have screened porches and fully equipped kitchens, sleep two to seven. There is a one-week minimum stay in July and August. ⌕ *Rte. 15, Box 176, 04478,* ☎ *207/ 534–7725. 8 cottages. Sauna, dock, boating. D, MC, V. $*

North Woods Essentials

Getting Around

BY CAR

A car is essential to negotiating this vast region but may not be useful to someone spending a vacation entirely at a wilderness camp. While public roads are scarce in the north country, lumber companies maintain private roads that are often open to the public (sometimes by permit only). When driving on a logging road, always give lumber company trucks the right of way. Be aware that loggers often take the middle of the road and will neither move over nor slow down for you.

BY PLANE

Charter flights, usually by seaplane, from Bangor, Greenville, or Millinocket to smaller towns and remote lake and forest areas can be arranged with flying services, which will transport you and your gear and help you find a guide: **Currier's Flying Service** (Greenville Junction, ☎ 207/695–2778), **Folsom's Air Service** (Greenville, ☎ 207/695– 2821), **Jack's Air Service** (Greenville, ☎ 207/695–3020), **Katahdin Air Service** (Millinocket, ☎ 207/723–8378), **Scotty's Flying Service** (Shin Pond, ☎ 207/528–2626).

Important Addresses and Numbers

EMERGENCIES

Charles A. Dean Memorial Hospital (Pritham Ave., Greenville, ☎ 800/ 260–4000 or 207/695–2223). **Mayo Regional Hospital** (75 W. Main St., Dover-Foxcroft, ☎ 207/564–8401). **Millinocket Regional Hospital** (200 Somerset St., Millinocket, ☎ 207/723–5161).

VISITOR INFORMATION

Baxter State Park Authority (64 Balsam Dr., Millinocket 04462, ☎ 207/ 723–5140). **Millinocket Area Chamber of Commerce** (1029 Central St., Millinocket 04462, ☎ 207/723–4443; ☉ Daily 8–5, Memorial Day–Sept.; weekdays 9–noon Oct.–Memorial Day.) **Moosehead Lake Region Chamber of Commerce** (Rtes. 6 and 15, Box 581, Greenville 04441, ☎ 207/695–2702; ☉ Daily Memorial Day–Columbus Day, call for hours). **North Maine Woods** (Box 421, Ashland 04732, ☎ 207/ 435–6213), a private organization, publishes maps, a canoeing guide for the St. John River, and lists of outfitters, camps, and campsites.

Maine Sporting Camp Association (Box 89, Jay 04239, no ☎) publishes a list of its members, with details on the facilities available at each camp.

MAINE ESSENTIALS

Arriving and Departing

By Boat

Marine Atlantic (☎ 207/288–3395 or 800/341–7981) operates a car-ferry service year-round between Yarmouth (Nova Scotia) and Bar Harbor; **Prince of Fundy Cruises** (☎ 800/341–7540 or, in ME, 800/482–0955) operates a car ferry between Portland and Yarmouth (May–Oct.).

By Bus

Vermont Transit (☎ 207/772–6587), a subsidiary of **Greyhound,** connects towns in southwestern Maine with cities in New England and throughout the United States. **Concord Trailways** (☎ 800/639–3317) has daily year-round service between Boston and Bangor (via Portland), with a coastal route connecting towns between Brunswick and Searsport.

By Car

Interstate 95 is the fastest route to and through the state from coastal New Hampshire and points south, turning inland at Brunswick and going on to Bangor and the Canadian border. Route 1, more leisurely and scenic, is the principal coastal highway from New Hampshire to Canada.

By Plane

Both of Maine's major airports, **Portland International Jetport** (☎ 207/774–7301) and **Bangor International Airport** (☎ 207/947–0384), have scheduled daily flights by major U.S. carriers.

Hancock County Airport (☎ 207/667–7329), in Trenton, 8 miles northwest of Bar Harbor, is served by Colgan Air (☎ 207/667–7171 or 800/272–5488). **Knox County Regional Airport** (☎ 207/594–4131), in Owls Head, 3 miles south of Rockland, has flights to Boston on Colgan Air (☎ 207/596–7604 or 800/272–5488).

By Train

Amtrak (☎ 800/872–7245) is expected to have added service between Boston and Portland by late 1995. Plans are for three round-trip runs daily with four stops in Maine and three in New Hampshire; round-trip fare will be about $30.

Getting Around

By Boat

Casco Bay Lines (☎ 207/774–7871) provides ferry service from Portland to the islands of Casco Bay, and **Maine State Ferry Service** (☎ 207/596–2202 or 800/491–4883) provides ferry service from Rockland, Lincolnville, and Bass Harbor to islands in Penobscot and Blue Hill bays.

By Car

In many areas a car is the only practical means of travel. The *Maine Map and Travel Guide,* available for a small fee from offices of the Maine Publicity Bureau, is useful for driving throughout the state; it has directories, mileage charts, and enlarged maps of city areas.

By Plane

Regional flying services, operating from regional and municipal airports (*see above*), provide access to remote lakes and wilderness areas as well as to Penobscot Bay islands.

By Train

During the ski season, **Sunday River Ski Resort** operates the *Sunday River Silver Bullet Ski Express* (☎ 207/824–7245) through scenic terrain between Portland and Bethel. No reservations are necessary for the once-a-day run; lift tickets can be purchased aboard the train.

Guided Tours

Golden Age Festival (5501 New Jersey Ave., Wildwood Crest, NJ 08260, ☎ 609/522–6316 or 800/257–8920) offers a four-night bus tour geared to senior citizens, with shopping at Kittery outlets and L. L. Bean, a Boothbay Harbor boat cruise, and stops at Kennebunkport, Mount Battie in Camden, and Acadia National Park. Tours operate May to mid-October.

Skiing

Weather patterns that create snow cover for Maine ski areas may come from the Atlantic or from Canada, and Maine may have snow when other New England states do not—and vice versa. In recent years ski-area operators in Maine have embraced snowmaking with a vengeance, and they now have the capacity to cover thousand-foot-plus mountains. In turn, more skiers have discovered Maine skiing, yet in most cases this has still not resulted in crowds, hassles, or lines. Ski-area acquisition wars produced positive results: S-K-I Inc., which owns a number of ski areas in New England, including Killington in Vermont, became part owner of Sugarloaf/USA and immediately put in a new high-speed quad chairlift and announced plans for new trails. This should enable this granddaddy of Maine resorts to compete with Sunday River, which has become a huge, well-managed attraction and one of New England's most popular ski destinations.

Further good news for Maine ski areas is the building of more and better lodging; best news of all is that skiers generally find lower prices here for practically every component of a ski vacation or a day's outing: lift tickets, accommodations, lessons, equipment, and meals. A further result of the ski acquisition wars is that Sugarloaf/USA and Sunday River skiers now can buy lift ticket packages good for these areas as well as their sister resorts in New Hampshire and Vermont.

Dining

For most visitors, Maine means lobster. As a general rule, the closer you are to a working harbor, the fresher your lobster will be. Aficionados eschew ordering lobster in restaurants, preferring to eat them "in the rough" at classic lobster pounds, where you select your lobster swimming in a pool and enjoy it at a waterside picnic table. Shrimp, scallops, clams, mussels, and crab are also caught in the cold waters off Maine, and the better restaurants in Portland and the coastal resort towns prepare the shellfish in creative combinations with lobster, haddock, salmon, and swordfish. Blueberries are grown commercially in Maine, and Maine cooks use them generously in pancakes, muffins, jams, pies, and cobblers. Full country breakfasts of fruit, eggs, breakfast meats, pancakes, and muffins are commonly served at inns and bed-and-breakfasts.

CATEGORY	COST*
$$$$	over $35
$$$	$25–$35
$$	$15–$25
$	under $15

average cost of a three-course dinner, per person, excluding drinks, service, and 7% restaurant sales tax

Lodging

Bed-and-breakfasts and Victorian inns furnished with lace, chintz, and mahogany have joined the family-oriented motels of Ogunquit, Boothbay Harbor, Bar Harbor, and the Camden-Rockport region. Two world-class resorts with good health club and sports facilities are on the coast near Portland and on Penobscot Bay near Rockland. Although accommodations tend to be less luxurious away from the coast, Bethel, Center Lovell, and Rangeley offer sophisticated hotels and inns. In the far north the best alternative to camping is to stay in a rustic wilderness camp, most of which serve hearty meals. For a list of camps, write to the **Maine Sporting Camp Association** (Box 89, Jay 04239).

At many of Maine's larger hotels and inns with restaurants, Modified American Plan (includes breakfast and dinner) is either an option or required during the peak summer season.

CATEGORY	COST*
$$$$	over $100
$$$	$80–$100
$$	$60–$80
$	under $60

Prices are for a standard double room during peak season, excluding 7% lodging sales tax.

Important Addresses and Numbers

Visitor Information

Maine Publicity Bureau (325B Water St., Box 2300, Hallowell 04347, ☎ 207/623–0363 or, outside ME, 800/533–9595; ℻ 207/623–0388).
Maine Innkeepers Association (305 Commercial St., Portland 04101, ☎ 207/773–7670) publishes a statewide lodging and dining guide.

3 Vermont

Southern Vermont has farms, freshly starched New England towns, quiet back roads, bustling ski resorts, and strip-mall sprawl. Central Vermont's trademarks include marble quarries north of Rutland and pastures that create the patchwork of the Champlain Valley. The heart of the area is the Green Mountains. The state's largest city (Burlington) and the nation's smallest state capital (Montpelier) are in northern Vermont, as are some of the most remote areas of New England. Much of the state's logging, dairy farming, and skiing take place here.

EVERYWHERE YOU LOOK around Vermont, the evidence is clear: This is not the state it was 25 years ago.

By Mary H. Frakes and Tara Hamilton, with an introduction by William G. Scheller

Updated by Tara Hamilton

That may be true for the rest of New England as well, but the contrasts between the present and recent past seem all the more sharply drawn in the Green Mountain State, if only because an aura of timelessness has always been at the heart of the Vermont image. Vermont was where all the quirks and virtues outsiders associate with up-country New England were supposed to reside. It was where the Yankees were Yankee-est and where there were more cows than people.

Not that you should be alarmed, if you haven't been here in a while; Vermont hasn't become southern California, or even, for that matter, southern New Hampshire. This is still the most rural state in the Union (meaning that it has the smallest percentage of citizens living in statistically defined metropolitan areas), even if there are, finally, more people than cows. It's still a place where cars occasionally have to stop while a dairy farmer walks cows across a secondary road; and up in Essex County, in what George Aiken dubbed the Northeast Kingdom, there are townships with zero population. And the kind of scrupulous, straightforward, plainspoken politics practiced by Governor (later Senator) Aiken for 50 years has not become outmoded in a state that still turns out on town-meeting day.

How has Vermont changed? In strictly physical terms, the most obvious transformations have taken place in and around the two major cities, Burlington and Rutland, and near the larger ski resorts, such as Stowe, Killington, Stratton, and Mt. Snow. Burlington's Church Street, once a paradigm of all the sleepy redbrick shopping thoroughfares in northern New England, is now a pedestrian mall complete with chic bistros; outside the city, suburban development has supplanted dairy farms in towns where someone's trip to Burlington might once have been an item in a weekly newspaper. As for the ski areas, it's no longer enough simply to boast the latest in chairlift technology. Stratton has an entire "Austrian Village" of restaurants and shops, while a hillside adjacent to Bromley's slopes has sprouted instant replica Victorians for the second-home market. The town of Manchester, convenient to both resorts, is awash in designer-fashion discount outlets.

But the real metamorphosis in the Green Mountains has to do more with style, with the personality of the place, than with the mere substance of development. The past couple of decades have seen a tremendous influx of outsiders—not just skiers and "leaf peekers," but people who've come to stay year-round—and many of them are determined either to freshen the local scene with their own idiosyncrasies or to make Vermont even more like Vermont than they found it. On the one hand, this translates into the fact that one of the biggest draws to the tiny town of Glover each summer is an outdoor pageant that promotes leftist political and social causes; on the other, it means that sheep farming has been reintroduced into the state, largely to provide a high-quality product for the hand-weaving industry.

This ties in with another local phenomenon, one best described as Made in Vermont. Once upon a time, maple syrup and sharp cheddar cheese were the products that carried Vermont's name to the world. The market niche that they created has since been widened by Vermonters— a great many of them refugees from more hectic arenas of commerce

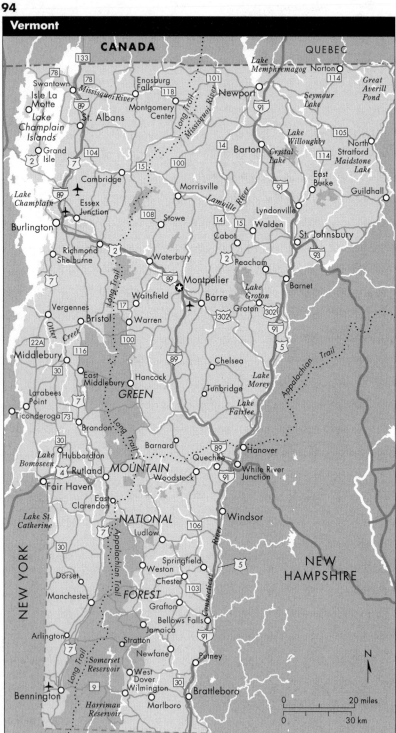

CANADA

QUEBEC

133

78   78

Swanton

Isle La Motte

Mississquoi River

Enosburg Falls

101

Lake Memphremagog

Norton

114

Lake Champlain Islands

St. Albans

Montgomery Center

118

Newport

91

Seymour Lake

Great Averill Pond

2   Grand Isle

104

15

100

Long Trail

Mississquoi River

14   Barton

Crystal Lake

Lake Willoughby

105

North Stratford

Lake Champlain

89

Cambridge

Morrisville

91

East Burke

Maidstone Lake

114

Essex Junction

108   Stowe

Lamville River

Lyndonville

Guildhall

Burlington

2

Waterbury

14   15   Walden

St. Johnsbury

Richmond   Shelburne

Montpelier

Barre

Cabot

2   Peacham

93

7

Long Trail

Waitsfield

302

Lake Groton

Groton

302

Barnet

Vergennes

17

Warren

89

91

Bristol

Otter Creek

100

Chelsea

5

Appalachian Trail

22A

116

East Middlebury

Hancock

Lake Morey

Middlebury

30

GREEN

Tunbridge

Lake Fairlee

Larabees Point

7

Brandon

Barnard

89   Hanover

Ticonderoga   73

Long Trail

Quechee

Woodstock

White River Junction

Lake Bomoseen

Hubbardton

MOUNTAIN

91

Fair Haven   4   Rutland

East Clarendon

NATIONAL

106   Windsor

Lake St. Catherine

30

7

Ludlow

Appalachian Trail

5

Weston

Springfield

Dorset

Chester

FOREST

103

Manchester

Grafton

Arlington

7

Bellows Falls

Jamaica   91

Long Trail

Stratton

Newfane

Putney

Somerset Reservoir

West Dover   Wilmington

30

Brattleboro

Bennington

9

Marlboro

Harriman Reservoir

NEW YORK

NEW HAMPSHIRE

Connecticut River

N

0   20 miles

0   30 km

in places like Massachusetts and New York—offering a dizzying variety of goods with the ineffable cachet of Vermont manufacture. There are Vermont wood toys, Vermont apple wines, Vermont chocolates, even Vermont gin. All of it is marketed with the tacit suggestion that it was made by Yankee elves in a shed out back on a bright autumn morning.

The most successful Made in Vermont product is the renowned Ben & Jerry's ice cream. Neither Ben nor Jerry comes from old Green Mountain stock, but their product has benefited immensely from the magical reputation of the place where it is made. Along the way, the company (which started in Burlington under the most modest circumstances in 1979) has become the largest single purchaser of Vermont's still considerable dairy output. Proof that the modern and the traditional—wearing a red-plaid cap and a Johnson Woolen Mills hunting jacket—can still get along very nicely in Vermont.

SOUTHERN VERMONT

The Vermont tradition of independence and rebellion began in southern Vermont. Many towns founded in the early 18th century as frontier outposts or fortifications were later important as trading centers. In the western region the Green Mountain Boys fought off both the British and the claims of land-hungry New Yorkers—some say their descendants are still fighting. In the 19th century, as many towns turned to manufacturing, the eastern part of the state preserved much of its farms and orchards.

Exploring

Numbers in the margin correspond to points of interest on the Southern Vermont map.

The first thing you'll notice upon entering the state is the conspicuous lack of billboards along the highways and roads. The foresight back in the 1960s to prohibit their proliferation has made for a refreshing lack of aggressive visual clutter; their absence allows travelers unencumbered views of working farmland, freshly starched New England towns, and quiet back roads, but doesn't hide the reality of abandoned dairy barns, bustling ski resorts, and strip-mall sprawl. We begin in the east, south of the junction of I–91 and Route 9.

1 At the confluence of the West and Connecticut rivers, **Brattleboro,** a town of about 13,000, originated as a frontier scouting post and became a thriving industrial center and resort town in the 1800s. More recently, the area has become a haven for left-leaning political activists and those pursuing one form of alternative lifestyle or another. Its downtown, bustling with activity, is the center of commerce for southeastern Vermont.

A former railroad station, the **Brattleboro Museum and Art Center** has replaced locomotives with art and historical exhibits as well as an Estey organ from the days when the city was home to one of the world's largest organ companies. *Canal and Bridge Sts.,* ☎ *802/257–0124.* ☛ *$2 adults, $1 senior citizens.* ⊙ *May–Oct., Tues.–Sun. noon–6.*

Larkin G. Mead, Jr., a Brattleboro resident, stirred 19th-century America's imagination with an 8-foot snow angel he built at the intersection of Routes 30 and 5. **Brooks Memorial Library** has a replica of the angel as well as rotating art exhibits. *224 Main St.,* ☎ *802/254–5290.* ⊙ *Mon.–Thurs. 9–9, Fri. 9–6, Sat. 9–5.*

Southern Vermont

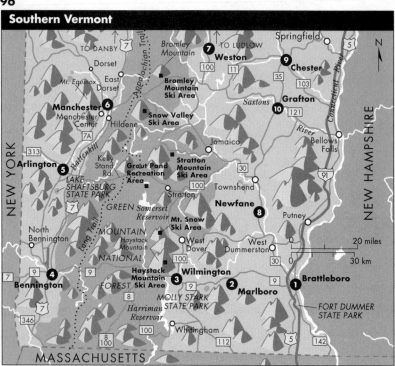

TIME OUT **Hamelmann's Bakery** (Elliot St.) creates crusty country breads in hand-shaped loaves, as well as thick napoleons and delicate fruit and almond tarts.

From Brattleboro head north along the eastern edge of the state to **Putney,** where **Harlow's Sugar House** (Rte. 5, 2 mi north of Putney, ☎ 802/387–5852) has horse-drawn sleigh or wagon rides into the sugar bush to watch the maple sugaring in spring, berry picking in summer, and apple picking in autumn. You can buy the fruits of these labors in the gift shop. Crafts afficionados will want to visit **Basketville** (Main St., Box 710, Putney 05346, ☎ 802/387–5509), to witness the traditional production methods employed in constructing the incredible number of baskets that are for sale; and **Green Mountain Spinnery** (Depot Rd., at Exit 4 of I-91, Putney 05346, ☎ 802/387–4528), where yarn is made from local wool and mohair. (*See* Shopping, *below.*)

❷ Nearly 10 miles west of Brattleboro on Route 9 is **Marlboro,** a tiny town that draws musicians and audiences from around the world each summer to the Marlboro Music Festival, founded by Rudolf Serkin and led for many years by Pablo Casals. Perched high on a hill just off Route 9, **Marlboro College** is the center of musical activity. The demure white-frame buildings have an outstanding view of the valley below, and the campus is studded with apple trees.

❸ **Wilmington,** the shopping and dining center for the Mt. Snow ski area to the north, lies 8 miles west of Marlboro on Route 9. Strolling up and down Main Street's cohesive assemblage of 18th- and 19th-century buldings—many of them listed on the National Register of Historic Places—is made more interesting and educational by picking up a copy of the walking-tour guide from the Chamber of Commerce (E. Main St., Box 3, Wilmington 05363, ☎ 802/464–8092).

To begin a scenic (though well-traveled) 35-mile circular tour that affords panoramic views of the region's mountains, farmland, and abundant cow population, drive west on Route 9 to the intersection with Route 8. Turn south and continue to the junction with Route 100; follow Route 100 through Whitingham (the birthplace of the Mormon prophet Brigham Young), and stay with the road as it turns north again and takes you back to Route 9. On this last leg you can visit the **North River Winery,** which occupies a converted farmhouse and barn on Route 112 and produces such fruit wines as Green Mountain Apple. *Rte. 112, 6 mi south of Wilmington,* ☎ *802/368–7557.* ☛ *Free.* ☉ *Late Apr.–Dec., daily 10–5; Jan.–late Apr., Fri.–Sun. 11–5.*

❹ Take Route 9 west through the Green Mountain National Forest to see **Bennington,** the state's third-largest city and the commercial focus of Vermont's southwest corner. It has retained much of the industrial character it developed in the 19th century, when paper mills, grist mills, and potteries formed the city's economic base. It was in Bennington, at the Catamount Tavern, that Ethan Allen organized the Green Mountain Boys, who helped capture Ft. Ticonderoga in 1775. Here also, in 1777, American general John Stark urged his militia to attack the Hessians across the New York border: "There are the Redcoats; they will be ours or tonight Molly Stark sleeps a widow!"

A chamber of commerce brochure (*see* Visitor Information *in* Vermont Essentials, *below*) describes an interesting, self-guided walking tour of **Old Bennington,** a National Register Historic District just west of downtown, where impressive white-column Greek Revival and sturdy brick Federal homes stand around the village green. In the graveyard of the **Old First Church,** at the corner of Church Street and Monument Avenue, the tombstone of the poet Robert Frost proclaims, "I had a lover's quarrel with the world."

The **Bennington Battle Monument,** a 306-foot stone obelisk with an elevator to the top, commemorates General Stark's victory over the British, who attempted to capture Bennington's stockpile of supplies. The battle, which took place near Walloomsac Heights in New York State, helped bring about the surrender two months later of the British commander, "Gentleman Johnny" Burgoyne. *15 Monument Ave.,* ☎ *802/447–0550.* ☛ *$1 adults, 50¢ children 6–11.* ☉ *Mid-Apr.–late Oct., daily 9–5.*

The **Bennington Museum**'s rich collections of early Americana include vestiges of rural life, a good percentage of which are packed into towering glass cases. The decorative arts are well represented; one room is devoted to early Bennington pottery, then known as Norton pottery, the product of one of the first ceramic makers in the country. Another room covers the history of American glass and contains fine Tiffany specimens. Devotees of folk art will want to see the largest public collection of the work of Grandma Moses, who lived and painted in the area. Among the 30 paintings and assorted memorabilia is her only self-portrait and the famous painted caboose window. *W. Main St. (Rte. 9),* ☎ *802/447–1571.* ☛ *$5 adults, $4 senior citizens, children under 12 free, $12 family.* ☉ *Daily 9–5.*

TIME OUT Pop into **Alldays and Onions** (519 E. Main St. ☎ 802/447-0043) for scrumptious sandwiches on homemade bread or for desserts, which are baked on the premises.

Contemporary stone sculpture and white-frame neo-Colonial dorms, framed by acres of cornfields, punctuate the green meadows of **Bennington College**'s deceptively placid campus. The small coeducational liberal arts college, one of the most expensive in the country, is noted for its progressive program in the arts, as well as a recent, controversial faculty upheaval that sent shockwaves through academia nationwide. To reach the campus, take Route 67A off Route 7 and look for the stone entrance gate.

 Don't be surprised to see familiar-looking faces among the roughly 2,200 people of **Arlington,** about 15 miles north of Bennington on Route 7A. The illustrator Norman Rockwell lived here for 14 years, and many of the models for his portraits of small-town life were his neighbors. Settled first in 1763, Arlington was called Tory Hollow for its Loyalist sympathies—even though a number of the Green Mountain Boys lived here, too. Smaller than Bennington and more down-to-earth than upper-crust Manchester to the north, Arlington displays a certain Rockwellian folksiness. It's also known as the home of Dorothy Canfield Fisher, a novelist popular in the 1930s and 1940s.

There are no original paintings at the **Norman Rockwell Exhibition.** Instead, the exhibition rooms are crammed with reproductions, arranged in every way conceivable: chronologically, by subject matter, and juxtaposed with photos of the models—some of whom work here. *Rte. 7A, Arlington,* ☎ *802/375–6423.* ☛ *$1, children under 6 free.* ☺ *May–Oct., daily 9–5; Nov.–Apr., daily 10–4.*

⑥ **Manchester,** where Ira Allen proposed financing Vermont's participation in the American Revolution by confiscating Tory estates, has been a popular summer retreat since the mid-19th century. Manchester Village's tree-shaded marble sidewalks and stately old homes reflect the luxurious resort lifestyle of a century ago, while Manchester Center's upscale factory outlets appeal to the affluent 20th-century ski crowd drawn by nearby Bromley and Stratton mountains. Warning: The town has become extremely popular with the shopping-inclined in recent years and can take on the overwhelming feel of a crowded New Jersey mall the weekend before Christmas.

Hildene, the summer home of Abraham Lincoln's son Robert, is a 412-acre estate that the former chairman of the board of the Pullman Company built for his family and their descendants; Mary Lincoln Beckwith, Robert's granddaughter, lived here as recently as 1975. With its Georgian Revival symmetry, gracious central hallway, and grand curved staircase, the 24-room mansion is unusual in that its rooms are not roped off. When "The Ride of the Valkyries" is played on the 1,000-pipe Aeolian organ, the music emanates from the mansion's very bones. Tours include a short film on the owner's life and a walk through the elaborate formal gardens. *Rte. 7A, Manchester,* ☎ *802/362–1788.* ☛ *$7 adults, $4 children 6–15.* ☺ *Mid-May–Oct., daily 9:30–4.*

If you've been swept up by the recent passionate fly-fishing resurgence or have been fishing for years, stop by the **American Museum of Fly Fishing,** which displays more than 1,500 rods, 800 reels, 30,000 flies, and the tackle of such celebrities as Bing Crosby, Daniel Webster, and Winslow Homer. Its 2,500 books on angling comprise the largest public library devoted to fishing. *Rte. 7A, Manchester,* ☎ *802/362–3300.* ☛ *$2 adults, children under 12 free.* ☺ *May–Oct., daily 10–4; Nov.–Apr., weekdays 10–4.*

The **Southern Vermont Art Center**'s 10 rooms are set on 375 acres dotted with contemporary sculpture. A popular retreat for local patrons of the arts, the nonprofit educational center has a permanent collection, changing exhibits, and a serene botany trail that passes by a 300-year-old maple tree. The graceful Georgian mansion is also the frequent site of concerts, dramatic performances, and films (call for current programs). *West Rd., Box 617, Manchester,* ☎ *802/362–1405.* 🖝 *$3 adults, 50¢ students.* ☉ *Memorial Day–Oct. 15, Tues.–Sat. 10–5, Sun. noon–5; Dec.–mid-Apr., Mon.–Sat. 10–4.*

TIME OUT   At the **Gourmet Deli** (Factory Point Square, Rte. 7A) you'll find homemade soups, sandwiches, and baked goods that can be eaten at outdoor tables with umbrellas in summer.

You may want to keep your eye on the temperature gauge of your car as you drive the 5-mile toll road to the top of 3,825-foot **Mt. Equinox.** Remember to look out the window periodically for views of the Battenkill trout stream and the surrounding Vermont countryside. Picnic tables line the drive, and there's an outstanding view down both sides of the mountain from a notch known as "the Saddle." *Rte. 7A, Manchester,* ☎ *802/362–1114.* 🖝 *$4.50 car.* ☉ *May–Oct., daily 8 AM–dark.*

❼ One can also head east on Route 11, from Manchester, and then north on Route 100 to reach **Weston,** perhaps best known for the **Vermont Country Store** (Rte. 100, ☎ 802/362–4667), which may be more a way of life than a shop. For years the retail store and its mail-order catalogue have carried such nearly forgotten items as Lilac Vegetal aftershave, Monkey Brand black tooth powder, Flexible Flyer sleds, pickles in a barrel, and tiny wax bottles of colored syrup. Nostalgia-invoking implements dangle from the store's walls and ceiling.

The **Mill Museum** (Rte. 100, ☎ 802/824–6781) just down the road has numerous hands-on displays depicting the engineering and mechanics of one of the town's mills, as well as enlightening photo exhibits of life in the mid- to late 1800s.

From Weston you might head south on Route 100 through Jamaica and then down Route 30 through Townshend to Newfane, all pretty hamlets typical of small-town Vermont. Just south of Townshend, near the Townshend Dam on Route 30, is the state's longest single-**❽** span bridge, now closed to traffic. **Newfane,** with its crisp white buildings surrounding the village green, is especially attractive. The 1939 **First Congregational Church** and the **Windham County Court House,** with its 17 green-shuttered windows and rounded cupola, are often open. The building with the four-pointed spire is **Union Hall,** built in 1832.

Another option from Weston is to travel east to Route 11, which will **❾** take you to **Chester,** where gingerbread Victorians frame the town green. Look for the **stone village** on North Street on the outskirts of town—two rows of buildings constructed from quarried stone, built by two brothers and said to have been used during the Civil War as stations on the Underground Railroad. The **National Survey Charthouse** (Main St., ☎ 802/875–2121) is a map-lover's paradise: It's good for a rainy-day browse even if maps aren't your passion. The local pharmacy down the street has been in continuous operation since the 1860s.

❿ It's 8 miles south on Route 35 from Chester to **Grafton,** the almost-too-picturesque village that got a second lease on life when the Windham Foundation provided funds for its restoration: It's now one of the best-kept in the state. Grafton's **Historical Society** documents the change and has other exhibits. *Townshend Rd.,* ☎ *802/843–2255.* 🖝 *Free.* ☉ *Memorial Day–Columbus Day, Sat. 2:30–4:40; July–Aug., Sun. 2:30–4:40.*

What to See and Do with Children

Battle Monument and Museum, Bennington
Harlow's Sugar House, Putney
Luman Nelson New England Wildlife Museum, Marlboro
Mt. Equinox, Manchester

Off the Beaten Path

A boardwalk winds through the **North Springfield Bog** (just off Fairground Rd., 2½ mi north of Riverside School, ☎ 802/885–2779), a 10,000-year-old bog with some of the finest examples of bog plants in the state. The area encourages amateur naturalists and is ideal for a nature walk. Nearby, **Spring Weather Nature Area** (Reservoir Rd., off Rte. 106, N. Springfield), has trails that wind through 70 acres of fields, forest, and flood plains.

Shopping

Shopping Districts

Candle Mill Village's (Old Mill Rd., off Rte. 7A, E. Arlington, ☎ 802/375–6068 or 800/772–3759) shops specialize in community cookbooks from around the country, bears in all forms, music boxes, and, of course, candles. The nearby waterfall makes a pleasant backdrop for a picnic. **Manchester Commons** (Rtes. 7 and 11/30, ☎ 802/362–3736), the largest and spiffiest of three large factory-direct minimalls, has such big-city names as Joan and David, Coach, Boston Trader, Ralph Lauren, Hickey-Freeman, and Cole-Haan. Not far off are **Factory Point Square** (Rte. 7) and **Battenkill Place** (Rte. 11). **Wilmington Flea Market** (Rtes. 9 and 100 S, ☎ 802/464–3345; ⊙ Weekends Memorial Day–mid-Oct.) is a cornucopia of leftovers and never-solds. The **Newfane Flea Market** (Rte. 35, 802/365–7771) happens every weekend during summer and fall and is the selling venue for collectible dealers from all over the state.

Food and Drink

Allen Bros. (Rte. 5 south of Bellows Falls, ☎ 802/722–3395) bakes apple pies, cider doughnuts, and an array of Vermont foods. **Equinox Nursery** (Rte. 7A, between Arlington and Manchester, ☎ 802/362–2610) carries a wide selection of produce and local foods, including ice cream. **H & M Orchard** (Dummerston Center, ☎ 802/254–8100) lets you watch sugaring and pick your own fruit seasonally. **Vermont Country Store** (Rte. 100, Weston, ☎ 802/824–3184) sets aside one room of its old-fashioned emporium for Vermont Common Crackers and bins of fudge and other candy.

Specialty Stores
ART AND ANTIQUES
Carriage Trade (☎ 802/362–1125) and **1812 House** (☎ 802/362–1189), just north of Manchester Center on Route 7, contain room after room of Early American antiques; Carriage Trade has especially fine collections of clocks and ceramics. **Danby Antiques Center** (⅛ mi off Rte. 7, 13 mi north of Manchester, ☎ 802/293–9984) has 11 rooms and a barn filled with furniture and accessories, folk art, textiles, and stoneware. **Four Corners East** (307 North St., Bennington, ☎ 802/442–2612) has Early American antiques. **Gallery North Star** (Townshend Rd., Grafton, ☎ 802/843–2465) focuses on oils, watercolors, and lithographs by Vermont artists, as well as sculpture. **Newfane Antiques Center** (Rte. 30, south of Newfane, ☎ 802/365–4482) displays antiques from 20 dealers on three floors. **Tilting at Windmills Gallery**

(Rte. 11/30, ☎ 802/362–3022) displays paintings from many well-known artists.

BOOKS

The Book Cellar (120 Main St., Brattleboro, ☎ 802/254–6026), with three floors of books, is strong on Vermont and New England volumes. **Johnny Appleseed** (next to The Equinox hotel, Manchester Village, ☎ 802/362–2458) specializes in Vermont lore and the hard-to-find. **Northshire Bookstore** (Main St., Manchester, ☎ 802/362–2200) has a large inventory of travel and children's books.

CRAFTS

Anton of Vermont Quilts (Rte. 100, 9 mi north of Mt. Snow) has a rich collection of hand-crafted fabrics and quilts. **Basketville** (Rte. 5, Putney, ☎ 802/387–5509) is, appropriately, an immense space filled with baskets. **Bennington Potters Yard** (324 County St., ☎ 802/447–7531) has seconds from the famed Bennington Potters. Prepare to get dusty digging through the bad stuff to find an almost-perfect piece at a modest discount. The complex of buildings also houses a glass factory outlet and John McLeod woodenware. **Green Mountain Spinnery** (Exit 4, I–91, Putney, ☎ 802/387–4528; tour is $1 adults, 50¢ children) offers yarns, knit items, and tours of its yarn factory at 1:30 on the first and third Tuesday of each month. **Handworks on the Green** (Rte. 7, Manchester, ☎ 802/362–5033) deals in contemporary crafts—ceramics, jewelry, glass—with an emphasis on sophisticated, brightly colored decorative work. **Newfane Country Store** (Rte. 30, Newfane, ☎ 802/365–7916) has an immense selection of quilts—they can be custom ordered as well—and homemade fudge. **Vermont Artisan Design** (115 Main St., Brattleboro, ☎ 802/257–7044), one of the state's best crafts shops, displays contemporary ceramics, glass, wood, and clothing. **Weston Bowl Mill** (Rte. 100, Weston, ☎ 802/824–6219) has finely crafted wood products at mill prices.

MEN'S AND WOMEN'S CLOTHING

Orvis Retail Store (Rte. 7A, Manchester, ☎ 802/362–3622) carries the outdoor clothing and home furnishings featured in its popular mail-order catalog. A nearby outlet (Union St., ☎ 802/362–6455), housed in what was Orvis's shop in the 1800s, has relatively good bargains. **Anne Klein, Liz Claiborne, Donna Karan, Esprit, Giorgio Armani,** and **Jones New York** are among the shops on Routes 11/30 and 7 South in Manchester—a center for designer factory stores.

Skiing

Bromley Mountain

Box 1130, Manchester Center 05255
☎ *snow conditions 802/824–5522; lodging 800/865–4786*

Venerable Bromley, whose first trails were cut in 1936, is where thousands of skiers learned to ski and learned to love the sport. Today, Bromley attracts families who enjoy its friendly attitude as well as experienced skiers who seek their skiing roots. The area has a comfortable red-clapboard base lodge, built when the ski area first opened more than 50 years ago, with a large ski shop and a condominium village adjacent to the slopes. Bromley completed a major overhaul of its snowmaking system in 1994.

DOWNHILL

While most ski areas are laid out to face the north or east, Bromley faces south, making it one of the warmer spots to ski in New England.

About 35% of its 35 trails are beginner and 34% intermediate; the 31% that has some surprisingly good advanced-expert terrain is serviced by the Blue Ribbon quad chair on the east side. The vertical drop is 1,334 feet. Five double chairlifts, one quad lift, a J-bar, and two surface lifts for beginners provide transportation. A reduced-price, two-day lift pass is available. Kids are still kids (price-wise) up to age 14, but they ski free with a paying adult on nonholiday weekdays. Eighty-four percent of the area is covered by snowmaking.

CROSS-COUNTRY

The Nordic Inn (Landgrove, ☎ 802/824–6444) grooms all 26 kilometers of its trails and is an intimate, idyllic setting for the sport.

OTHER ACTIVITIES

Karl Pfister Sleigh Rides (Landgrove, ☎ 802/824–6320) has a 12-person Travis sleigh with bench seats; call for reservations.

CHILD CARE

Bromley was one of the first ski areas to have a nursery, and it has maintained its reputation as one of the region's best places to bring children. Besides a nursery for children from one month to age 6, there is ski instruction for children ages 3–14.

Mt. Snow/Haystack Ski Resort

400 Mountain Rd., Mt. Snow 05356
☎ 802/464–3333; lodging, 800/245–7669; snow conditions, 802/464–2151

In its present form, Mt. Snow is unpretentious; but it hasn't always been this way. Established in the 1950s, Mt. Snow has come a long way since the 1960s, when its dress-up-and-show-off ski scene earned it the nickname Mascara Mountain. Purchased in 1977 by SKI, Ltd., which also owns Killington (90 minutes away), Mt. Snow's service and facilities reveal its parent's highly professional management—from the parking lot and ticket booths to the day-care center and ski-rental area. You may encounter crowds at the ski lifts (and on a weekend you most certainly will), but Mt. Snow knows how to handle them. Your lift ticket can be used not only at Killington (and vice versa) but also at Haystack (2½ miles away), which SKI Ltd. bought in 1994 after leasing for several years. A free shuttle connects the two areas by road.

At Mt. Snow, both the bustling Main Base Lodge and the Sundance Base Lodge have food service and other amenities. The Carinthia Base Lodge (site of the old Carinthia ski area, absorbed by Mt. Snow in 1986) is usually the least crowded and most easily accessible from the parking lot.

Haystack—the southernmost ski area in Vermont—is much smaller than Mt. Snow, but offers a more personal atmosphere. A modern base lodge is close to the lifts.

DOWNHILL

Mt. Snow is a remarkably well-formed mountain. From its 1,700-foot vertical summit, most of the trails down the face are intermediate, wide, and sunny. Toward the bottom and in the Carinthia section are the beginner slopes; most of the expert terrain is on the North Face, where there's a bounty of excellent fall-line skiing. In all, there are 84 trails, of which about two-thirds are intermediate. The trails are served by two quad, six triple, and eight double chairlifts, plus two surface lifts. The ski school's EXCL instruction program is designed to help advanced and expert skiers.

Most of the 43 trails at Haystack are pleasantly wide with bumps and rolls and straight fall lines—good cruising, intermediate runs. There's also a section with three double-black-diamond trails—very steep but short. A beginner section, safely tucked below the main-mountain trails, provides a haven for lessons and slow skiing. Three triple and two double chairlifts and one T-bar service Haystack's 1,400 vertical feet.

CROSS-COUNTRY

Four cross-country trail areas within 4 miles of the resort provide more than 150 kilometers of varied terrain. The Hermitage (Coldbrook Rd., ☎ 802/464–3511) and the White House (Rtes. 9 and 100, ☎ 802/464–2135) both have 50 kilometers of groomed trails; Timber Creek (Rte. 100, just north of Mt. Snow entrance, ☎ 802/464–0999) is appealingly small with 16 kilometers of thoughtfully groomed trails, and Sitzmark (East Dover Rd., Wilmington 05363, ☎ 802/464–3384) has 40 kilometers of trails, with 12 kilometers of them machine tracked.

OTHER ACTIVITIES

Sleigh rides and winter nature walks head the list of nonskiing winter activities at Mt. Snow. Adams Farm (Higley Hill, ☎ 802/464–3762) has three double-traverse sleighs drawn by Belgian draft horses. Rides include a narrated tour and hot chocolate; call for reservations. The Memorial Park Skating Rink (☎ 802/257-2311) in Brattleboro has rentals.

CHILD CARE

The lively, well-organized child care center (reservations necessary) takes children ages 6 weeks through 12 years in three separate sections: a nursery for those under 18 months, a playroom complex for toddlers up to 30 months, and, adjacent, an even bigger room for older kids. Each has age-appropriate toys and balances indoor play—including arts and crafts—with trips outdoors. Most youngsters sign up for full- or half-day sessions of the ski school–sponsored SKIwee program, designed for those between 4 and 12.

Okemo Mountain
R.F.D. 1, Ludlow 05149
☎ 802/228–4041; lodging, 800/786–5366; snow conditions, 802/228–5222

Okemo has evolved and emerged in recent years to become popular as a major resort and an ideal ski area for families with children. The main attraction is a long, broad, gentle slope with two beginner lifts just above the base lodge. All the facilities at the bottom of the mountain are close together, so family members can regroup easily during the ski day. The net effect of the village area is efficient and attractive—it even boasts today's obligatory clock tower.

DOWNHILL

Above the broad beginner's slope at the base, the upper part of Okemo has a varied network of trails: long, winding, easy trails for beginners, straight fall-line runs for experts, and curving, cruising slopes for intermediates. The 72 trails are served by an efficient lift system of six quads, two triple chairlifts, and two surface lifts; 95% are covered by snowmaking. From the summit to the base lodge, the vertical drop is 2,150 feet. The ski school offers a complimentary Ski Tip Station, where intermediate or better skiers can get an evaluation and a free run with an instructor.

CROSS-COUNTRY

Fox Run (Fox Lane, RSD 1, Box 123, Ludlow 05149, ☎ 802/228–8871) has 26 kilometers of trails, all groomed.

OTHER ACTIVITES

Brickyard Farm (South Hill, ☎ 802/228–5032) is the place for sleigh rides in the area with its large 12–14 passenger traveler and smaller 4-person sleigh; call to reserve.

CHILD CARE

The area's nursery, for children 6 weeks–8 years, has a broad range of indoor activities and supervised outings. Children 3 and up can get brief introduction-to-skiing lessons; those ages 4–8 can take all-day or half-day SKIwee lessons.

Stratton

Stratton Mountain 05155
☎ *802/297–2200 or 800/843–6867; snow conditions, 802/297–4211; lodging, 800/787–2886*

Since its creation in 1961, Stratton has undergone several physical transformations and upgrades, yet the area's sophisticated character has been retained. It has been the special province of well-to-do families and, more recently, young professionals from the New York–southern Connecticut corridor. Since the mid-80s, an entire village, with a covered parking structure for 700 cars, has arisen at the base of the mountain: Adjacent to the base lodge are a condo-hotel, restaurants, and about 25 shops lining a pedestrian mall. Stratton is a self-contained center 4 miles up its own access road off Route 30 in Bondville, about 30 minutes from Manchester's popular shopping zone.

DOWNHILL

Stratton's skiing comprises three sectors. The first is the lower mountain directly in front of the base lodge-village-condo complex; a number of lifts reach mid-mountain from this entry point, and practically all skiing is beginner or low-intermediate. Above that, the upper mountain, with a vertical drop of 2,000 feet, is graced with a high-speed, 12-passenger gondola, *Starship XII.* Down the face are the expert trails, while on either side are intermediate cruising runs with a smattering of wide beginner slopes. The third sector, the Sun Bowl, is off to one side with two quad chairlifts and two new expert trails, a full base lodge, and a lot of intermediate terrain. A new Ski Learning Park with 10 trails and 5 lifts has its own "Park Packages" available for novice skiers. In all, Stratton has 92 slopes and trails served by the gondola and four quad, one triple, six double chairlifts, and two surface lifts.

CROSS-COUNTRY

The Stratton area has 22 kilometers (12 miles) of cross-country skiing on the Sun Bowl side of the mountain.

OTHER ACTIVITIES

The area's sports center has two indoor tennis courts, three racquetball courts, a 25-meter indoor swimming pool, a hot tub, a steam room, a fitness facility with Nautilus equipment, and a restaurant.

CHILD CARE

The day-care center takes children ages 6 weeks through 5 years for indoor activities and outdoor excursions. The ski school has programs for ages 4–12; both are daylong with lunch. SKIwee instruction programs are also available for ages 4–12. A junior racing program and special instruction groups are aimed at more experienced young skiers.

Other Sports

Biking

The 20-mile Dorset–Manchester trail runs from Manchester Village north on West Street to Route 30, turns west at the Dorset village green onto West Road, and heads back south to Manchester. **Battenkill Sports** (Rte. 7, at Rte. 11/30, ☎ 802/362–2634) and **Pedal Pushers** (Rte. 11/30, ½ mi east of Rte. 7A, ☎ 802/362–5200) in Manchester rent bikes.

A 26-mile loop out of Chester follows the Williams River along Route 103 to Pleasant Valley Road north of Bellows Falls. At Saxtons River, turn west onto Route 121 and follow along the river to connect with Route 35. When the two routes separate, follow Route 35 north back to Chester. **Neal's Wheels** (Rte. 11, ☎ 802/875–3627) has rentals.

In Bennington **Mountain Bike Peddlers** (954 E. Main St., ☎ 802/447–7968) and **Up and Downhill** (160 Benmont Ave., ☎ 802/442–8664) offer rentals and repairs.

Vermont Mountain Velo (☎ 802/362–1326) leads inn-to-inn mountain biking trips in and around the Green Mountain National Forest. Mountain biking at **Stratton** (☎ 800/842–6867) has something for everyone, as long as you don't mind the institutionalized feeling of biking at a mammoth ski resort; rentals, guided tours, and accessories are available.

Canoeing

The Connecticut River between Bellows Falls and the Massachusetts border, interrupted by one dam at Vernon, is relatively easy. A good resource is *The Complete Boating Guide to the Connecticut River,* available from **CRWC Headquarters** (125 Combs Rd., Easthampton, MA 01027, ☎ 413/584–0057). **Connecticut River Safari** (Rte. 5, Brattleboro, ☎ 802/257–5008) has guided and self-guided tours as well as canoe rentals. **Battenkill Canoe, Ltd.** (Rte. 7A, Arlington, ☎ 802/362–2800) has rentals and day trips on the Battenkill and can arrange custom inn-to-inn tours.

Fishing

The Orvis Co. (Manchester Center, ☎ 802/362–3900) hosts a nationally known fly-fishing school on the Battenkill, the state's most famous trout stream, with three-day courses given weekly, April–October. **Battenkill Anglers** (☎ 802/362–3184) teaches the art and science of fly fishing. They have both private and group lessons. **Strictly Trout** (☎ 802/869–3116) will arrange a fly-fishing trip on any Vermont stream or river.

The Connecticut River contains small-mouth bass, walleye, and perch; shad are returning via the fish ladders at Vernon and Bellows Falls. Harriman and Somerset reservoirs in the central part of the state offer both warm- and cold-water species; Harriman has a greater variety.

Hiking

One of the most popular segments of the Long Trail starts at Route 11/30 west of Peru Notch and goes to the top of Bromley Mountain (four hours). About 4 miles east of Bennington, the Long Trail crosses Route 9 and runs south to the summit of Harmon Hill (two–three hours). On Route 30 about 1 mile south of Townshend is Townshend State Park; from here the hiking trail runs to the top of Bald Mountain, passing an alder swamp, a brook, and a hemlock forest (two hours).

The **Mountain Goat** (Rte. 7A just south of Rte. 11/30, Manchester, ☎ 802/362–5159) sells hiking, backpacking, and climbing equipment; it also offers climbing clinics. The **Green Mountain Club** (Rte. 100, Box 650, Waterbury Center 05677, ☎ 802/244–7037) publishes a number of helpful hiking maps and guides.

Recreation Areas

Summertime facilities at **Stratton** include 15 outdoor tennis courts, 27 holes of golf, horseback riding, and mountain biking. Instruction programs in tennis and golf are offered. The area hosts a summer entertainment series and is home of an LPGA golf tournament and the Women's Hardcourt Tennis Championships.

Water Sports

Lake Whittingham (Harriman Reservoir) is the largest lake in the state; there are boat launch areas at Wards Cove, Whitingham, Mountain Mills, and the Ox Bow. **Lake Front Restaurant** (☎ 802/464–5838) rents sailboats, canoes, and rowboats by the hour or day. **West River Canoe** (Rte. 100, off Rte. 30, Townshend, ☎ 802/896–6209) has sailboard rentals and lessons.

National Forests and State Parks

The 275,000 acres of Green Mountain National Forest extend down the center of the state, providing scenic drives, picnic areas, 95 campsites, lakes, and hiking and cross-country ski trails. Grout Pond Recreation Area and Somerset Reservoir are two idyllic boating and hiking destinations—it's worth the wear on your car's struts and shocks driving dirt roads (closed in winter) to get to them. The national forest also has trail heads for the Appalachian and Long trails. Contact the **Forest Supervisor, Green Mountain National Forest** (151 West St., Box 519, Rutland 05701, ☎ 802/773–0300).

The waterfalls at the Lye Brook Wilderness Area are popular. Contact the **U.S. Forest Service** (Rte. 11/30, east of Manchester, ☎ 802/362–2307; ☺ Weekdays 8–4:30).

The following state parks have camping sites and facilities as well as picnic tables. **Emerald Lake State Park** (Rte. 7, 9 mi north of Manchester, ☎ 802/362–1655; 430 acres) has a marked nature trail, an on-site naturalist, boat and canoe rentals, and a snack bar. The hiking trails at **Fort Dummer State Park** (S. Main St., 2 mi south of Brattleboro, ☎ 802/254–2610; 217 acres) afford views of the Connecticut River Valley. **Lake Shaftsbury State Park** (Rte. 7A, 10½ mi north of Bennington, ☎ 802/375–9978; 101 acres) is one of a few parks in Vermont with group camping; it has a swimming beach, self-guided nature trails, and boat and canoe rentals. **Molly Stark State Park** (Rte. 9, east of Wilmington, ☎ 802/464–5460; 158 acres) has a hiking trail to a vista from a fire tower on Mt. Olga. **Townshend State Park** (3 mi north of Rte. 30, between Newfane and Townshend, ☎ 802/365–7500; 856 acres), the largest in southern Vermont, is popular for the swimming at Townshend Dam and the stiff hiking trail to the top of Bald Mountain. **Woodford State Park** (Rte. 9, east of Bennington, ☎ 802/447–4169; 400 acres) has an activities center on Adams Reservoir, a playground, boat and canoe rentals, and marked nature trails.

Dining and Lodging

There are a number of rambling, luxurious inns in Manchester and Arlington; they share a lodging referral service (☎ 802/824–6915). Mt. Snow, Stratton, and Bromley ski areas have fostered a profusion of exemplary B&Bs.

Arlington
DINING AND LODGING

$$–$$$ **West Mountain Inn.** Many couples find this inn a romantic spot to get
★ married: It has a llama ranch on the property, African violets and llama-
shape chocolates in the rooms, quilted bedspreads, and a front lawn
with a spectacular view of the countryside. This former farmhouse of
the 1840s, restored over the last several years, sits on 150 acres, seemingly a world apart from civilization. Rooms 2, 3, and 4 in the front
of the house overlook the front lawn; the three small nooks of room
11 resemble railroad sleeper berths and are perfect for kids. A low-
beamed, paneled, candlelit dining room is the setting for six-course prix-
fixe dinners featuring such specialties as veal chops topped with
sun-dried tomatoes and Asiago cheese. Aunt Min's Swedish rye and
other toothsome breads, as well as desserts, are all made on the
premises. Tables by the windows are front row to the glorious view of
the mountains. ⌹ *Rte. 313, 05250,* ☎ *802/375–6516,* FAX *802/375–
6553. 13 rooms with bath, 3 suites. Restaurant (reservations advised),
bar, hiking, skiing. AE, MC, V. MAP.*

$$–$$$ **Arlington Inn.** The Greek Revival columns at the entrance to this rail-
★ road magnate's home of 1848 give it an imposing presence, yet the inn
is more welcoming than forbidding. The charm is created by linens that
coordinate with the Victorian-style wallpaper, clawfoot tubs in some
bathrooms, and the house's original moldings and wainscoting. The
carriage house, built at the turn of the century and renovated in 1985,
has country French and Queen Anne furnishings. Having changed
hands twice in as many years, the restaurant struggles to retain its reputation as one of the most respected in the state. Polished hardwood
floors, green tablecloths and rose walls, and soft candlelight comple-
ment the food; so might a bottle of wine from the extensive collection.
⌹ *Rte. 7A, 05250,* ☎ *802/375–6532 or 800/443–9442. 10 rooms
with bath, 3 cottages. Restaurant (reservations advised), bar, tennis
courts. AE, MC, V. MAP.*

LODGING

$–$$ **Hill Farm Inn.** This homey inn still has the feel of the country farm-
house it used to be. In fact, the surrounding farmland was deeded to
the Hill family by King George in 1775 and is said to be one of the
oldest in the state. It is now protected from development by the Vermont Land Trust. The beefalo that roam the 50 acres, the fireplace in
the informal living room, the mix of sturdy antiques, the spinning wheel
in the upstairs hallway—all convey a relaxed, friendly atmosphere. Room
7 has a beamed cathedral ceiling, and from its porch you can see Mt.
Equinox; the rooms in the 1790 guest house are very private; the cabins are rustic and fun. ⌹ *Just off Rte. 7, Box 2015, 05250,* ☎ *802/375–
2269 or 800/882-2545. 6 rooms with bath, 5 doubles share 3 baths,
2 suites, 4 cabins in summer. AE, D, MC, V. MAP.*

Bennington
DINING

$$$ **Main Street Café.** Since it opened in 1989, this small storefront with
polished hardwood floors, candlelit tables, and fresh flowers has drawn
raves, its Northern Italian cuisine judged well worth the few minutes'
drive from downtown Bennington. Favorites include the rigatoni tossed
with Romano, Parmesan, broccoli, and sausage in a cream sauce and
the chicken stuffed with ham, provolone, and fresh spinach and served
in a Marsala-onion sauce. The look is casual chic, like that of a Man-
hattan loft transplanted to a small town. ✕ *Rte. 67A, N. Bennington,*
☎ *802/442–3210. Reservations advised. AE, DC, MC, V. No lunch.
Closed Mon. and Tues.*

$$ **The Brasserie.** The Brasserie's fare is some of the city's most creative. A mozzarella loaf swirls cheese through bread topped with anchovy-herb butter, and the soups are filling enough for a meal. The decor is as clean-lined and contemporary as the Bennington pottery that is for sale in the same complex of buildings. ✕ *324 County St.,* ☎ *802/447–7922. MC, V. Closed Tues.*

$ ★ **Blue Benn Diner.** Breakfast is served all day in this authentic diner. The eats include turkey hash and breakfast burritos that wrap scrambled eggs, sausage, and chiles in a tortilla. Pancakes, of all imaginable varieties, are a favorite. There can be a long wait, especially on weekends. ✕ *Rte. 7 N,* ☎ *802/442–8977. No credit cards. No dinner Sun.–Tues.*

LODGING

$$–$$$ **South Shire Inn.** Canopy beds in lushly carpeted rooms, ornate plaster moldings, and a dark mahogany fireplace in the library create turn-of-the-century grandeur; fireplaces and hot tubs in some rooms add warmth. Furnishings are antique except for the reproduction beds that provide contemporary comfort. The inn is in a quiet residential neighborhood within walking distance of the bus depot and downtown stores. Breakfast is served in the peach-and-white wedding cake of a dining room. ⌂ *124 Elm St., 05201,* ☎ *802/447–3839. 9 rooms with bath. AE, MC, V. MAP.*

$–$$ ★ **Molly Stark Inn.** This gem of a B&B will make you so comfortable you'll feel like you're staying with an old friend. Tidy blue plaid wallpaper, gleaming hardwood floors, antique furnishings, and a wood-burning stove in a brick alcove of the sitting room add country charm to this 1860 Queen Anne Victorian. Molly's Room, at the back of the building, gets less noise from Route 9; the attic suite is most spacious. A new secluded cottage with a 16-foot ceiling, a king-size brass bed, and a two-person whirlpool bath surrounded by windows that look out to the woods is as romantic as it gets. The innkeeper's genuine hospitality and quirky charisma delight guests, as does the full country breakfast that's been known to feature cinnamon-apple cheddar cheese quiche. ⌂ *1067 E. Main St., 05201,* ☎ *802/442–9631 or 800/356–3076. 6 rooms, 2 with bath. MC, V. MAP.*

Brattleboro

DINING

$ **Common Ground.** The political posters and concert fliers that line the staircase make you conscious of Vermont's strong progressive element as you ascend into the loftlike, rough-hewned dining rooms. Owned cooperatively by the staff, this vegetarian restaurant serves the likes of cashew burgers, veggie stir-fries, and the "humble bowl of brown rice." A chocolate cake with peanut butter frosting and other desserts (sans white sugar, of course) will lure confirmed meat-eaters. ✕ *25 Elliot St.,* ☎ *802/257–0855. No credit cards. Closed Tues.*

$ **Mole's Eye Cafe.** Built in the 1930s as the tavern for the long gone old Brooks Hotel, this local gathering place is pretty much an institution. The appeal of this cozy basement establishment is its neighborly hospitality—not to mention the home-baked turkey melts, Mexican munchies, and hearty, homemade soups and desserts. ✕ *High St.,* ☎ *802/257–0771. MC, V. No reservations.*

DINING AND LODGING

$–$$ **Latchis Hotel.** Restoration of the downtown landmark's Art Deco grandeur was completed in 1989, and everything old is new again: black-and-white-check bathroom tiles, painted geometric borders along the ceiling, multicolored patterns of terrazzo on the lobby floor. All deluxe rooms have refrigerator, complimentary Continental breakfast, movie passes, and shopping discounts at Brattleboro stores. Odd-numbered rooms have views of the Connecticut River and Main Street. The Latchis Grille is home to the Windham Brewery and serves rich ales and lagers, as well as an eclectic array of pub grub—grilled chicken and fish sandwiches, fried calamari, burgers, salads, and the like. ⌨ *50 Main St., 05301, ☎ 802/254–6300. 35 rooms with bath. Restaurant. AE, MC, V. CP.*

Chester

LODGING

$$$ Inn at Long Last. An army of toy soldiers fills a glass case beside the enormous fieldstone fireplace in the pine-floor lobby of this Victorian inn, where guests like to gather for after-dinner drinks before the fire. Bookshelves in the large wood-panel library/pub hold volumes in literature, science, biography, music, history, and labor economics; one entire shelf is devoted to George Orwell. Individual rooms are named after people, places, and things important to innkeeper Jack Coleman, former president of Haverford College in Pennsylvania, and are decorated simply with personal memorabilia. Some bathrooms are fairly small. The quietest section of the inn is at the back. Although its atmosphere is not overly warm, this grand old inn musters respect—characteristics curiously reflected in the innkeeper as well. ⌨ *Main St., Box 589, 05143, ☎ 802/875–2444. 30 rooms, 1 with bath in hall. Restaurant, tennis courts. MC, V. MAP.*

Dorset

DINING AND LODGING

$$$ **Barrows House.** Jim and Linda McGinniss' 200-year-old Federal-style
★ inn is a long-time favorite with those who wish to escape the commercial hustle of Manchester (Bromley is about 8 miles away). Originally built as the home of Dorset's minister, it has always been a focal point of town. Carrying on this tradition, the superb dining now draws people from surrounding communities. The deep-red woodwork and library theme of the pub room makes it an intimate venue in which to sample the elegant country fare, while the greenhouse room, embellished with terra cotta and deep blue hues, is a pleasant summer eating spot. In addition to the 12 guest rooms in the main building, there are rooms in carriage houses that have easy access to the pool and tennis courts. ⌨ *Rte. 30, Dorset 05251, ☎ 802/867–4455 or 800/639–1620, FAX 802/867–0132. 18 rooms with bath, 10 suites. Pool, sauna, bicycles, tennis courts. Full breakfast included; MAP available. MC, V.*

$$–$$$ **Marble West Inn.** The serenity of the grounds—rambling gardens and ponds, rockers on a porch facing meadows and mountains—equals the hospitality and warmth emanating from within this inn on a quiet back road just outside of town. A baby grand piano, fireplaces in both sitting rooms, and afternoon tea greet guests seeking repose, as do rooms highlighted with delicate stenciling, hardwood floors, and well-preserved antiques. Breakfast may feature banana-stuffed French toast or an egg strada. ⌨ *Dorset West Rd., Dorset 05251, ☎ 802/867–4155. 8 rooms with bath. AE, MC, V.*

Grafton

DINING AND LODGING

$$–$$$ **The Old Tavern at Grafton.** The white-column porches on both stories of the main building wrap around this commanding inn that dates to 1801 and has hosted Daniel Webster and Nathaniel Hawthorne. There are 14 rooms in the main building and 22 rooms in two houses across the street. The rooms in the older part of the inn are furnished in antiques, and evoke New England's 18th-century frontier days. Two dining rooms, one with formal Georgian furniture and oil portraits, the other with rustic paneling and low beams, serve such hearty traditional New England dishes as venison stew or grilled quail; cheeses, made just down the road, show up in some dishes. A popular gathering spot is the Phelps Barn Bar, which is filled with authentic English pub furniture. Cross-country ski trails are nearby. ☎ *Rte. 35, 05146,* ☎ *802/843–2231 or 800/843–1801,* 🖷 *802/843–2245. 35 rooms with bath. Restaurant, bar, pond, tennis courts, recreation room. AE, MC, V. Closed Apr.*

LODGING

$$ **Eaglebrook of Grafton.** A mix of antiques and abstract art give this
★ small country inn an air of city sophistication. The cathedral-ceilinged sun room, built overlooking the Saxtons River, the seven fireplaces with soapstone mantels, and the watercolor stencils in the hallways warrant this elegant retreat's feature in a glossy interior-design magazine. Blue-checked fabric gives one of the three bedrooms a French provincial air; another leans toward American country; the third has a Victorian flavor. Outside, the landscaped stone terrace is a perfect place to sit with a bottle of wine on a summer evening. The lush furnishings and care extended by the innkeepers toward their guests assure an indulgent stay. ☎ *Main St., 05146,* ☎ *802/843–2564. 1 room with bath, 2 rooms share bath. CP. No credit cards.*

Londonderry
DINING AND LODGING

$$$ **The Highland House.** "No request is too big" is the credo of the innkeepers of this 1842 country inn. The inn is surrounded by 32 private acres and is just 10 minutes by car from Bromley Mountain. The guest rooms are simple, with reproduction furniture, dried-flower wall ornaments, and quilts. The breakfast is hearty New England style; in the evenings the six-table dining area becomes a candlelit room where duck with a ginger or raspberry sauce is popular. ☎ *Rte. 100, Londonderry 05148,* ☎ *802/824–3019,* 🖷 *802/824–3657. 17 rooms with bath. Pool, cross-country skiing, tennis courts. Rates include full breakfast. AE, MC, V. Restaurant closed Mon. and Tues.*

Ludlow
LODGING

$$$ **Okemo Mountain Lodge.** The three-story, brown-clapboard building has balconies and fireplaces in all guest rooms, and the one-bedroom condominiums clustered around the base of the ski lifts are close to restaurants, shops, and the resort's clock tower. Also available are Kettlebrook and Winterplace slopeside condominiums, run by Okemo Mountain Lodging Service. ☎ *Rte. 100, RFD 1, Ludlow 05149,* ☎ *802/228–5571, 802/228–4041, or 800/780–5366;* 🖷 *802/228–2079. 76 rooms with bath. Restaurant, bar. AE, D, MC, V.*

Manchester
DINING

$$$–$$$$ **Chantecleer.** Five miles north of Manchester, intimate dining rooms have been created in a converted dairy barn with a large fieldstone fireplace. The menu reflects the chef's Swiss background: The appetizers include *Bündnerfleisch* (air-dried Swiss beef) and frogs' legs in garlic butter; chateaubriand and Wiener schnitzel are typical entrées. ✗ *Rte. 7, E. Dorset,* ☎ *802/362–1616. Reservations required. DC, MC, V. No lunch. Closed Mon. and Tues.*

$$–$$$ **Bistro Henry's.** Just outside of town, this new restaurant attracts a devoted clientele for its authentic French bistro fare and attention to detail. The dining room is spacious and open, and a bar sits off in a corner.

Recently on the menu were an Alsatian onion tart, eggplant and mushroom terrine Provençal, and sweetbreads with mustard crust and cognac. Breakfast, lunch, and Sunday brunch are also served. ✕ *Rte. 11/30, Manchester,* ☎ *802/362–4982. Reservations recommended. D, MC, V. Closed Mon.*

$–$$ **Quality Restaurant.** Gentrification has reached the down-home neighborhood place that was the model for Norman Rockwell's *War News* painting. The Quality now has Provençal wallpaper and polished wood booths, and the sturdy New England standbys of grilled meat loaf and hot roast beef or turkey sandwiches have been joined by tortellini Alfredo with shrimp and smoked salmon. Breakfast is always popular. ✕ *Main St.,* ☎ *802/362–9839. AE, MC, V.*

DINING AND LODGING

$$$–$$$$ **The Equinox.** This grand white-column resort was a fixture even before Abe Lincoln's family began summering here; it's worth a look around even if you don't stay here. A complete overhaul in 1992 restored the guest rooms, public spaces, and the golf course. Rooms and dining areas are furnished in the casually elegant Vermont grand country style. Dining in the Marsh Tavern, you can feel like you're sitting in the middle of a Ralph Lauren Polo ad: spiral-based floor lamps accompany rich, supple upholstered settees and stuffed arm chairs; high bow-back chairs sit around tables with fluted columns; sconces light paneled ceilings; and several fireplaces create a dreamy glow. The food is equally aesthetically pleasing: Devonshire shepherd's pie, and the woodland supper of roast duck, venison sausage, and wild mushrooms are popular; a grains, greens, and beans entrée is offered as well. The Colonnade, where jackets are required, is as elegant as dining can be and is open only during summer months. The resort is often the site of large conferences. ▦ *Rte. 7A, Manchester Village 05254,* ☎ *802/362–4700 or 800/362–4747,* ▩ *802/362–4861. 119 rooms with bath, 18 suites, 9 3-bedroom town houses. 2 restaurants, bar, indoor and outdoor pools, sauna, steam room, health club, golf, tennis courts. AE, D, DC, MC, V.*

$$$–$$$$ **Reluctant Panther.** The spacious bedrooms have goose-down duvets and Pierre Deux linens; they are colored in soft, elegant grays and peaches, and styled with an eclectic mix of antique, country, and contemporary furnishings. Ten rooms have fireplaces—the Mary Porter suite has two—and all suites have whirlpools. The best views are from rooms B and D. In Wildflowers, the restaurant long known for its sophisticated cuisine, a huge fieldstone fireplace dominates the larger of the two dining rooms; the other is a small greenhouse with five tables. Glasses and silver sparkle in the candlelight, the service is impeccable, and the menu, which changes daily, might include boneless stuffed chicken with spinach, Gruyère, and Chardonnay-thyme sauce, or fricassee of lobster with Nantucket Bay scallops and Gulf shrimp. ▦ *West Rd., Box 678, 05254,* ☎ *802/362–2568 or 800/822–2331,* ▩ *802/362–2586. 16 rooms with bath, 4 suites. Restaurant (reservations required; closed Tues. and Wed.), bar, meeting room. AE, MC, V. MAP.*

LODGING

$$$ **1811 House.** The atmosphere of an elegant English country home can
★ be enjoyed without crossing the Atlantic. A pub-style bar that serves 26 kinds of single-malt scotches and is decorated with horse brasses; the Waterford crystal in the dining room; equestrian paintings; and the English floral landscaping of three acres of lawn all make this an inn worthy of royalty. The rooms contain period antiques; six have fireplaces, and many have four-poster beds. Bathrooms are old-fashioned but serviceable, particularly the Robinson Room's marble-enclosed tub.

🖼 *Rte. 7A, 05254,* ☎ *802/362–1811 or 800/432–1811,* FAX *802/362–2443. 11 rooms with bath, 3 cottages. Bar. AE, MC, V. MAP.*

$$ The Battenkill Inn. The hearts carved into the outside trim were final touches added to this architectural gem, when it was built in 1840 as a wedding present; the 50 rose bushes that ring the property are a modern-day toast to that romance. Recently taken over by an enthusiastic young couple, Mary and Ramsay Gourd, this recently refurbished inn has all the elements you'd expect from a New England B&B. Deep red wallpaper contrasting with dark green prints lure guests into the dining and sitting rooms. Original wooden doors and window frames, polished oak floors, and a grand curving walnut staircase encourage guests to forgive the rather small bathrooms—a hindrance that often plagues 1800s farmhouses-turned-inns. Rooms in the rear have decks that look out toward a meadow and the Battenkill; some rooms have fireplaces. Attentive hospitality and the memorable breakfasts are fast becoming this inn's trademarks: raspberry and cream cheese–filled French toast is a favorite; everything is made with low- or non-fat ingredients when possible. 🖼 *Box 948, Rte. 100, Manchester Village 05254,* ☎ *802/362–4213 or 800/441–1628. 10 rooms with bath. MAP.*

$$ Manchester Highlands Inn. Almost all the guest rooms in this 1898 inn
★ have at least one rocking chair—a detail that reflects innkeepers Patricia and Pat Eichorn's intention to make relaxing their guests' foremost pastime. There are five sitting rooms, including an amiable pub downstairs and a plant-filled sun room that looks out over the pool and the mountains beyond. Lots of woodwork, including several sets of original pocket doors between rooms downstairs, contributes to the warm atmosphere. Rooms in the main inn are spacious and light, and all rooms have delicate lace curtains and featherbeds; the Turret and Tower rooms are especially romantic. Rooms in the carriage house are less appealing, but good for skiers and families. 🖼 *Highland Ave. 05255,* ☎ *802/362–4565 or 800/743–4565. 15 rooms with bath. Pool, recreation room. Rates include full breakfast. MC, V.*

Newfane

DINING AND LODGING

$$$–$$$$ The Four Columns. Erected 150 years ago for a homesick Southern bride, the majestic white columns of the Greek Revival mansion are more intimidating than the Colonial-style rooms inside. Room 1 in the older section has an enclosed porch overlooking the town common; three rooms and a suite are annexed. All rooms have antiques, brass beds, and quilts; some have fireplaces. The third-floor room in the old section is the most private. In the restaurant, chef Greg Parks has introduced such nouvelle American dishes as mixed grilled game sausages, jumbo shrimp with poblano butter and tapenade toast, and grilled marinated quail with pesto couscous. The classy dining room is decorated with antique tools and copper pots, and the tables sport such coverings as Towle place settings and Limoges china. 🖼 *West St., Box 278, 05345,* ☎ *802/365–7713. 17 rooms with bath. Restaurant (reservations advised; closed Tues., weekdays Apr., early Dec.), hiking. AE, MC, V. CP; MAP in foliage season.*

LODGING

$$ The Candle and the Rose. This is a tiny house reminiscent of European B&Bs, where guests really feel as if their hosts have invited them personally to spend the night at their place in the country. The innkeeper moved from sunny California to fulfill her dream of running a guesthouse. She has livened up what was once, according to some, the old town jail with bright lavenders and teals. The hallways are a little cramped, but the rooms are spacious. Breakfast is served at an antique cherry table in the parlor room that looks out onto Newfane's idyllic town green. ⊞ *West St., Box 477, 05345,* ☏ *802/365–7204. 2 rooms with bath, 2 rooms share bath. No credit cards.*

Putney
DINING AND LODGING
$–$$ **The Putney Inn.** The main building of this inn dates from the 1790s and was part of a farming estate owned by an English army captain. It later became a seminary—the present-day pub was once the chapel. Two fireplaces dominate the lobby, while wedgwood blue and mahogany hues complement the hand-hewn post-and-beam structure of the sitting areas. The guest rooms have Queen Anne mahogany reproductions. The exterior of the adjacent building is disheartening, but the rooms are spacious and modern and are 100 yards from the banks of the Connecticut River. Guests dine in what was once the attached barn, where massive original beams are also part of the charm. The cuisine is regionally inspired, with innovative flourishes, and includes New England pot pies, wild game mixed grill, and burgers with Vermont cheddar. ⊞ *Depot Rd., 05346,* ☏ *802/387–5517 or 800/653–5517,* ℻ *802/387–5211. 25 rooms with bath. MAP. AE, MC, V.*

LODGING
$ **Hickory Ridge House.** The unusually spacious guest rooms of this stately 1808 Federal mansion reflect the original owner's fortune. They have a country-farmhouse decor that is simple yet comfortable; four have fireplaces. Rag rugs cover pine floors, white lace curtains hang at the windows, and walls are cheerful pastels; bathrooms have large tubs. Putney was once a focus of the back-to-the-land movement; traces of that ethos are reflected in the vegetarian breakfasts that might include stuffed pumpkin pancakes or an inspired soufflé. ⊞ *Hickory Ridge Rd., R.D. 3, Box 1410, 05346,* ☏ *802/387–5709. 3 rooms with bath, 4 rooms share 3 baths. MAP. MC, V.*

Stratton
DINING AND LODGING
$$$ **Stratton Mountain Inn and Village Lodge.** The complex includes a 125-room inn—the largest on the mountain—and a 91-room lodge with studio units. Ski packages that include lift tickets bring down room rates. ⊞ *Stratton Mountain Rd., 05155,* ☏ *802/297–2500 or 800/777–1700,* ℻ *802/297–1778. 216 rooms with bath. 2 restaurants, pool, 2 hot tubs, sauna, racquetball, golf course, tennis courts. AE, D, DC, MC, V.*

West Dover
DINING
$$$ **Doveberry Inn.** The red carpet sets the tone in the two candlelit, intimate dining rooms for the authentic Northern Italian cuisine, including roast pork stuffed with red peppers; venison served with spinach, provolone cheese, and whole garlic over polenta; and farfalle with smoked chicken and pesto. ✕ *Rte. 100, W. Dover,* ☏ *802/464–5652 or 800/722–3204. Reservations advised. AE, MC, V.*

DINING AND LODGING
$$$ **Deerhill Inn.** Up on a ridge, this English Country inn's wall of west-facing windows afford the public areas views of the valley below and the ski slopes across the way. A huge fireplace and a garden-scene mural dominate the living room, while English hand-painted yellow wallpaper, an emerald green carpet, and collections of antique plates accent the dining rooms. The guest rooms are in transition, emerging gradu-

ally from the influence of the previous innkeeper who had a heavy hand with '70s decor. Each has an endearing quality: One has an Oriental bedroom set, another is done all in plaids. The four balcony rooms are the most spacious and have great views. All but one room has a tub. The fare is upscale comfort food and includes meat pies, homemade sausage, and fish. No French wines are served. ⌂ *Valley View Rd., Box 136, 05356,* ☎ *802/464–3100 or 800/993–3379. 17 rooms with bath. Pool. AE, MC, V.*

West Townsend

DINING AND LODGING

$$$–$$$$ **Windham Hill Inn.** In the converted, turn-of-the-century dairy barn, two rooms share an enormous deck that overlooks the West River Valley. Rooms in the main building are more formal. Personal touches abound throughout the inn: Guest rooms have cherry pencil-post canopy beds made by a local artisan, and there's a restored Steinway piano for guests to try their hand. Near Stratton, this is a perfect place to foster one's craving for the genteel after a reckless day of abandon on the slopes. ⌂ *West Townshend 05359,* ☎ *802/874–4080 or 800/944–4080,* FAX *802/874–4702. 15 rooms with bath. Restaurant, bar, pond, ice-skating, cross-country skiing. AE, MC, V. Closed in early spring and Nov. 27–Dec. 26.*

Weston

DINING AND LODGING

$–$$$ **The Inn at Weston.** The fairly basic guest rooms of the inn, spread between two farmhouses that date from the 1830s, are furnished with early American reproductions. A fireplace and two wood-burning stoves grace the living rooms, while an intimate wood-paneled pub greets guests after a hard day of shopping at the Vermont Country Store across the street. The fare featured in the large candlelit room includes lamb sautéed with mushrooms and Dijon mustard sauce and grilled chicken breast marinated in olive oil and lemon and served with raspberry sauce. Breads and desserts are made on the premises. ⌂ *Main St.,* ☎ *802/824–6789 or 800/754–5804. 12 rooms with bath, 7 rooms share 3 baths. Restaurant (reservations advised, no lunch, closed Mon.). Full breakfast included; MAP available. AE, MC, V. Closed last wk of Apr. and around Thanksgiving.*

Wilmington

DINING AND LODGING

$$$$ **The White House of Wilmington.** The grand staircase in this Federal-style mansion leads to spacious rooms that are individually decorated and have antique bathrooms, brass wall sconces, mah-jongg sets, and in some cases the home's original wallpaper. The newer section has more contemporary plumbing; some rooms have fireplaces and lofts. A description of the public rooms—heavy velvet drapes, tufted leather wingchairs—suggests formality, yet the atmosphere is casual and comfortable. Although it's just a 10-minute drive to Mt. Snow–Haystack, the White House is primarily a cross-country ski touring center, with a rental shop and 43 kilometers (about 28 miles) of trails. Instruction is also available. ⌂ *Rte. 9, 05363,* ☎ *802/464–2135 or 800/541–2135,* FAX *802/464–5222. 12 rooms with bath. Restaurant, bar, indoor and outdoor pools, sauna. Breakfast and MAP available. AE, DC, MC, V.*

$$$–$$$$ **The Hermitage.** Staying in this 19th-century inn is a bit like visiting an
★ English country manor in hunting season. English setters prance about the grounds amid various collections of decoys, while game birds roam the fields near a duck pond—don't get too attached to the birds, however; you'll probably have one for dinner during your stay. The most

formal rooms are in the Colonial-style main inn, where every room has a fireplace. You can also stay in the adjacent Wine House, built in 1980; and about ½ mile down the road in the Brook Bound Inn, which has more modest rooms and is much less expensive. Furnishings in all are simple turn-of-the-century New England: muslin curtains, white shutters. Beds are four poster or have towering oak headboards. The restaurant has a traditional Continental menu that showcases home-raised game birds and venison—and a 2,000 label wine list. ☎ *Coldbrook Rd., Box 457, 05363, ☎ 802/464–3511. 25 rooms with bath, 4 share 2 baths. Restaurant (reservations advised), pool, sauna, cross-country skiing, tennis courts. MAP. AE, DC, MC, V.*

LODGING

$$ Trail's End. In the 10 years since they became innkeepers, Bill and Mary Kilburn have taken what was once a bare-bones ski dorm and created a warm, user-friendly, four-season lodge. The inn's centerpiece is the cathedral-ceiling living room with catwalk loft seating, and an immense, 21-foot fieldstone fireplace. Guest rooms are comfortable, if somewhat simple, though two suites have fireplaces and whirlpool tubs. The real draw is the Kilburns themselves, whose enthusiasm and genuine interest will have you sitting and talking over coffee all morning. Breakfast is served at one of three immense round pine tables. ☎ *Smith Rd., 05363, ☎ 802/464–2727 or 800/859–2585. 15 rooms with bath. Pool, fishing, tennis court. MAP. MC, V.*

The Arts

Music
Marlboro Music Festival (Marlboro Music Center, ☎ 802/257–4333) presents a broad range of classical and contemporary music in weekend concerts in July and August. **New England Bach Festival** (Brattleboro Music Center, ☎ 802/257–4523), with a chorus under the direction of Blanche Moyse, is held in fall. **Vermont Symphony Orchestra** (☎ 802/864–5741) performs in Bennington and Arlington in winter, in Manchester and Brattleboro in summer.

Opera
Brattleboro Opera Theatre (☎ 802/254–6649) stages a complete opera once a year and holds an opera workshop.

Theater
Dorset Playhouse (north of Manchester, ☎ 802/867–5777) hosts a community group in winter and a resident professional troupe in summer. **Oldcastle Theatre Co.** (Southern Vermont College, Bennington, ☎ 802/447–0564) performs from April through October. **Weston Playhouse** (☎ 802/824–5288) is the oldest professional summer theater in Vermont. **Whetstone Theatre** (River Valley Playhouse, Putney, ☎ 802/387–5678) stages six productions from April through December.

Nightlife

Much of southern Vermont nightlife centers on Wilmington and the Mt. Snow ski area and around Manchester. During ski season you'll find live entertainment most nights; in summer it will be limited to weekends. Check local newspapers for listings.

Convenient to Bromley, the **Park Bench Café** (☎ 802/362–2557), in Manchester, has live entertainment on Friday and Saturday nights; **Avalanche** (Manchester, ☎ 802/362–2622) has a little of everything—country, blues, soft rock; and the **Marsh Tavern** (☎ 802/362–4700) at the Equinox Hotel has more subdued cabaret music and jazz Tuesday through Saturday in summer. **Mulligan's** (☎ 802/297–9293 and 802/362–3663) two locations are popular hang-out spots at both Stratton Mountain and in Manchester; they have American cuisine, and DJs and live bands in the late afternoon and on weekends. **Haig's** (☎ 802/297–1300) in Bondville, 5 miles from Stratton, has a unique indoor simulated golf course for those who can't wait for summer. **The Red Fox Inn** (☎ 802/297–2488), also 5 miles from Stratton, has a DJ and occasional live music in the tavern.

At **Poncho's Wreck** (Wilmington, ☎ 802/464–9320), in the Mt. Snow area, acoustic jazz or mellow rock is the standard lineup. The **Snow Barn** (☎ 802/464–3333), near the base of the resort, has live entertainment weekends during the season; a little farther down Route 100, **Deacon's Den Tavern** (☎ 802/464–9361) and the **Sitzmark** (☎ 802/464–3384) have live bands on weekends. For a quieter après-ski experience, there's **Le Petit Chef** (☎ 802/464–8437) or the **Dover Forge** (☎ 802/464–2114).

In Brattleboro, the **Mole's Eye Cafe** (☎ 802/257–0771; cover charge, Fri.–Sat.) has live bands: perhaps acoustic or folk on Wednesday, danceable R&B, blues, or reggae weekends; **Common Ground** (☎ 802/257–0855) often has folk or performance art on weekends.

Southern Vermont Essentials

Getting Around
BY BUS
Vermont Transit (☎ 802/864–6811, 800/451–3292, or, in VT, 800/642–3133) links Bennington, Manchester, Brattleboro, and Bellows Falls.

BY CAR
In the south the principal east–west highway is Route 9, the Molly Stark Trail, from Brattleboro to Bennington. The most important north–south roads are Route 7; the more scenic Route 7A; Route 100, which runs through the state's center; I–91; and Route 5, which runs along the state's eastern border. Route 30 from Brattleboro to Manchester is a scenic drive. All routes are heavily traveled during peak tourist seasons.

BY TRAIN
In Bellows Falls, on the Connecticut River at the eastern edge of the state, you can board the **Green Mountain Flyer** for a 26-mile two-hour round-trip to Chester's restored 1872 train station. The journey, in superbly restored cars that date from the golden age of railroading, takes you through scenic countryside past covered bridges and along the Brockway Mills gorge. You can also start your journey from the Chester depot. A six-hour tour is also offered, in fall only. *Island St. off Bridge St. (Rte. 12)*, ☎ 802/463–3069. ☛ *2-hr. trip: $10 adults, $6 children 3–12.* ☉ *Mid-June–early Sept., Tues.–Sun.; early Sept.–mid Oct., daily. Train departs 11, 12:10, 2:00; call to confirm.*

Important Addresses and Numbers
EMERGENCIES
Brattleboro Memorial Hospital (9 Belmont Ave., ☎ 802/257–0341).

VISITOR INFORMATION
Bennington Area Chamber of Commerce (Veterans Memorial Dr., Bennington 05201, ☎ 802/447–3311; ☉ Weekdays 9–5). **Brattleboro Chamber of Commerce** (180 Main St., Brattleboro 05301, ☎ 802/254–4565; ☉ Weekdays 8–5). **Chamber of Commerce, Manchester and the Mountains** (Adams Park Green, Box 928, Manchester 05255, ☎ 802/362–2100; ☉ Weekdays 9–5, Sat. 10–4). **Mt. Snow/Haystack Region Chamber of Commerce** (E. Main St., Box 3, Wilmington 05363, ☎ 802/

464–8092; ⊗ Weekdays 9–noon and 1–4:45). **Windsor Area Chamber of Commerce** (Box 5, Windsor 05089, ☎ 802/672–5910; ⊗ Weekdays 9–5).

CENTRAL VERMONT

Service jobs in tourism and recreation have increased while those in manufacturing have dwindled in central Vermont. Although some industry is still found, particularly in the west around Rutland, the state's second-largest city, it is the southern tip of Lake Champlain—as well as many other, smaller lakes—and several major ski resorts, that really make the area economically viable. Local trademarks include the state's famed marble quarries, just north of Rutland, and large dairy herds and pastures that create the quilted patchwork of the Champlain Valley. The heart of the area is the Green Mountains, running up the state's spine, and the surrounding wilderness of the Green Mountain National Forest, which offers countless opportunities for outdoor recreation and soulful pondering of the region's intense natural beauty—even for those inclined not to venture beyond the confines of their vehicles.

Exploring

Numbers in the margin correspond to points of interest on the Central Vermont map.

Our tour begins in Windsor, on Route 5 near I–91, at the eastern edge of the state, winds westward toward Route 100, up along the spine of the Green Mountains, and crosses over the ridge at two points, both inspiring passes.

❶ **Windsor** was the delivery room for the birth of Vermont. The **Old Constitution House,** where, in 1777, grant holders declared Vermont an independent republic, was moved to its present site, where it contains 18th- and 19th-century furnishings, American paintings and prints, and Vermont-made tools, toys, and kitchenware. *Rte. 5, ☎ 802/674–6628. ☛ $1. ⊗ Late May–mid-Oct., Wed.–Sun. 10–4.*

The firm of Robbins & Lawrence became famous for applying the "American system"—the use of interchangeable parts—to the manufacture of rifles. Although the company no longer exists, the **American Precision Museum,** in the restored 1846 Windsor House, extols the Yankee ingenuity that created a major machine-tool industry here in the 19th century. The museum contains the largest collection of historically significant machine tools in the country. The Windsor House also houses the **Vermont State Crafts Center** (☎ 802/674–6729), a gallery of juried, skillfully made Vermont crafts. *196 Main St., ☎ 802/674–5781. ☛ $2 adults, 75¢ children 6–12. ⊗ Weekdays 9–5, weekends and holidays 10–4.*

The **covered bridge** just off Route 5 that spans the Connecticut River between Windsor and Cornish, New Hampshire, is—at 460 feet—the longest in the state.

❷ The industrial town of **White River Junction,** on the Connecticut River 14 miles north of Windsor, is the home of the **Catamount Brewery,** one of the state's several microbreweries. Catamount has become immensely popular in the Northeast; it brews golden ale, a British-style amber, a dark porter, and such seasonal specialties as a hearty Christmas ale. Samples are available at the tour's conclusion, and there's a company store. *58 S. Main St., ☎ 802/296–2248. ☛ Free. ⊗ Mon.–Sat. 9–5, Sun. 1–5. 3 tours Mon.–Sat., 2 tours Sun.*

A bit farther north along Route 5 or I–91 is **Norwich,** just across the river from Dartmouth College. There's a model of the original 1791 Oliver Evans Mill and historic photographs of flour being delivered by horsecart in the **King Arthur Flour Baker's Store** (Rte. 5, Norwich, ☎ 802/649–3361), both a museum and a retail outlet for all things baking-oriented, including baking tools and hard-to-find grains and specialty flours. The company has been in business since 1790.

The new **Montshire Museum of Science** has numerous hands-on exhibits that explore space, nature, and technology; there are also living habitats, several aquariums, many children's programs, and a maze of trails to investigate its 100 acres of pristine woodland. One of the finest museums in New England, it's an ideal destination for a rainy day. *Montshire Rd., Box 170,* ☎ *802/649–2200.* ☛ *$5 adults; $3 children 3–17.* ☉ *Daily 10–5.*

TIME OUT   **Jasper Murdock's Alehouse** (☎ 802/649–1143), America's smallest brewery, serves hearty fare in addition to its home-brewed stouts, porters, and ales in the 1797 Norwich Inn on Main Street.

❸   **Quechee,** 6 miles west of White River Junction, is perched astride the Ottauquechee River. Nearby, 165-foot-deep **Quechee Gorge** is impressive, though overrun by tourists. You can see the mile-long gorge, carved by a glacier, from Route 4, but many visitors picnic nearby or scramble down one of several descents for a closer look. More than a decade ago **Simon Pearce** set up an eponymous glassblowing factory in an old mill by the bank of a waterfall here, using the water power to drive his furnace. The glass studio produces exquisite wares and houses a pottery workshop, a shop, and a restaurant; visitors can watch the artisans at work. *Main St.,* ☎ *802/295–2711.* ☉ *Workshops: weekdays 10–5; store: daily 9–9.*

❹   Four miles east of Quechee on Route 4, **Woodstock** realizes virtually every expectation of a quaint New England town (except for the crowds). Perfectly preserved Federal houses surround the tree-lined village green, and streams flow around the town center, which is anchored by a covered bridge. The town owes much of its pristine appearance to the Rockefeller family's keen interest in historic preservation and land conservation.

Other town shapers include the 19th-century forerunner to modern environmentalism, George Perkins Marsh, who is credited largely with the creation of the Smithsonian Institute in Washington, D.C., and Frederick Billings, for whom the **Billings Farm and Museum** is named. Exhibits in the reconstructed Queen Anne farmhouse, school, general store, workshop, and former Marsh homestead demonstrate the lives and skills of early Vermont settlers. Splitting logs doesn't seem nearly so quaint when you've watched the effort that goes into it! *Rte. 12, ½ mi north of Woodstock,* ☎ *802/457–2355.* ☛ *$6 adults, $3.50 children 6–12.* ☉ *Early May–late Oct., daily 10–5.*

Period furnishings of the Woodstock Historical Society fill the rooms of the white clapboard **Dana House** (ca. 1807). Exhibits include the town charter, furniture, maps, and locally minted silver. The elaborate sleigh once owned by Frederick Billings, displayed in the barn, conjures up visions of romantic rides through the snow. *26 Elm St.,* ☎ *802/ 457–1822.* ☛ *$3.50 adults, $2.50 senior citizens, $1 children 12–18.* ☉ *May–late Oct., Mon.–Sat. 10–5, Sun. 2–5.*

Near Woodstock, the **Raptor Center** of the **Vermont Institute of Natural Science** houses 26 species of birds of prey, among them a bald eagle,

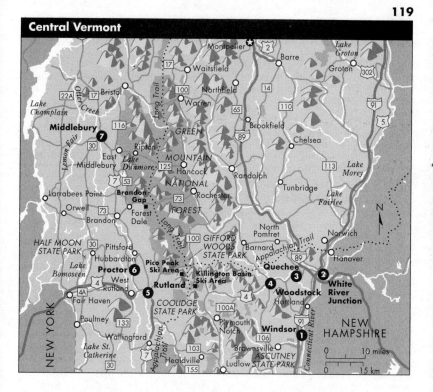

a peregrine falcon, and the 3-ounce saw-whet owl. All the caged birds have been found injured and unable to survive in the wild. This non-profit, environmental research and education center is on a 77-acre nature preserve with self-guided walking trails. *Church Hill Rd.,* ☎ *802/457–2779.* ☛ *$5 adults, $2 children 5–15.* ☉ *Daily 10–4; closed Sun, Nov.–Apr.*

TIME OUT Relax at one of the outdoor tables at the **Dunham Hill Bakery** (Central St.) and enjoy a light lunch or pastry and cappuccino.

Former U.S. President Calvin Coolidge was born and buried in **Plymouth Notch,** a town that shares his character: low-key and quiet. South of Route 4 on Route 100A, the small cluster of state-owned buildings looks more like a large farm than a town; in addition to the homestead there's the general store once run by Coolidge's father, a visitor center, an operating cheese factory, a one-room schoolhouse, and the former summer White House. Coolidge's grave is in the cemetery across Route 100A. *Rte. 100A, 6 mi south of Rte. 4, east of Rte. 100,* ☎ *802/672–3773.* ☛ *$3.50 adults, children under 12 free.* ☉ *Memorial Day–mid-Oct., daily 9:30–5:30.*

The intersection of Routes 4 and 100 is at the heart of central Vermont's ski country, with the Killington, Pico, and Okemo resorts nearby. For a side trip into the area's principal city, **Rutland,** continue west 10 miles on Route 4.

❺ In **Rutland** the homes of blue-collar workers vastly outnumber the mansions of the marble magnates who made the town famous, as do strips of shopping centers and a seemingly endless row of traffic lights. Rutland's traditional economic ties to railroading and marble, the latter an industry that supplied stone to such illustrious dwellings as the central research building of the New York Public Library in New York City, have been rapidly eclipsed by the growth of the Pico and Killington ski areas to the east.

 The highlight of the area is the **Vermont Marble Exhibit,** 4 miles north of Rutland in **Proctor,** where visitors can not only watch the sculptor-in-residence transform stone into finished works of art, but can also choose first-hand the marble they want to use for their custom-built kitchen counter. The gallery illustrates various industrial applications of marble—note the hall of presidents and the replica of Leonardo da Vinci's *Last Supper* in marble—and depicts the industry's history via exhibits and slide shows. You can buy factory seconds and both foreign and domestic marble items here, too. *62 Main St., Proctor (follow signs off Rte. 3),* ☎ *802/459–3311 or 802/459–2300 for orders.* ☛ *$3.50 adults, $1.50 children 6–12.* ☉ *Memorial Day–Oct., daily 9–5:30; Nov.–Memorial Day, Mon.–Sat. 9–4.*

The scenic drive north on Route 100 leads into the heart of the Green Mountains. The intersection of Routes 100 and 125 in Hancock has two of Vermont's most inspiring mountain drives. The shorter one runs west on Route 125, passing nature trails and the picnic spot at Texas Falls Recreation Area. It then traverses a moderately steep mountain pass before reaching Middlebury. This is Robert Frost country; Vermont's late poet laureate spent 23 summers at a farm just east of Ripton. The mustard-color buildings of Middlebury College's Breadloaf Campus are home of the renowned writer's conference begun by Frost; go a mile farther to hike the easy ¾-mile **Robert Frost Interpretive Trail,** which winds through quiet woodland. Plaques along the way bear quotations from Frost's poems. There's a picnic area across the road from the trailhead.

For a longer run, continue on Route 100 and, after snaking through the Granville Gulf Nature Reserve, enter the **Mad River Valley,** home to the Sugarbush and Mad River Glen ski areas. Although in close proximity to these popular resorts, the valley towns of **Warren** and **Waitsfield** have maintained a decidedly low-key atmosphere. The gently carved ridges cradling the valley and the swell of pastures and fields lining the river seem to keep further notions of ski-resort sprawl at bay. Pick up a map from the Sugarbush Chamber of Commerce (*see* Important Addresses and Numbers *in* Central Vermont Essentials, *below*) and investigate the back roads that spur off Route 100 for some exhilarating valley views.

TIME OUT The **Bridge Street Bakery** (Bridge St.) in Waitsfield has innovative soups, a variety of breads, and pastries that you can savor at tables outside while taking in the goings-on of a small town.

Route 17 winds westward up and over the Appalachian Gap, one of Vermont's most panoramic mountain passes: The views from the top and on the way down the other side toward the quiet town of Bristol are a just reward for the challenging drive.

In the late 1800s **Middlebury** was the largest Vermont community west of the Green Mountains: an industrial center of river-powered wool, grain, and marble mills. Otter Creek, the state's longest river, traverses the town center. Still a cultural and economic hub amid the Champlain Valley's serene pastoral patchwork, the town and countryside beckon a day of exploration.

Smack in the middle of town, **Middlebury College** (☎ 802/388–3711), founded in 1800, was conceived as an accessible alternative to the more worldly University of Vermont—although the two schools have since traded reputations. The provocative contrast of early 19th-century stone buildings against the postmodern architecture of the Fine Arts Building and sports center make for an opinion-provoking campus stroll. The **Johnson Memorial Art Gallery** has a permanent collection of paintings and sculpture that includes work by Rodin and Hiram Powers. *Fine Arts Bldg.,* ☎ *802/388–3711, ext. 5235.* ☛ *Free.* ⊙ *Tues.–Fri. 10–5, weekends noon–5.*

The **Vermont Folklife Center** is in the basement of the restored 1801 home of Gamaliel Painter, the founder of Middlebury College. The rotating exhibits explore all facets of Vermont life using means as diverse as contemporary photography, antiques, paintings by folk artists, and manuscripts. *2 Court St.,* ☎ *802/388–4964.* ☛ *Donations accepted.* ⊙ *Weekdays 9–5 and, May–Oct., Sat. noon–4.*

Take the guided tour at the **Sheldon Museum,** an 1829 marble-merchant's house whose period rooms contain furniture, toys, clothes, kitchen tools, and paintings that span from colonial times to the early 20th century. *1 Park St.,* ☎ *802/388–2117.* ☛ *$3.50 adults, $3 senior citizens and students, 50¢ children under 12.* ⊙ *June–Oct., Mon.–Sat. 10–5; Nov.–May, weekdays 10–5.*

TIME OUT Calvi's (Merchants Row, Middlebury) has an old-fashioned marble-counter soda fountain and an extensive menu of ice-cream dishes.

More than a crafts store, the **Vermont State Craft Center at Frog Hollow** is a juried display of the work of more than 250 Vermont artisans. The center sponsors classes with some of those artists. *Mill St.,* ☎ *802/388–3177.* ⊙ *Jan.–May, Mon.–Sat. 9:30–5; June–Dec., Mon.–Sat. 9:30–5, Sun. noon–5.*

The Morgan horse—the official state animal—is known for its even temper and stamina even though its legs are a bit truncated in proportion to its body. The University of Vermont's **Morgan Horse Farm,** about 2½ miles from Middlebury, is a breeding and training farm where, in summer, you can tour the stables and paddocks. *Follow the sign off Rte. 23,* ☎ *802/388–2011.* ☛ *$3.50 adults, $1 children 13–19.* ⊙ *May–Oct., daily 9–4:30; Nov.–Apr., weekdays 9–4:30, Sat. 9–noon.*

What to See and Do with Children

Icelandic Horse Farm, Waitsfield
Morgan Horse Farm, Middlebury
Montshire Museum of Science, Norwich
Raptor Center, Woodstock

Off the Beaten Path

Crossing the **floating bridge at Brookfield** feels like driving on water. The bridge, supported by almost 400 barrels, sits at water level and is the scene of the annual ice harvest festival in January (the bridge is closed in winter). Take Route 65 off I–89 to Brookfield and follow the signs.

The **Green Mountain Audubon Nature Center** (Huntington-Richmond Rd., Richmond, ☎ 802/434–3068) bursts with great things to do, see, and learn; this is a wonderful place to orient yourself to Vermont's outdoor wonders. The center's 230 acres of diverse habitats are a sanctuary for all things wild, and the 5 miles of trails beg you to explore and understand the workings of differing natural communities. The center offers such events as dusk walks, wildflower and birding rambles, nature workshops, and educational activities for both kids and adults.

Shopping

Shopping Districts

Historic Marble Works (Middlebury, ☎ 802/388–3701), a renovated marble manufacturing facility, is a collection of unique shops set amid quarrying equipment and factory buildings. **The Marketplace at Bridgewater Mills** (Rte. 4, west of Woodstock, ☎ 802/672–3332), set in a three-story converted woolen mill, houses such crafts boutiques as Vermont Clock Craft and Vermont Marble, as well as The Mountain Brewers, producers of Long Trail Ale, where tours and tastings are available. **Timber Rail Village** (Rte. 4, Quechee, ☎ 802/295–1550) bills itself as an antiques mall and stocks inventory from 225 dealers in its immense reconstructed barn. A small-scale working railroad will take the kids for a ride while Mom and Dad browse.

Food and Drink

Bristol Market (28 North St., Bristol, ☎ 802/453–2448), open since the early 1900s, proffers gourmet health foods and local products. **Green Mountain Coffee Roasters** (Mad River Green, Waitsfield. ☎ 802/496–5470), utopia for coffee lovers, has beans from all the world that are roasted in their Waterbury headquarters. **The Village Butcher** (Elm St., Woodstock, ☎ 802/457–2756) is an emporium of Vermont comestibles.

Specialty Stores

ART AND ANTIQUES

The **Antiques Center at Hartland** (Rte. 5, Hartland, ☎ 802/436–2441), one of the best known in Vermont, displays, in two 18th-century houses, inventory from 50 dealers. The **Chaffee Art Gallery** (16 S. Main St., ☎ 802/775–0356) exhibits and sells the work of more than 250 Vermont artists who work in a variety of media. **Luminosity** (Rte. 100, Waitsfield, ☎ 802/496–2231) is in a converted church and, fittingly, specializes in stained glass, among other wares. **Minerva** (61 Central St., Woodstock, ☎ 802/457–1940) is a cooperative of eight artisans whose work includes stoneware, porcelain, and jewelry, as well as handwoven clothing, rugs, and blankets. **North Wind Artisans' Gallery** (81 Central St., Woodstock, ☎ 802/457–4587) has contemporary, mostly Vermont-made, artwork with sleek, jazzy designs. **Windsor Antiques Market** (53 N. Main St., Windsor, ☎ 802/674–9336) occupies a Gothic Revival church and sells Oriental, Native American, and military items in addition to American furniture, folk art, and accessories.

BOOKS

Charles E. Tuttle (28 S. Main St., Rutland, ☎ 802/773–8930) is a major publisher of books on Asia, particularly Asian art. In addition to its own publications, Tuttle has rare and out-of-print books, genealogies, and local histories.

CLOTHING

Scotland by the Yard (Rte. 4, Quechee, ☎ 802/295–5351) has authentic Scottish kilts, kilt pins in imaginative designs, and jewelry bearing traditional Scottish emblems and symbols. **Who Is Sylvia?** (26 Central St., Woodstock, ☎ 802/457–1110) stocks vintage clothing and antique linens and jewelry.

CRAFTS

All Things Bright and Beautiful (Bridge St., Waitsfield, ☎ 802/496–3997) is a 12-room Victorian house jammed to the rafters with stuffed animals of all shapes, sizes, and colors. **East Meets West** (Rte. 7 at Sangamon Rd., north of Rutland, ☎ 802/443–2242) shows carvings, masks, statues, textiles, pottery, and baskets from the Third World, the American Southwest, the Pacific Northwest, and the Arctic. **Folkheart** (18 Main St., Bristol, ☎ 802/453–4101; 71 Main St., Middlebury, ☎ 802/388–0367) carries an unusual selection of jewelry, toys, and crafts from around the world. **Holy Cow** (52 Seymour St., Middlebury, ☎ 802/388–6737) is where Woody Jackson creates and sells his infamous Holstein cattle-inspired T-shirts and memorabilia. **Log Cabin Quilts** (9 Central St., Woodstock, ☎ 802/457–2725) has an outstanding collection of quilts in traditional designs and supplies. **Warren Village Pottery** (Main St., Warren, ☎ 802/496–4162) sells unique, handcrafted wares from its home-based retail shop.

Skiing

Ascutney Mountain Resort
Rte. 44 (Box 699), Brownsville 05037
☎ *802/484–7711; lodging, 800/243–0011*

Rescued by an extraordinary auction, Ascutney launched its 1993–94 season after being closed for several years due to bankruptcy. It's now owned by the Plausteiner family, whose patriarch, John, was instrumental in operations at Mt. Snow, Vermont, and White Face Mountain in Lake Placid, New York. Now with a low debt load, Ascutney's future is much brighter, with its real estate development—once its downfall—now its centerpiece. There's a resort village in five buildings, with hotel suites and condominium units spread throughout. Perhaps the best feature for weary travelers is that the resort is right off I–91.

DOWNHILL
Thirty-one trails with varying terrain are covered by nearly 65% snow-making. Like a stereotypical ski mountain cutout, this one reaches a wide peak, and gently slopes to the bottom. Beginner and novice skiers stay toward the base, while intermediates enjoy the band that wraps the mid-section; and for experts there are tougher black diamond runs topping the mountain. One disadvantage to Ascutney, however, is that there is no easy way down from the summit, so novice skiers should not make the trip. For intermediate and advanced skiers, though, the Summit Chair is an enjoyable ride up. Trails are serviced by one double and three triple chairs. Ascutney is popular with families because it offers some of the least expensive junior lift tickets in the region.

CROSS-COUNTRY
There are 32 kilometers (18 miles) of groomed cross-country trails at the resort; lessons, clinics, and rentals are provided.

OTHER ACTIVITIES
Ascutney Mountain Resort Hotel has its own sports and fitness center with full-size indoor and outdoor pools, racquetball, aerobics facilities and classes, weight training, and massage, as well as ice skating on the pond. Conference facilities can accommodate up to 400 people.

CHILD CARE
Day care is available for children ages 6 months to 6 years, with learn-to-ski options and rental equipment available for toddlers and up (children 6 and under ski free). There are half- and full-day instruction programs for children 3–6.

Killington
400 Killington Rd., Killington 05751
☎ *802/422–3333; lodging, 800/621–6867; snow conditions, 802/422–3261*

"Megamountain," "Beast of the East," and just plain "huge" are appropriate descriptions of Killington. Despite its extensive facilities and terrain, lift lines on weekends (especially holiday weekends) can be downright dreadful. It has the longest ski season in the East and some of the best package plans anywhere. With a single telephone call skiers can select price, date, and type of ski week they want; choose accommodations; book air or railroad transportation; and arrange for rental equipment and ski lessons.

DOWNHILL

It would probably take a skier a week to test all 155 trails on the six mountains of the Killington complex, even though everything interconnects. About 63% of the 829 acres of skiing can be covered with machine-made snow, and that's still more snowmaking than any other area in the world can manage. Transporting skiers to the peaks of this complex are a 3½-mile gondola plus seven quads, four triples, and five double chairlifts, as well as two surface lifts. That's a total of 19 ski lifts, a few of which reach the area's highest elevation, at 4,220 feet off Killington Peak, and a vertical drop of 3,150 feet to the base of the gondola. The range of skiing includes everything from Outer Limits, one of the steepest and most challenging trails anywhere in the country, to the 10-mile-long, super-gentle Juggernaut Trail.

OTHER ACTIVITIES

Killington proper is for skiing; the Cortina Inn (802/773–3333) has an ice-skating rink with rentals and offers sleigh rides from 6–9 PM; you can also skate on Summit Pond (802/422–4476).

CHILD CARE

Nursery care is available for children from infants to 8 years old. There's a one-hour instruction program for youngsters 3–8; those 6–12 can join an all-day program, with a break for lunch.

Mad River Glen
Rte. 17, Waitsfield 05673
☎ 802/496–3551; snow conditions, 802/496–2001 or 800/696–2001

Mad River Glen was developed in the late 1940s and has changed relatively little since then; the single chairlift may be the only lift of its vintage still carrying skiers. There is an unkempt aura about this place that for 40 years has attracted a devoted group of skiers from wealthy families in the East as well as rugged individualists looking for a less-polished terrain. Remember that most of Mad River's trails (85%) are covered only by natural snow. The apt area motto is "Ski It If You Can."

DOWNHILL

Mad River is steep. Terrain changes constantly on 33 interactive trails, of which 75% are intermediate to superexpert. Intermediate and novice terrain are regularly groomed. Four chairs (including the famed single) service the mountain's 2,000-foot vertical.

CHILD CARE

The nursery (☎ 802/496–2123) takes children 3 weeks to 5 years, while the ski school has classes for children 4–12. Junior racing is available weekends and during holiday periods.

Pico Ski Resort
2 Sherburne Pass, Rutland 05701
☎ 802/775–4346; snow conditions, 802/775–4345; lodging, 800/848–7325

Although it's only 5 miles down the road from Killington, venerable Pico has long been a favorite among people looking for uncrowded, wide-open cruiser skiing. When modern lifts were installed and a village square was constructed at the base, some feared that friendly patina would be threatened, but the relatively new condo-hotel, restaurants, and shops have not altered the essential nature of Pico.

DOWNHILL

From the area's 4,000-foot summit, most of the trails are advanced to expert, with two intermediate bail-out trails for the timid. The rest of the mountain's 2,000 feet of vertical terrain is mostly intermediate or easier. The lifts for these slopes and trails are two high-speed quads, two triples, and three double chairs, plus two surface lifts. The area has 82% snowmaking coverage.

CROSS-COUNTRY

Mountain Meadows (☎ 802/775–7077) has 40 kilometers of groomed trails and 10 kilometers of marked outlying trails; Mountain Top (☎ 802/483–6089) is mammoth with 120 kilometers of trails, 80 of which are groomed.

OTHER ACTIVITIES

A sports center (☎ 802/773–1786) at the base of the mountain has fitness facilities, a 75-foot pool, whirlpool tub, saunas, and a massage room.

CHILD CARE

The nursery takes children from 6 months through 6 years old and provides indoor activities and outdoor play. The ski school has full- and half-day instruction programs for children 3–12.

Sugarbush

Box 350, Warren 05674
☎ 802/583–2381; lodging, 800/537–8427; snow conditions, 802/583–7669

In the early 1960s Sugarbush had the reputation of being an outpost of an affluent and sophisticated crowd from New York. While that reputation has faded, Sugarbush has maintained a with-it attitude—not that anyone would feel uncomfortable here. The resort, recently bought by LBO Holdings, which also owns Sunday River in Maine and Attitash in New Hampshire, is undergoing quite a few changes. Snowmaking should be increasing to more than 70% coverage by the 1996 season, with the installation of a new state-of-the-art, computer-controlled system that the resort has fought long and hard for: Environmental restrictions, land-use permits, and the fact that part of the resort is on National Forest land have made acquiring the snowmaking capacity enjoyed by other major resorts difficult. The base of the mountain has a village of condominiums, restaurants, shops, bars, and a sports center.

DOWNHILL

Sugarbush is two distinct mountain complexes. The Sugarbush South area is what old-timers recall as Sugarbush Mountain: With a vertical of 2,400 feet, it is known for formidable steeps toward the top and in front of the main base lodge. South has three triple, four double, and two surface lifts that together serve 110 trails. Sugarbush North offers what South has in short supply—beginner runs. North also has steep fall-line pitches and intermediate cruisers off its 2,600 vertical feet. This mountain has three quads (including a high-speed version), two double chairlifts, and two surface lifts. Snowmaking at Sugarbush South is now up to 57%, greatly improving early and late season skiing. By 1996, favorite runs, including Castlerock, Twist, and Middle

Earth will be covered. There are plans to connect the two mountains with a horizontal "people mover" by the 1996 season.

CROSS-COUNTRY
More than 25 kilometers (15 miles) of groomed cross-country trails are adjacent to the Sugarbush Inn. **Blueberry Lake** cross-country ski area (Plunkton Rd., Warren, ☎ 802/496–6687) has 23 kilometers of groomed trails through thickly wooded glades. **Ole's** (Airport Rd., Warren, ☎ 802/496–3430) runs a cross-country center out of the tiny Warren airport; it has 64 kilometers of trails—42 groomed—that span out into the surrounding woods from the open fields of the landing strips.

OTHER ACTIVITIES
A sports center (Sugarbush Sports Center, ☎ 802/583–2391) near the ski lifts has Nautilus and Universal equipment; tennis, squash, and racquetball courts; whirlpool, sauna, and steam rooms; and two indoor pools. A smaller sports center (The Pavilion, ☎ 802/538–2605) has all the activities listed above save the racquet sports. The town of Waitsfield recently built a new skating rink (☎ 802/496–9199) and intends to put a lid on it soon for skating year-round. **Lareau Farm** (Rte. 100, Waitsfield, ☎ 802/496–4949) has a 100-year-old sleigh that cruises along the Mad River.

CHILD CARE
The Sugarbush Day School accepts children ages 6 weeks through 6 years; older children have indoor play and outdoor excursions. There's half- and full-day instruction available for children ages 4–11.

Suicide Six
Woodstock 05091
☎ *802/457–1666; lodging, 800/448–7900; snow conditions, 802/457–1622*

Suicide Six, site of the first ski tow in the United States (1934), is owned and operated by the Woodstock Inn and Resort. The inn, in lovely Woodstock Village, 3 miles from the ski area, offers package plans that are remarkably inexpensive, considering the high quality of the accommodations. In addition to skiers interested in exploring Woodstock, the area attracts students and racers from nearby Dartmouth College.

DOWNHILL
Despite Suicide Six's short vertical of only 650 feet, there is challenging skiing here: There are several steep runs down the mountain's face and intermediate trails that wind around the hill. Beginner terrain is mostly toward the bottom. The 19 trails are serviced by two double chairlifts and one surface lift.

CROSS-COUNTRY
The ski touring center has 60 kilometers (37 miles) of trails. Equipment and lessons are available.

OTHER ACTIVITIES
A sports center at the Woodstock Inn and Resort (☎ 802/457–1100) has an indoor lap pool; indoor tennis, squash, and racquetball courts; whirlpool, steam, sauna, and massage rooms; and exercise and aerobics rooms.

CHILD CARE
Although the ski area has no nursery, baby-sitting can be arranged through the Woodstock Inn if you're a guest; lessons for children are given by the ski-school staff. There's a children's ski-and-play park for those ages 3–7.

Other Sports

Biking

The popular 14-mile Waitsfield–Warren loop begins when you cross the covered bridge in Waitsfield. Keep right on East Warren Road to the four-way intersection in East Warren; continue straight, then bear right, riding down Brook Road to the village of Warren; return by turning right (north) on Route 100 back toward Waitsfield. **Mad River Bike Shop** (Rte. 100, Waitsfield, ☎ 802/496–9500) offers rentals, mountain bike tours, and maps.

A more challenging, 32-mile ride starts in Bristol: Take North Street from the traffic light in town and continue north to Monkton Ridge and on to Hinesburg; to return, follow Route 116 south through Starksboro and back to Bristol. The **Bike and Ski Touring Center** (74 Main St., Middlebury, ☎ 802/388–6666) offers rentals.

A bike trail runs alongside Route 106 south of Woodstock. Visit **Cyclery Plus** (36 Rte. 4 W, West Woodstock, ☎ 802/457–3377) to rent equipment and get help planning an extended trip in the area.

Canoeing

Otter Falls Outfitters (Marble Works, Middlebury, ☎ 802/388–4406) has maps, guides, and gear. **North Star Canoes** (Balloch's Crossing, ☎ 603/542–5802) in Cornish, New Hampshire, rents canoes for half-day, full-day, and overnight trips on the Connecticut River.

Fishing

Central Vermont is the heart of the state's warm-water lake and pond fishing. **Lake Dunmore** produced the state-record rainbow trout; **Lakes Bomoseen** and **St. Catherine** are good for rainbows and largemouth bass. In the east, **Lakes Fairlee** and **Morey** feature bass, perch, and chain pickerel, while the lower part of the **Connecticut River** has bass, pickerel, walleye, and perch. **The Vermont Fly Fishing School** (Quechee Inn, Clubhouse Rd., Quechee 05059, ☎ 802/295–7620) provides workshops, and **Yankee Charters** (20 S. Pleasant St., Middlebury 05753, ☎ 802/388–7365) sets up trips on Lake Champlain; both rent gear.

Golf

Spectacular views and challenging play are the trademarks of the Robert Trent Jones–designed 18-hole course at **Sugarbush Resort** (Golf Course Rd., Warren, ☎ 802/583–2722). Jones also designed the 18-hole course at **Woodstock Country Club** (South St., Woodstock, ☎ 802/457–2112), run by the Woodstock Inn.

Hiking

Several day hikes in the vicinity of Middlebury take in the Green Mountains. About 8 miles east of Brandon on Route 73, one trail starts at Brandon Gap and climbs steeply up **Mt. Horrid** (1 hour). On Route 116, about 5½ miles north of East Middlebury, a U.S. Forest Service sign marks a dirt road that forks to the right and leads to the start of the hike to **Abbey Pond,** which has a view of Robert Frost Mountain (two–three hours).

About 5½ miles north of Forest Dale on Route 53, a large turnout marks a trail to the **Falls of Lana** (two hours). Three other trails—two short ones of less than a mile each and one of 2½ miles—lead to the old abandoned fortifications at **Mt. Independence;** to reach them, take Route 22A west of Orwell for 3½ miles and continue on the right fork almost 2 miles to a parking area.

Horseback Riding
Kedron Valley Stables (Rte. 106, S. Woodstock, ☎ 802/457–2734) has lessons and guided trail rides.

Polo
Quechee Polo Club (Dewey's Mill Rd., ½ mi off Route 4, Quechee, ☎ 802/295–7152) draws several hundred spectators on summer Saturdays to its matches near the Quechee Gorge. Admission is $2 adults, $1 children, or $5 per car.

Recreation Areas
At **Suicide Six,** outdoor tennis courts, lighted paddle courts, croquet, and an 18-hole golf course are available in the summer.

Water Sports
There are many lakes in the western region of the state including Bomoseen, St. Catherine, Dunmore, the Chittenden Resevoir, and of course, Lake Champlain. Rent boats from **Chipman Point Marina** (Rte. 73A, Middlebury, ☎ 802/948–2288), where there is dockage for 60 boats.

State Parks

The following state parks have camping and picnicking facilities: **Ascutney State Park** (Rte. 5, 2 mi north of I–91 [Exit 8], ☎ 802/674–2060) has a scenic mountain toll road and snowmobile trails. **Coolidge State Park** (Rte. 100A, 2 mi north of Rte. 100, ☎ 802/672–3612), in Calvin Coolidge National Forest, includes the village where Calvin Coolidge was born and is great for snowmobiling. **Gifford Woods State Park**'s Kent Pond (Rte. 100, ½ mi north of Rte. 4, ☎ 802/775–5354) is a terrific fishing hole. **Half Moon State Park**'s principal attraction is Half Moon Pond (Town Rd., 3½ mi off Rte. 30 west of Hubbardton, ☎ 802/273–2848). The park has approach trails, nature trails, and a naturalist, as well as boat and canoe rentals.

Dining and Lodging

Country inns and bed-and-breakfasts abound in Woodstock and near the Sugarbush and Killington ski areas, although accommodations are found in even the smallest towns as well. The **Woodstock Area Chamber of Commerce** (☎ 802/457–2389) and **Sugarbush Reservations** (☎ 800/537–8427) provide lodging referral services.

Bristol
DINING

$$$ **Mary's at Baldwin Creek.** One of the most inspired eating experiences
★ in the state, Mary's is settling into its new location in a 1790 farmhouse on the outskirts of town. They have traded the intimate, yet somewhat cramped, quarters on Main Street for four distinct dining rooms that unfold each into the next. The "summer kitchen," with a blazing fireplace and rough-hewn barn-board walls, and the lighter, pastel-colored main room provide breathing room; secluded corner tables abound. The innovative, ever-changing cuisine includes a legendary garlic soup, Vermont rack of lamb with a rosemary-mustard sauce, duck cassis smoked over applewood, and Mako shark with a banana salsa. For dessert, the raspberry gratin is a favorite. Sunday brunch is a local ritual. ✗ *Rte. 116, north of Bristol,* ☎ *802/453–2432. Reservations advised. AE, MC, V. Closed Mon.*

Brookfield

DINING AND LODGING

$$–$$$ **Autumn Crest Inn.** Technically not in Brookfield, this inn is really out in the middle of nowhere atop a knoll that has a nearly 180-degree-view of a 46-acre work-horse farm and the surrounding valley. One could spend the whole day on the Queen Anne–style porch that graces the front of the 1790 inn, although both the dining and living rooms also have tremendous views. Early risers can see the sunrise in the winter. The overall feel of the inn is casual, like relaxing in a friend's living room. Guest rooms in the older part of the house have more character: the Davenport Room, highlighted with periwinkle hues, is named after Tom Davenport, who invented the electric engine and was born in this house. The newer section feels a bit too motel-like, although the suites are spacious and comfortable. The creative dinner menu is seasonal and often spotlights various ethnic cuisines. Seafood is predominant: Caribbean night often includes conch chowder and spicy lime chicken or shrimp curry. Breakfast might be peach-schnapps French toast or gingerbread pancakes. ☎ *RFD 1, Clark Rd., Box 150, Williamstown 05679,* ☎ *802/433–6627 or 800/339-6627. 18 rooms with bath. Dining room, pond, horseback riding, cross-country skiing, sleigh rides, 2 tennis courts. MAP. AE, MC, V. Reservations requested.* ☺ *Restaurant: Wed.–Sun.*

$–$$ **Green Trails Inn.** This inn comprises 1790 and 1830 farmhouses that
★ are the focal point of a sleepy, yet stubborn town that has voted several times to keep the village roads dirt and the nation's only wooden floating bridge still floating. Everything about this place is an expression of the friendliness of the innkeepers: The massive fieldstone fireplace that dominates the living and dining area of the inn is symbolic of the stalwart, down-to-earth hospitality. The rooms are furnished simply with quilts and a spattering of early American antiques. The meals (for guests only) are home-cooking at its best—Vermont chicken pie is a favorite. Taking a walk down a tree-shaded country road was never so pleasant. ☎ *Main St., 05036,* ☎ *802/276–3412 or 800/243–3412. 15 rooms, 9 with bath. Full breakfast included; MAP available in winter. Cross-country skiing, ski shop, sleigh rides. MC, V.*

Brownsville

DINING AND LODGING

$$–$$$$ **Ascutney Mountain Resort Hotel.** One of the big attractions of this five-
❄ building resort hotel–condo complex is that the lift is literally outside the main door. The comfortable, well-maintained hotel suites come in different configurations and sizes—some with kitchen, fireplace, and deck. Slope-side multilevel condos have three bedrooms, three baths, and private entries. The Ascutney Harvest Inn, an attractive restaurant serving Continental and traditional cuisine, is within the complex. ☎ *Box 699, Brownsville, 05037,* ☎ *802/484–7711 or 800/243–0011,* FAX *802/484–3117 or 800/243–0011. 240 suites and condos. Restaurant, 2 bars, health club, billiards. AE, MC, V.*

LODGING

$–$$ **Millbrook Bed and Breakfast.** This Victorian farmhouse, built in 1880,
★ is now directly across from the Ascutney ski slopes. Making après-ski idleness easy are the five sitting rooms, eclectically decorated with antiques and contemporary furnishings. ☎ *Rte. 44 (Box 410), Brownsville 05037,* ☎ *802/484–7283. 4 rooms with bath, 2 rooms share bath, 1 suite. Hot tub. Full breakfast and afternoon snacks included. MC, V.*

Killington/Pico

DINING AND LODGING

$$$ **Cortina Inn.** This large luxury lodge and miniresort is very comfortable
❄ and the location is prime. About two-thirds of the rooms have private
balconies, although the views aren't spectacular. Sleigh rides, ice skat-
ing, and guided snowmobile tours are some off-the-slopes activities.
The New England Culinary Institute is in residence. ☎ *Rte. 4, Mendon
05751,* ☎ *802/773–3331 or 800/451–6108,* FAX *802/775–6948. 98
rooms with bath. Restaurant, bar, outdoor hot tub, indoor pool, health
club, saunas, 8 tennis courts. AE, D, DC, MC, V.*

$$$ **Summit Lodge.** This rambling, rustic two-story country lodge on an
❄ access road, just 3 miles from Killington Peak, caters to a varied crowd
of ski enthusiasts who are warmly met by the lodge's mascots—a pair
of Saint Bernards. Country decor and antiques blend with modern conveniences to create a relaxed atmosphere. Two restaurants allow both
formal and informal dining. ☎ *Killington Rd., Killington 05751,* ☎
802/422–3535 or 800/635–6343, FAX *802/422–3536. 45 rooms with
bath, 2 suites. 2 restaurants, bar, fireplace lounge, pool, pond, hot tub,
massage, saunas, racquetball, ice-skating, recreation rooms, nightclub.
AE, DC, MC, V.*

$$ **The Inn at Long Trail.** This 1938 skier and hiker lodge is just ¼ mile
❄ from the Pico ski slopes and even closer to the Appalachian/Long
Trail. The unusual decor (i.e., massive boulders—inside the inn!), has
nature as a prevailing theme. Gaelic charm is on hand with Irish music,
darts, and Guinness always on tap. The Irish hospitality is extended
particulary toward end-to-end hikers who get a substantial break in
the rates. Dinner is served on weekends only. ☎ *Rte. 4 (Box 267), Killing-
ton 05751,* ☎ *802/775–7181 or 800/325–2540. 17 rooms with bath,
5 suites with fireplaces. MAP. MC, V.*

Middlebury

DINING AND LODGING

$$–$$$ **Swift House Inn.** The white-panel wainscoting, elaborately carved ma-
★ hogany and marble fireplaces, and cherry paneling in the dining room
give this Georgian home of a 19th-century governor and his philan-
thropist daughter a formal elegance. Rooms, each with Oriental rugs
and nine of them with fireplaces, are decorated with such antique re-
productions as canopy beds, swag curtains, and clawfoot tubs. Some
bathrooms have double whirlpool tubs. Rooms in the house by the road
suffer from street noise. In the dining room, the adventurous menu might
include angel-hair pasta with imported mushrooms in a macadamia
pesto sauce, or smoked pheasant salad with a raspberry vinaigrette.
☎ *25 Stewart La., 05753,* ☎ *802/388–9925,* FAX *802/388–9927. 21
rooms with bath. Restaurant, pub, sauna, steam room. MAP. AE, D,
MC, V.*

$$ **Waybury Inn.** The Waybury Inn may look familiar; it appeared as the
"Stratford Inn" on television's *Newhart.* Guest rooms, some of which
have the awkward configuration that can result from the conversion
of a building of the early 1800s, have quilted pillows, antique furnishings,
and middle-age plumbing. Comfortable sofas around the fireplace create a homey living room, and the pub—which serves more than 100
different kinds of beer—is a favorite local gathering spot. ☎ *Rte. 125,
05740,* ☎ *802/388–4015 or 800/348–1810. 14 rooms with bath.
Restaurant, pub. AE, MC, V.*

Quechee

DINING

$$$ **Simon Pearce.** Candlelight, sparkling glassware from the studio down-
stairs, contemporary dinnerware, exposed brick, and large windows that

No matter where you go, travel is easier when you know the code.^{SM}

dial **1 8 0 0**
C A L L
A T T®

AT&T **Phone**

Dial 1 800 CALL ATT and you'll always get through from any phone with any card* and you'll always get AT&T's best deal.** It's the one number to remember when calling away from home.

*Other long distance company calling cards excluded.
**Additional discounts available.

AT&T
Your True Choice

overlook the roaring Ottauquechee River below coalesce to form an ideal setting. Sesame-crusted tuna with noodle cakes and wasabi and roast duck with mango chutney sauce are specialties of the house; more than 700 choices on the wine list assure finding that perfect vintage. ✗ *Main St.,* ☎ *802/295–1470. Reservations advised. AE, MC, V.*

DINING AND LODGING

$$–$$$ **Parker House.** The spacious peach-and-blue rooms of this renovated
★ 1857 Victorian mansion are named for former residents: Emily boasts a marble fireplace and an iron-and-brass bed; the armoire and dressing table in Rebecca have delicate faux inlays; Walter is the smallest room; and Joseph has a spectacular view of the Ottauquechee River. All rooms on the third floor are air-conditioned. Lace window panels, high-back chairs, and traditional wall stenciling enhance the dining room's elegant atmosphere. The menu features such entrées as roast local rabbit with homemade plum chutney as well as lighter bistro fare. In warm weather, there is dining on the terrace with its spectacular river view. 🏠 *16 Main St., Box 0780, 05059,* ☎ *802/295–6077. 7 rooms with bath. MAP. MC, V.*

LODGING

$$–$$$ **Quechee Bed and Breakfast.** Dried herbs hang from the beams in the
★ living room, where a wood settee sits before a floor-to-ceiling fireplace that dates to the original structure of 1795. In the guest rooms, hand-woven throws cover the beds and soft pastels coordinate linens and decor. Jessica's Room is the smallest; the Bird Room, with its exposed beams, is one of four that overlook the Ottauquechee River. Rooms at the back are farther from busy Route 4. The wide front porch is adorned with seasonal decorations such as luminarias and cornstalks, and the inn is within walking distance of Quechee Gorge. 🏠 *Rte. 4, 05059,* ☎ *802/295–1776. 8 rooms with bath. MC, V. MAP.*

Rutland

DINING

$$ **Ernie's Hearthside.** Known also as Royal's Hearthside, Royal's Grill and Bar, and Ernie's Grill and Bar, this Rutland institution features an open hearth with hand-painted tiles, behind which the staff prepares mesquite-grilled chicken with basil, tomato, and mushrooms; roast prime rib; and lamb chops grilled with ginger and rosemary. ✗ *37 N. Main St.,* ☎ *802/775–0856. Reservations advised. AE, DC, MC, V.*

$–$$ **Back Home Cafe.** Wood booths, black-and-white linoleum tile, and ex-
★ posed brick give this second-story café the air of a hole-in-the-wall in New York City—where the owners come from. Dinner might be baked stuffed fillet of sole with spinach, mushrooms, feta cheese, and tarragon sauce, or any of a number of Italian specialties. Daily lunch specials offer soup, entrée, and dessert for less than $5. ✗ *21 Center St.,* ☎ *802/775–2104. MC, V.*

DINING AND LODGING

$$–$$$ **Vermont Marble Inn.** The innkeepers are the sort of people who beg
★ you to put on your coat so you don't catch cold; they also present an elaborate afternoon tea on a sterling silver service. Two ornate Carrara marble drawing room fireplaces look and feel as though they were carved from solid cream. Guest rooms are named for authors (Byron, Elizabeth Barrett Browning), whose works are placed beside the bed. The antique furnishings may include canopy beds, working fireplaces, and antique trunks; the bathrooms are large enough to have accommodated the full, flowing dresses of 1867, when the inn was built as a private home. Anything less than the classical music, crystal chandelier, and candlelight in the dining room would scarcely do justice to

a meal that might include veal loin sautéed in saffron oil with sweet peppers and olives in a chive pesto, or braised duckling in port and raspberry sauce with wild rice. A vegetarian plate may offer lentil-and-vegetable-stuffed zucchini and grilled polenta. 🖭 *Fair Haven, 05743,* ☎ *802/265–8383. 12 rooms with bath. AE, MC, V.*

LODGING

$–$$ **The Inn at Rutland.** There *is* an alternative to motel and hotel chain ac-
❋ commodations in Rutland—at this renovated Victorian mansion. The ornate oak staircase lined with heavy embossed gold and leather wainscoting leads to rooms that blend modern bathrooms with turn-of-the-century touches: botanical prints, elaborate ceiling moldings, frosted glass, pictures of ladies in long white dresses. Second-floor rooms are larger than those on the third (once the servants' quarters). 🖭 *70 N. Main St., 05701,* ☎ *802/773–0575 or 800/808–0575,* 🖷 *802/775–3506. 11 rooms with bath. CP. AE, D, MC, V.*

Waitsfield

DINING

$$–$$$ **Chez Henri.** Tucked in the shadows of Sugarbush ski area, this bistro has garnered a year-round following with traditional French dishes such as grilled swordfish with a coulis, rabbit in red wine sauce, and fillet of beef with peppercorns. Locals frequent the congenial bar and dine al fresco next to a tumbling stream. ✗ *Sugarbush Village,* ☎ *802/583–2600. AE, MC, V.*

$ **Richard's Special Vermont Pizza (RSVP).** Walk through the door, and you're immediately transported through time (to the 1950s) and space (to anywhere but Vermont). The pizza—legendary around these parts with its paper-thin crust and toppings like cilantro pesto, cob-smoked bacon, pineapple, and sautéed spinach—has become known for transport as well: Richard will Federal Express a frozen pie almost anywhere in the world overnight. And there are plenty of takers. Salads and sandwiches are also available. ✗ *Bridge St.,* ☎ *802/496–7787. MC, V.*

DINING AND LODGING

$$ **Lareau Farm Country Inn.** Surrounded by 67 acres of pastures and
❋ woodland, and just an amble away from Mad River, this collection of
★ old farm buildings (the oldest part dates from 1790) appeals to outdoor enthusiasts as well as to those simply seeking a rejuvenating retreat in the country. There's a lot of history here—the original settler is buried on the property—which innkeepers Susan and Dan Easley love to share; you can explore it yourself on a mile-long stroll, with the help of a detailed walking guide they've put together. The furnishings in the inn are an eclectic mix of Victorian sofas and Oriental rugs. Susan made the quilts in each of the guest rooms, and Dan often plays the piano that was made in Burlington. The many-windowed dining room is the most inviting room in the house where the family-style breakfast is served to guests at one of the four massive oak and cherry tables. Sit on the covered porch in an Adirondack chair that faces horses grazing in pastures out back, explore the large jazz collection, swim in the river, take a horse or sleigh ride, or stroll in the beautiful gardens. American Flatbread, the restaurant in the barn next door is a recommended experience. 🖭 *Rte. 100, Box 563,* ☎ *802/496-4949. 11 rooms with bath, 2 share bath. Restaurant, sleigh rides. MC, V.*

$–$$ **Tucker Hill Lodge.** Attempts to maintain its 1940s-ski-lodge ambience have succeeded at this inn that opened the same year as Mad River Glen ski area. Pine-panelling and otherwise simple furnishings suffice as most guests here are more interested in skiing all day than in Victorian frills. Georgio's Café occupies two dining rooms: one upstairs, with red tablecloths and a deep blue ceiling, and one downstairs, with a bar, open stone oven, and fireplace. Both have a warm Mediterranean feel. *Pettini alla Veneziana* (stone-seared scallops with raisins and pine nuts), and *saltimbocca alla Valdostana* (roulades of beef with fontina cheese and prosciutto) are two specialties. Fondue, pasta dishes, and pizza round out the menu. ☎ *Rte. 17, 05673,* ☎ *802/496–3983 or 800/543–7841,* FAX *802/496–3203. 16 rooms with bath, 6 share bath. Restaurant, pool, hiking, tennis court. MAP. AE, MC, V.*

LODGING

\$\$\$–\$\$\$\$ **The Inn at the Round Barn Farm.** Art exhibits have replaced cows in the big round barn here (one of only 12 in the state), but the Shaker-style building still dominates the farm's 85 countryside acres. The inn's guest rooms are in the 1806 farmhouse, where books line the walls of the cream-color library (unfortunately, the only sitting room). The rooms are sumptuous and elegant, with eyelet-trimmed sheets, elaborate four-poster beds, rich-colored wallpapers, and brass wall lamps for easy bedtime reading. Breakfast is served in a cheerful solarium that overlooks landscaped ponds and rolling acreage. ☎ *E. Warren Rd., R.R. 1, Box 247, 05673,* ☎ *802/496–2276,* FAX *802/496–8832. 11 rooms with bath. Pool. MAP. AE, MC, V.*

\$–\$\$ **Beaver Pond Farm Inn.** A peaceful drive down a country lane lined with
★ sugar maples leads to this small, restored 1840 farmhouse overlooking rolling meadows, a golf course, and cross-country ski trails. Guest rooms are decorated simply, and bathrooms are ample. The focal point of the inn is the huge deck, where, after active days, guests gaze at the mountains and meadows. A full breakfast, which might include orange-yogurt pancakes, is served at an oblong walnut table; a low wooden buffet lines the wall and holds china belonging to four generations. The inn, which has a 180-yard driving range, is next door to the Robert Trent Jones–designed Sugarbush Golf Course and is less than a mile from Sugarbush Mountain. ☎ *R.D. Box 306, Golf Course Rd., 05674,* ☎ *802/583–2861,* FAX *802/583–2860. 4 rooms with bath, 2 share bath. Dining room. MC, V. Full breakfast included. MAP available Tues., Thurs., and Sat.*

Windsor

DINING

\$\$ **Windsor Station.** This converted main-line railroad station serves such main-line entrées as chicken Kiev, filet mignon, and prime rib. The booths, with their curtained brass railings, were created from the high-back railroad benches in the depot. ✕ *Depot Ave.,* ☎ *802/674–2052. AE, MC, V. Closed early Nov.*

DINING AND LODGING

\$\$ **Juniper Hill Inn.** An expanse of green lawn with Adirondack chairs and
❄ a garden of perennials sweeps up to the portico of this Greek Revival mansion, built at the turn of the century and now on the National Register of Historic Places. The central living room, with its hardwood floors, oak paneling, Oriental carpets, and thickly upholstered wing chairs and sofas, has a stately feel. Spacious bedrooms have antiques; some have fireplaces. The four-course dinners served in the candlelit dining room may include roast pork glazed with mustard and brandy sauce. The inn is just 7 miles from Mt. Ascutney. ☎ *Juniper Hill Rd., Box 79, 05089,* ☎ *802/674–5273 or 800/359–2541,* FAX *802/674–5273. 16 rooms with bath. Restaurant, pool, hiking. MC, V. MAP.*

Woodstock

DINING

$$$–$$$$ **The Prince and the Pauper.** Here is a romantically candlelit Colonial set-
★ ting, a prix fixe menu, and nouvelle French fare with a Vermont accent.
The roast duckling might be served with a black cherry or Cointreau
glaze; escalopes de veau could have a Madeira demiglace or creamed
onions with tarragon vinegar. Homemade lamb and pork sausage in puff
pastry with a honey-mustard sauce is another possibility. ✕ *24 Elm St.,*
☎ *802/457–1818. Reservations advised. D, MC, V. No lunch. Closed
Sun.–Mon. Apr.–May and Nov.*

$$–$$$ **Bentley's.** In addition to the standards—burgers, chili, homemade
soups, omelets, croissants with various fillings—entrées at this infor-
mal and often busy restaurant include duck in raspberry purée, almonds,
and Chambord, and tournedos with red zinfandel sauce. Remy rum-
raisin ice cream is one of the tempting desserts. You'll find jazz or blues
here on weekends. ✕ *3 Elm St.,* ☎ *802/457–3232. AE, MC, V.*

DINING AND LODGING

$$$–$$$$ **Kedron Valley Inn.** In 1985, Max and Merrily Comins began renovat-
★ ing what, in the 1840s, had been the National Hotel. Many rooms have
either a fireplace or a Franklin stove, and each has a quilt. Two rooms
have private decks, another has a private veranda, and a fourth has a
private terrace overlooking the stream that runs through the inn's 15
acres. Exposed-log walls make the motel units in back more rustic than
the rooms in the main inn, but they're decorated similarly. The classi-
cally trained chef creates such French masterpieces as fillet of Norwe-
gian salmon stuffed with herb seafood mousse in puff pastry and shrimp,
scallops, and lobster with wild mushrooms sautéed in shallots and
white wine and served with a Fra Angelico cream sauce. The decor here,
too, is striking; a terrace looking onto the grounds is open in summer.
▣ *Rte. 106, 05071,* ☎ *802/457–1473,* ℻ *802/457–4469. 28 rooms
with bath. Restaurant, bar, pond, beach, horseback riding. MAP. D, MC,
V. Closed Apr.*

$$$–$$$$ **Woodstock Inn and Resort.** The hotel's lobby, with its massive wood-
beam mantel and floor-to-ceiling fieldstone fireplace, embodies the spirit
of New England. It comes as no surprise to learn that the resort is owned
by the Rockefeller family. The rooms' modern ash furnishings are
high-quality institutional, enlivened by patchwork quilts: The inoffensive
decor is designed to please the large clientele of corporate conference
attendees. Some of the newer rooms, constructed in 1990, have fire-
places. The dinner fare is nouvelle New England; the menu changes
seasonally and may include such entrées as salmon steak with avocado
beurre blanc, beef Wellington, and prime rib. The wall of windows af-
fords diners a view over the inn's putting green. ▣ *Rte. 4, 05091,* ☎
802/457–1100 or 800/448–7900, ℻ *802/457–6699. 146 rooms with
bath. Restaurant (reservations advised), bar, indoor pool, outdoor
pools, saunas, croquet, health club, racquetball, squash, golf, skiing,
tennis courts, meeting rooms. AE, MC, V.*

LODGING

$$$$ **Twin Farms.** At the center of this exclusive 235-acre resort stands the
1795 farmhouse where Sinclair Lewis and Dorothy Thompson lived.
In recent years the stone-and-pine house has been fully renovated and
four stone cottages have been added. Rooms and cottages have such
luxurious touches as original watercolors, ample bookshelves, fireplaces,
needlepoint rugs, and wood-and-stone furniture. One avant-garde stu-
dio has huge arch windows, a cathedral-ceiling living room done in
spare classical furnishings, and a king-size bed covered in woven raf-
fia in a loft overhead. Chef Neil Wigglesworth prepares a prix-fixe menu

of rich contemporary cuisine that draws regularly on local recipes. ⌶ *Rte. 12, 8 mi north of Woodstock (Box 115, Barnard, VT 05031),* ☎ *802/234–9999 or 800/894–6327,* ℻ *802/234–9990. 4 rooms with bath, 8 cottages. 2 bars, dining room, exercise room, boating, bicycles, recreation room, meeting rooms. AE, MC, V.*

$$–$$$ **The Woodstocker.** Just a short stroll from the covered bridge and the village green, this 1830s B&B offers the grace and elegance you'd expect in a town like Woodstock. The rooms are large and light, and furnished with a hodgepodge of antiques, like brass and iron four-poster beds and mahogany highboys. The cheerful grandfather clock, a year-round holiday tree that's decorated differently each season, and an intriguing piece with fake drawers carved into the front panel are centerpieces of the common areas. Breakfast might include bananas Foster, French toast, or an egg strada. ⌶ *61 River St. (Rte. 4), 05091,* ☎ *802/457–3896 or 800/457–3896. 9 rooms with bath. MAP. MC, V.*

$–$$ **The Winslow House.** This farmhouse built in 1872 once presided over
★ a dairy farm that reached down to the banks of the Ottauquechee River. Although this B&B has only four guest rooms and the common area is small, the two upstairs quarters are uncommonly spacious and have separate sitting rooms: Room 3 is dominated by mahogany furnishings, while the English oak bed, armoire, and mission desk in Room 4 transport you to a more luxurious era. A comfortable, unpretentious place with great cross-country skiing and golf nearby, this B&B is just far enough outside of town to feel secluded. ⌶ *38 Rte. 4, 05091,* ☎ *802/ 457–1820. 4 rooms with bath. MAP. D, MC, V.*

The Arts

Green Mountain Cultural Center (Inn at the Round Barn, E. Warren Rd., Waitsfield, ☎ 802/496–7722), a nonprofit organization, brings concerts and art exhibits, as well as educational workshops, to the Mad River Valley. **Middlebury College** (☎ 802/388–3711) sponsors music, theater, and dance performances throughout the year at Wright Memorial Theatre. The **Pentangle Council on the Arts** (☎ 802/457–3981) in Woodstock organizes performances of music, theater, and dance at the Town Hall Theater. In Rutland, the **Crossroads Arts Council** (☎ 802/775–5413) presents music, opera, dance, jazz, and theater events.

Music
Vermont Symphony Orchestra (☎ 802/864–5741) performs in Rutland and, during the summer, in Woodstock.

Opera
Opera North (Norwich, ☎ 802/649–1060) does three opera productions annually at locations throughout the state.

Theater
The Valley Players (Rte. 100, Waitsfield, ☎ 802/496–3485) presents a year-round mix of musicals, dramas, follies, and holiday shows. **Vermont Ensemble Theater** (☎ 802/388–2676 or 802/388–3001) has a three-week summer season in a tent on the Middlebury College campus.

Nightlife

Most nighttime activity takes place around the ski resorts of Killington, Pico, and Sugarbush.

Giorgio's Café (Tucker Hill Lodge, Rte. 17, Waitsfield, ☎ 802/496–3983) is a cozy spot to warm by the fire to the sounds of soft folk and jazz on weekends. **Gallaghers** (Rtes. 100 and 17, Waitsfield, ☎ 802/496–8800) is a popular spot, with danceable local bands. **The Back Room at Chez Henri** (Sugarbush Village, ☎ 802/583–2600) is popular with the après-ski and late-night dance crowd. **Inn at Long Trail** (Rte. 4, Killington, ☎ 802/775–7181) has a comfortable pub that hosts Irish music on weekends. **The Pickle Barrel** (Killington Rd., Killington, ☎ 802/422–3035), a favorite with the après-ski crowd, presents up-and-coming acts and can get pretty rowdy. Try the hot, spicy chicken wings to warm up after skiing at **Casey's Caboose** (☎ 802/422–3795), halfway up the access road. The **Wobbly Barn** (☎ 802/422–3392), with dancing to blues and rock, is open during ski season. **Bentleys** (3 Elm St., Woodstock, ☎ 802/457–3232), a popular restaurant, also has live jazz and blues on weekends. **Crow's Nest Club** (☎ 802/484–7711), in the Ascutney Mountain Resort Hotel, has live entertainment on weekends. **Destiny** (☎ 802/674–6671), in the town of Ascutney, has rock entertainment with live bands during the week and a DJ on Sunday.

Central Vermont Essentials

Getting Around

BY BUS

Vermont Transit (☎ 802/864–6811, 800/451–3292, or, in VT, 800/642–3133) links Rutland, White River Junction, Burlington, and many smaller towns.

BY CAR

The major east–west road is Route 4, which stretches from White River Junction in the east to Fair Haven in the west. Route 125 connects Middlebury on Route 7 with Hancock on Route 100; Route 100 splits the region in half along the eastern edge of the Green Mountains. Route 17 travels east–west from Waitsfield over the Appalachian Gap through Bristol and down to the shores of Lake Champlain. Interstate 91 and the parallel Route 5 follow the eastern border; Routes 7 and 30 are the north–south highways in the west. Interstate 89 links White River Junction with Montpelier to the north.

Guided Tours

Country Inn Along the Trail (R.R. 3, Box 3115, Brandon 05733, ☎ 802/247–3300) leads skiing and hiking trips from inn to inn in Central Vermont. **The Icelandic Horse Farm** (Common Rd., Waitsfield, ☎ 802/496–6707) offers year-round guided riding expeditions on easy-to-ride Icelandic horses. Full-day and half-day rides, weekend tours, and inn-to-inn treks are available. **Land o' Goshen Farm** (Rte. 73, Brandon, ☎ 802/247–6015; ⊘ Mid-May–mid-Oct.) raises llamas for sale and offers guided day or overnight trips in which llamas carry the luggage. Day trips cost $75 per person (two-person minimum), overnight trips $210–$250 (six-person minimum).

Important Addresses and Numbers

EMERGENCIES

Rutland Medical Center (160 Allen St., Rutland, ☎ 802/775–7111). **Porter Medical Center** (South St., Middlebury, ☎ 802/388–7901).

VISITOR INFORMATION

The following offices are open weekdays 9–5: **Addison County Chamber of Commerce** (2 Court St., Middlebury 05753, ☎ 802/388–7951), **Quechee Chamber of Commerce** (Box 106, Quechee 05059, ☎ 802/295–7900), **Rutland Region Chamber of Commerce** (7 Court Sq., Box 67, Rutland 05701, ☎ 802/773–2747), **Sugarbush Chamber of Commerce** (Rte. 100, Box 173, Waitsfield 05673, ☎ 802/496–3409), **Windsor Area**

NORTHERN VERMONT

Both the state's largest city (Burlington) and the nation's smallest state capital (Montpelier) are in this region, as are some of the most rural and remote areas of New England. Much of the state's logging and dairy farming take place in the northern stretches of the state, where the state's most snow falls (hence the profusion of ski areas—Jay, Burke, Bolton, Smugglers' Notch, and Stowe). Cradled between the population centers of Burlington and Montpelier to the south and the border with Canada to the north, the Northeast Kingdom stretches vast and untamed, where the harsh reality of rural life and moose sightings are much more common than microbreweries and hip cafés (Budweiser and diners are more the norm). With Montréal only an hour from the border, the Canadian influence is strong, and Canadian accents and currency common (the closer you get to the border, the more bilingual signs you'll encounter).

Exploring

Numbers in the margin correspond to points of interest on the Northern Vermont map.

You'll find plenty to do in the region's cities: Burlington, Montpelier, St. Johnsbury, and Barre; in the bustling resort area of Stowe; in the Lake Champlain islands; and in the wilds of the Northeast Kingdom.

❶ The Vermont legislature anointed **Montpelier** as the state capital in 1805. Today, with fewer than 10,000 residents, the city is the country's least populous seat of government. Built in 1859, following its predecessor's destruction (the first time by the legislators themselves, the second time by fire), the current **Vermont State House**—with its gleaming gold dome and granite columns 6 feet in diameter (plucked from the ground right next door in Barre)—is more impressive than one might think for a city this size. The interior of the building just had a face-lift in 1994, but most of the original furnishings are still in place and continue to reflect the intimacy of the state's citizen legislature. Tour the building on your own or with a guide; tours are offered on the half hour. *115 State St., ☎ 802/828–2228. ☛ Free. ☉ Weekdays 8–4; tours July–mid-Oct. 10–3:30, Sat. 11–2:30.*

Perhaps you're wondering what the last panther shot in Vermont looked like? Why New England bridges are covered? What a niddy-noddy is? Or what Christmas was like for a Bethel boy in 1879? ("I skated on my new skates. In the morning Papa and I set up a stove for Gramper.") The **Vermont Museum,** on the ground floor of the Vermont Historical Society offices in Montpelier, satisfies the curious with intriguing informative exhibits. *109 State St., ☎ 802/828–2291. ☛ $3 adults, $2 senior citizens. ☉ Tues.–Fri., 9–4:30, Sat. 9–4, Sun. noon–4.*

The intersection of State and Main streets is the city hub, bustling with the activity of state and city workers during the day. It's an endearing place to spend an afternoon browsing in the local shops; in true, small-town Vermont fashion, the streets become deserted at night.

Northwest of Montpelier, in **Waterbury,** one of Vermont's best-loved attractions is **Ben & Jerry's Ice Cream Factory,** the mecca, nirvana, and

Valhalla for ice-cream lovers. Ben and Jerry, who began selling ice cream from a renovated gas station in the 1970s, have created a business that has grown to one of the most influential voices in community-based activism in the country. Their social and environmental consciousness have made the company a model of corporate responsibility. Fifty percent of tour proceeds go to Vermont community groups. The plant tour is a bit self-congratulatory and only skims the surface of the behind-the-scenes goings-on that many would no doubt like to learn more about—a flaw forgiven when the free samples are offered. *Rte. 100, 1 mi north of I–89,* ☎ *802/244–5641.* ☛ *Tour: $1 adults, children under 12 free.* ☼ *Daily 9–5 (till 9 in summer and fall). Tour every ½ hr.*

❷ To many, **Stowe**—northwest of Montpelier on Route 100, 10 miles north of I–89—rings a bell as the place the von Trapp family, of *Sound of Music* fame, chose to settle after fleeing Austria. Set amid acres of pastures that fall away dramatically and allow for wide-angle panoramas of the mountains beyond, the **Trapp Family Lodge** (Luce Hill Rd., ☎ 802/253–8511) is the site of a popular outdoor music series in summer and an extensive cross-country ski trail network in winter.

For more than a century the history of Stowe has been determined by the town's proximity to **Mt. Mansfield,** the highest elevation in the state. As early as 1858, visitors were trooping to the area to view the mountain whose shape suggests the profile of the face of a man lying on his back. If hiking to the top isn't your idea of a good time, in the summer months you can take the 4½-mile **toll road** to the top for a short scenic walk and a magnificent view. *Mountain Rd., 7 mi from Rte. 100,* ☎ *802/253–3000.* ☛ *$9 car, $6 motorcycle.* ☼ *Late May–early Oct., daily 10–5.*

An alternative means of reaching Mt. Mansfield's upper reaches is the eight-seat **gondola** that shuttles continuously up to the area of "the Chin," which has a small restaurant (dinner reservations required). *Mountain Rd., 8 mi from Rte. 100,* ☎ *802/253–3000 or 800/253–4754.* ☛ *$10 adults, $5 children 6–12.* ☼ *June–early Oct., daily 10–5; Dec.–Apr., daily 8:30–4 for skiers; Oct.–Nov. and May, weekends 10–5.*

When you tire of shopping on Stowe's Main Street and on Mountain Road (most easily accomplished by car), head for the town's **recreational path** that begins behind the Community Church in the center of town and meanders for 5⅓ miles along the river valley. There are many entry points along the way; whether you're on foot, ski, bike, or in-line skates, it's a tranquil means of enjoying the outdoors.

TIME OUT   The **Blue Moon Café** on Stowe's School Street serves affordable, eclectic bistro fare in a renovated landmark building; dine on the patio in the summer.

Northwest of Stowe is an exciting and scenic, although indirect, route

 ❸ to Burlington: **Smugglers' Notch,** the narrow pass between Mt. Mansfield and Madonna Peak that is said to have sheltered 18th-century outlaws in its rugged, bouldered terrain. Weaving around the huge stones that shoulder the road, you'd hardly know you're on state highway Route 108. There are parking spots and picnic tables at the top. The notch road is closed in winter.

Follow Route 108 to Route 15 in Jeffersonville, where you'll find the **Brewster River Mill,** Vermont's only steam-powered grist mill. It is worth a stop to view this fascinating but almost-extinct process. The creatively packaged stone-ground flour and meal make a fun, alternative Vermont keepsake. *Rte. 108,* ☎ *802/644–2987.* ☼ *Daily 9–5.*

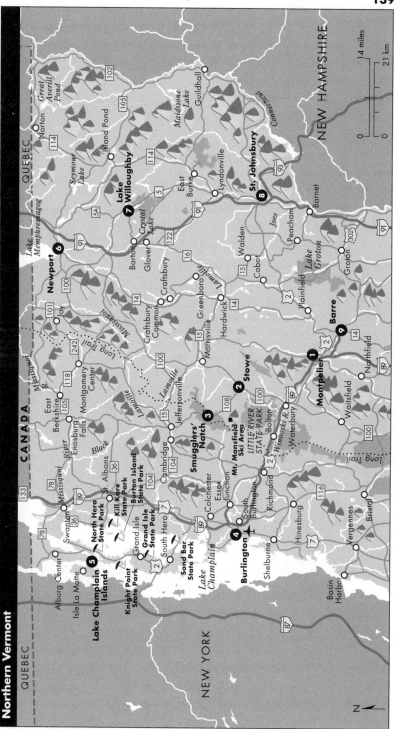

Northern Vermont

The junction of Routes 15 and 108 presents some intriguing choices: Head east on Route 15 for a pleasant antiques-store-dotted drive through the towns of Johnson (home of Johnson Woolen Mills) and Morrisville and loop back toward Stowe; continue farther east on Route 15, turning north 4 miles outside of Morrisville toward **Craftsbury Common** or north on Route 126 in Hardwick toward **Greensboro,** two idyllic towns with long histories as vacation destinations; or turn west in Jeffersonville on Route 15 toward Burlington and attractions to the southwest.

TIME OUT **Dinner's Dunn at the Windridge Bakery** (Main St. Jeffersonville, ☎ 802/644-8219) will fill you up with savory breads, homemade soups, and turkey pot pie. The massive bread oven that dominates the room has been turning out the loaves since 1948.

❹ Vermont's largest population center, **Burlington** was founded in 1763 and had a long history as a trade center following the growth of shipping on Lake Champlain in the 19th century. More recently, energized by the roughly 20,000 students from the area's five colleges, including the University of Vermont, and an abundance of culture-hungry, transplanted urban dwellers, Burlington draws an eclectic element. It was for years the only city in America with a socialist mayor—now the nation's sole socialist congressional representative. The **Church Street Marketplace**—a pedestrian mall of funky shops, intriguing boutiques, and an appealing menagerie of sidewalk cafés, food and craft vendors, and street performers—is an animated downtown focal point. Burlington's festive town center is where most people in central and northern Vermont are drawn at least occasionally to do errands or see a show.

Crouched on the shores of Lake Champlain, which shimmers in the shadows of the Adirondacks to the west, Burlington's recently revitalized **waterfront** teems with outdoor enthusiasts in summer who stroll along its recreation path and ply the waters in sailboats and motorcraft. A replica of an old Champlain paddlewheeler, The Spirit of Ethan Allen, hosts narrated cruises on the lake and, in the evening, dinner and moonlight dance sailings that drift by the Adirondacks and the Green Mountains. *Perkins Pier,* ☎ *802/862–9685.* ☛ *$8 adults, $4 children 5–11.* ✆ *Cruises June–mid-Oct., daily 10–9.*

TIME OUT Need a pick-me-up? Stop by **Speeder & Earl's Espresso Bar** (104 Church St.) for a cup o' joe.

After emerging from the built-up strip heading south out of Burlington, Route 7 gives way to the fertile farmland of the Champlain Valley, affording chin-dropping views of the rugged Adirondacks across the lake. Five miles from the city, one could trace all New England history simply by wandering the 45 acres of the **Shelburne Museum,** whose 37 buildings seem an anthology of individual museums. The large collection of Americana contains 18th- and 19th-century period homes and furniture, fine and folk art, farm tools, more than 200 carriages and sleighs, Audubon prints, even a private railroad car from the days of steam. And an old-fashioned jail. And an assortment of duck decoys. And an old stone cottage. And a display of early toys. And the *Ticonderoga,* an old sidewheel steamship, curiously misplaced, grounded amid lawn and trees. *Rte. 7, 5 mi south of Burlington,* ☎ *802/985–3346.* ☛ *2 consecutive days: $16 adults, $7 children 6–14.* ✆ *Mid-May–mid-Oct., daily 10–5; limited winter hours, call ahead.*

Nearby **Shelburne Farms** has a history of improving the farmer's lot by developing new agricultural methods. Founded in the 1880s as a private estate, the 1,000-acre property is now an educational and cultural resource center. Here you can see a working dairy farm, listen to nature lectures, or simply stroll the immaculate grounds on a scenic stretch of Lake Champlain waterfront. The original landscaping, designed by Frederick Law Olmsted, the creator of Central Park and Boston's Emerald Necklace, gently channels the eye to expansive vistas and aesthetically satisfying views of such buildings as the five-story, 2-acre Farm Barn. *East of Rte. 7, 6 mi south of Burlington,* ☎ *802/985–8686.* ☛ *$5.50 adults, $5 senior citizens, $2.50 children 6–15. Guided tour $2.50.* ۞ *Visitor center and shop daily 9:30–5, last tour at 3:30; tours given Memorial Day–mid-Oct.*

At the 6-acre **Vermont Wildflower Farm,** the display along the flowering pathways changes constantly: violets in the spring, daisies and black-eyed Susans for summer, and fall colors that rival the trees' foliage. You can buy wildflower seeds, crafts, and books here. *Rte. 7, 5 mi south of the Shelburne Museum,* ☎ *802/425–3500.* ☛ *$3 adults, $1.50 senior citizens.* ۞ *Mid-May–Oct., daily 10–5.*

Retrace Route 7 back through Burlington and head north, where more of the state's history is revealed. Ethan Allen, Vermont's famous early settler, is a figure of some mystery. The visitor center at his **homestead** by the Winooski River answers questions about his flamboyant life, and raises some you may not have thought of. The house, about 70% original, has such frontier hallmarks as nails pointing through the roof on the top floor, rough saw-cut boards, and an open hearth for cooking. *North Ave., off Rte. 127, north of Burlington,* ☎ *802/865–4556.* ☛ *$3.50 adults, $3 senior citizens, $2 children 6–12, $10 family.* ۞ *Mid-May–mid-June, Tues.–Sun. 1–5; mid-June–Labor Day, Mon.–Sat 10–5, Sun. 1–5; Labor Day–late Oct., daily 1–5.*

Samuel de Champlain's claim on the islands dotting the northern expanses of Lake Champlain is represented on Isle La Motte by a granite statue that looks south toward the site of the first French settlement **⑤** and its shrine to St. Anne. Today the **Lake Champlain Islands** are a center of water recreation in summer, and ice fishing in winter. North of Burlington, the scenic drive through the islands on Route 2 begins at I–89 and travels north through South Hero, Grand Isle, and Isle La Motte to Alburg Center, 5 miles from the Canadian border. Here Route 78 will take you east to the mainland.

To cross northern Vermont, take Route 78 east through the **Missisquoi National Wildlife Refuge** (☎ 802/868–4781)—5,800 acres of federally protected wetlands, meadows, and woods—to Route 105. Continue to Route 118 in East Berkshire, and follow that to Route 242 in Montgomery Center and the Jay Peak area. From the top of the mountain pass there are vast views of Canada to the north and of Vermont's rugged **Northeast Kingdom** to the east.

The descent from Jay Peak on Route 101 leads to Route 100, which can be the beginning of a scenic loop tour of routes 14, 5, 58, and back **⑥** to 100, or take you east to the city of **Newport** on Lake Memphremagog. The waterfront is the dominant view of the city, which is built on a peninsula. The grand hotels of the last century are gone, yet the buildings still drape dramatically along the lake's edge and climb the hills behind.

You will encounter some of the most unspoiled areas in all Vermont on the drive south from Newport on either Route 5 or I–91 (I–91 is faster, Route 5 is prettier). This region, the Northeast Kingdom, is named for the remoteness and stalwart independence that has helped to preserve its rural nature.

➐ On the northern shore of **Lake Willoughby,** 7 miles northeast of Barton on Route 16, the cliffs of surrounding Mts. Pisgah and Hor drop to water's edge and give this glacially carved, 500-foot-deep lake a striking resemblance to a Norwegian fjord. The lake is popular for both summer and winter recreation, and the trails to the top of Mt. Pisgah reward hikers with glorious views.

If a taste of real Vermont is what you're after, from the northern shores of the lake head along the eastern edge on Route 5A to the twin towns of West Burke and East Burke, where a jam-packed general store, a post office, and a couple of great places to eat are about all you'll find. If it's a moose sighting you're after, head north on Route 114 toward Island Pond, an outpost of a town, where the beasts are all but common. From Barton, you can also continue south down Route 5 or Route 122 (both beautiful drives), to the town of Lyndonville, where you'll want to hop on the interstate to avoid the strip-mall drudge that bogs down this section of Route 5.

TIME OUT If you have a hankering for good, old-fashioned barbecued ribs and chicken (weekends only) or for the equally satisfying burgers and fries, stop into **Big Bertha's** (West Burke, ☎ 802/467-3032) after a day's skiing or hiking. This is a place for those with big appetites!

➑ The southern gateway to the Northeast Kingdom is the city of **St. Johnsbury,** directly off I–91. Though chartered in 1786, St. Johnsbury's identity was not firmly established until 1830, when Thaddeus Fairbanks invented the platform scale, a device that revolutionized weighing methods that had been in use since the beginning of recorded history. The impact of his company on the city is still pervasive: a distinctly 19th-century industrial feel onto which a strong cultural and architectural imprint has been superimposed, the result of the Fairbanks family's philanthropic bent. Opened in 1891, the **Fairbanks Museum and Planetarium** attests to the family's inquisitiveness about all things scientific. The redbrick building in the squat Romanesque architectural style of H. H. Richardson houses collections of Vermont plants and animals and an intimate 50-seat planetarium. *Main and Prospect Sts.,* ☎ *802/748–2372.* ☛ *$4 adults, $2.50 children, $9 family; planetarium $1.50.* ☉ *July–Aug., Mon.–Sat. 10–6, Sun. 1–5; Sept.–June, Mon.–Sat. 10–4, Sun. 1–5. Planetarium shows: July–Aug., daily at 11, 1:30; Sept.–June, weekends at 1:30.*

The **St. Johnsbury Athenaeum,** with its dark rich paneling, polished Victorian woodwork, and ornate circular staircases that rise to the gallery around the perimeter, is a tiny gem. The gallery at the back of the building has the overwhelming *Domes of Yosemite* by Albert Bierstadt and a lot of sentimental 19th-century material. *30 Main St.,* ☎ *802/748–8291.* ☛ *Free.* ☉ *Mon., Wed. 10–8; Tues., Thurs., Fri. 10–5:30; Sat. 9:30–4.*

Heading west from St. Johnsbury along Route 2, an 8-mile detour to the south leads to the village of **Peacham.** This tiny hamlet's stunning scenery and 18th-century charm have made it a favorite for urban refugees and artists seeking solitude and inspiration, as well as for movie directors looking for the quintessential New England village. The largely ignored, yet laudable *Ethan Frome* was filmed here.

TIME OUT Stop into the **Peacham Store** (Main St.) for a quirky combination of Yankee Vermont sensibility and Hungarian eccentricity. Transylvanian goulash, stuffed peppers, and lamb-and-barley soup are among the take-out specialties. Browse through the locally made crafts while waiting for your order.

 Barre has been famous as the source of Vermont granite ever since two men began working the quarries in the early 1800s; the large number of immigrant laborers attracted to the industry made the city prominent in the early years of the American labor movement. Although the town itself may lack charm and appeal to visitors, it's a classic example of real working-class New England life.

The attractions of the **Rock of Ages granite quarry** (Exit 6 off I–89, follow Rte. 63) range from the awe-inspiring (the quarry resembles the Grand Canyon in miniature) to the absurd (the company invites you to consult a directory of tombstone dealers throughout the United States). The view from the artisan center, which you pass on the drive to the visitor center, seems like a scene out of Dante's *Inferno:* A dusty, smoky haze hangs above the acres of people at work, with machines screaming as they bite into the rock. The process that transfers designs to the smooth stone and etches them into it is fascinating. *Rte. 63, ☎ 802/476–3115. ☉ Quarry and visitor center May–mid-Oct., daily 8:30–5; artisan center weekdays 8–3:30. Quarry shuttle bus tour weekdays 9:30–3:30;* ☛ *$2 adults, $1 children 5–12.*

What to See and Do with Children

Ben & Jerry's Ice Cream Factory, Waterbury
Lamoille Valley Railroad, Morrisville
The Spirit of Ethan Allen, Burlington

Off the Beaten Path

The **Lake Champlain Maritime Museum** commemorates the days when steamships sailed along the coast of northern Vermont carrying logs, livestock, and merchandise bound for New York City. The exhibits housed here in a one-room stone schoolhouse 25 miles south of Burlington include historic maps, nautical prints, and a collection of small craft. *Basin Harbor Rd., 5 mi west of Vergennes, ☎ 802/475–2317.* ☛ *$3 adults. ☉ Memorial Day–mid-Oct., daily 10–5.*

South of I–91 (Exit 25), in the town of Glover, is the **Bread and Puppet Museum,** an unassuming, ramshackle barn that houses a surrealistic collection of props used in past performances by the world-renowned Bread and Puppet Theater. The troupe, whose members live communally on the surrounding farm, have been performing social and political commentary with the towering (they're supported by people on stilts), eerily expressive puppets for almost 30 years. *Rte. 122, Glover, 1 mi east of Rte. 16, ☎ 802/525–3031.* ☛ *Free. Call for hours.*

North of Route 2, midway between Barre and St. Johnsbury, the biggest cheese producer in the state, the **Cabot Creamery Cooperative** (☎ 800/639–4031), has a visitor center with an audiovisual presentation about the state's dairy and cheese industry, tours of the plant, and—best of all—samples. *Cabot, 3 mi north of Rte. 2, ☎ 802/563–2231.* ☛ *$1. ☉ Mon.–Sat. 8–4:30.*

Shopping

Shopping Districts
Church Street Marketplace (Main St.–Pearl St., Burlington, ☎ 802/863–1648), a pedestrian thoroughfare, is lined with boutiques, cafés, and

street vendors. **Burlington Square Mall,** off Church Street, has Porteous (the city's major department store) and some 50 shops. **The Champlain Mill** (Rte. 2/7, northeast of Burlington, ☎ 802/655–9477), a former woolen mill on the banks of the Winooski River, has three floors of stores. The **Mountain Road** in Stowe is lined with shops from town up toward the ski area.

Food and Drink

Cabot Creamery Annex (Rte. 100, 2½ mi north of I–89, Waterbury, ☎ 802/244–6334) is the retail store and tasting center for Vermont's king of cheese (*see* Off the Beaten Path, *above*). **Cold Hollow Cider Mill** (Rte. 100, Waterbury Center, ☎ 802/244–8771) sells cider, baked goods, and Vermont produce; they offer tastes of the fresh-pressed cider. **Green Mountain Chocolate Co.** (Rte. 100, Duxbury, ☎ 802/244–1139) greets you with cases and cases of hand-rolled truffles, extravagant pastries, and umpteen-zillion types of candies.

Specialty Stores

ANTIQUES

Architectural Salvage Warehouse (212 Battery St., Burlington, ☎ 802/658–5011) has clawfoot tubs, stained-glass windows, mantels, andirons, and the like. **Barton & Boardman Interiors** (184 Battery St., Burlington, ☎ 802/865–4406) is a beautiful store filled to the rafters with fine collectibles and gifts. **Great American Salvage** (3 Main St., Montpelier, ☎ 802/223–7711) supplies architectural detailing: moldings, brackets, stained-glass and leaded windows, doors, and trim retrieved from old homes. **Tailor's Antiques** (68 Pearl St., Burlington, ☎ 802/862–8156) carries small primitive paintings as well as glass and china for collectors. On Route 15, 2 miles west of Johnson, **The Buggy Man** (☎ 802/635–2110) and **Mel Siegel** (☎ 802/635–7838) both have affordable, quality antiques.

BOOKS

Both locations of **Bear Pond Book** (77 Main St., Montpelier, ☎ 802/229–0774; Main St., Stowe, ☎ 802/253–8236) are inviting stores with comfy browsing areas and comprehensive selections. **Chassman & Bem Booksellers** (1 Church St., Burlington, ☎ 802/862–4332), probably the best bookstore in Vermont, has more than 40,000 titles, with a discriminating selection of children's books and a large magazine rack.

CLOTHING

Handblock (97 Church St., Burlington, ☎ 802/962–8211) carries a fun collection of casual yet indulgent women's clothing; it also specializes in rich, hand-dyed linens and colorful stoneware. **Johnson Woolen Mills** (Main St., Johnson, ☎ 802/635–2271) is an authentic factory store with great deals on woolen bankets, yardgoods, and the famous Johnson outerwear. **Vermont Trading Company** (2 State St., Montpelier, ☎ 802/223–2142; 151 N. Main St., Barre, ☎ 802/476–6865) has natural-fiber clothing and funky accessories.

COUNTRY STORES

Baily's Country Store (Rte. 114, East Burke, ☎ 802/626–3666), a veritable institution, supplies locals and visitors alike with baked goods, wine, clothing, and other sundries. At the **Shelburne Country Store** (Village Green, Shelburne, ☎ 802/985–3657), step back in time as you walk past the potbellied stove and take in the aroma emanating from the fudge neatly piled behind huge antique glass cases; candles, weather vanes, glassware, and Vermont food products are its specialties. **Wiley's Store** (Main St., Greensboro, ☎ 802/533–2621), with wooden floors and tin ceilings that boast of its old-time authenticity, warrants attentive exploration; you never know what you might find in this packed-to-the-rafters emporium.

CRAFTS

Bennington Potters North (127 College St., Burlington, ☎ 802/863–2221) has, in addition to the popular pottery, interesting gifts, glassware, furniture, and other housewares. **Vermont State Craft Center** (85 Church St., Burlington, ☎ 802/863–6458) is an elegant gallery displaying contemporary and traditional crafts by more than 200 Vermont artisans. **Vermont Rug Makers** (Route 100C, E. Johnson, ☎ 802/635–2434) features handwoven rugs of every shape and size; custom orders are a specialty. **Yankee Pride** (Champlain Mill, Winooski, ☎ 802/655–0500) has more than 1,200 calico quilts. **By Vermont Hands** (Rte. 15, 1 mi west of Johnson, ☎ 802/635–7664) displays works by more than 50 Vermont artisans.

Skiing

Bolton Valley Resort

Box 300, Bolton 05477
☎ 802/434–2131; lodging, 800/451–3220

Although some skiers come for the day, most people who visit Bolton Valley (20 miles west of Montpelier) stay at one of the hotels or condominium complexes at the base of the mountain. Because of this proximity and the relatively gentle skiing, Bolton attracts more beginners and family groups than singles. The mood is easygoing, the dress and atmosphere casual; there is a ski shop, a country store, deli, post office, eight restaurants and lounges, sports club, and meeting and convention space.

DOWNHILL

Many of the 48 interconnecting trails on Bolton's two mountains, each with a vertical drop of 1,625 feet, are rated intermediate and novice. However, some 23% of the Bolton terrain is rated expert. In fact, as a note of credibility, the DesLauriers brothers of Warren Miller–movie fame ski and work here. Timberline Peak trail network, with a vertical of 1,000 feet, is where you'll find some of the wider slopes and more challenging terrain. Serving these trails are one quad chair, four doubles, and one surface lift—enough to prevent long lift lines on all but the most crowded days. Top-to-bottom trails are lit for night skiing 4–10 PM every evening except Sunday. The area has 70% snowmaking coverage.

CROSS-COUNTRY

Bolton Valley, with its more than 100 kilometers (62 miles) of cross-country trails, 20 kilometers of which are machine tracked, is a favorite of Vermonters. Lessons and rentals (including telemark) are available.

OTHER ACTIVITIES

The sports center has an indoor pool, whirlpool, sauna, one indoor tennis court, and an exercise room. Weekly events and activities include sleigh rides and races.

CHILD CARE

The child care center has supervised play and games, indoors and outdoors, for infants and children up to 6 years old. Child care is also available three nights per week. For children who want to learn to ski, there are programs for ages 5–15.

Burke Mountain
Box 247, East Burke 05832
☏ *802/626–3305; lodging, 800/541–5480; snow conditions, 800/922–2875*

Burke has a reputation for being a low-key, family mountain that draws most of its skiers from Massachusetts and Connecticut. In addition to having plenty of terrain for tenderfeet, intermediate skiers, experts, racers, telemarkers, and snowboarders are stimulated here as well on the time-honored New England narrow trails that the resort has endeavored to preserve. Many of Burke's packages are significantly less expensive than those at other Vermont areas. Burke Mt. Academy has contributed a number of notable racers to the U.S. Ski Team, including Olympians Diann Roffe-Steinrotter, Julie Parisien, Matt Grosjean, and Casey Puckett.

DOWNHILL
With a 2,000-foot vertical drop, Burke is something of a sleeper among the larger eastern ski areas. Although there is limited snowmaking (35%), the mountain's northern location and exposure assure plenty of natural snow. It has one quad, one double chairlift, and two surface lifts. Lift lines, even on weekends and holidays, are light to nonexistent.

CROSS-COUNTRY
Burke Mountain Ski Touring Center has more than 60 kilometers (37 miles) of trails (54 groomed); some lead to high points with scenic views.

OTHER ACTIVITIES
The Wildflower Inn (Darling Hill Rd., ☏ 800/627–8310) has 15-passenger sleighs drawn by Belgian draft horses.

CHILD CARE
The nursery here takes children ages 6 months to 6 years. SKIwee lessons through the ski school are available to children ages 4–16.

Jay Peak
Rte. 242, Jay 05859
☏ *802/988–2611 or 800/451–4449*

Jay Peak boasts the most natural snow of any ski area in the East. Sticking up out of the flat farmland, Jay catches an abundance of precipitation from the maritime provinces of Canada. Its proximity to Québec attracts Montréalers, and discourages Eastern seaboarders; hence, some bargain packages.

DOWNHILL
Jay Peak is in fact two mountains with 50 trails, the highest reaching nearly 4,000 feet with a vertical drop of 2,153 feet, served by a 60-passenger tram (the only one in Vermont). The area also has a quad, a triple, and a double chairlift, and two T-bars. The smaller mountain has more straight-fall-line, expert terrain, while the tram-side peak has many curving and meandering trails perfectly suited for intermediate and beginning skiers. Jay is known for its glade skiing and now has 13 gladed trails. Every morning at 9 AM the ski school offers a free tour, from the tram down one trail. The area has 80% snow-making coverage.

CROSS-COUNTRY
A touring center at the base of the mountain has 40 kilometers (25 miles) of cross-country trails, 20 kilometers of which are groomed.

CHILD CARE
The child care center for youngsters 2–7 is open from 9 to 4. Guests of Hotel Jay or the Jay Peak Condominiums get this nursery care free,

as well as evening care and supervised dining at the hotel. Children 5–12 can participate in an all-day SKIwee program, which includes lunch.

Smugglers' Notch Resort

Smugglers' Notch 05464
☎ *802/644–8851 or 800/451–8752*

This resort complex has most everything you might need at the base of the lifts. Most skiers stay at the resort. Smugglers' has long been respected for its family programs and, therefore, attracts such clientele.

DOWNHILL

Smugglers' is made up of three mountains. The highest, Madonna, with a vertical drop of 2,610 feet, is in the center and connects with a trail network to Sterling (1,500-foot vertical). The third mountain, Morse (1,150-foot vertical), is more remote, but you can visit all three without removing your skis. The wild, craggy landscape lends a pristine, wilderness feel to the skiing. The tops of each of the mountains have expert terrain—a couple of double black diamonds make Madonna memorable—while intermediate trails fill the lower sections. Morse specializes in beginner trails. The 56 trails are served by five double chairlifts, including the new Mogul Mouse Magic Lift in 1993, and one surface lift. There is now top-to-bottom snowmaking on all three mountains, allowing for 61% coverage.

CROSS-COUNTRY

The area has 37 groomed and tracked kilometers (23 miles) of cross-country trails.

OTHER ACTIVITIES

Management committed itself to developing an activities center long before the concept was adopted by other ski resorts. The self-contained village has ice skating, sleigh rides, and horseback riding. Vermont Horse Park (☎ 802/644–5347) also offers rides on authentic horse-drawn sleighs. For indoor sports, there are hot tubs, tennis courts, and a pool.

CHILD CARE

The child care center is a spacious facility that takes children from 6 weeks through 6 years old. Children ages 3–17 have ski camps that have instruction, and movies, games, and story-time for the little ones.

Stowe Mountain Resort

5781 Mountain Rd., Stowe 05672
☎ *802/253–3000; lodging, 800/247–8693; snow conditions, 802/253–2222*

To be precise, the name of the village is Stowe and the name of the mountain is Mt. Mansfield, but to generations of skiers, the area, the complex, and the region are just plain Stowe. This classic resort dates to the 1930s, when the sport of skiing was a pup. Even today the area's mystique attracts more serious skiers than social skiers. In recent years, on-mountain lodging; free shuttle buses that gather skiers from lodges, inn, and motels along the Mountain Road; improved snowmaking; and new lifts have added convenience to the Stowe experience. Yet the traditions remain: the Winter Carnival in January, the Sugar Slalom in April, ski weeks all winter. So committed is the ski school to improvements that even noninstruction package plans include one free ski lesson. Three base lodges provide plenty of essentials, including two on-mountain restaurants.

DOWNHILL

Mt. Mansfield, with a vertical drop of 2,360 feet, is one of the giants among Eastern ski mountains. Its symmetrical shape allows skiers of all abilities long, satisfying runs from the summit. The famous Front Four runs (National, Liftline, Starr, and Goat) are the intimidating centerpieces for tough, expert runs, yet there is plenty of mellow intermediate skiing and one long beginner trail from the top that ends at the Toll House, where there is easier terrain. Mansfield's satellite sector is a network of intermediate and one expert trail off a basin served by a gondola. Spruce Peak, separate from the main mountain, is a teaching hill and a pleasant experience for intermediates and beginners. In addition to the new high-speed, eight-passenger gondola, Stowe has one quad, one triple, and six double chairlifts, plus one handle tow and poma, to service its 45 trails. Night skiing has been added on a trial basis; trails are accessed by the gondola. The resort has 73% snowmaking coverage.

CROSS-COUNTRY

The resort has 40 kilometers (24 miles) of groomed cross-country trails and 40 kilometers of back-country trails. There are four interconnecting cross-country ski areas with over 100 kilometers of groomed trails within the town of Stowe.

OTHER ACTIVITIES

The Jackson Arena (☎ 802/253–6148) is a public ice-skating rink that rents skates. Charlie Horse Carriage and Sleigh Rides (☎ 802/253–2215), is open daily 11–4; evening group rides are by reservation.

CHILD CARE

The child care center takes children ages 2 months through 12 years. Children's Adventure Center on nonthreatening Spruce Peak is headquarters for all children's programs, ages 3–12.

Other Sports

Biking

The often-deserted roads of the Northeast Kingdom that seem to regularly bring yet another more-beautiful-than-the-last vista are ideal for cycling. Pick up a copy of the *Vermont Life* "Bicycle Vermont" map and guide (from any Chamber of Commerce) to get you started.

In Burlington a recreational path runs 9 miles along the waterfront. South of Burlington, a moderately easy 18½-mile trail begins at the blinker on Rte. 7, Shelburne, and follows Mt. Philo Road, Hinesburg Road, Route 116, and Irish Hill Road. **Earl's** (135 Main St., ☎ 802/862–4203) and **North Star Cyclery** (100 Main St., ☎ 802/863–3832) rent equipment and provide maps.

The junction of Routes 100 and 108 is the start of a 21-mile tour with scenic views of Mt. Mansfield; the course takes you along Route 100 to Stagecoach Road, to Morristown, over to Morrisville, and south on Randolph Road. The **Mountain Bike Shop** (Mountain Rd., ☎ 802/253–7919) supplies equipment and offers guided tours.

Canoeing

Sailworks (176 Battery St., Burlington, ☎ 802/864–0111) rents canoes and gives lessons at Sand Bar State Park in summer. **Umiak Outdoor Outfitters** (849 S. Main St., Stowe, ☎ 802/253–2317) specializes in canoes and rents them for day trips; they also lead guided overnight excursions. The **Village Sport Shop** (Lyndonville, ☎ 802/626–8448) rents canoes for plying the Connecticut River.

Fishing

Rainbow trout inhabit the Missisquoi, Lamoille, Winooski, and Willoughby rivers, and there's warm-water fishing at many smaller lakes and ponds. Lakes Seymour, Willoughby, and Memphremagog and Great Averill Pond in the Northeast Kingdom are good for salmon and lake trout. The **Fly Rod Shop** (Rte. 100, 3 mi south of Stowe, ☎ 802/253–7346) rents and sells equipment.

Lake Champlain, stocked annually with salmon and lake trout, has become the state's ice-fishing capital; walleye, bass, pike, and channel catfish are also taken. Ice fishing is also popular on Lake Memphremagog.

Marina services are available north and south of Burlington. **Malletts Bay Marina** (228 Lakeshore Dr., Colchester, ☎ 802/862–4077) and **Point Bay Marina** (Thompson's Point, Charlotte, ☎ 802/425–2431) both provide full service and repairs.

Groton Pond (Rte. 302, off I–91, 20 mi south of St. Johnsbury, ☎ 802/584–3829) is a popular spot for trout fishing; boat rentals are available.

Hiking

Stop into the headquarters of the **Green Mountain Club,** 1 mile north of Waterbury Center (Rte. 100, R.R. 1, Box 650, Waterbury Center 05677, ☎ 802/244–7037), which maintains the Long Trail—the north–south border-to-border footpath that runs the length of the spine of the Green Mountains—as well as other trails nearby. They sell a number of maps and guides and are helpful with suggestions.

Mount Mansfield State Forest and **Little River State Park** (Rte. 2, 1½ mi west of Waterbury) provide an extensive trail system, including one that reaches the site of the Civilian Conservation Corps unit that was here in the 1930s.

For the climb to **Stowe Pinnacle,** go 1½ miles south of Stowe on Route 100 and turn east on Gold Brook Road opposite the Nichols Farm Lodge; bear left at the first fork, continue through an intersection at a covered bridge, turn right after 1.8 miles, and travel 2.3 miles to a parking lot on the left. The trail crosses an abandoned pasture and takes a short, steep climb to views of the Green Mountains and Stowe Valley (two hours).

Llama Trekking

Cold Hollow Llamas (Belvedere, ☎ 802/644–5846) leads trips through the Vermont countryside; their gourmet picnic lunches are a highlight.

Tennis

Bolton Valley has eight outdoor tennis courts; **Smugglers'** has two. The **Stowe Area Association** (☎ 802/253–7321), which hosts a grand prix tennis tournament in early August, can recommend nearby public courts.

Water Sports

Smugglers' has a water playground and an outdoor pool. **Burlington Community Boathouse** (foot of College St., Burlington Harbor, ☎ 802/865–3377) has sailboard and boat rentals (some captained) and lessons. **Chiott Marine** (67 Main St. Burlington, ☎ 802/862–8383) caters to all realms of water sports with two floors of hardware, apparel, and accessories. The yacht Intrepid, an America's Cup winner, can be chartered from **International Yacht Sales** (Colchester, ☎ 802/864–6800).

Beaches

Some of the most scenic Lake Champlain beaches are on the Champlain islands. **North Hero State Park** (☎ 802/372–8727) has a children's play area nearby; **Knight Point State Park** (☎ 802/372–8389) is the reputed home of "Champ," Lake Champlain's answer to the Loch Ness monster; and **Sand Bar State Park** (☎ 802/372–8240) is near a waterfowl preserve. Arrive early to beat summer crowds. ☞ *$1 adults, 50¢ children.* ☉ *Mid-May–Oct.*

The **North Beaches** are on the northern edge of Burlington: North Beach Park (North Ave., ☎ 802/864–0123), Bayside Beach (Rte. 127 near Malletts Bay), and Leddy Beach, which is popular for sailboarding.

State Parks

The following have camping and picnicking facilities: **Burton Island State Park** (Rte. 105, 2 mi east of Island Pond, then south on marked local road, ☎ 802/524–6353; 253 acres) is accessible only by ferry or boat; at the nature center a naturalist discusses the island habitat. There's a 100-slip marina with hookups and 20 moorings, and a snack bar. **Grand Isle State Park** (Rte. 2, 1 mi south of Grand Isle, ☎ 802/372–4300; 226 acres) has a fitness trail and a naturalist. **Kill Kare State Park** (Rte. 36, 4½ mi west of St. Albans Bay, then south on town road 3½ mi, ☎ 802/524–6021; 17.7 acres) is popular for sailboarding; there is ferry service to Burton Island. **Little River State Park** (Little River Rd., 3½ mi north of Rte. 2, 2 mi east of Rte. 100, ☎ 802/244–7103; 12,000 acres) has marked nature trails for hiking on Mt. Mansfield and Camel's Hump, boat rentals, and a ramp. **Smugglers' Notch State Park** (Rte. 108, 10 mi north of Mt. Mansfield, ☎ 802/253–4014; 25 acres) is good for picnicking and hiking on wild terrain among large boulders.

Dining and Lodging

There's an odd dearth of inns and B&Bs in Burlington, although a plethora of chain hotels provides dependable accommodations. The Stowe area has a **lodging referral service** (☎ 800/247–8693).

Bolton Valley

DINING AND LODGING

$$–$$$ **Bolton Valley Resort.** Like the ski area, this self-contained resort is geared
❄ to families. Hotel units are ski-in, ski-out, and have either a fireplace or a kitchenette; condominium units have as many as four bedrooms. Children under six ski and stay free. ▣ *Mountain Rd., Bolton 05477, ☎ 802/434–2131 or 800/451–3220,* ℻ *804/434–4547. 146 rooms with bath. 5 restaurants, deli, pub, indoor and outdoor pools, sauna, health club, 9 tennis courts. AE, D, DC, MC, V.*

$–$$ **Black Bear Inn.** Within the walls of this mountaintop country inn are
❄ 24 guest rooms; each has a quilt made by the innkeeper, in-room
★ movies (a different one each night), and—you guessed it—bears! Be sure to ask for a room with a balcony, many of which overlook the Green Mountains and ski trails. ▣ *Mountain Rd., 05477, ☎ 802/434–2126 or 800/395–6335,* ℻ *802/434–5761. 24 rooms with bath. Restaurant, pool. MC, V.*

Burlington

DINING

$$ **The Daily Planet.** Contemporary plaid oilcloth, an old jukebox playing Aretha Franklin, a solarium, and a turn-of-the-century bar add up to one of Burlington's hippest restaurants. This is Marco Polo cuisine—basically Mediterranean with Oriental influences: lobster risotto with peas; braised lamb loin with polenta and chutney; various stir-fries. ✕ *15 Center St., ☎ 802/862–9647. Reservations advised. AE, DC, MC, V.*

$$ Isabel's. In part of an old lumber mill, this eclectic, inspired Ameri-
★   can-cuisine restaurant notable for its artful presentation has high ceil-
     ings, exposed-brick walls, and knockout views spanning west from its
     Lake Champlain frontage. The menu changes weekly and has included
     salmon stuffed with spinach and feta wrapped in a phyllo pastry with
     béchamel sauce, and New Zealand lamb with walnut pesto. Lunch and
     Sunday brunch are popular; outdoor patio dining beckons on warm
     days. ✕ *112 Lake St.,* ☎ *802/865–2522. Reservations advised. AE,
     DC, MC, V. No lunch weekends; no dinner Mon.–Wed.*

$–$$ Bourbon Street Grill. With a 1–10 heat scale where three is "everyone
     else's medium," you know this place takes itself seriously—even if the
     chef is a Yankee and the guests wear ski parkas instead of Mardi Gras
     beads. If New England's cold has you yearning for spicy food, try the
     jambalaya or Cajun grilled flank steak. The menu offers a bunch of grill
     entrées, Jamaican jerk chicken, and shrimp popcorn—most can be spiced
     according to the number of taste buds you have left. ✕ *213 College St.,*
     ☎ *802/865–2800. Reservations advised. AE, DC, MC, V.*

$–$$ Sweet Tomatoes. The wood-fired oven of this bright and boisterous trat-
★   toria sends off a mouth watering aroma. With hand-painted ceramic
     pitchers, bottles of dark olive oil perched against a backdrop of exposed
     brick, and crusty, bull-headed bread that comes with a bowl of oil and
     garlic for dunking, this soulful eatery beckons you to Italy's country-
     side. The selections on the extensive, exclusively Italian wine list have
     been thoroughly tested—vineside—by the owners. The menu includes
     caponata (roasted eggplant with onions, capers, olives, parsley, celery,
     and tomatoes), *cavatappi* (pasta with roasted chicken and sautéed
     mushrooms, peas, and walnuts in a pecorino-romano-carbonara sauce),
     and an extensive selection of pizzas. ✕ *83 Church St.,* ☎ *802/660–9533.
     Reservations accepted for large parties. MC, V.*

DINING AND LODGING

$$–$$$$ The Inn at Shelburne Farms. This is storybook land: Built at the turn
★   of the century as the home of William Seward and Lila Vanderbilt Webb,
     the Tudor-style inn perches on Saxton's Point overlooking Lake Cham-
     plain, the distant Adirondacks, and the sea of pastures that make up
     this 1,000-acre working farm. Each guest room is different, from the
     wallpaper to the period antiques. The two dining rooms define elegance.
     A seasonal menu features home-grown products that might include loin
     of pork with an apple-cider–sundried-cranberry chutney, or rack of lamb
     with spinach-and-roasted-garlic pesto. The inn's profits help support
     the farm's environmental education programs for local schools. ⌖ *Har-
     bor Rd., Shelburne 05482,* ☎ *802/985–8498,* FAX *802/985–8123. 24
     rooms, 17 with bath. Restaurant (reservations advised), lake, hiking,
     boating, fishing, tennis courts, recreation rooms. AE, DC, MC, V.
     Closed mid-Oct.–mid-May.*

$$$ Inn at Essex. This Georgian-style hotel that sits back from the subur-
     ban sprawl encircling Burlington—about 10 miles from downtown—
     is a state-of-the-art conference center dressed in country-inn clothing.
     Attentive staff, individually decorated rooms with flowered wallpaper,
     working fireplaces in some rooms, and library books on the reproduction
     desks lend character. The two restaurants—the refined Butler's and the
     more casual Birchtree Cafe—are run by the New England Culinary In-
     stitute. Students are coached by an executive chef and rotate through
     each position, from sous-chef to waitstaff—these are great chefs in the
     making. The updated New England style shows off sweet dumpling
     squash with ginger-garlic basmati rice, and lobster in yellow corn
     sauce with spinach pasta at Butler's; chicken pot pie and seafood stew
     with saffron risotto in the café. ⌖ *70 Essex Way, off Rte. 15, Essex*

Junction 05452, ☎ *802/878–1100 or 800/288–7613,* ⨳ *802/878–0063. 97 rooms with bath. Restaurant (reservations advised), pool, library. AE, D, DC, MC, V.*

$$$ **Radisson Hotel–Burlington.** This sleek corporate giant is the hotel closest to downtown shopping, and it faces the lakefront. Odd-numbered rooms have the view; rooms whose number end in 1 look onto both lake and city. Girard's, the hotel's restaurant, serves traditional, yet inspired, Continental fare. ☏ *60 Battery St., 05401,* ☎ *802/658–6500 or 800/333–3333,* ⨳ *802/658–4659. 256 rooms with bath. Restaurant, bar, indoor pool, airport shuttle, parking. AE, D, DC, MC, V.*

Craftsbury
DINING AND LODGING
$–$$$ **Craftsbury Inn.** Just down the road from Craftsbury Common's traditional New England green, this 1850 Greek revival country inn with a two-tiered porch is a well-situated base for outdoor enthusiasts and those in search of real respite. Antiques, Oriental rugs, leaded floor-to-ceiling windows, and dark blue and mauve accents create a warm ambiance; two bird's eye maple hutches, gleaming pine floors, and embossed tin ceilings embellish the sitting rooms. The guest rooms have brass, iron, and canopy beds; all have custom-made quilts. The wood-burning stove, bright yellow wallpaper, and picture windows in the dining room herald the inn's exceptional fare, which includes butternut-squash-and-apple soup, smoked trout with cucumber caper sauce, and rack of lamb with Roquefort sauce. ☏ *Main St., 05826,* ☎ *802/586–2848 or 800/336–2848. 10 rooms, 6 with bath. Restaurant (closed Mon. and Tues.), bar, cross-country skiing. MAP. MC, V.*

East Burke
DINING
$–$$ **The Pub Outback.** A huge copper bar with rough-hewn beams and rafters overhead set the tone in this casual, friendly restaurant. Appealing to both the après-ski crowd and families, it serves the likes of warm spinach salad, black bean cakes, burgers, and shrimp and chicken piccata. ✕ *Rte. 114,* ☎ *802/626–5187. D, DC, MC, V.*

$–$$ **River Garden Café.** Eat outdoors on the enclosed porch or the patio and enjoy the perennial gardens that rim the grounds of the area's newest eatery. The café is bright and cheerful on the inside as well; one notes the difference between a café and a restaurant. The healthful fare includes lobster-and-scallop casserole, Vermont smoked trout, bruschetta, and stir-fries. ✕ *Rte. 114,* ☎ *802/626–3514. MC, V.*

DINING AND LODGING
$–$$ **Old Cutter Inn.** Only ½ mile from the Burke Mountain base lodge is ❄ this small converted farmhouse that will fulfill your quest for the quaint-inn experience. The restaurant features fare that reflects the Swiss chef/owner's heritage, as well as other superb Continental cuisine. ☏ *R.R. 1 (Box 62), 05832,* ☎ *802/626–5152. 10 rooms, 5 with bath. Restaurant, bar, pool. MAP available. MC, V. Closed Apr., Nov.*

LODGING
$–$$$ **Burke Mountain Resort.** A variety of modern accommodations are ❄ available at this resort, from economical to luxurious, fully furnished slopeside town houses and condominiums with full kitchens and TVs. Some have fireplaces, others have wood-burning stoves. Two-night minimum stay required. ☏ *Box 247, 05832,* ☎ *800/541–5480,* ⨳ *802/626–3364. AE, MC, V.*

Greensboro

DINING AND LODGING

$$–$$$ **Highland Lodge.** Tranquility defined: An 1860 rambling lakefront house that overlooks a pristine lake, with 120 acres of rambling woods and pastures laced with hiking and skiing trails (ski rental available). Widely touted as having one of the best front porches in the state, this quiet family resort is part refined elegance, of the preppy New England sort, and part casual country, of the summer camp sort. Comfortable guest rooms have Victorian-style furnishings and most have views of the lake; cottages are more private, simply furnished, and great for families. Swimming, fishing, and boating are big pastimes here, and if you haven't whiled enough of your day away, lunch on the porch is a must. The dinner menu is fairly traditional and might include entrées such as roasted Vermont leg of lamb and grilled Black Angus sirloin. ⊡ *Caspian Lake, Greensboro 05841,* ☎ *802/533–2647,* FAX *802/533–7494. 11 rooms with bath, 10 cottages. Restaurant, hiking, boating, cross-country skiing, swimming, tennis court, recreation room. Full breakfast included; MAP available. D, MC, V.*

Jay

DINING AND LODGING

$$–$$$ **The Black Lantern.** Built in 1803 as a hotel for mill workers, the inn has ❋ been providing bed and board ever since. Though the feeling is country, little touches of sophistication abound: Provençal print wallpaper in the dining room, a subtle rag-roll finish in the rooms in the renovated building next door. All suites have whirlpools and most have fireplaces. The restaurant's menu includes pan-seared salmon served with a red pepper sauce and grilled lamb Margarite. ⊡ *Rte. 118, Montgomery Village, 05470,* ☎ *802/326–4507,* FAX *802/326–4077. 10 rooms with bath, 6 suites. Restaurant. AE, MC, V.*

$$–$$$ **Hotel Jay & Condominiums.** Ski-lodge simplicity sets the tone in the hotel, ❋ with wood paneling in the rooms, built-in headboards, and vinyl wallpaper in the bathroom. Right at the lifts, the hotel is very convenient for people who plan to spend most of their time on the slopes. Rooms on the southwest side have a view of Jay Peak, those on the north overlook the valley, and upper floors have balconies. The 84 condominiums have one to three bedrooms and modern kitchens, washers-dryers, and spacious living areas with fireplaces. Most are slope-side. Summer rates are very low. ⊡ *Rte. 242, 05859,* ☎ *802/988–2611 or 800/451–4449,* FAX *802/988–4049. 48 rooms with bath, 84 condos. Restaurant, bar, pool, sauna, tennis courts, recreation room. MAP. (Lift tickets included in rates). AE, D, DC, MC, V.*

$$ **The Inn on Trout River.** The wood-burning stove is often the center of ❋ attention in the two-tiered living and dining area of this 100-year-old inn, although the piano, the library, the pub with a U-shaped bar, or the pool table down in the recreation room could equally draw your attention. The guest rooms are decorated in the English country cottage style and all have down quilts and flannel sheets in winter; the largest has a Franklin pot-belly stove, a dressing area, and a clawfoot tub. The back lawn rambles down to the river and llama treks are offered in warm months. The restaurant serves hearty New England fare. ⊡ *Main St., Montgomery Center, 05471,* ☎ *802/326–4391 or 800/338-7049. 10 rooms with bath. Restaurant, pub, library, recreation room. MAP. AE, D, MC, V.*

Jeffersonville

DINING

$$$$ **Le Cheval D'Or.** Easily one of the most renowned restaurants in the state, this institution carries the requisite attitude that goes along with such a reputation. A world-famous chef, incredible food, elegant atmosphere, and jackets, please! ✕ *Main St. (Box 426),* ☎ *802/644–5556. Reservations required. Jacket and tie. MC, V.*

DINING AND LODGING

$$$–$$$$ **Smugglers' Notch Resort.** The large year-round resort has contem-
❄ porarily furnished condos, most with fireplaces and decks. ⊞ *Rte. 108, 05464,* ☎ *802/644–8851 or 800/451–8752,* FAX *802/644–5913. 350 condos. 3 restaurants, bar, indoor pool, exercise room, hot tub, saunas, ice-skating, 10 tennis courts, baby-sitting, children's programs, nursery, playground, recreation room. AE, DC, MC, V.*

LODGING

$$ **The Highlander Motel.** Although most of the rooms are motel-style, the
❄ Highlander also has three inn-style, antiques-filled units that have views of the mountain. No matter what configuration you choose, you won't be far from Smugglers' Village, 2½ miles away. You can enjoy breakfast and dinner by the fire. ⊞ *Rte. 108 S, 05464,* ☎ *802/644–2725 or 800/367–6471,* FAX *802/644–2725. 15 rooms with bath. Restaurant, recreation room. MC, V.*

Lake Willoughby
DINING AND LODGING

$$–$$$ **WillowVale.** The innkeeper insists it's the Lucerne of America, while others think of Norway's fjords or Scotland's craggy landscape. In any case, Lake Willoughby is stunning; the best thing about this inn is its location. The guest rooms are somewhat uninspired—furnished with functional reproductions—but the comfortable pub with its long, attractive bar and the huge veranda bedecked with rockers and Adirondack chairs are appealing gathering places. The popular, elegant dining room, with its polished wood floor, black bow-back chairs, and green linens, has windows on three sides, so watching the sun set is often an integral part of dinner. The cuisine is traditional Continental. ⊞ *Rte. 5A, Westmore, 05860,* ☎ *802/525–4123 or 800/541–0588. 7 rooms with bath, 4 cottages. Restaurant, pub. CP. D, MC, V.*

LODGING

$–$$ **Fox Hall Inn.** Throughout this 1890 Cottage Revival, listed on the Na-
★ tional Register of Historic Places, furnishings and rooms are embellished by moose miscellany—a response to northern Vermont's passionate interest in these once-scarce creatures. The generous wraparound veranda overlooking Lake Willoughby is dotted with swinging seats and comfortable chairs and is perfect for a summer evening spent listening to the loons. The two corner turret rooms are the most distinctive and spacious, with lake views; the other rooms are also bright and furnished with wicker and quilts. ⊞ *Rte. 16, 05822,* ☎ *802/525–6930. 9 rooms, 4 with bath. Hiking, boating, cross-country skiing. Full breakfast and afternoon snacks included; MAP available. MC, V.*

Lyndonville
DINING AND LODGING

$$–$$$ **Wildflower Inn.** Nearly every room in the inn's four buildings gets a
★ piece of the 500 acres of incredible views. Sitting atop a long ridge that affords panoramic vistas in every direction, this rambling complex of old farm buildings—which date from 1796—was a working dairy farm until 1985. Guest rooms in the restored Federal-style main house, as well as in the carriage houses, are decorated simply with both reproductions and contemporary furnishings. The most spacious rooms are the suites called the Meadows, which are in what used to be the blacksmith shop. In warm weather, the inn is family-oriented in every

respect: There's a petting barn, planned children's activities, a kid's swimming pool; the inn quiets down a bit in winter when it caters more to cross-country skiers. Meals feature hearty, country-style food with homemade breads and vegetables from the garden. ⌑ *Darling Hill Rd., 05851,* ☎ *802/626–8310 or 800/627–8310,* ℻ *802/626–3039. 15 rooms with bath, 7 suites. Restaurant, pool, pond, hot tub, sauna, fishing, ice-skating, cross-country skiing, sleigh rides, tennis court, recreation room, nursery. MC, V. Closed Apr. and Nov.*

Montpelier

DINING

$$$ **Tubb's.** Nearly everyone working here is a student at the New England
★ Culinary Institute. Although this is their training ground, the quality and inventiveness are anything but beginner's luck. The menu changes daily. Tips are *verboten!* ✕ *4 Elm St.,* ☎ *802/229–9202. Reservations advised. MC, V. Closed Sun.*

DINING AND LODGING

$$$–$$$$ **The Inn at Montpelier.** This spacious inn built in the early 1800s was ren-
★ ovated in 1988 with the business traveler in mind; yet the architectural detailing, antique four-poster beds, Windsor chairs, stately upholstered wing chairs, and the classical guitar on the stereo attract non-business folks. The formal sitting room has a Federal feel to it, and the wide wraparound Colonial Revival porch is perfect for reading a good book or watching the town go by. The rooms in the annex across the street are equally elegant. There's also an outstanding restaurant. ⌑ *147 Main St., 05602,* ☎ *802/223–2727,* ℻ *802/223–0722. 19 rooms with baths. Restaurant (reservations suggested), meeting rooms. CP. AE, MC, V.*

St. Johnsbury

DINING AND LODGING

$$$–$$$$ **Rabbit Hill Inn.** Guests are welcomed into a warmth that melts away
★ even the most stressful of journeys. In the formal, Federal parlor, mulled cider is served from the fireplace crane on chilly afternoons. The low wooden beams of the Irish pub next door are a casual contrast to the rest of the inn. Rooms are each as stylistically different as they are consistently indulgent: The Loft, with its 8-foot Palladian window, king canopy bed, double whirlpool bath, and corner fireplace, is one of the most requested. Rooms toward the front of the inn get views of the Connecticut River and New Hampshire's White Mountains. Eclectic, regional cuisine is served in the low-ceiling dining room—perhaps grilled sausage of Vermont pheasant with pistachios or smoked chicken and red lentil dumplings nestled in red pepper linguine. Meat and fish are smoked on the premises, and the herbs and vegetables often come from gardens out back. ⌑ *Rte. 18, Lower Waterford 05848,* ☎ *802/ 748–5168 or 800/762–8669. 15 double rooms with bath, 5 suites. Restaurant (reservations advised), pub, boating, hiking, cross-country skiing. MAP. MC, V. Closed Apr. and 1st 3 wks in Nov.*

Stowe

DINING

$$ **Foxfire Inn.** A restored Colonial building might seem an unusual place in which to find such superb Italian delicacies as veal rollatini, steak saltimbocca, and *tartufo* (vanilla and chocolate gelato in a chocolate cup with a raspberry center). However, this old farmhouse a couple of miles north of Stowe proper blends the two well, and its popularity with locals proves it's worth the short drive. ✕ *Rte. 100,* ☎ *802/253– 4887. MC, V.*

$$ **Villa Tragara.** A converted farmhouse has been carved into intimate
★ dining nooks where romance reigns over such specialties as ravioli filled
with four cheeses and served with a half-tomato, half-cream sauce. The
tasting menu is a five-course dinner for $35 (plus $15 for coordinat-
ing wines). ✗ *Rte. 100, south of Stowe,* ☎ *802/244–5288. Reserva-
tions advised. AE, MC, V.*

DINING AND LODGING

$$$$ **Topnotch at Stowe.** This resort, built in the 1970s, just 3 miles from
❄ the base of the mountain, is one of the state's most posh. Floor-to-ceil-
ing windows, a freestanding circular stone fireplace, and cathedral ceil-
ings make the lobby an imposing setting. Rooms have thick rust-color
carpeting, a small shelf of books, and perhaps a barn-board wall or
an Italian print. ⌂ *Mountain Rd., 05672,* ☎ *802/253–8585 or 800/
451–8686,* 𝖥𝖠𝖷 *802/253–9263. 92 rooms with bath, 14 2–3 bedroom
town homes, 8 suites. 3 restaurants, bar, indoor pool, outdoor pools,
health spa, horseback riding, 14 tennis courts. AE, D, MC, V.*

$$–$$$ **Edson Hill Manor.** This French Canadian–style manor built in 1940 sits
❄ atop 225 acres of rolling hills. Oriental rugs accent the dark wide-board
floors and a tapestry complements the rich, burgundy-patterned sofas
that face the huge stone fireplace in the living room. The comfortable
guest rooms are pine panelled, and have fireplaces, canopy beds, and
down comforters; bathrooms are livened up with artwork. The dining
room is really the heart of the place: The walls of windows allowing
contemplation of the inspiring view compete for diners' attention with
paintings of a wildflower, an ivy-covered stone arch, and vines climb-
ing to the ceiling. The highly designed, sculpted food is coined "eclec-
tic American" and is served on hand-painted plates. ⌂ *1500 Edson Hill
Rd., 05672,* ☎ *802/253–7371 or 800/621–6084,* 𝖥𝖠𝖷 *802/253–4036.
25 rooms with bath. Restaurant (dinner only; ⊘ Fri. and Sat. Apr. and
May, daily rest of yr), pool, hiking, cross-country skiing, horseback rid-
ing. AE, D, MC, V.*

LODGING

$$$ **The Gables Inn.** The converted farmhouse is a rabbit warren of charm-
❄ ing, antiques-filled rooms. The four rooms in the carriage house have
cathedral ceilings, fireplaces, TVs, and whirlpool tubs. There is a porch
with comfortable chairs on which you can enjoy the view of Mt. Mansfield. The tiny plant-filled sunroom is perfect for lazy mornings, and
the generous breakfasts are legendary. ⌂ *Mountain Rd., 05672,* ☎ *802/
253–7730 or 800/422–5371,* 𝖥𝖠𝖷 *802/253–8989. 17 rooms with bath;
2 suites. Dining room, bar, pool, hot tub. B&B and MAP rates available. AE, D, MC, V.*

$$ **The Inn at the Brass Lantern.** Home-baked cookies in the afternoon, a
❄ basket of logs by your fireplace, and stenciled hearts along the wain-
scoting reflect the care taken in turning this 18th-century farmhouse
into a place of welcome. An understated atmosphere settles into the
building's corners: you'll find no pretentions here. All rooms have
quilts and country antiques; most are oversize. And although the inn
(really a B&B) is precariously close to the Grand Union supermarket
next door, the breakfast room (and some guest rooms) have a terrific
view of Mt. Mansfield. ⌂ *Rte. 100, ½ mi north of Stowe, 05672,* ☎
802/253–2229 or 800/729–2980, 𝖥𝖠𝖷 *802/253–7425. 9 rooms with
bath. Breakfast room. MAP. AE, MC, V.*

Waterbury
DINING AND LODGING

$$–$$$ **Thatcher Brook Inn.** There were once two sawmills across the street from
❄ this 1899 mansion, which was the residence for the sawyers and their fam-

ilies—it's hard now to picture their lives, with the hub of activity centered around Ben & Jerry's ice cream factory next door. Twin gazebos are poised on either end of the front porch, which is graced with Adirondack chairs and black rockers; and stands of giant white pines bolster the inn, defining its space on busy Route 100. Comfortable guest rooms have modern bathroom fixtures and floral wallpaper. The pine panelling, fireplace, framed *Life* magazines, and tables with backgammon boards painted right on them make the pub a popular socializing spot. Classic French cuisine is served in the dining room where dark green walls and mauve linens accent original woodwork. The inn's central location makes it a perfect base for exploring some of the state's most popular tourist attractions. ⚓ *Rte. 100, 05676,* ☎ *802/244–5911 or 800/292–5911 or 800/336–5911,* FAX *802/244–1294. 24 rooms with bath. Pub. Full breakfast included. AE, D, DC, MC, V.*

The Arts

Barre Opera House (City Hall, Main St., Barre, ☎ 802/476–8188) hosts music, opera, theater, and dance performances. **Catamount Arts** (60 Eastern Ave., St. Johnsbury, ☎ 802/748–2600) brings avant-garde theater and dance performances to the Northeast Kingdom, as well as classical music and frequent film screenings.

Flynn Theatre for the Performing Arts, a grandiose old structure, is the cultural heart of Burlington; it schedules the Vermont Symphony Orchestra, theater, dance, big-name musicians, and lectures. *153 Main St., Burlington,* ☎ *802/864–8778 for information; 802/863–5966 for tickets.*

Music

Stowe Performing Arts (☎ 802/253–7321) sponsors a series of classical and jazz concerts during July and August in a meadow high above the village, next to the Trapp Family Lodge. **Vermont Symphony Orchestra** (☎ 802/864–5741) performs at the Flynn Theatre in Burlington in winter and outdoors at Shelburne Farms in summer.

Theater

Champlain Shakespeare Festival performs each summer at the Royall Tyler Theater (☎ 802/656–0090) at the University of Vermont. **St. Michael's Playhouse** (☎ 802/654–2281) is the state's old equity theater company. **Stowe Stage Co.** (Stowe Playhouse, Mountain Rd., Stowe, ☎ 802/253–7944) does musical comedy, July to early October. **Vermont Repertory Theater** (☎ 802/655–9620) mounts five productions in a season, which runs from September through May.

Nightlife

Nighttime activities are centered in Burlington, with its college students and business travelers, and in the ski areas where many of the restaurants and bars have après-ski entertainment.

Vermont Pub and Brewery (College and St. Paul Sts., Burlington, ☎ 802/865–0500) makes its own beer and fruit seltzers and is arguably the most popular spot in town. It serves a full lunch and dinner menu, and folk musicians play here regularly. **Last Elm Cafe** (N. Winooski Ave., Burlington, no ☎), a good old-fashioned coffeehouse, is a good bet for folk music. **Club Metronome** (188 Main St., Burlington, ☎ 802/865–4563) stages an eclectic musical mix that ranges from the newest in cutting edge to funk, blues, reggae, and the occasional big name. **Nectar's** (188 Main St., Burlington, ☎ 802/658–4771) never charges a cover and is always jumping to the sounds of local bands.

Bolton Valley Resort's **James Moore Tavern** (☎ 802/434–2131) has live entertainment. The **Pub Out Back** (☎ 802/626–5187) in East Burke is a congenial gathering place, its oval copper bar a welcome sight to Burke Mountain skiers and moose seekers. In the Smugglers' area, most après-ski action centers around the afternoon bonfires and nightly live entertainment in the **Meeting House** (☎ 802/644–8851) or **Smugglers' Lounge** (Village Restaurant, ☎ 802/644–2291); sleigh rides, fireworks, and torch-light parades occur twice weekly. Around Stowe, the **Matterhorn Night Club** (☎ 802/253–8198) has live music and dancing; **BK Clark's** (☎ 802/253–9300) also has live music. Other options include the lounges at **Topnotch at Stowe** (☎ 802/253–8585), for live weekend entertainment, and the less-expensive **Stoweflake Inn** (☎ 802/253–7355).

Northern Vermont Essentials

Getting Around

BY BUS
Vermont Transit (☎ 802/864–6811, 800/451–3292, or, in VT, 800/642–3133) links Burlington, Stowe, Montpelier, Barre, St. Johnsbury, and Newport.

BY CAR
In north-central Vermont, I–89 heads west from Montpelier to Burlington and continues north to Canada. Interstate 91 is the principal north–south route in the east, and Route 100 runs north–south through the center of the state. North of I–89, routes 104 and 15 provide a major east–west transverse.

Lake Champlain Ferries (☎ 802/864–9804), in operation since 1826, operates three ferry crossings during the summer months and one in winter through thick lake ice. Ferries leave from the King Street Dock in Burlington. This is a convenient means of getting to and from New York, as well as a pleasant way to spend an afternoon. Call for the current schedule.

Guided Tours

The **Lamoille Valley Railroad,** a working line, augments its income by carrying passengers on one- and two-hour excursions along the Lamoille River, where the green and gold cars crisscross the water and pass through the Fischer Bridge, the only covered railroad bridge in the country. *Stafford Ave., Morrisville, ☎ 802/888–7183.* ☛ *$10 adults, $5 children 5–12.* ☉ *July–early Sept., Fri. and Sat. 10, 1:00, and 2:30; mid-Sept.–mid-Oct., Mon.–Sat. 10, 1:00, and 2:30.*

Important Addresses and Numbers

EMERGENCIES
Medical Center Hospital of Vermont (Colchester Ave., Burlington, ☎ 802/656–2345) is the most comprehensive medical facility in the region.

VISITOR INFORMATION
The following offices are open weekdays 9–5: **Greater Newport Area Chamber of Commerce** (The Causeway, Newport 05855, ☎ 802/334–7782); **Lake Champlain Regional Chamber of Commerce** (209 Battery St., Box 453, Burlington 05402, ☎ 802/863–3489); **St. Johnsbury Chamber of Commerce** (30 Western Ave., St. Johnsbury 05819, ☎ 802/748–3678); **Smugglers' Notch Area Chamber of Commerce** (Box 3264, Jeffersonville 05464, ☎ 802/644–2239). The **Stowe Area Association** (Main St., Box 1320, Stowe 05672, ☎ 802/253–7321 or 800/247–8693) is open April–October, weekdays 9–5; November–March, weekdays 9–9, Saturday 10–6, Sunday 10–4.

VERMONT ESSENTIALS

Arriving and Departing

By Bus

Vermont Transit (☎ 802/864–6811, 800/451–3292, or, in VT, 800/642–3133) connects Bennington, Brattleboro, Burlington, Rutland, and other Vermont cities and towns with Boston, Springfield, Albany, New York, Montréal, and cities in New Hampshire. **Bonanza** (☎ 800/556–3815) connects New York City with Bennington.

By Car

Interstate 91, which stretches from Connecticut and Massachusetts in the south to Québec (Hwy. 55) in the north, reaches most points along Vermont's eastern border. Interstate 89, from New Hampshire to the east and Québec (Hwy. 133) to the north, crosses central Vermont from White River Junction to Burlington. Southwestern Vermont can be reached by Route 7 from Massachusetts and Route 4 from New York.

By Plane

Burlington International Airport (☎ 802/863–2874) has scheduled daily flights on Continental, Delta, United, and USAir. West of Bennington and convenient to southern Vermont, **Albany–Schenectady County Airport** in New York State is served by 10 major U.S. carriers.

By Train

Amtrak's (☎ 800/872–7245) new *Vermonter,* a daytime service linking Hartford, CT, with Brattleboro, Bellows Falls, Claremont, White River Junction, Montpelier, Waterbury, Essex Junction, and St. Albans, replaces the *Montrealer.* The *Adirondack,* which runs from New York City to Montréal, serves Albany, Ft. Edward (near Glens Falls), Ft. Ticonderoga, and Plattsburgh, allowing relatively convenient access to western Vermont.

Getting Around

By Car

The official speed limit in Vermont is 50 mph, unless otherwise posted; on the interstates it's 65 mph. You can get a state map, which has mileage charts and enlarged maps of major downtown areas, free from the Vermont Travel Division. *The Vermont Atlas and Gazetteer,* sold in many bookstores, shows nearly every road in the state and is great for driving on the back roads.

By Plane

Aircraft charters are available at Burlington International Airport from **Inotech Aviation** (☎ 802/658–2200) and **Valley Air Services** (☎ 802/863–3626).

Southern Vermont Helicopter (W. Brattleboro, ☎ 802/257–4354) provides helicopter transportation throughout New England.

Guided Tours

Biking

Vermont is great bicycle-touring country, and a number of companies offer weekend tours and week-long trips that range throughout the state. Most chambers of commerce have brochures highlighting good cycling routes in their area, and many bookstores sell *25 Bicycle Tours in Vermont* by John Freidin, the founder of **Vermont Bicycle Touring** (Box 711, Bristol 05443, ☎ 802/453–4811). The first bike tour operator in the

United States, and one of the most respected, it operates numerous tours throughout the state. **Bicycle Holidays** (Box 2394, Munger St., Middlebury 05753, ☎ 802/388–2453) creates custom-designed bike trips, and will help you put together your own inn-to-inn tour by providing route directions and booking your accommodations.

Canoeing

Umiak Outdoor Outfitters (849 S. Main St., Stowe 05672, ☎ 802/253–2317) has shuttles to nearby rivers for day excursions as well as customized overnight trips. **Vermont Canoe Trippers/Battenkill Canoe, Ltd.** (Box 65, Arlington 05250, ☎ 802/362–2800) organizes canoe tours and fishing trips.

Educational

Vermont Off Beat (Box 4366, S. Burlington 05406, ☎ 802/863–2535) has an extraordinary lineup of special-interest workshops. These weekend getaways can be on anything from studying Robert Frost (in Middlebury) to planting perennials (in Craftsbury Common) to gathering Vermont mushrooms (in Waitsfield).

Hiking

North Wind Touring (Box 46, Waitsfield 05673, ☎ 802/496–5771) offers guided walking tours through Vermont's countryside. **Vermont Hiking Holidays** (Box 750, Bristol 05443, ☎ 802/453–4816) leads guided walks from May through October, with lodging in country inns. **Walking Tours of Southern Vermont** (R.R. 2, Box 622, Arlington, ☎ 802/375–1141) specializes in historical inn-to-inn tours; several are for women only.

Horseback Riding

Kedron Valley Stables (Box 368, South Woodstock 05071, ☎ 802/457–1480) has one- to six-day riding tours with lodging in country inns.

Skiing

The Green Mountains run through the middle of Vermont like a bumpy spine, visible from almost every point in the state; generous accumulations of snow make the mountains an ideal site for skiing. Recent increased snow-making capacity and improved, high-tech computerized equipment at many areas virtually assures a good day on the slopes. Vermont has 21 alpine ski resorts with nearly 900 trails and some 4,000 acres of skiable terrain. Combined, the resorts offer some 175 lifts and have the capacity to carry a total of more than 200,000 skiers per hour. In addition, the state offers a wide variety of accommodations and dining options, from inexpensive dormitories to luxurious inns, at the base of most ski mountains or within an easy drive. Though grooming is sophisticated at all Vermont areas, conditions usually range from hard pack to icy, with powder a rare luxury. The best advice for skiing in Vermont is to keep your skis well tuned.

Route 100 is well known as the "Skier's Highway," passing by 13 of the state's ski areas. Vermont's major resorts are Stowe, Jay Peak, Sugarbush, Killington, Okemo, Mt. Snow, and Stratton. Midsize, less hectic areas to consider include Ascutney, Bromley, Bolton Valley, Smugglers' Notch, Pico, Mad River Glen, and Burke Mountain.

Dining

Vermont restaurants have not escaped common efforts in the northeast to adapt traditional New England fare to the ways of nouvelle cuisine. The New England Culinary Institute, based in Montpelier, has trained a number of Vermont chefs who have now turned their attention to such native New England foods as fiddlehead ferns (available only for a short time in the spring); maple syrup (Vermont is the largest U.S. producer); dairy products, especially cheese; native fruits and berries that are often transformed into jams and jellies; "new Vermont" products such as salsa and salad dressings; and venison, quail, pheasant, and other game.

Your chances of finding a table for dinner vary dramatically with the season: Many restaurants have lengthy waits during peak seasons (when it's always a good idea to reserve ahead) and then shut down during the slow months of April and November. Some of the best dining is found in country inns.

CATEGORY	COST*
$$$$	over $35
$$$	$25–$35
$$	$15–$25
$	under $15

average cost of a three-course dinner, per person, excluding drinks, service, and 7% sales tax

Lodging

Vermont's largest hotels are in Burlington and near the major ski resorts. Elsewhere you'll find a variety of inns, bed-and-breakfasts, and small motels. Rates are highest during foliage season, from late September to mid-October, and lowest in late spring and November, when many properties close. Many of the larger hotels offer package rates. Some antiques-filled inns discourage bringing children.

Bed-and-breakfast referral services include **American Country Collection of Bed and Breakfast** (984 Gloucester Pl., Schenectady, NY 12309, ☎ 518/370–4948) and **American–Vermont Bed and Breakfast Reservation Service** (Box 1, E. Fairfield 05448, ☎ 802/827–3827). You can also try calling the chambers of commerce in many ski areas.

The **Vermont Chamber of Commerce** (*see* Visitor Information, *below*) publishes the *Vermont Travelers' Guidebook,* which is an extensive list of lodgings, and additional guides to country inns and vacation rentals. The **Vermont Travel Division** (*see* Visitor Information, *below*) has a brochure that lists lodgings at working farms.

CATEGORY	COST*
$$$$	over $150
$$$	$100–$150
$$	$60–$100
$	under $60

All prices are for a standard double room during peak season, with no meals unless noted, and excluding service charge.

Important Addresses and Numbers

Emergencies

Vermont State Police (☎ 800/525–5555),Vermont's **Medical Health Care Information Center** (☎ 802/864–0454), and **Telecommunications Device for the Deaf** (TDD) (☎ 802/253–0191) have 24-hour hotlines.

Visitor Information

Vermont Travel Division (134 State St., Montpelier 05602, ☎ 802/828–3237; ⊘ Weekdays 7:45–4:30). **Vermont Chamber of Commerce** (Box 37, Montpelier 05601, ☎ 802/223–3443; ⊘ Weekdays 8:30–5).

Information centers are on the Massachusetts border at I–91, the New Hampshire border at I–89, the New York border at Route 4A, and the Canadian border at I–89.

4 New Hampshire

Portsmouth, star of New Hampshire's 18-mile coastline, has great restaurants, theater, and an impressive historic district; Exeter is an enclave of Revolutionary War history. The lakes region, rich with historic landmarks, also has good restaurants, hiking trails, and antiques shops. People come to the White Mountains to hike, ski, and photograph vistas and vibrant foliage. Mt. Washington's peak claims the harshest winds and lowest temperatures ever recorded. Western and central New Hampshire are the unspoiled heart of the state.

By Michelle
Seaton, with
an introduction
by William G.
Scheller

WHEN GENERAL JOHN STARK coined the expression Live Free or Die, he knew what he was talking about. Stark had been through the Revolutionary War battles of Bunker Hill and Bennington—where he was victorious—and was clearly entitled to state the choice as he saw it. It was, after all, a choice he was willing to make. But Stark could never have imagined that hundreds of thousands of his fellow New Hampshire men and women would one day display the same fierce sentiment as they traveled the streets and roads of the state: Live Free or Die is the legend of the New Hampshire license plate, the only state license plate in the Union to adopt a sociopolitical ultimatum instead of a tribute to scenic beauty or native produce.

The citizens of New Hampshire are a diverse lot who cannot be tucked neatly into any pigeonhole. To be sure, a white-collar worker in one of the high-tech industries that have sprung up around Nashua or Manchester is no mountaineer defending his homestead with a muzzle-loader, no matter what it says on his license plate.

Yet there is a strong civic tradition in New Hampshire that has variously been described as individualistic, mistrustful of government, even libertarian. This tradition manifests itself most prominently in the state's long-standing aversion to any form of broad-based tax: There is no New Hampshire earned-income tax, nor is there a retail sales tax. Instead, the government relies for its revenue on property taxes, sales of liquor and lottery tickets, and levies on restaurant meals and lodgings—the same measures that other states use to varying degrees. Nor are candidates for state office likely to be successful unless they declare themselves opposed to sales and income taxes.

Another aspect of New Hampshire's suspiciousness of government is its limitation of the gubernatorial term of service to two years: With the running of the reelection gauntlet ever imminent, no incumbent is likely to take the risk of being identified as a proponent of an income or a sales tax—or any other similarly unpopular measure.

And then there's the New Hampshire House of Representatives. With no fewer than 400 members, it is the most populous state assembly in the nation and one of the largest deliberative bodies in the world. Each town with sufficient population sends at least one representative to the House, and he or she had better be able to give straight answers on being greeted—on a first-name basis—at the town hardware store on Saturday.

Yankee individualism, a regional cliché, may or may not be the appropriate description here, but New Hampshire does carry on with a quirky, flinty interpretation of the Jeffersonian credo that the government governs best that governs least. Meanwhile, visitors to New Hampshire see all those license plates and wonder whether they're being told that they've betrayed General Stark's maxim by paying an income tax or a deposit on soda bottles—still another indignity the folks in the Granite State have spared themselves.

THE COAST

The first VIP to vacation on the New Hampshire coast was George Washington in 1789. By all accounts he had a pretty good time, although a bizarre fishing accident left him with a nasty black eye. President Wash-

New Hampshire

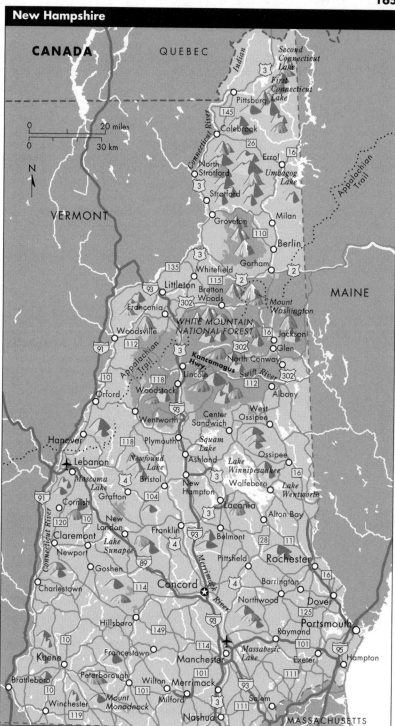

CANADA QUEBEC

Indian

Second Connecticut Lake

First Connecticut Lake

Pittsburg
145

Connecticut River

Colebrook
26

Errol
16

North Stratford

Umbagog Lake

3

Stratford

Milan

VERMONT

Groveton

110

Berlin

3

Gorham

Whitefield
135

115

2

MAINE

Littleton
93

Bretton Woods

302

Mount Washington

Franconia

WHITE MOUNTAIN NATIONAL FOREST

Woodsville
91

112

16

Jackson

Appalachian Trail

302

Glen

Kancamagus Hwy
3

North Conway

118

Woodstock

Lincoln

Swift River

302
112

Albany

Orford
10

93

Wentworth

Center Sandwich

West Ossipee

Hanover

118

Plymouth

Squam Lake

Lebanon

Newfound Lake

Ashland

Lake Winnipesaukee

Ossipee

Mascoma Lake

4

Bristol

New Hampton

Wolfeboro
16

91

Cornish

Grafton

104

3

Laconia

Lake Wentworth

120

New London

Franklin

Belmont

Alton Bay

Connecticut River

Claremont

Lake Sunapee

4

93

28

11

Newport

89

Pittsfield

Rochester

Goshen

114

Concord

4

Barrington

16

Charlestown

Merrimack River

Northwood

Dover

Hillsboro

149

125

Portsmouth

Keene
10

Francestown

114

Raymond

101

95

Peterborough

Manchester
101

Massabesic Lake

Exeter

Hampton

Wilton

Merrimack

111

Brattleboro

Mount Monadnock

Milford

3

93

Salem

Winchester
119

Nashua

111

MASSACHUSETTS

0 — 20 miles
0 — 30 km

N

Appalachian Trail

ington couldn't have had nearly as much fun as today's traveler. Accompanied as he was by 14 generals (all in full dress uniform), he couldn't walk barefoot along the sandy beaches, or picnic at Odiorne Point overlooking the ocean. He probably did get a nice look at the homes of John Paul Jones and John Langdon, however, both of which still stand.

Today's visitor will find swimming, boating, fishing, and water sports amid the beaches and state parks of New Hampshire's 18-mile coastline. Hampton Beach features a 1940s-style boardwalk, complete with arcade and nightly entertainment. Portsmouth has it all: the shopping, the restaurants, the music, the theater, and one of the best historic districts in the nation. In Exeter, New Hampshire's enclave of Revolutionary War history, visitors can take a walking tour that explores the 18th- and early 19th-century homes clustered around Phillips Exeter Academy. If President Washington could do it all again, he would probably leave the generals at home and enjoy a leisurely dinner at a quiet seaside inn.

Exploring

Numbers in the margin correspond to points of interest on the New Hampshire Coast map.

New Hampshire shares a mere 18 miles of its border with the ocean, yet a tour of the coast can take as long as a Sunday afternoon or last for several days. On Route 1, about 2 miles north of the Massachusetts bor-
❶ der, is the old town of **Seabrook,** which is the site of the controversial nuclear power plant of the same name. Adjacent is the **Seabrook Nature & Science Center** (Lafayette Rd., ☎ 800/338–7482; ☉ Mon.–Sat. 10–4), where you can see control-room operators in training and tour an extensive exhibit on the science of power. Here you can pedal a bike to create electricity and use interactive computer games to learn about nuclear power. On the nature side, the center maintains a ¾-mile nature trail, a touch pool for kids, and several large aquariums of local sea life.

❷ Two miles farther north, in **Hampton Falls,** where Route 1 meets Route 88, is the **Applecrest Farm Orchards,** a pick-your-own apple grove and berry patch and bakery where you can buy fresh fruit pies and cookies. In winter you can follow a cross-country ski trail through the orchard. *Rte. 88, Hampton Falls,* ☎ *603/926–3721.* ☉ *Daily 10–dusk.*

If you prefer raspberries, try the **Raspberry Farm** (Rte. 84, Hampton Falls, ☎ 603/926–6604), 3 miles inland on Route 84. The farm offers eight varieties of pick-your-own berries, including blackberries and black raspberries. They also sell fresh berry tarts, jams, vinegars, and sauces.

Return to Route 1, where, at the junction of Route 101, the coastal Route
❸ 1A veers east and passes near **Hampton Beach,** the liveliest on the coast. An estimated 150,000 people visit on the 4th of July alone. If you like fried dough, loud music, arcade games, palm readers, parasailing, and tens of thousands of bronze bodies, don't miss it. The 3-mile boardwalk looks like it was snatched out of the 1940s. Here kids can play games and see how saltwater taffy is made. Free outdoor concerts are held many evenings along with a once-a-week fireworks display. There are talent shows and karaoke performances in the Seashell Stage— right on the beach. Big names perform in the club of the 7-acre, multiple-arcade **Hampton Beach Casino and Ballroom** (☎ 603/926–4541). Each summer locals crown a Miss Hampton Beach, hold a children's festival, and celebrate the end of the season with a huge seafood feast the weekend after Labor Day. For a quieter time, stop by for a sunrise stroll, when only seagulls and the odd jogger interrupt the serenity.

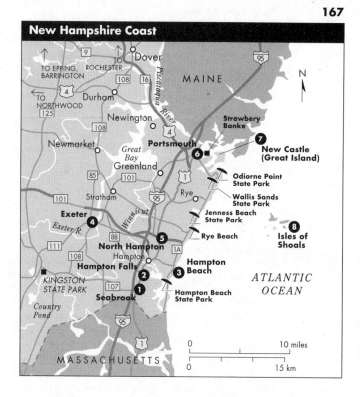

New Hampshire Coast

From here you can take Route 101 a few miles inland to the quiet town
❹ of **Exeter.** In 1638 the town's first settlers built their homes around the
falls where the freshwater Exeter river meets the salty Squamscot.
During the Revolutionary War, Exeter was the state capitol, and it was
here that the first state constitution and the first declaration of independence from Great Britain were put to paper. **Phillips Exeter Academy**
opened its doors in 1783 and is still one of the nation's most esteemed
prep schools. The **American Independence Museum,** in the Ladd-
Gilman House (adjacent to the campus), celebrates the birth of our nation. Built by Nathaniel Ladd and the first brick house in town, it was
eventually converted into a governor's mansion for John Taylor Gilman.
The story of the revolution unfolds during each guided tour, which shows
off drafts of the U.S. Constitution and the first Purple Heart. *1 Governor's La., Exeter,* ☎ *603/772–2622.* ☛ *$4 adults, $3 senior citizens,
$2 children 6–12.* ☼ *May–Oct., Wed.–Sun. noon–5.*

TIME OUT **Masseno's, the Cook's Choice** (33 Water St., Exeter, ☎ 603/778–
7585) serves up such gourmet picnic items as roast beef–and–Boursin
sandwiches or curried chicken with apples and walnuts. You can also
have a seat in the bright café for some coffee and pastries.

❺ Route 101 takes you back to Route 1A north and a scenic drive to **North
Hampton** and Rye Beach. Just north of Hampton Beach sits a group
of immodest mansions known as Millionaires' Row. Because of the way
the road curves, the drive south along this route is even more breathtaking than the drive north. The **Fuller Gardens** bloom all summer long
with 1,500 rosebushes of every shade and type, a Hosta display garden, and a serenity-inspiring groomed Japanese garden. *10 Willow Ave.,
N. Hampton,* ☎ *603/964–5414.* ☛ *$4 adults, $3.50 senior citizens.*
☼ *Early May–mid-Oct., daily 10–6.*

Jenness Beach and **Wallis Sands State Park,** north of Rye Beach, are swimmers' beaches with bright white sand and ample parking. Farther north you'll find the **Odiorne Point State Park** and the Seacoast Science Center. In 1623 the first European settlers landed here, making Odiorne Point the birthplace of New Hampshire. Today the park encompasses more than 300 acres of protected land. You can pick up an interpretive brochure on any one of the nature trails or simply stroll and enjoy the beautiful vistas of the nearby Isles of Shoals. The tidal pools here are considered the best in New England and show off crabs, periwinkles, and sea anemones. The Science Center houses a small museum, which organizes lectures, guided bird walks, and interpretive programs. Exhibits include a two-pool touch tank and historical displays that trace Odiorne point to the Ice Ages. *Rte. 1A, Rye,* ☎ *603/436–8043.* ☛ *Parking: $2.50.* ⊙ *Daily 11–5.*

6 Routes 1, 1A, and 1B, and I–95 all converge on **Portsmouth,** the largest city and the cultural epicenter of the coast. Here you will find restaurants of every stripe and in every price range, plus theater, music, art galleries, and an excellent historic district. Originally settled in 1623 as Strawbery Banke, it became a prosperous port until the Revolutionary War. Many of the homes built prior to the war still stand as part of the Portsmouth Historic District, which includes the **Portsmouth Trail** and a section of town still called Strawbery Banke. Pick up a map from the information kiosk on Market Square or from any of the marked historic houses, which are all within walking distance of one another.

On Little Harbor Road at the South Street Cemetery stands the **Wentworth-Coolidge Mansion** (☎ 603/436–6607), originally the residence of Benning Wentworth, New Hampshire's first Royal Governor. Notable among the period furnishings is the carved pine mantelpiece in the council chamber; also notice Wentworth's own imported lilac trees, which bloom each May.

The **Portsmouth Historical Society,** in the **John Paul Jones House** (Middle and State Sts., ☎ 603/436–8420), contains costumes, glass, guns, portraits, and documents of the late 18th century. It's now one of six houses on the Portsmouth Trail, a historic walking tour that opens on the third Friday in August and lasts through October 15. Tickets cost $4 per house and may be purchased at any of the houses.

TIME OUT   Gourmet coffee shops abound in Portsmouth. **Breaking New Grounds** (16 Market St.) serves cappuccino, espresso, and all the hybrids along with cheesecake and cookies. The **Ceres Street Bakery** (51 Penhallow St.) offers elaborate tarts and tortes, as well as soups and light lunches.

Bring a picnic lunch to historic **Prescott Park,** on the waterfront between Strawbery Banke and the Piscataqua river. The large formal garden, with lively fountains, is the perfect place to while away an afternoon. The park also contains the Point of Graves, Portsmouth's oldest burial ground, and two historic warehouses that date from the early 17th century. One of them, the Sheafe warehouse, was where John Paul Jones outfitted the USS *Ranger,* one of the U.S. Navy's earliest ships. *Prescott Park, Marcy St.,* ☎ *603/431–8748.* ☛ *Free.* ⊙ *Sheafe Museum: Memorial Day–Labor Day, Wed.–Sun. 8–4.*

The **Port of Portsmouth Maritime Museum,** in Albacore Park, is home of the USS *Albacore,* which was built here in 1953 as a prototype submarine—a floating laboratory assigned to test a new hull design, dive brakes, and sonar systems for the Navy. A documentary prior to the tour shows visitors how the 55 crew members lived and worked. The nearby Memorial Garden and its reflecting pool have been dedicated as a memorial to the crews and officers lost in submarine service. *600 Market St., ☎ 603/436–3680. ☛ $4 adults, $3 senior citizens, $2 children 7–17, $10 families. ⊘ May–Columbus Day, daily 9:30–5:30; call for winter hrs.*

TIME OUT For light lunch, gourmet ice cream, or coffee, try **Annabelle's** (Ceres St.). The health conscious might like **Izzy's Frozen Yogurt** (corner Bow and Ceres Sts.), which has such frozen delights as low-fat sundaes and an amazing sugar- and fat-free hot fudge sauce.

The first English settlers named this area for the abundant wild strawberries they found along the shore of the Piscataqua River. Today **Strawbery Banke** is a 10-acre outdoor museum with period gardens and more than 40 buildings that date from 1695 to 1820. The district was slated for urban renewal in the late 1950s, but a group of concerned residents successfully fought to preserve it. The museum is now a study in the evolution of a neighborhood, with nine furnished homes representing several different time periods. For example, the Drisco House, built in 1795, was first used as a dry-goods store, and one room still depicts this history; the living room, on the other hand, is decorated just as it was in the 1950s. The boyhood home of Thomas Bailey Aldrich (author of *The Story of a Bad Boy*) is still called **Nutter House,** the name he gave it in that novel—it's been restored just as it was when he wrote about it, right down to the wallpaper and hanging bookshelves. In the **Wheelwright House** you can see daily demonstrations of 18th-century cooking. Continental breakfast, lunch, and Sunday brunch are served at the **Washington Street Eatery** (61 Washington St., ☎ 603/430–9442). *Marcy St., ☎ 603/433–1100 or 603/433–1106. ☛ $10 adults, $9 senior citizens, $7 children 7–17, children under 6 free, $25 families. Tickets good for 2 consecutive days. ⊘ May–Oct., daily 10–5; weekend after Thanksgiving, 10–4; 1st 2 weekends in Dec., 3:30–8:30.*

❼ The small island of **New Castle,** just east of Portsmouth, was once known as Great Island, although it's made up of a single square mile of land. To get here, follow Route 1B (New Castle Avenue). The narrow roads lined with pre-Revolutionary houses make the island perfect for walking. On the way here you'll pass the old **Wentworth By The Sea,** the last of the great seaside resorts. It sits empty today and overlooks a golf course; it was the site of the signing of the Russo-Japanese Treaty in 1905, a fact that attracts many Japanese tourists. **Ft. Constitution** was originally Ft. William and Mary, a British stronghold overlooking Portsmouth Harbor. The fort was raided by rebel patriots in 1774 in one of the first overt acts of defiance against the King of England. The rebels later used the stolen munitions against the British at the Battle of Bunker Hill. Interpretive panels throughout the park further explain its history. *Ft. Constitution, Great Island. ⊘ Mid-June–Labor Day, daily 9–5; Labor Day–mid-June, weekends 9–5.*

Island Excursions

Ten miles off the coast lie nine small islands (eight at high tide): the
❽ **Isles of Shoals.** Many, like Hog Island, Smuttynose, and Star Island, retain the earthy names given them by the transient fishermen who first visited in the early 17th century. A colorful history of piracy, murder, and ghosts surrounds the archipelago, long populated by an independent lot who, according to one writer, hadn't the sense to winter on the mainland (there remains a small summer population). Not all of the islands lie within the New Hampshire border: After an ownership

dispute between Maine and New Hampshire, they were divvied up between the two states (five went to Maine, four to New Hampshire).

Celia Thaxter, a native islander, romanticized these islands with her poetry in *Among the Isles of Shoals,* published in 1873. In her time, **Appledore Island** became an offshore retreat for her coterie of writers, musicians, and artists. The island is now used by the Marine Laboratory of Cornell University, but Thaxter's lovely garden still blooms each summer, tended by volunteers.

Star Island houses a nondenominational conference center. In summer, scheduled cruises take visitors to Star in the morning for a picnic and a narrated walking tour (only conference attendees may stay overnight).

The **Isles of Shoals Steamship Company** runs island cruises and whale-watching expeditions. Captain Bob Whittaker hosts these voyages aboard the MV *Thomas Laighton,* a replica of a Victorian steamship, on which he regales passengers with tall tales. Breakfast, lunch, and light snacks are available on board, or you can bring your own. Some trips include a stopover and historic walking tour on Star Island. *Barker Wharf, 315 Market St., Portsmouth, ☎ 603/431–5500 or 800/ 441-4620. Reservations advised. ☉ Tour cruises mid-June–Labor Day, Oct. Whale-watching cruises May–Oct.*

What to See and Do with Children

Children's Museum of Portsmouth. Hands-on exhibits explain such subjects as lobstering, geography, computers, recycling, and outer space. Some programs require advance reservations. *280 Marcy St., ☎ 603/ 436–3853. ☛ $3.50 adults and children over 1, $3 senior citizens. ☉ Tues.–Sat. 10–5, Sun. 1–5. Also Mon. 10–5 in summer and during school vacations.*
Hampton Playhouse, Hampton (*see* The Arts, *below*)
Port of Portsmouth Maritime Museum and Albacore Park, Portsmouth

Off the Beaten Path

Bird-watchers will love the **Great Bay Estuary,** 4 miles west of Portsmouth. Here, among the 4,471 acres of tidal waters, mud flats, and about 48 miles of inland shoreline, visitors can see the Great Blue Heron, Osprey, and the Snowy Egret, especially conspicuous during the spring and fall migrations. The area is most famous, however, for having New Hampshire's largest concentration of winter eagles. Hikers will find trails at Adam's Point and at Sandy Point, and canoeists can put in at Chapman's Landing (Route 108) on the Squamscot River. Access to the Great Bay is a bit tricky and parking limited, but the Fish and Game Department's **Sandy Point Discovery Center** (Depot Rd. off Rte. 101, Greenland, ☎ 603/778–0015) distributes maps and information, and has displays about the estuary.

Shopping

Shopping Districts
Portsmouth's Market Square has gift and clothing boutiques, card shops, and exquisite crafts stores. Portsmouth has two shopping malls and an outlet center, although the serious outlet shoppers head to Maine.

Antiques
Antiques shops line Route 1 in **Hampton Falls,** including **Antiques New Hampshire** (☎ 603/926–9603), a group shop with 35 dealers. **Antiques One** (☎ 603/926–5332) carries everything but furniture, in-

cluding a wide selection of books and maps. **Antiques at Hampton Falls** (☎ 603/926–1971), has silver, jewelry, and collectibles. The **Barn at Hampton Falls** (☎ 603/926–9003) is known for its American and European furniture. **Northwood,** along Route 4, also has dozens of antiquaries. **Portsmouth** has several funky consignment shops and antiquarian bookstores near the town square. Sunday flea markets are held in the **Star Center** (25 Fox Run Rd., Newington, ☎ 603/431–9403).

In addition to the **Applecrest** and **Raspberry** farms in Hampton Falls (*see* Exploring, *above*), country and farm products, such as homemade jams and pickles, are available at **Emery Farm** (Rte. 4, Durham, ☎ 603/742–8495), **Tuttle's Farm** (Dover Point Rd., Dover, ☎ 603/742–4313), and **Calef's Country Store** (Rte. 9, Barrington, ☎ 603/664–2231).

Factory Outlets

For shoppers who don't care to drive north to Kittery, the **North Hampton Factory Outlet Center** (Lafayette Rd. , N. Hampton, ☎ 603/964–9050) offers tax-free goods and discounts on such brand names as Van Heusen, Famous Footwear, and American Tourister. The center has a diverse group of stores including the Leather Outpost, and the Sports Outpost. Bass has its own factory outlet there as well.

Galleries and Crafts Shops

Alie Jewelers (1 Market St., Portsmouth, ☎ 603/436–0531) carries gold, silver, and gemstone jewelry designed by New England artisans. **Country Curtains** (2299 Woodbury Ave., Newington, ☎ 603/431–2315), on the Old Beane Farm, sells curtains, bedding, furniture, and folk art. **Exeter League of New Hampshire Craftsmen** (61 Water St., Exeter, ☎ 603/778–8282) showcases original jewelry, woodworking, and pottery produced by select, juried members. The **Museum Shop at the Dunaway Store** (Marcy St., Portsmouth, ☎ 603/433–1114) stocks reproduction and contemporary furniture, quilts, crafts, candy, gifts, postcards, and books about the history of the area. **N. W. Barrett** (53 Market St., Portsmouth, ☎ 603/431–4262) specializes in fine art and crafts from both local and nationally acclaimed artists. The second floor showcases furniture in every price range from affordable steam-bent oak to one-of-a-kind lamps and rocking chairs. On the first floor you can browse the leather, jewelry, pottery, and fiber displays. **Pierce Gallery** (105 Market St., ☎ 603/436-1988) sells reasonably priced prints and paintings of both the Maine and New Hampshire coast. **A Picture's Worth a Thousand Words** (65 Water St., Exeter, ☎ 603/778–1991) sells antique and contemporary prints and frames them in-house. You can also choose from a wonderful collection of old maps, town histories, and rare books. **Salmon Falls Stoneware** (Oak Street Engine House, Dover, ☎ 603/749–1467 or 800/621–2030) produces handmade, salt-glaze stoneware, using a method that was popular among early American potters. Potters are on hand if you want to place a special order or just watch them work. **Tulips** (19 Market St., Portsmouth, ☎ 603/431–9445) was Portsmouth's first crafts gallery and still specializes in wood crafts and quilts.

Malls

Fox Run Mall (Fox Run Rd., Newington, ☎ 603/431–5911) is huge and generic, as a mall should be. This one houses Filene's, Jordan Marsh, JCPenney, Sears, and 100 other stores. **Newington Mall** (45 Gosling Rd., Newington, ☎ 603/431-4104) has Bradlees, Montgomery Ward, Porteuos, and 40 more stores—as well as Friendly's and Papa Ginos.

Sports and the Outdoors

Bicycling

The volume of traffic along Route 1 and the major highways on the Seacoast makes cycling difficult and dangerous for people unfamiliar with the area. The safest route is the bike path along Route 1A, for which you can park at Odiorne point and follow the road 14 miles south to Seabrook. Avoid Route 1, Route 4, and Route 101. Some bikers begin at Prescott Park and take Route 1B into Newmarket, but beware of the traffic. Another pretty route is from Newington Town Hall to the Great Bay Estuary.

Boating

Between April and October, deep-sea fishermen head out for cod, mackerel, and bluefish. There are rentals and charters aplenty, offering half- and full-day cruises, as well as some night fishing at Hampton, Portsmouth, Rye, and Seabrook piers. Try **Eastman Fishing & Marine** (Seabrook, ☎ 603/474–3461), **Atlantic Fishing Fleet** (Rye Harbor, ☎ 603/964–5220), **Al Gauron Deep Sea Fishing** (Hampton Beach, ☎ 603/926–2469), and **Smith & Gilmore** (Hampton Beach, ☎ 603/926–3503).

Camping

Exeter Elms Family Campground (188 Court St., Exeter 03833, ☎ 603/778-7631) has riverfront sites. **Pine Acres Family Campground** (74 Freetown Rd., Raymond 03077, ☎ 603/895–2519) has a giant water slide. There is also **Tidewater Campground** (160 Lafayette Rd., Hampton 03842, ☎ 603/926–5474) and **Tuxbury Pond Camping Area** (W. Whitehall Rd., S. Hampton 03842, ☎ 603/394–7660).

Hiking

An excellent 1-mile trail climbs to the summit of **Blue Job Mountain** (Crown Point Rd. off Rte. 202A, 1 mi from Rochester), where there is a firetower with a good view. The **Urban Forestry Center** (45 Elwyn Rd., Portsmouth, ☎ 603/431–6774), the **Great Bay Estuary,** and the **Odiorne Point State Park** also have several marked trails. The **New Hampshire Division of Parks and Recreation** (☎ 603/271–3254) has the Rockingham Recreation Trail, which wends 27 miles from Epping to Manchester and is open to hikers, bikers, snowmobiles, and cross-country skiers.

Beaches

The beaches tend to be crowded on weekends and more comfortable midweek, with the sun worshipers arriving in droves around 10. Changing rooms and showers are available at the southern end of **Hampton Beach State Park.** You'll usually find the beaches in **Jenness, Rye,** and **Wallis Sands** less congested than in Hampton, but you can view them and take your pick as you cruise Route 1A; they're all within 18 miles of each other. For freshwater swimming, try **Kingston State Park** (☎ 603/642–5471) at Kingston on Great Pond (not to be confused with Great Bay). Coastal beaches outside the state park system include **Foss Beach, Rye,** and **New Castle Common, New Castle.** The state maintains some metered parking spaces near Hampton Beach, but these tend to be scarce. Private lots charge around $5 a day along the coast.

Dining and Lodging

Portsmouth is considered by many to be the restaurant capital of New England. And yet every other small town in the region has its own favorite restaurant that will leave a unique culinary taste in your mouth. Inns and hotels are most crowded from mid-June to mid-October, so reserve well ahead. Restaurants, too, appreciate reservations on summer weekends and throughout October, or until the last leaf falls.

Dover

DINING

$$ **Newick's Lobster House.** Rumor has it that Newick's serves the best lobster roll on the New England coast, but regulars cherish the onion rings, too. This casual lobster shack serves seafood and atmosphere in heaping portions. Picture windows allow terrific views over Great Bay. ✕ *431 Dover Point Rd.,* ☎ *603/742–3205. AE, D, MC, V.*

Durham

DINING AND LODGING

$–$$ **New England Center Hotel.** Set in a lush wooded area on the campus of the University of New Hampshire, this hotel is large enough to be a full-service conference center, but quiet enough to feel like a retreat. You'll find larger rooms in the new wing, each with two queen-size beds. Decor is typical of most chain hotels. ☎ *15 Strafford Ave., 03824,* ☎ *603/862–2800,* ℻ *603/862–4351. 115 rooms with bath. 2 restaurants, lounge, exercise room. AE, DC, MC, V.*

Exeter

DINING

$ **Loaf and Ladle.** This understated café serves hearty chowders, soups, stews, and huge sandwiches on homemade bread—all cafeteria-style. Check the blackboard for the ever-changing rotation of stews, breads, and desserts. Overlooking the river, the café is handy to the shops, galleries, and historic houses along Water Street. ✕ *9 Water St.,* ☎ *603/ 778-8955. No reservations. AE, D, DC.*

DINING AND LODGING

$$–$$$ **Exeter Inn.** This three-story brick, Georgian-style inn, set on the campus of Phillips Exeter Academy, is furnished lavishly with antique and reproduction pieces but possesses every modern amenity. It's been the choice of visiting Phillips Exeter parents for the past half century. The dining room's house specialty is the chateaubriand served on an oaken plank with duchess potatoes and a béarnaise sauce, although the chef also boasts of a showstopping veal culinaire, the preparation of which changes daily. On Sunday, the line forms early for a brunch of more than 60 delicious options. Sit in the big, bright sunporch and admire the fig tree growing in the center of the room. ☎ *90 Front St., 03833,* ☎ *603/772–5901 or 800/782–8444,* ℻ *603/778–8757. 50 rooms with bath. Restaurant (reservations advised; not accepted for Sun. brunch), fitness room. AE, D, DC, MC, V.*

Hampton

DINING

$$–$$$ **Ron's Beach House.** Here you'll discover not one but seven fresh fish dishes of the day. Order any one of them prepared in any way you can imagine: baked, steamed, blackened, pan-seared. Ingredients are from the sea—even the mariner's chicken is stuffed with seafood. Start with the cioppino (Italian seafood stew). The restaurant occupies a renovated summer cottage in the Plaice Cove section of Hampton, 3 miles north of the main beach. ✕ *965 Ocean Blvd.,* ☎ *603/926–1870. Reservations advised. AE, D, DC, MC, V.*

LODGING

$$ **Victoria Inn.** Built as a carriage house in 1875, this romantic bed-and-breakfast is done in the style Victorians loved best: wicker, chandeliers, and lace. One room is done all in lilac; the honeymoon suite has white eyelet coverlets and a private sunroom. Innkeepers Bill and Ruth Muzzey have named one room in honor of Franklin Pierce, the former U.S. president who for years summered in the home next door. Full breakfast includes unusual dishes such as broiled grapefruit and orange French toast. ⊞ *430 High St. (½ mi from Hampton Beach), 03842,* ☎ *603/929–1437. 6 rooms, 3 with bath. Full breakfast included. MC, V.*

Hampton Beach
DINING AND LODGING

$$–$$$ Ashworth by the Sea. This hotel was built across the street from Hampton Beach in 1912; most rooms have private decks, and the furnishings vary from period to contemporary. The beachside rooms have a breathtaking ocean view, while the others look out onto the pool or the quiet street, offering solitude from the noisy beach. ⊞ *295 Ocean Blvd., 03842,* ☎ *603/926–6762 or 800/345–6736,* FAX *603/926–2002. 105 rooms with bath. 3 restaurants, pool. AE, D, DC, MC, V.*

Newmarket
LODGING

$ Moody Parsonage Bed and Breakfast. The first things guests notice about this red-clapboard Colonial are the original paneling, beautiful old staircases, and wide pine floors. With a fire crackling on chilly evenings and a spinning wheel in the living-room corner, some think they've stepped back in time. The house was built in 1730 for John Moody, the first minister of Newmarket, and if he came back today, he'd recognize it inside and out. One bedroom and bath are on the first floor. The three rooms upstairs share a bath. Innkeeper Debbie Reed serves summer breakfasts on the front porch, which looks out over a nearby golf course. Located 2 miles south of Newmarket center, the inn is just across the street from the Rockingham Ballroom. ⊞ *15 Ash Swamp Rd., 03857,* ☎ *603/659–6675. 4 rooms, 1 with bath. CP. No credit cards.*

Portsmouth
DINING

$$$$ Blue Strawberry Restaurant. This restaurant was opened 20 years ago by a chef who never used recipes but cooked by inspiration alone. Though he's long gone, the restaurant retains his inventive spirit. The menu changes daily according to the freshest available ingredients. ✕ *29 Ceres St.,* ☎ *603/431–6420. Reservations required. D, MC, V. No lunch. Closed Mon.–Wed. Oct. 15–July 3.*

$$$ Library at the Rockingham House. This Portsmouth landmark was once a luxury hotel and the site of the press signing of the Russo-Japanese Treaty in 1905. Most of the building has been converted to condominiums, but the restaurant retains the original atmosphere, with hand-carved Spanish-mahogany paneling and bookcases on every wall. Here even the dividers between booths are stacked with old tomes, and the waitresses present each bill in the pages of a vintage best-seller. The food, too, seems to belong in a social club of another century. Don't miss the roasted Long Island duckling with a maple-bourbon glaze, or the roasted, brine-cured pork loin chop stuffed with apples, sage, and walnuts. ✕ *401 State St.,* ☎ *603/431–5202. Reservations advised on weekends. AE, DC, MC, V.*

$$$ Oar House and Deck. With a deck beside the Heritage Cruise dock—perfect for romantic dinners or nightcaps—the Oar House is a hub of Portsmouth summer nightlife. Try the bouillabaisse, the rack of lamb, or the veal Barbara (with avocado, crab, cheese, and mushroom topping). ✕ *55 Ceres St.,* ☎ *603/436–4025. Reservations advised. AE, MC, V.*

$$ Porto Bello. Owner Yolanda Desario and her mother have brought the tastes of Naples to downtown Portsmouth. In this second-story dining room overlooking the harbor, you can enjoy daily antipasto specials ranging from grilled portobello mushrooms to stuffed calamari. Pastas include spinach gnocchi and homemade ravioli filled with eggplant, walnuts, and Parmesan and Romano cheeses. Choose from other entrées such as lamb; fish; and their specialty, veal *carciofi*—a 4-ounce center-cut steak served with artichokes. The tastes are so simple and the ingredients so fresh, you won't have trouble finishing four courses. ✗ *67 Bow St., 2nd Floor,* ☎ *603/431–2989. Reservations advised. D, MC, V. Closed Sun., Mon.*

$–$$ **B.G.'s Boathouse Restaurant.** Another local favorite, this place looks like an old fisherman's shack but serves the best seafood in town and plenty of it. Many customers arrive by boat. ✗ *Rte. 1B,* ☎ *603/431–1074. No reservations. AE, D, MC, V.*

$–$$ **The Brewery.** You can watch the brewing process of 15 different kinds of ale through the interior windows of this in-house brewery. The pub-style fare includes spicy shrimp, stir-fry combinations, burritos, fresh tuna steak au poivre, and fish-and-chips. Live entertainment is offered Wednesday through Saturday. ✗ *56 Market St.,* ☎ *603/431–1115. AE, D, MC, V.*

$–$$ **Karen's.** Pass through the purple door and into the restaurant that locals would like to keep secret. Karen's specializes in light, simple seafood dishes prepared to perfection. The dinner menu changes completely every few days, according to the chef's whims. The lunch menu features a lot of sautés, stir-fries, such sandwiches as open-face blackened swordfish, and a few pasta choices. For Sunday brunch look for the eggs Sardou or the eggnog French toast, but even on an ordinary morning you can design your own omelet and enjoy homemade corn-beef hash. ✗ *105 Daniel St.,* ☎ *603/431–1948. No reservations. AE, D, MC, V. No smoking. No lunch Sun.–Wed.*

DINING AND LODGING

$$–$$$ **Sheraton Portsmouth Hotel.** Portsmouth's only luxury hotel, this five-story redbrick building offers a nice harbor view and a central location. The hotel houses the area's main conference center, making it a perfect choice for business travelers. Suites have full kitchens and living rooms. ⊡ *250 Market St., 03801,* ☎ *603/431–2300 or 800/325–3535,* FAX *603/433–5649. 148 rooms with bath, 29 suites. Restaurant, 2 lounges, indoor pool, health spa, nightclub. AE, D, DC, MC, V.*

LODGING

$$$ **Sise Inn.** If you can't decide between a hotel and a small inn with period decor, stay at this Queen Anne town house in Portsmouth's historic district, which captures the best of both worlds. Each room is individually decorated with silks, rubbed woods, and antique reproductions, but has cable TV and whirlpool baths as well. Victorian style meets postmodern, with a Continental breakfast thrown in. The inn is close to the Market area and within walking distance of the theater district and several nice restaurants. ⊡ *40 Court St., 03801,* ☎ *and* FAX *603/433–1200, or 800/267–0525. 34 rooms with bath. In-room VCRs, hot tubs. CP. AE, DC, MC, V.*

$$–$$$ **Governor's House B&B.** This 1917 Georgian mansion was for more than 30 years home to New Hampshire's Governor, Charles Dale. Innkeepers Nancy and John Grossman reopened it in 1992 as a bed-and-breakfast and have fully restored the four rooms with period antiques—right down to the canopy beds. Nancy's hand-painted mosaic tiles in the bathrooms justify at least a visit. Guests enjoy a gourmet, low-fat breakfast each morning. ⊡ *32 Miller Ave., 03801,* ☎ *603/431–6546,* FAX *603/427–0803. 4 rooms with bath. Air-conditioning, fans, tennis. Full breakfast included. AE, MC, V.*

$$ Martin Hill Inn. Set in two buildings downtown, this charming inn is within walking distance of the historic district and waterfront; quiet rooms are comfortably furnished with antiques. ⌧ *404 Islington St.,* ☎ *603/436–2287. 4 rooms with bath, 3 suites. MC, V.*

Rochester

DINING AND LODGING

$$ Governor's Inn. Enjoy a quiet, candlelit dinner on the weekends or a lively theme-oriented dinner mid-week, which could involve a murder mystery, a cabaret, or a performance by the singing wait staff. The prix fixe menu, by reservation only, changes weekly but may include appetizers of black sturgeon caviar or summer-squash bisque, grilled beef tenderloin stuffed with Danish blue cheese, and a light dessert of lemon meringue. The new à la carte lunch, served weekdays, offers a very popular seafood lasagna. ⌧ *78 Wakefield St., 03867,* ☎ *603/332–0107. AE, MC, V.*

Rye

LODGING

$$ Rock Ledge Manor. Built out on a point and offering a 270° ocean view from a full wraparound porch, this mid-19th-century mansion was once part of a resort colony and just predates the houses along Millionaire's Row. It is the only area inn directly on the ocean, and all rooms have water views. The owners speak French and English and serve a huge breakfast each morning in the sunny dining room overlooking the Atlantic. ⌧ *1413 Ocean Blvd. (Rte. 1A), 03870,* ☎ *603/431–1413. 4 rooms, 2 with bath. Full breakfast included. No credit cards.*

The Arts

Music

Music in Market Square (☎ 603/436–9109) is a summer series of free concerts given on Fridays at noon. Classical musicians, both vocal and instrumental, perform inside the North Church in Market Square. **Prescott Park Arts Festival** (Marcy St., Portsmouth, ☎ 603/436–2848), kicks off with the Independence Day pops concert and then continues for eight weeks featuring the art of more than 100 regional artists, as well as music, dance, and one outdoor production four nights weekly. Don't miss the Chowder Festival or the jazz picnic on Sunday. Free admission.

Theater

Hampton Playhouse (357 Winnacunnet Rd., Rte. 101E, Hampton, ☎ 603/926–3073) brings familiar Hollywood and New York theater faces to the Seacoast with its summer theater July through September. Matinees are Wednesday and Friday at 2:30; children's shows are Saturday at 11 and 2. Schedules and tickets are available at the box office or at the Chamber of Commerce Sea Shell (Ocean Blvd., ☎ 603/926–8717). The **Music Hall** (28 Chestnut St., Portsmouth, ☎ 603/436–2400) is the 14th oldest operating theater in the country (ca. 1878), and its mission is to bring the best touring events to the Seacoast—from classical and pop to dance and theater. The hall also hosts an ongoing art-house film series. The **Seacoast Repertory Theatre** (125 Bow St., Portsmouth, ☎ 603/433–4472 or 800/639–7650) is one of the top regional theaters in the country and the coast's only year-round professional live theater. The Portsmouth Academy of Performing Arts, the Bow Street Theater, and the Portsmouth Youth Theatre combine to fill its calendar with musicals, classic dramas, and new works by upcoming playwrights.

Nightlife

The **Hampton Beach Casino Ballroom** (Ocean Beach Blvd., Hampton Beach, ☎ 603/926–4541; ☉ Apr.–Oct.) has been bringing name entertainment to the Hampton Beach area for more than 30 years. Tina Turner, the Monkees, Jay Leno, and Loretta Lynn have all played here. Expect a crowd of as many as 2,500 people. The **Portsmouth Gaslight Co.** (64 Market St., Portsmouth, ☎ 603/430–8582; courtyard opens at 5; the band starts at 7) is a popular brick-oven pizzeria and restaurant by day. But on summer nights, this place transforms itself into a party. That's when the management opens up the back courtyard, brings in live local rock bands, and serves a special punch in plastic sandpails. By midnight, not only is the courtyard full, but the three-story parking garage next door has become a makeshift auditorium. People come from as far away as Boston and Portland to hang out at the **Press Room** (77 Daniel St., Portsmouth, ☎ 603/431–5186; name entertainment weekends; open gig Tues.–Sat.), in an old three-story brick building, for folk, jazz, blues, and bluegrass performances. Tuesday night features an open mike; on Sunday the jazz starts at 7. UNH students tend toward Portsmouth and the several bars along Durham's Main Street.

Coast Essentials

Getting Around

BY CAR

For coastal scenery, follow Route 1A, which shows off the water, the beaches, and some breathtaking summer estates. For convenience, follow Route 1, which wends slightly inland. Route 1B tours the island of Newcastle, and Route 4 connects Portsmouth with Dover, Durham, and Rochester.

Guided Tours

Audubon Society of New Hampshire (3 Silk Farm Rd., Concord 03301, ☎ 603/224–9909) schedules monthly field trips throughout the state and a special fall bird-watching tour to Star Island and the Isles of Shoals.

Insight Tours (☎ 603/436–4223 or 800/745–4213) gives one- to three-hour bus tours focusing on the history and architecture of Portsmouth, in addition to guided walking tours.

New Hampshire Seacoast Cruises (☎ 603/964–5545) offers narrated tours of the Isles of Shoals and whale-watching expeditions from June to Labor Day out of Rye Harbor Marina.

Portsmouth Harbor Cruises (☎ 603/436–8084 or 800–776–0915) takes passengers on a historic tour of the 14 islands of Portsmouth harbor and the Isles of Shoals. Ask about the inland estuary tours of the Great Bay and about sunset and foliage cruises.

Portsmouth Livery Company (☎ 603/427–0044) provides narrated horse-and-carriage tours of Colonial Portsmouth and Strawbery Banke.

Important Addresses and Numbers

EMERGENCIES

New Hampshire State Police (☎ 603/271–3636 or 800/852–3411). **Portsmouth Regional Hospital** (333 Borthwick Ave., ☎ 603/436–5110 or 603/433–4042). **Exeter Hospital** (10 Buzzell Ave., ☎ 603/778–7311).

VISITOR INFORMATION

Hours are generally Monday through Friday, 9–5. **Exeter Area Chamber of Commerce** (120 Water St., Exeter 03833, ☎ 603/772–2411). **Greater Dover Chamber of Commerce** (299 Central Ave., Dover 03820,

☎ 603/742–2218). **Greater Portsmouth Chamber of Commerce** (500 Market St., Portsmouth 03801, ☎ 603/436–1118). **Hampton Beach Area Chamber of Commerce** (836 Lafayette Rd., Hampton 03842, ☎ 603/926–8717). **Seacoast Council on Tourism** (235 West Rd., Suite 10, Portsmouth 03801, ☎ 603/436–7678 or 800/221–5623).

LAKES REGION

Lake Winnipesaukee, a Native American name for "Smiling Water," is the largest of the dozens of lakes scattered across the eastern half of central New Hampshire. In fact, with 283 miles of shoreline, it's the largest in the state. Dotted as it is with so many islands, some claim Winnipesaukee has an island for every day of the year. In truth, there are 274 of them, which fails this speculation by about three months.

Unlike Winnipesaukee, which hums with activity all summer long, the more secluded Squam Lake, with a dearth of public-access points, seems to shun visitors. Perhaps it was this tranquility that attracted producers of the 1981 film *On Golden Pond,* several of whose scenes were shot here. Nearby Lake Wentworth is named for the first Royal Governor of the state, who, in building his country manor here, established North America's first summer resort.

This region is rich with historic landmarks, including some well-preserved Colonial and 19th-century villages. Eating and recreational opportunities abound, too: There are dozens of good restaurants, several golf courses, hiking trails, and good antiquing along the way. But to experience the Lakes Region to its fullest, you'll want to enjoy some form of water play, whether it be swimming, fishing, sailing, or just sitting on an old dock dangling your toes in any of these icy lakes.

Exploring

Numbers in the margin correspond to points of interest on the New Hampshire Lakes map.

This tour begins at Lake Winnipesaukee's southernmost tip, and moves clockwise through the lakeside towns, starting on Route 11. Neither quiet nor secluded, the lake's southern shore is alive with tourists from the moment the first flower blooms until the last maple has shed its leaves.

① Two mountain ridges hold 7 miles of Winnipesaukee in Alton Bay. At the southern extremity of the lake you'll find the town of **Alton Bay.** Aside from the lake's cruise boats, which dock here, there are a dance pavilion, minigolf, a public beach, and a Victorian-style bandstand for summer concerts.

A few miles east on Route 11A is the **Gunstock Recreation Area** (☎ 603/293–4341), a sprawling park with an Olympic-size pool, a children's playground, hiking trails, horses, paddleboats, and a campground with 300 tent and trailer sites. A major downhill-skiing center, it once claimed the longest tow rope in the country—an advantage that helped local downhill skier and Olympic silver medalist Penny Pitou perfect her craft.

② One of the larger public beaches is at the resort community of **Gilford.** When incorporated in 1812, the town decided to ask its oldest resident to name it. A veteran of the Battle of the Guilford Courthouse, in North Carolina, he borrowed that town's name—though apparently he didn't know how to spell it. The town today is as quiet and peaceful as it must have been then. Commercial development has been shunned here; you couldn't buy a T-shirt or piece of pottery if you tried.

❸ North of Gilford on Route 11A, **Weirs Beach**—dubbed New Hampshire's Coney Island—forms the lake's center for arcade activity. Anyone who loves souvenir shops, fireworks, bumper cars, and hordes of children will be right at home. Several cruise ships (*see* Guided Tours *in* Lakes Region Essentials, *below*) depart from this dock, and the **Winnipesaukee Railroad** (☎ 603/279–5253) picks up passengers here for an hour-long tour of the shore. You'll find water slides in town at **Surf Coaster** (☎ 603/366–4991) and **Water Slide** (☎ 603/366–5161), or you can spend all night working your way through the minigolf course, 20 lanes of bowling, and more than 500 games at **Funspot** (☎ 603/366–4377).

TIME OUT **Kellerhaus** (Daniel Webster Hwy., ☎ 603/366–4466), just north of Weirs Beach and overlooking the lake, is an alpine-style building that has been selling homemade chocolates, hard candy, and ice cream since 1906. Kids love the ice-cream smorgasbord, which has a great variety of toppings. Fortunately, the price is based not on the number of scoops but on the size of the dish.

❹ **Meredith,** on Route 3 at the western extremity of Winnipesaukee, is known primarily as the home of **Annalee's Doll Museum** (☎ 603/279–4144). Visitors can view a vast collection of the famous felt dolls and learn about the woman behind their creation. The town has a fine collection of crafts shops and art galleries. An information center is across from the Town Docks. On rainy days you can visit the **Children's Museum and Shop,** where kids can make bubbles and play instruments, among other activities. *28 Lang St., Meredith, ☎ 603/279–1007.* ☛ *$5 adults and children over 2.* ۞ *Tues.–Sat. 9:30–5, Sun. noon–5.*

❺ The town of **Center Harbor,** set on the middle of three bays at the northern end of Winnipesaukee, also borders lakes Squam, Waukewan, and Winona.

To detour around Squam Lake: Route 25B will take you to Route 25, which leads to the town of Holderness. At the junction of routes 113 and 25, on the shores of the lake, is the 200-acre **Science Center of New Hampshire** (☎ 603/968–7194). This nature center maintains a ¾-mile trail that features such wildlife as black bears, bobcats, otter, and snowy owls. It also sponsors educational events, including a daily "Up Close to Animals" series in which visitors get a closer look at such species as the Red Shouldered Hawk. ☛ *$6 adults, $3 children 5–15 (admission is slightly higher July–Aug.).* ۞ *May–Oct., daily 9:30–4:30.*

From here you can take Route 113 east up and around Squam Lake, through the beautiful village of Center Sandwich. Its **Historical Society Museum** (Maple St., ☎ 603/284–6269; ۞ June–Sept., Mon.–Sat. 11–5) traces the history of the town largely through the faces of its inhabitants. Mid-19th-century portraitist and town son Albert Gallatin Hoit has eight works here; they are hung alongside a local photographer's exhibit portraying the town's mothers and daughters.

❻ From here, take Route 109 south to **Moultonborough,** which claims 6½ miles of shoreline on Lake Kanasatka, as well as a piece of Squam. Although people love to browse in the **Old Country Store** (Moultonborough Corner, ☎ 603/476–5750) and its museum of antique farming and forging tools (admission free), the best-known attraction is the **Castle in the Clouds.** Construction began in 1911 on this odd, elaborate mansion and went on for three years; owner Thomas Gustave Plant pumped $7 million into this dwelling, which, amazingly, was built without nails. It has 16 rooms, eight bathrooms, and doors made of lead. Unfortunately, Plant spent the bulk of his huge fortune on this project

New Hampshire Lakes

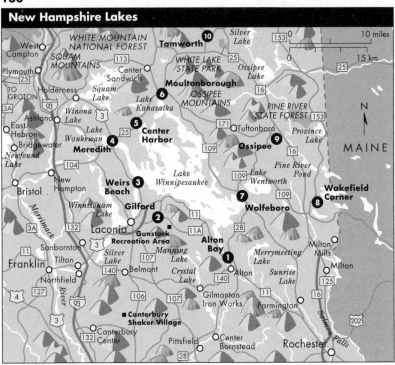

and died penniless in 1946. *Rte. 171, Moultonborough, ☎ 603/476–2352 or 800/729–2468. ☉ Mid-June–mid-Oct., daily 9–5; mid-May–mid-June, weekends 10–4.*

7 **Wolfeboro,** 15 miles southeast of Moultonbourough, has been a resort since John Wentworth built his summer home on the shores of Lake Wentworth in 1763. The original Wentworth house burned in 1820, but you can see some salvaged items at the **Libby Museum** (Rte. 109, Wolfeboro, ☎ 603/569–1035; ☉ Memorial Day–Labor Day, Tues.–Sun. 10–4), along with an unusual natural-history collection. The **Clark House Historical Exhibit and Museum** (S. Main St., ☎ 603/569–4997; ☉ July–Aug., Mon.–Sat. 10–4) takes a more conventional look at the town's history; one exhibit re-creates a late-19th-century fire station, complete with a red fire engine. Wolfeboro's downtown area is right on Winnipesaukee, attracting droves of tourists summer-long: The chamber of commerce estimates that the population increases tenfold each June.

Wolfeboro is also headquarters to the **Hampshire Pewter Company** (☎ 603/569-4944), where artisans still use 17th-century techniques to make pewter hollowware and accessories. Shop tours begin on the hour, weekdays in summer, less often off-season. A few miles north on Route 109 is the trailhead to **Abenaki Tower.** A short (¼-mile) hike to the 100-foot post-and-beam tower, followed by a more rigorous climb to the top, rewards you with a vast view of Winnipesaukee and the Ossipee mountain range.

East of Winnipesaukee lie several villages that, thankfully, lack the lakeside towns' bustle of tourism. **Wakefield Corner,** on the Maine border, **8** is a registered historic district, with a church, houses, and an inn looking just as they did in the 18th century. The nearby town of Wakefield encompasses 10 lakes. Here you'll find the charming **Museum of Childhood,** where exhibits include a one-room schoolhouse from 1890, model trains, a collection of antique children's sleds, and 3,000 dolls. *Off Rte. 16 in Wakefield Corner,* ☎ *603/522–8073.* ☛ *$3 adults, $1.25 children under 9.* ☻ *Memorial Day–Columbus Day, Mon., Wed.–Sat. 11–4, Sun. 1–4.*

❾ From here, Route 16N leads to the three **Ossipee** villages. Or you can take Route 153, the slower road among the scenic lakes on Maine's border. Between Ossipee and West Ossipee, Route 16N passes sparkling Lake Ossipee, known for fine fishing and swimming. Among these hamlets you'll also find several antiques shops and galleries. **Tamworth,**
❿ northwest of Ossipee on Route 113, also has a clutch of villages within its borders. The view through the birches of Chocorua Lake has been so often photographed that you may get a sense of having been here before.

What to See and Do with Children

Annalee's Doll Museum, Meredith
Children's Museum and Shop, Meredith
Funspot, Surf Coaster, and **Water Slide,** Weirs Beach
Museum of Childhood, Wakefield
New Hampshire Farm Museum. It's not just a collection of farm implements and tools, but a living museum with weekend events demonstrating farm-related crafts. *Rte. 125, Milton,* ☎ *603/652–7840.* ☛ *$5 adults, $1.50 children under 13.* ☻ *Mid-June–Columbus Day, Tues.–Sat. 10–4, Sun. noon–4.*
Science Center of New Hampshire, Holderness
Winnipesaukee Railroad, Meredith and Weirs beaches

Off the Beaten Path

Expert tour guides at the **Canterbury Shaker Village** kindly welcome visitors to this historic village with a detailed 90-minute tour of the grounds. Guides will answer questions about the history and philosophy of the Shakers. Established in 1792, this religious community flourished in the 1800s. It was the sixth of 19 self-contained Shaker villages that practiced equality of the sexes and races, common ownership, celibacy, and pacifism. Shakers were known for the perfection of their artistry and for the simplicity and integrity of their design, especially in household furniture. Because they believed in efficient work, they became prolific inventors of indispensable time-savers, such as the clothespin and the flat broom. This outdoor museum has crafts demonstrations and a large shop of books and fine Shaker reproductions. The Creamery Restaurant brings to life Shaker recipes for Sunday brunch, lunch daily, and candlelight dinners before the 7 PM tour on Friday and Saturday nights. Most visitors spend the better part of a day here. *288 Shaker Rd., 7 mi from Exit 18 off I–93, Canterbury,* ☎ *603/783–9511.* ☛ *$8 adults, $4 children 6–16.* ☻ *May–Oct., daily 10–5; Apr., Nov., Dec., Fri.–Sun. 10–5.*

Shopping

The area's crafts shops, galleries, and boutiques are all geared to the summer influx of tourists. Many close in the off-season (late October–mid-April), and the wares tend toward T-shirts and somewhat tacky trinkets. You'll find most antiques shops along the eastern side of Winnipesaukee near Wolfeboro and around Ossipee.

Specialty Shops

ART AND ANTIQUES

Dow's Corner Shop (Rte. 171, Tuftonboro Corner, ☎ 603/539–4790) has not one but two of everything. So crowded with historic memorabilia, this antiques shop could pass as a museum. At the **Old Print Barn** (Meredith, ☎ 603/279–6479), choose from 1,000 rare prints from around the world in this huge barn. This is the largest print gallery in northern New England. From Route 104 in Meredith follow Winona Road and look for "Lane" on the mailbox.

CRAFTS

Keepsake Quilting & Country Pleasures (Senter's Marketplace on Rte. 25, Center Harbor, ☎ 603/253–4026) calls itself America's largest quilt shop and proves it with 5,000 bolts of fabric, hundreds of quilting books, and countless supplies, plus a wide selection of yarn and needlework kits. The **Meredith League of New Hampshire Craftsmen** (Rte. 3, ½ mi north of the junction of Rtes. 3 and 104, Meredith, ☎ 603/279–7920) sells the juried work of area artisans. The **Old Country Store and Museum** (Moultonborough Corner, ☎ 603/476–5750) has been selling everything from handmade soaps to antiques, maple products, aged cheeses, and penny candy since 1781. **Sandwich Home Industries** (Rte. 109, Center Sandwich, ☎ 603/284–6831), the 65-year-old grandparent of the League of New Hampshire Craftsmen, was formed to foster cottage crafts. There are crafts demonstrations in July and August and sales of home furnishings and accessories mid-May–October.

CRYSTAL

Pepi Hermann Crystal (3 Waterford Pl., Gilford, ☎ 603/528–1020) sells hand-cut crystal chandeliers and stemware; you can also take a tour and watch the artists at work.

Shopping Malls

Mill Falls Marketplace (☎ 603/279–7006), on the bay in Meredith, contains nearly two dozen shops, as well as restaurants and an inn. **Belknap Mall** (☎ 603/524–5651), on Route 3 in Laconia, has boutiques, crafts stores, and a New Hampshire state liquor store.

Skiing

Gunstock

Box 1307, Laconia 03247
☎ *603/293–4341 or 800/486–7864*

High above Lake Winnipesaukee, the pleasant, all-purpose ski area of Gunstock attracts some skiers for overnight stays and others—many from Boston and its suburbs—for day skiing. Gunstock allows skiers to return lift tickets for a cash refund for any reason—weather, snow conditions, health, equipment problems—within an hour and 15 minutes of purchase. That policy plus a staff of customer-service people give class to an old-time ski area; Gunstock dates to the 1930s.

DOWNHILL

Clever trail cutting, and trail grooming and surface sculpting three times daily have made this otherwise pedestrian mountain an interesting place for intermediates. That's how the 41 trails are rated, with designated sections for slow skiers and learners. The 1,400 feet of vertical has one quad, two triple, and two double chairlifts and two surface tows. Gunstock has the third largest night-skiing facility in New England, with 12 trails lit for night and five lifts operating.

CROSS-COUNTRY
The Gunstock ski area offers 40 kilometers (25 miles) of cross-country trails.

CHILD CARE
The nursery takes children from six months; the ski school teaches the SKIwee system to children 3–12.

Other Sports

Boating

The **Lakes Region Association** (Box 589, Center Harbor 03226, ☎ 603/253–8555) gives boating advice. Power boats can be rented in Meredith from **Meredith Marina and Boating Center** (☎ 603/279–7921). You'll find pontoon boats, power boats, and personal watercraft at **Thurston's Marina** (☎ 603/366–4811) in Weirs Beach.

Camping

Gunstock (Rte. 11A, Gilford, ☎ 603/293–4344) is a protected woodland in which you can ski, hike, bike, swim, and take guided horseback tours. **Meredith Woods** (Meredith 03253, ☎ 603/279–5449 or 800/848–0328) offers year-round camping and RV facilities, as well as an indoor heated pool. **Yogi Bear's Jellystone Park** (Ashland 03217, ☎ 603/968–3654) is especially good for families. **Clearwater Campground** (Meredith 03253, ☎ 603/279–7761) is a wooded, tent and RV campground on Lake Pemigewasset. **Squam Lakeside Camp Resort and Marina** (Rte. 3, Holderness 03245, ☎ 603/968–7227) is open year-round and has full hookups and cable TV. **White Lake State Park** (Tamworth 03886, ☎ 603/323–7350), between Tamworth and Ossipee, has two camping areas with 200 tent sites and a camp store, a shaded picnic area, swimming, and canoe rentals.

Fishing

You'll find lake trout and salmon in Winnipesaukee, trout and bass in the smaller lakes, and trout in various streams all around the area. Alton Bay has an "Ice Out" salmon derby in spring. In winter, on all the lakes, intrepid ice fishers fish from huts known as "ice bobs." For up-to-date fishing information, call the **New Hampshire Fish and Game** office (☎ 603/744–5470).

Golf

The area's one 18-hole golf course is at **White Mountain Country Club** (N. Ashland Rd., Ashland, ☎ 603/536–2227).

Hiking

The region is full of beautiful trails. Contact the Alexandria headquarters of the **Appalachian Mountain Club** (☎ 603/744–8011) or the **Laconia Office of the U.S. Forest Service** (☎ 603/528–8721) for advice and information. **Red Hill,** a trail on Bean Road off Route 25, northeast of Center Harbor, really does turn red in autumn. The reward at the end of the trail in any season is a beautiful view of Squam Lake and the mountains; try also **Mt. Major** in Alton, **Squam Range** in Holderness, and **Pine River State Forest,** east of Route 16.

Water Sports

The lake is teeming with boats in summer. Look for waterskiing regulations at every marina. Scuba divers can explore a 130-foot-long cruise ship that sunk in 30 feet of water off Glendale in 1895. **Dive Winnipesaukee Corp.** (4 N. Main St., Wolfeboro, ☎ 603/569–2120) runs charters out to this and other wrecks and offers instruction, rentals, repairs, and scuba sales. They also give lessons in waterski-ing and windsurfing.

State Parks

White Lake State Park (Rte. 16, Tamworth) has a 72-acre stand of na-tive pitch pine, which is a National Natural Landmark. The park also has hiking trails, a sandy beach, trout fishing, canoe rentals, and two separate camping areas. Both the **Plummer Ledge Natural Area** (Town Rd., Wentworth) and the **Sculptured Rocks Natural Area** (between Rte. 3A and 118, Groton) show off striking glacial potholes that vary in size from 2 feet to more than 10 feet across.

Beaches

Ellacoya State Beach (Rte. 11, Gilford) consists of 600 feet along the southwestern shore of Lake Winnipesaukee and offers views of the Os-sipee and Sandwich mountain ranges. **Wentworth State Beach** (Rte. 109, Wolfeboro) has good swimming and picnicking areas, as well as a bath house. One of the most beautiful area beaches is the **Wellington State Beach** (off Rte 3A, Bristol), on the western shore of Newfound Lake. You can swim or picnic along the ½-mile sandy beach or take the scenic walking trail. Among the free beaches are **Bartlett Beach** (Winnisquam Ave., Laconia), **Opechee Park** (N. Main St., Laconia), and the **Alton Bay Beach** (Alton Bay).

Dining and Lodging

Because restaurants around the lakes serve throngs of visitors in sum-mer, be sure to call for reservations. In peak season, everything is booked. Off-season, whole communities seem to close for the winter.

Belmont

DINING AND LODGING

$–$$ **Hickory Stick Farm.** The specialty is roast duckling with country herb stuffing and orange-sherry sauce, which you order by portion—the quar-ter, half, or whole duck. Dinner includes salad, orange rolls, a vegetable, and potato. Consider also seafood, beef tenderloin, rack of lamb, or a vegetarian casserole. The 200-year-old Cape-style inn has two large, old-fashioned upstairs bed-and-breakfast rooms with cannonball beds, stenciled wallpaper, lace curtains, and full bathrooms. Breakfast is on the sunporch and offers such goodies as peach–and–cream cheese stuffed French toast. It's 4 miles from Laconia. ☎ *60 Bean Hill Rd., 03246,* ☎ *603/524–3333. 2 rooms with bath. Restaurant (reservations accepted; no lunch). Full breakfast included. AE, D, MC, V. Closed Mon.–Wed., mid-Oct.–late Apr.*

Center Barnstead

DINING

$$$ **Crystal Quail.** The namesake quail dish is only available in season, but this tiny restaurant, in an 18th-century farmhouse, is worth the drive in any season. The prix-fixe menu is presented verbally with a couple of choices for appetizer, main dish, and dessert. Those choices may in-clude saffron-garlic soup, a house pâté, quenelle-stuffed sole, or duck in crisp potato shreds. They don't serve wine or beer, so bring your own. Seating just 12 patrons, this is the most intimate dining experience in New Hampshire. ✗ *Pitman Rd.,* ☎ *603/269–4151. Reservations re-quired. No credit cards. BYOB. No lunch. Closed Mon., Tues.*

Center Harbor

DINING AND LODGING

$$-$$$ **Red Hill Inn.** Chef Elmer Davis loves dessert. On any given night, the wait staff must recite close to a dozen choices, including his famous vinegar pie (which is sweeter than it sounds), his windswept chocolate torte, and his Kentucky high pie. But before you get that far, try one of his special appetizers, maybe the baked brie wrapped in phyllo, or any one of two dozen entrées featuring seafood, lamb, and duck. The inn was once the entire campus of Belknap College. Before that, it was a rambling summer mansion with a history of interesting past owners, including an artist who painted nursery-rhyme characters on the walls of one of the rooms. The current owners have carefully renovated the house and grounds. The large bay window in the common room overlooks "Golden Pond." Furnished with Victorian pieces and country furniture, many of the rooms have fireplaces, and some have whirlpool baths. The popular Runabout Lounge is an antique speedboat halved to form a pub. ☎ *RD 1, Box 99M (Rte. 25B), 03226, ☎ 603/279–7001, FAX 603/279–7003. 21 rooms with bath. Restaurant (reservations advised). Full breakfast included. AE, D, DC, MC, V.*

Center Sandwich

DINING AND LODGING

$$ **Corner House Inn.** This quaint Victorian inn serves home-cooked meals in a converted barn. Before you get to the white chocolate cheesecake with key-lime filling, you may want to try the chef's lobster-and-mushroom bisque, or the mouthwatering crab cakes. The room's mood mixes exposed beams with candlelight and a whimsical decor of local arts and crafts. Come by on Thursday to hear storytellers perform in the glow of the wood stove. The three comfortable, old-fashioned rooms upstairs display the original paintings and quilted wall hangings of local artists. ☎ *Rtes. 109 and 113, 03277, ☎ 603/284–6219, FAX 603/284–6220. 3 rooms with bath. Restaurant (reservations advised). Full breakfast included. AE, MC, V. Closed Mon. and Tues. Nov.–mid-June.*

Gilford

DINING AND LODGING

$$-$$$ **B. Mae's Resort Inn.** All the rooms in this resort and conference cen-
✳ ter are large; some one-bedroom condominiums have kitchens. ☎ *Rte. 11A, Gilford 03246, ☎ 603/293–7526 or 800/458–3877, FAX 603/293–4340. 82 rooms with bath. Restaurant, lounge, indoor pool, exercise room, recreation room. AE, D, DC, MC, V.*

$$-$$$ **Gunstock Inn and Health Club.** This country-style resort and motor inn
✳ about a minute's drive from the Gunstock recreation area has rooms of various sizes furnished with American antiques and with views of the mountains and Lake Winnipesaukee. ☎ *580 Cherry Valley Rd. (Rte. 11A), Gilford 03246, ☎ 603/293–2021 or 800/654–0180, FAX 603/293–2050. 27 rooms with bath. Restaurant, indoor pool, spa, health club. AE, MC, V.*

Holderness

LODGING

$$$ **Manor on Golden Pond.** Built in 1913 as a private retreat for Mr. Isaac Van Horn, it thankfully retains a dignified air with well-groomed grounds, clay tennis courts, a swimming pool, a private dock with canoes, paddle boats, and a boathouse. Guests feast on a five-course prix-fixe dinner with such specialties as rack of lamb, filet mignon, shrimp Aegean, and nonpareil apple pie. Guests can stay in the main inn, the carriage-house suites, or one of the four housekeeping cottages. ☎ *Rte.*

3, 03245, ☎ *603/968–3348 or 800/545–2141,* ⓕⓐⓧ *603/968–2116. 27 rooms with bath. Restaurant, pub. AE, MC, V.*

$$ Inn on Golden Pond. This informal country home, built in 1879 and set on 50 wooded acres, is just across the road from Squam Lake. Visitors have lake access and can stroll among the property's many nature trails. The rooms have a traditional country decor of hardwood floors, braided rugs, easy chairs, and calico-print bedspreads and curtains. The quietest rooms are in the rear on the third floor. Breakfast includes homemade rhubarb jam, from rhubarb grown on the property. 🏠 *Rte. 3, Box 680, 03245,* ☎ *603/968–7269. 8 rooms with bath. Full breakfast included. AE, MC, V.*

Meredith

LODGING

$$ Nutmeg Inn. The white Cape-style house with black shutters was built in 1763 by a sea captain who obtained the dwelling's timber by dismantling his ship. He paneled the dining room with extra-wide "king's boards," which were supposed to be reserved for royal construction. An 18th-century ox yoke is bolted to the wall over a walk-in-size fireplace, and the wide-board floors are also original. All the rooms are named after spices and decorated accordingly. The inn is on a rural side street off Route 104, the main link between I–93 and Lake Winnipesaukee. 🏠 *Pease Rd., RFD 2, 03253,* ☎ *603/279–8811. 7 rooms with bath, 1 suite. Pool, meeting rooms. Full breakfast included. D, MC, V.*

Moultonborough

DINING

$$–$$$ Sweetwater Inn. Chef and owner Mike Love makes dishes from scratch, right down to the home-churned blackberry-honey butter. The breads, the demiglaces, the salad dressings, the desserts are all prepared here. He makes the pasta daily for the lobster ravioli (with a pepper-vodka sauce) and the fettuccine jambalaya (sautéed chicken, scallops, and andouille sausage with garlic, sherry, peppers, and Cajun spices). Although he calls the cuisine traditional French, he does offer some Spanish and nouvelle Italian dishes—paellas and pollo con gambas (chicken breast and shrimp sautéed with brandy). He uses only herbs and spices as seasonings; no salt. The decor is as eclectic as the menu. The formality of linen tablecloths and effusive service is cut by the wood stoves and proliferation of local art. ✕ *Rte. 25,* ☎ *603/476–5079. Reservations advised. AE, DC, MC, V.*

$$–$$$ The Woodshed. This 1860s barn and farmhouse looks like a woodshed, with farm implements and antiques hanging on the walls. You'll get hearty meals here, beef (including prime rib), lamb, and seafood— all cooked to order. Eat from the raw bar or try the New England section of the menu, which lists clam chowder, scrod, and Indian pudding; diners love the Denver chocolate pudding, a dense pudding-cake served warm with vanilla ice cream. ✕ *Lee's Mill Rd.,* ☎ *603/476–2311. Reservations advised. AE, D, DC, MC, V.*

Tamworth

DINING AND LODGING

$$ Tamworth Inn. The barn out back used to be home to the Barnstormer Theater, which has now moved to a bigger and more respectable stage across the street. The actors, though, still rehearse here. Summer guests never miss a theater performance, unless they're out hiking one of the trails in the nearby Hemenway State Forest. Every room is done in 19th-century American pieces and handmade quilts. In the dining room, the most popular appetizer among the pretheater set is the provolone-and-pesto terrine. Among entrées, try the pork tenderloin with apple-walnut corn-bread stuffing and an apple-cider sauce, or the roast duckling with the chef's sauce du jour. If you order the profiterole Tamworth (with the chef's own hot fudge sauce), your server should give warning: It is big enough for two. The pub offers lighter fare and a look at an antique sled collection. Sunday brunch is a summer favorite. ⊞ *Main St., Box 189, 03886, ☎ 603/323–7721 or 800/642–7352, FAX 603/323–2026. 15 rooms with bath. Restaurant (reservations advised; closed Sun., Mon. in summer and Sun.–Tues. in winter), pub, pool. Full breakfast included; MAP available. MC, V.*

Tilton

DINING

$$$ **Le Chalet Rouge.** On the west side of Tilton, this yellow house, with a modestly decorated dining room, is not unlike the country bistros of France. Neither the decor nor the menu is flashy, which most diners find refreshing. Choose from among a wonderful house pâté, escargots, or steamed mussels as a starter. Steak au poivre is one of the better entrées, but don't miss the duckling prepared with seasonal sauces: rhubarb in spring, raspberry in summer, orange in fall, creamy mustard in winter. ✗ *321 W. Main St., ☎ 603/286–4035. Reservations required. AE.*

Wakefield

LODGING

$ **Wakefield Inn.** The restoration of this 1804 stage-coach inn, in Wakefield's historic district, has been handled with an eye for detail. The dining room windows retain the original panes and Indian shutters. But the centerpiece of the building is the free-standing spiral staircase that rises three stories. Rooms are named for famous guests (such as John Greenleaf Whittier) or honor past owners. The large guest rooms have wide pine floors, big sofas, and handmade quilts. But guests can make their own quilt in one weekend with the Quilting Package course offered in late fall and early spring. ⊞ *R.R. 1, Box 2185, Mountain Laurel Rd., 03872, ☎ 603/522–8272 or 800/245–0841. 7 rooms with bath. Dinner by advance reservation only. Full breakfast included. MC, V.*

Wolfeboro

DINING

$$ **The Bittersweet.** This converted barn is decorated with an eclectic display of old quilts, pottery, sheet music, china, and other odd implements, all of which are for sale. Although it may feel like a cozy crafts shop, it's really a restaurant that locals love for the lamb-and-cider pie, duck with raspberry sauce, wiener schnitzel, and spinach salad. ✗ *Rte. 28, ☎ 603/569–3636. Reservations accepted. MC, V.*

DINING AND LODGING

$$–$$$ **Wolfeboro Inn.** This white-clapboard house on Main Street was built nearly 200 years ago but has 19th- and 20th-century additions, which extend to the waterfront of Wolfeboro Bay. The rooms have polished cherry and pine furnishings, and armoires (to hide the TVs), along with stenciled borders and country quilts. Wolfe's Tavern serves food cooked in a bake-oven fireplace, plus more than 45 brands of beer. Try the veal Wolfeboro, with its unlikely but delicious combination of veal, lobster, and shrimp sautéed and served with a cream sauce. The main dining room offers a very popular twin-lobster special. ⊞ *44 N. Main St., 03894, ☎ 603/569–3016 or 800/451–2389, FAX 603/569–5375. 38 rooms with bath, 5 suites. 2 restaurants, bar, beach, boating, bicycles. CP. AE, D, MC, V.*

The Arts

The **Belknap Mill Society** (Mill Plaza, Laconia, ☎ 603/524–8813) is a year-round cultural center housed in a 19th-century textile mill. The society sponsors concerts, exhibits, a lecture series, and workshops in arts and crafts and on history.

Music

Arts Council of Tamworth (☎ 603/323–7793) produces concerts—soloists, string quartets, revues, children's programs—from September through June, followed by a summer arts show the last weekend in July. **New Hampshire Music Festival** (88 Belknap Mountain Rd., Gilford, ☎ 603/524–1000) brings award-winning professional orchestras to the Lakes Region each summer from early July through mid-August.

Theater

Barnstormers (Main St., Tamworth, ☎ 603/323–8500), New Hampshire's oldest professional theater, performs Equity summer theater in July and August. The box office opens in June; before June, call the Tamworth Inn (*see* Dining and Lodging, *above*) for information. The **Lakes Region Theatre** (Interlakes Auditorium, Rte. 25, Meredith, ☎ 603/279–9933) has Broadway musicals six nights a week.

Nightlife

Funspot (Weirs Beach, ☎ 603/366–4377) is open 24 hours, July to Labor Day. You can bowl, snack, and play minigolf or any of the 500 arcade games all night long.

M/S Mount Washington (☎ 603/366–2628) has moonlight dinner-and-dance cruises Tuesday–Saturday evenings, with two bands and a different menu each night.

Lakes Region Essentials

Getting Around

BY BUS

Concord Trailways (☎ 800/639–3317) has daily stops in Tilton, Laconia, Meredith, Center Harbor, Moultonborough, and Conway.

BY CAR

On the western side of the region, I–93 is the principal north–south artery. Exit 20 leads to Route 11 and the southwestern side of Lake Winnipesaukee. Take Exit 23 to Route 104 to Route 25 and the northwestern corner of the region. From the coast, Route 16 stretches to the White Mountains, with roads leading to the lakeside towns.

BY PLANE

Moultonborough Airport Charter (Rte. 25, Moultonborough, ☎ 603/476–8801) offers chartered flights and tours.

Guided Tours

Cruising Golden Pond visits filming sites of the movie *On Golden Pond* aboard the *Lady of the Manor*, a 28-foot pontoon craft. *Manor Resort, Holderness, ☎ 603/279–4405.* ☛ *$10 adults, $5 children.* ☺ *Memorial Day–late Oct.*

Squam Lake Tours takes up to 20 passengers on a two-hour pontoon tour of "Golden Pond," with a visit to Church Island. The boat can also be chartered for guided fishing trips and wedding or anniversary parties, as well as for lake excursions. *Box 185, Holderness 03245, ☎ 603/968–7577.* ☺ *Late May–Oct.*

The **MS Mount Washington** (Box 5367, Weirs Beach 03247, ☎ 603/366–2628 or 603/366–5531) is a 230-foot craft that makes three-hour cruises of Lake Winnipesaukee. Departures are mid-May through mid-October, daily from Weirs Beach and Wolfeboro, three times weekly from Center Harbor, and four times weekly from Alton Bay. Ask about the moonlight dinner-and-dance cruises.

The **MV Sophie C.** (Weirs Beach, ☎ 603/366–2628) has been the area's floating post office for more than a century. It even has its own cancellation stamp. The boat departs Weirs Beach with both mail and passengers weekends from May 20 to June 11 and Monday through Saturday from June 12 to September 2.

The historic cars of the **Winnipesaukee Railroad** carry passengers along the lakeshore on an hour-long ride; boarding is at Weirs Beach or Meredith. *Box 9, Lincoln 03251, ☎ 603/279–5253. ☛ $7 adults, $4.50 children. ☉ Weekends Memorial Day–late June, late Sept.–mid-Oct.*

You can also see the area by air. **Sky Bright** (Laconia Airport, ☎ 603/528–6818) offers airplane and helicopter tours of the area and instruction on aerial photography.

Important Addresses and Numbers

EMERGENCIES
Lakes Region General Hospital (Highland St., Laconia, ☎ 603/524–3211).

VISITOR INFORMATION
Hours are generally weekdays 10–5. **Lakes Region Association** (Box 589, Center Harbor 03226, ☎ 603/253–8555). **Lakes Region Chamber of Commerce** (11 Veterans Sq., Laconia 03246, ☎ 603/524–5531 or 800/531–2347). **Wolfeboro Chamber of Commerce** (Railroad Ave., Wolfeboro 03894, ☎ 603/569–2200).

THE WHITE MOUNTAINS

Sailors approaching East Coast harbors frequently recognize the White Mountains—the highest range in the northeastern United States—towering in the distance, often mistaking these pale peaks for clouds. It was 1642 when explorer Darby Field could no longer contain his curiosity about one mountain in particular. He set off from his Exeter homestead and became the first man to climb what would eventually be called Mt. Washington, king of the Presidential range. More than a mile high, Mt. Washington must have presented Field with a slew of formidable obstacles—its peak claims the harshest winds and lowest temperatures ever recorded.

A few hundred years after Field's climb, curiosity about the mountains has not abated. People come here by the tens of thousands to hike and climb in spring and summer, to photograph the dramatic vistas and the vibrant sea of foliage in autumn, and to ski in winter. In this four-season vacation hub, many year-round resorts (some of which have been in business since the mid-1800s) are destinations in themselves, with golf, tennis, swimming, hiking, and cross-country skiing, and renowned restaurants.

Exploring

Numbers in the margin correspond to points of interest on the White Mountains map.

Although traveling at Mach One along I–93 is the fastest way to the White Mountains, it's hardly the most scenic. Try instead hopping off the interstate at Exit 32 in Lincoln and latching onto the **Kancamagus Highway** (a.k.a. "the Kank"), which allows classic White Mountains vistas. One caveat: This 34-mile trek erupts into fiery color each fall; photo-snapping drivers can really slow things down at this time. Prepare yourself for a leisurely pace, and enjoy the four scenic overlooks and picnic areas (all well marked).

A couple of short hiking trails off the Kank offer great rewards for relatively little effort. About 20 miles east of Exit 32, the parking and picnic area for **Sabbaday Falls** is the trailhead for an easy ½-mile trail to the falls, a multilevel cascade that plunges through two potholes and a flume. Travel another two miles east on the Kank for the **Russel Colbath Historic House** (ca. 1831), the only 19th-century homestead in the area and today a U.S. Forest Service information center. This marks the beginning of the **Rail 'N River Forest Trail,** a gentle ½-mile self-guided tour of White Mountains logging and geological history. It's wheelchair- and stroller-accessible.

❶ Continue on the Kank to Route 16 and **North Conway,** a shopper's paradise, with more than 150 outlet stores ranging from Anne Klein to Wallet Works to Joan & David. Most of them lie along Route 16.

Nonshoppers may wish to spend an hour on the **Conway Scenic Railroad,** which makes an 11-mile round-trip in vintage open-air trains pulled either by steam or diesel engines. Lunch is available in the dining car. The Victorian train station has displays of railroad artifacts, lanterns, and old tickets and timetables. *Main St.,* ☎ *603/356–5251 or 800/232–5251.* ☛ *$7.50 adults, $5 children 4–12.* ☉ *May–Oct., daily 9–6; Apr. and Nov.–late Dec., weekends 9–6. Reserve early during foliage season.*

You needn't be a rock climber to glimpse views from the 1,000-foot **White Horse** and **Cathedral** ledges. Two stoplights north of the Scenic Railroad's station, turn left onto River Road and then right onto West Side Road; then follow signs to the ledges. You can also drive up from **Echo Lake State Park** (N. Conway, ☎ 603/356–2672). From the top you'll see the entire valley in which Echo Lake shines like a diamond. Continue another ⁷⁄₁₀ mile on West Side Road to the unmarked trailhead to **Diana's Baths,** a spectacular series of waterfalls.

TIME OUT The **Thompson House Eatery** (Rte. 16, ☎ 603/383-9341), just south of Jackson, serves inventive fare that includes a ham-and-cheddar sandwich laced with apples and maple Dijon and the Currier & Ives salad of chicken, toasted almonds, tomatoes, and raisins over greens with a light curry dressing.

When the snow flies, the village of Jackson, just north of Glen on Route 16, becomes the state's cross-country skiing capital. **Jackson X-C** (Rte. 16A, Jackson, ☎ 603/383–9355 or 800/927–6697) offers a network of 64 trails of varying levels.

❷ Yes, you can drive to the top of **Mt. Washington,** the highest mountain (6,288 feet) in the northeastern United States and the spot where weather observers have recorded 231-mile-per-hour winds (the strongest in the world), but you'll have to endure the **Mt. Washington Auto Road** to get here. This toll road opened in 1861 and is said to be the nation's first manufactured tourist attraction. The road, which is closed in inclement weather, begins at Glen House, a gift shop and rest stop 15 miles north of Glen. Allow two hours round-trip and check your brakes first. Cars with automatic transmissions that can't shift down into first gear aren't allowed on the road at all. A better option is to

The White Mountains

0 ____ 10 miles
0 ____ 15 km

N

QUEBEC

CANADA

VERMONT

MAINE

Third Connecticut Lake

Second Connecticut Lake

First Connecticut Lake

Lake Francis

Pittsburg

145

Colebrook

Kidderville

Dixville Notch

DIXVILLE NOTCH STATE PARK

26

16

Errol

Umbagog L.

Connecticut River

3

Phillips

Strafford

Stark

West Milan

Groveton

Androscoggin

WHITE MOUNTAIN NATIONAL FOREST

Milan

110

16

Berlin

Lancaster

Gorham

2

91

135

Whitefield

Forest Lake

116

142

3

115

2

Gorham

Appalachian Trail

91

Littleton

93

Twin Mountain

302

Mt. Washington ❷

Bretton Woods ❺

Glen House

Bethlehem ❻

142

3

Pinkham Notch

Franconia ❼

Sugar Hill

18

Franconia Notch

CRAWFORD NOTCH STATE PARK

16

302

Lisbon

Cannon Mt.

3

302

Pemigewasset R.

Jackson

Woodsville

112

Franconia Notch State Park ❽

93

Lincoln

WHITE MOUNTAIN NATIONAL FOREST

North Woodstock

25

118

Woodstock

3

49

Kancamagus

Loon Mountain

Waterville Valley

Bear Notch Rd.

Sabbaday Falls

Hwy.

112

Bartlett ❹

ECHO LAKE STATE PARK

Swift

Glen ❸

Intervale

North Conway ❶

River

Mount Chocorua

16

Conway

302

TO SNOWVILLE, EAST MADISON

hop into one of the vans at Glen House for a 1½-hour guided tour. Up top, visit the **Sherman Adams Summit Building,** which contains a museum of memorabilia from each of the three hotels that have stood on this spot. There's also a nice display of native plant life and alpine flowers, as well as a glassed-in viewing area where you can hear the roar of that record-breaking wind. ☎ *603/466–3988.* ☛ *$14 car and driver, $5 adult passengers, $3 children 5–12. Van fare: $18 adults, $10 children 5–12.* ☉ *Daily mid-May–late Oct.*

❸ That cluster of fluorescent buildings on Route 16 in **Glen** is **Storyland,** a theme park with life-size storybook and nursery-rhyme characters, a flume ride, Cinderella's castle, a Victorian-theme river-raft ride, a farm-family variety show, and a simulated voyage to the moon. The kids will want to stay all day. *Rte. 16, Glen,* ☎ *603/383–4293.* ☛ *$15 (free under 4).* ☉ *Mid-June–Labor Day, daily 9–6; Labor Day–Columbus Day, weekends 10–5.*

Next door, a trip to **Heritage New Hampshire** is as close as you may ever come to experiencing time travel. Theatrical sets, sound effects, and animation usher you aboard the *Reliance* and carry you from a village in 1634 England over tossing seas to the New World. You will saunter along Portsmouth's streets in the late 1700s, applaud a speech by George Washington, and explore Portsmouth during the Industrial Revolution. Other exhibits include New England's largest historic mural. *Rte. 16, Glen,* ☎ *603/383–9776.* ☛ *$7.50 adults, $4.50 children 4–12.* ☉ *Mid-May–mid-Oct., daily 9–5.*

❹ From Glen, Route 302 follows the Saco River to **Bartlett** and the **Attitash Ski Area** (Rte. 302, ☎ 603/374–2368), which has a dry Alpine Slide, a water slide, a driving range, and a chairlift to the White Mountain Observation Tower, delivering 270° views of the Whites. Also in Bartlett, Bear Notch Road has the only midpoint access to the Kank (closed winter).

Route 302 passes through **Crawford Notch State Park** (☎ 603/374–2272), where you can stop for a picnic and a short hike to Arethusa Falls or the Silver and Flume cascades. Or you can just drive straight
❺ through to **Bretton Woods,** home of the Mount Washington, one of the nation's few remaining grand hotels. Early in this century, as many as 50 private trains a day brought the rich and famous from New York and Philadelphia to the hotel. In July 1944 the World Monetary Fund Conference convened here and established the American dollar as the basic unit of international exchange.

From Bretton Woods, take the marked road 6 miles northeast from Route 302 to the **Mt. Washington Cog Railway.** In 1858, when Reverend Thompson asked the state legislature for permission to build a steam railway up Mt. Washington, one legislator responded that he'd have better luck building a railroad to the moon. In spite of such skeptic views, the railway opened in 1869 and has since been giving tourists a thrilling alternative to driving or climbing to the top. Allow three hours round-trip. *Rte. 302, Bretton Woods,* ☎ *603/846–5404; outside NH, 800/922–8825, ext. 7.* ☛ *Round-trip $35. Reservations advised.* ☉ *May weekends for a limited schedule; June–Oct., daily 8:30–4:30, weather permitting.*

❻ In the 1920s the quiet town of **Bethlehem,** 25 miles west of Bretton Woods on Route 302, was known for only one thing: hay-fever relief. The crisp air at this elevation (1,462 feet) boasts a blissfully low pollen count. In the days before antihistamines, hay-fever sufferers arrived by the busload. The town also became home to a group of Hasidic Jews who established a kosher resort in the Arlington and Alpine hotels.

❼ Take Route 142 south to Route 18 to reach **Franconia,** where Route 116 leads south (follow the signs) to **The Frost Place,** Robert Frost's home from 1915 to 1920. It was here that he wrote his most remembered poem, "Stopping by Woods on a Snowy Evening." To be sure, the mountain views from this house would inspire any writer. Two rooms contain memorabilia and a few signed editions of his books. Outside, you can follow a short trail marked with lines of Frost's poetry. The house is still lived in by poets-in-residence and is the sight of occasional poetry readings. *Ridge Rd.,* ☎ *603/823–5510.* ☛ *$3 adults, $2 senior citizens, $1.25 children 6–15.* ☉ *Memorial Day–June, weekends 1– 5; July–Columbus Day, Wed.–Mon. 1–5.*

TIME OUT A short drive along Route 117, west of Franconia, to Sugar Hill leads to **Polly's Pancake Parlor** (☎ 603/823-5575), where you can sample whole wheat, buckwheat, cornmeal, and oatmeal-buttermilk pancakes with real maple syrup or a light lunch of baked beans and cob-smoked ham.

❽ Just south of Franconia on I–93 is **Franconia Notch State Park,** which contains a few of New Hampshire's best-loved attractions. The **Cannon Mountain Aerial Tramway** will lift you 2,022 feet for one more sweeping mountain vista. It's a five-minute ride to the top, where marked hiking trails lead from the observation platform. *Cannon Mountain Ski Area,* ☎ *603/823–5563.* ☛ *$8.* ☉ *Memorial Day–3rd weekend in Oct., daily 9–4.*

Just north of Cannon Mountain at the foot of the tramway, the **New England Ski Museum** has old trophies, skis and bindings, boots, and ski apparel dating from the late 1800s, as well as a collection of photos. ☎ *603/823–7177.* ☛ *Free.* ☉ *Dec. 1–Apr. 1 Thurs.–Tues. noon–5; Memorial Day–Columbus Day daily noon–5.*

No one should leave the White Mountains without seeing the granite profile of the **Old Man of the Mountains,** the icon of New Hampshire, located in the Franconia Notch State Park. Nathaniel Hawthorne wrote about it; New Hampshire resident Daniel Webster bragged about it; P. T. Barnum wanted to buy it. The two best places to view the giant stone face are the highway parking area on Route 3 or along the shores of Profile Lake.

The **Flume** is an 800-foot-long natural chasm discovered at about the same time as the Old Man by a local woman en route to her favorite fishing hole. Today the route through the flume has been built up with a series of boardwalks and stairways. The narrow walls give the gorge's running water a deeply eerie echo. *Exit 1 off I–93,* ☎ *603/745–8391.* ☛ *$6 adults, $3 children under 18.* ☉ *May–Oct., daily 9–5.*

What to See and Do with Children

Attitash Alpine Slide, Bartlett
Conway Scenic Railroad, North Conway
Mt. Washington Cog Railway, Bretton Woods
Storyland, Glen

Off the Beaten Path

Pittsburg lies just north of the White Mountains and contains the four Connecticut Lakes and the springs that form the Connecticut River.

In fact, the entire northern tip of the state—a chunk of about 250 square miles—lies within its town borders, the result of a border dispute between the United States and Canada in the early 19th century. The international border not yet fixed, the inhabitants of this region declared themselves independent of both countries in 1832 and wrote a constitution providing for an assembly, council, courts, and militia. They named their nation the Indian Stream Republic, after the river that passes through the territory—the capital of which was Pittsburg. In 1835 the feisty, 40-man Indian Stream militia invaded Canada—with only limited success. The Indian Stream war ended more by common consent than surrender; in 1842 the Webster-Ashburton Treaty fixed the international boundary. Indian Stream was incorporated as Pittsburg, making it the largest township in New Hampshire. Favorite uses of the land today are canoeing and photography; the pristine wilderness brims with moose. Contact the **Colebrook-Pittsburg Chamber of Commerce** (Colebrook 03576, ☎ 603/237–8939) for information about the region.

Dixville Notch. Just 12 miles from the Canadian border, this tiny community is known for only two things. It's the home of the Balsams Grand Resort Hotel, one of the oldest and most esteemed resorts (if also the most remote) in New Hampshire. Perhaps more important, Dixville Notch is also the first election district in the nation to vote in the presidential elections. Long before the sun rises on election day, the 34 or so voters gather in the little meeting room beside the hotel bar to cast their ballots and make national news.

Shopping

Some say that in the White Mountains, skiing is only the second-most popular sport, shopping being the hands-down favorite. Among the more than 200 area retail stores, you'll find custom-made hiking boots, sportswear (especially ski-related), one-of-a-kind boutiques, import shops, and outlets galore.

Specialty Shops

ANTIQUES

Antiques & Collectibles Barn (Rte. 16/302, 3425 Main St., North Conway, ☎ 603/356–7118), 1½ miles north of the village, is a 35-dealer colony with everything from furniture and jewelry to coins and other collectibles. **North Country Fair Jewelers** (Main and Seavy Sts., North Conway, ☎ 603/356–5819) carries diamonds, antique and estate jewelry, silver, watches, coins, and accessories. **Richard M. Plusch Fine Antiques** (Rte. 16/302, North Conway, ☎ 603/356–3333) deals in period furniture and accessories, including glass, sterling silver, Oriental porcelains, rugs, and paintings. **Sleigh Mill Antiques** (Snowville, off Rte. 153, ☎ 603/447–6791), an old sleigh and carriage mill 6 miles south of Conway, has become a shop specializing in 19th-century oil lighting and early gas and electric lamps.

CRAFTS

The **Basket & Handcrafters Outlet** (Kearsarge St., North Conway, ☎ 603/356–5332) bills itself as the shop your husband doesn't want you to find. It's perfect for those looking for gift baskets, dried-flower arrangements, and country furniture. **Handcrafters Barn** (Rte. 16, North Conway, ☎ 603/356–8996), a one-stop shopping emporium, features the work of 350 area artists and craftsmen, and has a shipping area for you to send your purchases home. **League of New Hampshire Craftsmen** (Main St., North Conway, ☎ 603/356–2441) features the area's best juried artisans.

SPORTSWEAR

You'll wait about a year for made-to-order **Limmer Boots** (Intervale, ☎ 603/356–5378) and pay more than $200 (plus shipping), but believers say they're worth the price.

Popular stores for skiwear include **Chuck Roast** (Rte. 16, North Conway, ☎ 603/356–5589), the **Jack Frost Shop** (Main St., Jackson Village, ☎ 603/383–4391), **Joe Jones** (Rte. 16, North Conway, ☎ 603/356–9411), and **Tuckerman's Outfitters** (Norcross Circle, North Conway, ☎ 603/356–3121).

Factory Outlets

Most of the area's more than 150 factory outlets huddle around Route 16 and North Conway, where you'll find the likes of Timberland, Pfaltzgraff, London Fog, Anne Klein, and Reebok; you can call the **Mount Washington Valley Visitors Bureau** (Box 2300, North Conway 03860, ☎ 603/356–5701) for further information.

Lincoln Square Outlet Stores (Rte. 112, Lincoln, ☎ 603/745–3883) stock predominantly factory seconds including London Fog, Van Heusen, and Bass—and there are a few restaurants as well. Take Exit 32 off I–93 and head 1½ miles east.

Malls

Millfront Marketplace, Mill at Loon Mountain (I–93 and the Kancamagus Hwy., Lincoln, ☎ 603/745–6261), a former paper factory, has become a full-service shopping center and inn, with restaurants, boutiques, a bookstore, a pharmacy, and a post office.

Skiing

Attitash
Rte. 302, Bartlett 03812
☎ *603/374–2368*

In the 1980s a new savvy management at Attitash directed the resort's appeal to active young people and families. Keeping a high and busy profile, the area hosts many activities, race camps, and demo equipment days. Lodging at the base of the mountain is available in condominiums and motel-style units a bit away from the hustle of North Conway. Attitash has a computerized lift-ticket system; skiers now go through turnstiles on their way to the lifts. In essence, the Smart Ticket allows you to pay by the run. Skiers can share the ticket, which is good for two years (including summer when it can be used on the slides).

DOWNHILL

Enhanced with massive snowmaking (98%), the trails now number 40. There are expert pitches at the top of the mountain (Idiot's Option, for example), but the bulk of the skiing is geared to advanced intermediates and below, with wide fall-line runs from mid-mountain. Beginners have a share of good terrain on the lower mountain. Serving the 23 kilometers (14½ miles) of trails and the 1,750-foot vertical drop are two triple, four doubles, and a quad chairlift.

CHILD CARE

Attitots Clubhouse takes children ages six weeks through five years. Other children's programs accommodate those up to 16 years of age.

Balsams/Wilderness
Dixville Notch 03576
☎ *603/255–3400 or 800/255–0600; in NH, 800/255–0800; snow conditions, 603/255–3951*

Maintaining the tradition of a grand resort hotel is the primary goal at Balsams/Wilderness. Skiing was originally provided as an amenity for hotel guests, but the area has since become popular with day-trippers, as well. Restoration of the large, sprawling structure that dates to 1866 has been continuous since the early 1970s. Guests will find many nice touches: valet parking, gourmet meals, dancing and entertainment nightly, cooking demonstrations, and other organized recreational activities.

DOWNHILL
Sanguinary, Umbagog, Magalloway are the tough-sounding slope names that are really only moderately difficult, leaning toward intermediate. There are trails from the top of the 1,000-foot vertical drop for every skill level. One double chairlift and two T-bars carry skiers up the mountain.

CROSS-COUNTRY
Balsams/Wilderness has 76 kilometers (45 miles) of cross-country skiing, tracked and also groomed for skating (a cross-country ski technique), with natural-history markers annotating some trails; there's also telemark and backcountry skiing.

OTHER ACTIVITIES
In winter, the area offers ice-skating, hayrides, sleigh rides, snowshoeing, and snowmobiling.

CHILD CARE
The nursery takes children up to age six at no charge to hotel guests. There are lessons for children three and up.

Black Mountain
Rte. 16B, Jackson 03846
☎ *603/383–4490 or 800/475–4669*

The setting is 1950s and the atmosphere is friendly and informal—skiers have fun here. There's a country feeling at the big base building, which resembles an old farmhouse, and at the skiing facilities, which generally have no lines. Black has the essentials for families and singles who want a low-key skiing holiday. The Family Passport allows two adults and two juniors to ski at discounted rates. Midweek rates here are usually the lowest in Mt. Washington Valley.

DOWNHILL
The bulk of the terrain is easy to middling, with intermediate trails that wander over the 1,150-vertical-foot mountain. Devil's Elbow on the Black Beauty trail—once a real zinger—has been expanded and is no longer as difficult to ski. The lifts are a triple and a double chairlift and two surface tows. Most of the skiing is user-friendly, particularly for beginners. The southern exposure adds to the warm atmosphere.

CROSS-COUNTRY
Black is near some of the finest cross-country skiing in the East. Contact the Jackson Ski Touring Foundation (Box 216, Jackson Village, NH 03846, ☎ 603/383–9355). JSTF has about 154 kilometers (94 miles) that wind through Jackson Village, along the Ellis River, and up into the backcountry.

OTHER ACTIVITIES
In addition to ski trails, snowboarders can use the halfpipe to practice their freestyle stunts.

CHILD CARE
The nonski nursery takes children up to six years old. The ski school has instruction for ages 3–12.

Bretton Woods

Rte. 302, Bretton Woods 03575
☎ *603/278–5000; information, 800/232–2972; lodging, 603/278–1000*

Bretton Woods has an attractive three-level, open-space base lodge, a convenient drop-off area, easy parking, and an uncrowded setting. On-mountain town houses are available with reasonably priced packages through the resort. The spectacular views of Mt. Washington itself are worth the visit; the scenery is especially beautiful from the Top o' Quad restaurant.

DOWNHILL

The skiing on the 30 trails is mostly gentle, with some intermediate pitches near the top of the 1,500-foot vertical, and a few expert runs. One quad, one triple, and two double chairlifts, and one T-bar service the trails. The area has night skiing Friday, Saturday, and holidays. A limited lift-ticket policy helps keep lines short.

CROSS-COUNTRY

A short distance from the base of the mountain is a large cross-country center with 90 kilometers (51 miles) of groomed and double-track trails.

OTHER ACTIVITIES

A recreation center has racquetball, saunas and whirlpools, indoor swimming, an exercise room, and a game room.

CHILD CARE

The nursery takes children ages two months through three years. The ski school has an all-day program for ages 3–12, using progressive instructional techniques. Rates include lifts, lessons, equipment, lunch, and supervised play.

Cannon Mountain

Franconia Notch State Park, Franconia 03580
☎ *603/823–5563; snow conditions, 603/823–7771 or 800/552–1234*

Nowhere is the granite of the Granite State more pronounced than at Cannon Mountain, where you'll find the essentials for feeling the thrill of downhill. One of the first ski areas in the United States, the massif has retained the basic qualities that make the sport unique—the camaraderie of young people who are there for challenge and family fun. The New England Ski Museum is adjacent to the base of the tramway. Cannon is owned and run by the state, and as a result, greater attention is paid to skier services, family programs, snowmaking, and grooming.

DOWNHILL

The tone of this mountain's skiing is reflected in the narrow, steep pitches off the peak of the 2,146 feet of vertical rise. Some trails marked intermediate may seem more difficult because of the sidehill slant of the slopes (rather than the steepness). Under a new fall of snow, Cannon has challenges not often found at modern ski areas. There is an 80-passenger tramway to the top, one quad, one triple, and two double chairlifts, and one surface lift.

CROSS-COUNTRY

Nordic skiing is available on a 13-kilometer (8.2-mile) bicycle path through Franconia Notch State Park.

CHILD CARE

Cannon's Peabody Base Lodge takes children one year and older. All-day and half-day SKIwee programs are available for children 4–12, and season-long instruction can be arranged.

King Pine Ski Area at Purity Spring Resort
Rte. 153, E. Madison, 03849
☎ *603/367–8896 or 800/367–8897; ski information, 800/373–3754*

King Pine, located a little more than 9 miles from Conway (past the white-steepled church town of Eaton), has been a family-run ski area for more than 100 years. The Hoyt family offers many ski-and-stay packages throughout the winter season, including free skiing to midweek resort guests.

DOWNHILL
King Pine's gentle slopes make it an ideal area for families just learning to ski. Because most of the terrain is geared for beginner and intermediate skiers, experts won't be challenged here except for a brief pitch on the Pitch Pine trail. Sixteen trails are serviced by a triple chair, double chair, and two J-bars. Night skiing is offered on Tuesday, Friday, Saturday, and holidays.

CROSS-COUNTRY
Twenty-five kilometers (15½ miles) of cross-country skiing is offered on King Pine's property.

OTHER ACTIVITIES
Facilities include an indoor pool and fitness complex; ice-skating and dogsledding are also available.

CHILD CARE
Children of all ages are welcome at the nursery (⊗ Daily 9–4) on the second floor of the base lodge. Lessons are offered to children ages four–six.

Loon Mountain
Kancamagus Hwy., Lincoln 03251
☎ *603/745–8111; snow conditions, 603/745–8100; lodging, 800/229–7829*

On the Kancamagus Highway and the Pemigewasset River is the modern Loon Mountain resort. Loon opened in the 1960s, and saw serious development in the 1980s, when more mountain facilities, base lodges, and a large hotel near the main lifts at the bottom of the mountain were added. The result attracts a broad cross-section of skiers. In the base lodge and around the mountain are a large number of food services and lounge facilities.

DOWNHILL
Wide, straight, and consistent intermediate trails prevail at Loon, making it ideal for plain fun or for advancing one's skills. Beginner trails and slopes are set apart, so faster skiers won't interfere. Most advanced runs are grouped on the North Peak section farther from the main mountain. The vertical is 2,100 feet; a four-passenger gondola, two triple and five double chairlifts, and one surface lift serve the 41 trails and slopes.

CROSS-COUNTRY
The touring center has 35 kilometers (22 miles) of cross-country trails.

OTHER ACTIVITIES
The Mountain Club has a fitness center with a whirlpool, lap pool, saunas, steam rooms, an exercise room, and racquetball and squash courts. Massages and aerobics classes are available.

CHILD CARE
The nursery takes children as young as six weeks; nonintensive ski instruction is offered to youngsters of nursery age. The ski school has a

program for children 9–12 and SKIwee for ages three–eight. Children five and under ski free every day, while those 6–12 ski free midweek during nonholiday periods when parents participate in a five-day ski week.

Mt. Cranmore
Box 1640, North Conway, 03860
☎ *603/356–5543; snow conditions, 800/786–6754; lodging, 800/543–9206*

The ski area at Mt. Cranmore, on the outskirts of North Conway, came into existence in 1938 when local residents saw an opportunity to make the most of their mountain. One early innovation, the clankety-clank Skimobile lift, has sadly been put out to museum pastures. An aggressive mountain-improvement program has been under way for several years, with new grooming equipment, a triple chair, expanded terrain, and base-restaurant services. A fitness center completes the "new" Cranmore with an indoor climbing wall.

DOWNHILL
The mountain and trail system at Cranmore is well laid out and fun to ski. Most of the runs are naturally formed intermediates that weave in and out of glades. Beginners have several slopes and routes from the 1,200-foot summit, while experts must be content with a few short but steep pitches. One triple and four double chairlifts carry skiers to the top. There is night skiing Thursday through Saturday and during holiday periods.

CROSS-COUNTRY
Sixty-five kilometers (40 miles) of groomed cross-country trails weave through North Conway and the countryside along the Mount Washington Valley Ski Touring Association Network (☎ 603/356–9920).

OTHER ACTIVITIES
Mt. Cranmore Recreation Center contains four indoor tennis courts, exercise equipment, an indoor pool, aerobics workout space, and a 40-foot indoor climbing wall. There's also outdoor skating and a halfpipe for snowboarders.

CHILD CARE
The nursery takes children one year and up. There's instruction for children 4–12.

Waterville Valley
Waterville Valley 03215
☎ *603/236–8311; snow conditions, 603/236–4144; lodging, 800/468–2553*

The area has been developed (with taste and regard for the New England sensibility) to resemble a small town: There are inns, lodges, and condominiums; restaurants, taverns, small cafés; shops, boutiques, and a grocery store; conference facilities; a post office; and a sports center. An array of three- to five-day vacation packages is available.

DOWNHILL
Mt. Tecumseh, a short shuttle ride from the Town Square and accommodations, has been laid out with great care and attention to detail. Most advanced skiers will find an adequate challenge, and there are slopes and trails for beginners, too; yet the bulk of the 53 trails are intermediate: straight down the fall line, wide, and agreeably long. Still, the variety is great enough that no one will be bored on a weekend visit. The lifts serving the 2,020 feet of vertical rise include one high-speed, detachable quad; three triple; and five double chairlifts; and four

surface lifts. A second mountain, Snow's, about 2 miles away, is open on weekends and takes some of the overflow; it has five fairly easy natural snow trails and one double chairlift off a 580-foot vertical. This ski area has hosted more World Cup races than any other in the East.

CROSS-COUNTRY

The cross-country network, with the ski center in the Town Square, has 105 kilometers (62 miles) of trails, 70 of them groomed.

OTHER ACTIVITIES

There's an ice-skating arena and a snowboard park; and the Sports Center has tennis, racquetball, and squash courts; a 25-meter indoor pool; jogging track; exercise equipment and classes; whirlpools, saunas, and steam rooms; massage service; and a games room.

CHILD CARE

The nursery takes children six weeks through four years old. There are SKIwee lessons and other instruction for children ages 3–12. The Kinderpark, a children's slope, has a slow-running lift and special props to hold children's attention. Children under six ski free anytime; midweek, those under 13 ski and stay free with a parent on five-day packages.

Wildcat Mountain

Pinkham Notch, Rte. 16, Jackson 03846
☎ *603/466–3326; snow conditions, 800/643–4521, lodging 800/255–6439*

Wildcat has been working hard to live down its reputation of being a difficult mountain. The 2¾-mile-long Polecat is where skiers who can hold a wedge should head, while experts can be found zipping down The Lynx, a run constantly voted by patrons of a local bar as the most popular in the Mt. Washington Valley. On a clear day, there is no better view than that of Mt. Washington (the highest peak in the Northeast) from here. Tuckerman Ravine, where skiers trek in spring to hike up and ski down, can also be seen. Trails are classic New England—narrow and winding.

DOWNHILL

Wildcat's expert runs deserve their designations and then some. Intermediates have mid-mountain-to-base trails, and beginners will find gentle terrain and a broad teaching slope. The 31 runs with a 2,100-foot vertical drop, are served by a two-passenger gondola and one double and four triple chairlifts.

CHILD CARE

The child care center takes children 18 months and up. All-day SKIwee instruction is offered to children 5–12. A separate slope is used for teaching children to ski.

Other Sports

Biking

Not surprisingly, the best way to cycle in the Whites is on a mountain bike. You'll find excellent routes detailed in the mountain-bike guide map "20 Off Road and Back Road Routes in Mt. Washington Valley," sold at area sports shops. There's also a bike path in Franconia Notch State Park, at the Lafayette Campground.

Camping

White Mountain National Forest (719 N. Main St., Laconia 03246, ☎ 603/528–8721) has 20 campgrounds, more than 900 camp sites, some available on a first-come first-served basis and some available by reservation. All sites are subject to a 14-day-limit.

The **Appalachian Mountain Club** (Box 298, Gorham 03581, ☎ 603/466–2721, 603/466–2725 for trail information, 603/466–2727 for reservations or for the free AMC guide to the huts and lodges) headquarters at Pinkham Notch was built in 1920 and now offers lectures, workshops, slide shows, and movies June–October. Accommodations include a 100-bunk main lodge and eight rustic cabins.

The **Lafayette Campground** (Franconia Notch State Park, 03580, ☎ 603/823–9513) has hiking and biking trails, 97 tent sites, showers, a camp store, and easy access to the Appalachian Trail. Other state parks have camping facilities, too. Reservations are not accepted.

Canoeing

River outfitter **Saco Bound & Downeast** (Box 119, Center Conway 03813, ☎ 603/447–2177 or 603/447–3801) offers gentle canoeing expeditions, guided kayak trips, white-water rafting on seven rivers, lessons, equipment and a full transportation service.

Fishing

The **North Country Angler** (N. Main St., North Conway, ☎ 603/356–6000) schedules intensive guided fly-fishing weekends and programs.

For trout and salmon fishing, try the Connecticut Lakes, though any clear stream in the White Mountains will do. Many are stocked, and there are 650 miles of them in the national forest alone. **Conway Lake** (Conway) is the largest of the area's 45 lakes and ponds; it's noted for smallmouth bass and—early and late in the season—good salmon fishing. The **New Hampshire Fish and Game Office** (☎ 603/788–3164) has up-to-date information.

Hiking

With 86 major mountains in the area, the hiking possibilities seem endless. Innkeepers can usually point you toward the better nearby trails; some inns schedule guided day trips for their guests. On a larger scale, **New England Hiking Holidays** (Box 1648, North Conway 03860, ☎ 603/356–9696 or 800/869–0949) offers inn-to-inn, guided hiking tours that include two, three, or five nights in country inns.

Some good hikes other than those mentioned throughout Exploring the New Hampshire Coast (*see above*) include the **Doublehead Ski Trail** (off Dundee Rd., Rte. 16B) in Jackson; **Artist's Bluff** (off Rte. 18), **Lonesome Lake** (Lafayette Pl.), and **Basin-Cascades Trails** (off Rte. 3) in Franconia Notch State Park; **Boulder Loop** and **Greeley Ponds** (off Kancamagus Hwy.); and **Sanguinari Ridge Trail** in Dixville Notch. The trail up **Mt. Chocorua** begins just north of Chocorua Lake, which is north of the Piper Trail building off Route 16.

Appalachian Mountain Club (*see* Camping, *above*) has information on hiking trails, hiking safety, and area wildlife; their hut system provides reasonably priced meals and dorm-style lodging on several different trails throughout the Whites.

White Mountain National Forest (U.S. Forest Service, 719 N. Main St., Laconia 03247, ☎ 603/528–8721 or 800/283–2267).

Llama Trekking

Snowvillage Inn (Snowville 03849, ☎ 603/447–2818 or 800/447–4345) conducts a guided trip up Foss Mountain. Your elegant picnic will include gourmet food from the inn's kitchen along with champagne.

Luckily you don't have to carry the food, the fine china, or the silver-ware—llamas do that for you. Reservations required.

White Mountain Llamas at the Stag Hollow Inn (Jefferson 03583, ☎ 603/586–4598) will introduce you to llama trekking, with one- to four-day hikes on beautiful, secluded trails. The hiking trips include picnic foods, but the primary focus is on the surrounding nature.

Recreation Areas

Bretzfelder Park (Bethlehem), a 77-acre nature and wildlife park, has a picnic shelter. At **Lost River Reservation** (N. Woodstock, ☎ 603/745–8031; ⊙ May–Oct.) you can tour the gorge and view such geo-logical wonders as the Guillotine Rock and the Lemon Squeezer. In ad-dition to the skiing, hiking, camping, and canoeing popular throughout the area, **Nestlenook Farm** (Dinsmore Rd., Jackson Village, ☎ 603/383–0845) offers romantic sleigh rides and maintains an outdoor ice-skating rink complete with music and a bonfire. You can rent skates here or get yours sharpened.

In summer, many area ski resorts have other attractions; for contact in-formation, *see* Skiing, *above*. **Attitash** has two Alpine slides and three water slides, horseback and pony riding, a golf driving range, and a scenic chairlift to the White Mountain observation tower. There are also con-certs, stock theater, rodeo, and a horse show held on premises. **Bal-sams/Wilderness** has 27 holes of golf; six tennis courts; two trap fields; a heated outdoor pool; boating, swimming, and fly fishing on Lake Glo-riette; and trails for hiking and climbing. At **Bretton Woods,** take advantage of in-line skating and lift-service mountain biking, as well as 27 holes of golf, 12 tennis courts, an outdoor pool, fly fishing, and hiking at the Mount Washington Hotel (☎ 603/278–1000). **King Pine**'s guests canoe, hike, fish, play tennis, and waterski. At **Loon Mountain,** facilities include an outdoor pool, tennis courts, horses, archery, in-line skates, and skeet. Take a mountain bike in a gondola to the summit and ride down. **Mt. Cran-more** has four outdoor tennis courts, and **Waterville Valley** has an out-door pool, 18 tennis courts, nine holes of golf, biking, horseback riding, in-line skating, and water sports on Corcoran's Pond.

State Parks

Crawford Notch State Park (Rte. 302, Harts Location), 6 miles of un-spoiled mountain pass, has scenic waterfalls perfect for picnicking, hik-ing, and photography. The Dry River Campground has 30 tent sites and is a popular base for hiking the White Mountain National Forest. **Dixville Notch State Park** (Rte. 26, Dixville, ☎ 603/788–3155), the northernmost notch, has a waterfall, picnic areas, and a hiking trail to Table Rock. **Echo Lake State Park** (Conway), the mountain lake be-neath White Horse Ledge, has swimming, picnicking, and a scenic road to the 700-foot Cathedral Ledge for a heart-stopping view of the White Mountains. **Franconia Notch State Park** (Franconia and Lincoln) is a 6,440-acre valley between the Franconia and Kinsman mountain ranges. Here you can swim, camp, picnic, bike, and hike on a 27-mile network of Appalachian-system trails, or view the Old Man of the Moun-tains, a 40-foot granite profile that's the official symbol of New Hamp-shire. The park also contains the Flume, Echo Lake, Liberty Gorge, the Cascades, the Basin, and the New England Ski Museum.

Dining and Lodging

Mt. Washington Valley has more than 100 hotels, lodges, and motels, many of which can be reached through the **Mount Washington Valley**

Chamber of Commerce Travel and Lodging Bureau (☎ 800/223–7669). The **Mt. Washington Valley Visitors Bureau** (☎ 603/356–3171 or 800/367–3364), **Country Inns in the White Mountains** (☎ 603/356–9460 or 800/562–1300), and the **Jackson Resort Association** (☎ 800/866–3334) are also reservation services.

Bartlett

DINING AND LODGING

$$$ **Attitash Mountain Village.** This condo-motel complex—just across the ❄ street from the mountain, via a tunnel under the road—has a glass-enclosed pool and units that will accommodate 2–14 people. Those quarters with fireplaces and kitchenettes are especially good for families. The style is Alpine-contemporary; the staff, young and enthusiastic. ⛣ *Rte. 302, Bartlett 03812-0358,* ☎ *603/374–6501 or 800/862–1600,* FAX *603/374–6509. 250 rooms with bath. Restaurant, pub, indoor pool, sauna, recreation room. AE, D, MC, V.*

Bethlehem

DINING AND LODGING

$$–$$$ **Adair.** In 1927 attorney Frank Hogan built this three-story Georgian Revival home as a wedding present for his daughter Dorothy Adair. Each of the guest rooms has a mountain view and is elegantly decorated in antique reproductions. Play pool downstairs in the tap room, or roam about the 200-acre estate. ⛣ *Old Littleton Rd., 03574,* ☎ *603/444–2600 or 800/441–2606,* FAX *603/444–4823. 8 rooms with bath, 1 suite. Restaurant, tennis. Full breakfast included. AE, MC, V.*

Bretton Woods

LODGING

$$$$ **Mount Washington Hotel.** The 1902 construction of this leviathan was ❄ one of the most ambitious projects of its day. It quickly became one of the nation's favorite grand resorts, most notable for its 900-foot-long veranda, which offers a full view of the Presidential range. With its stately public rooms and its large, Victorian-style bedrooms and suites, the atmosphere still courts a turn-of-the-century formality; jacket and tie are expected in the dining room at dinner and in the lobby after 6. This 2,600-acre property has an extensive recreation center. ⛣ *Rte. 302, 03575,* ☎ *603/278–1000 or 800/258–0330,* FAX *603/278–3457. 195 rooms with bath. 2 restaurants, indoor and outdoor pools, sauna, golf, tennis, hiking, horseback riding, bicycles, children's programs. MAP. AE, MC, V. Closed mid-Oct.–mid-May.*

$$–$$$ **Bretton Arms.** Built in 1896, this restored historic inn predates even ❄ the grande dame Mount Washington Hotel across the way, so you know that the trendsetters of the last century stayed here. Reservations are required in the dining room and should be made on arrival. Guests are invited to use the facilities of the Mount Washington Hotel during the summer and the Lodge at Bretton Woods year-round. ⛣ *Rte. 302, Bretton Woods 03575,* ☎ *603/278–1000 or 800/258–0330,* FAX *603/278–3457. 31 rooms with bath, 3 suites. Restaurant, lounge. AE, D, MC, V.*

$–$$ **Lodge at Bretton Woods.** Rooms have contemporary furnishings, a bal-❄ cony, and views of the Presidential Range. Darby's Restaurant serves Continental cuisine around a circular fireplace, and the bar is a hangout for après-skiers. The lodge, across the road from the Mount Washington Hotel, shares its facilities in summer. ⛣ *Rte. 302, Bretton Woods 03575,* ☎ *603/278–1000 or 800/258–0330,* FAX *603/278–3457. 50 rooms. Restaurant, lounge, indoor pool, sauna, recreation room. AE, D, MC, V.*

Conway

DINING AND LODGING

$$$ **Darby Field Inn.** After a day of cross-country skiing, snowshoeing, or
❄️ hiking in the White Mountain National Forest (which borders the prop-
erty), you can warm yourself before the living room's fieldstone fire-
place or by the woodstove in the bar. Built in 1826, this converted
farmhouse retains an unpretentious feel. Most of the rooms have moun-
tain views; the one with the queen-size mahogany bed is most popular.
In the restaurant, the prix-fixe menu usually features the inn's signa-
ture dish, chicken marquis (a sautéed breast of chicken with mushrooms,
scallions, tomatoes, and white wine), or roast Wisconsin duckling
glazed with Chambord or Grand Marnier. Don't leave without trying
the dark chocolate pâté with white-chocolate sauce or the famous
Darby cream pie. ☎ *Bald Hill, 03818,* ☎ *603/447–2181 or 800/426–*
4147, 𝔽𝔸𝕏 *603/447–5726. 15 rooms, 14 with bath, and 1 suite. Restau-*
rant (reservations advised), pool, cross-country skiing. Closed Apr.
Rates are MAP Jan.–Mar. AE, DC, MC, V.

Dixville Notch

DINING AND LODGING

$$$$ **Balsams Grand Resort Hotel.** This 232-room resort began as the Dix farm,
❄️ where, in 1866, a family could get a room and dinner for $2. Repeat
guests of this famed compound find a personalized bottle of maple syrup
in their rooms. The full slate of activities keeps families on the go—choose
from among magic shows, aerobics, cooking demonstrations, dancing,
skiing (lessons, too), and late-night games of broomball. The Tower Suite,
with its 20-foot conical ceiling, is in a Victorian-style turret and offers
360° views. Standard rooms have views of the 15,000-acre estate and
the mountains beyond as well as overstuffed chairs and soft queen-size
beds, which is exactly what you'll need after running around all day. In
summer the buffet lunch is heaped upon a 100-foot-long table. Given
this awesome amount of food, it's amazing that anyone has room left
for the stunning dinners—but they do. A starter might be chilled straw-
berry soup spiked with Grand Marnier, followed by poached fillet of
salmon with golden caviar sauce, and ending with chocolate hazelnut
cake. ☎ *Dixville Notch 03576,* ☎ *603/255–3400 or 800/255–0600,*
𝔽𝔸𝕏 *603/255–4221. 232 rooms with bath. Restaurant (reservations,*
jacket and tie), pool, golf, tennis, boating, bicycles, ice-skating, cross-
country skiing, downhill skiing, children's programs. Rates are AP in
summer, MAP in winter, and include sports and entertainment. AE, D,
MC, V. Closed late March–mid-May, mid-Oct.–mid-Dec.

East Madison

LODGING

$$ **Purity Spring Resort.** In the late 1800s, Purity Spring was a farm and
❄️ sawmill. Set on a private lake, since 1944 it's been a four-season resort
with swimming, fishing, hiking, tennis, and lawn games. The com-
pound consists of two colonial inns, a series of lakeside cottages, and
a ski lodge. In winter families take advantage of the King Pine Ski Area,
located on the property. You have a choice between hotel-style rooms
in the ski area or inn-style rooms in the main lodge. ☎ *Rte. 153, 03849,*
☎ *603/367–8896 or 800/367–8897,* 𝔽𝔸𝕏 *603/367–8664. 48 rooms, 38*
with bath. Restaurant, indoor pool, lake, hot tub, tennis, volleyball. Rates
are MAP or AP. AE, D, MC, V.

Franconia

DINING AND LODGING

$–$$$ **Franconia Inn.** This country resort has every manner of recreation for
❄️ all seasons. You can golf next door at Sunset Hill's nine-hole course,

play tennis, ride horseback, swim in the pool or sit in the hot tub, order your lunch to go for a day of hiking—even try soaring from the inn's own airstrip. Movies are shown evenings in the lounge. Rooms have designer chintzes, canopy beds, and country furnishings; some have whirlpool baths or fireplaces. The owners refer to the food here as French gourmet with an American twist, but its real focus is the family. The children choose from a separate menu, which includes the "Young Epicurean Cheeseburger" and a "Petite Breast of Chicken." Adults stick to such specialties as medallions of veal with apple-mustard sauce or filet mignon with sun-dried tomatoes. ☎ *Easton Rd., 03580,* ☎ *603/ 823–5542 or 800/473–5299,* FAX *603/823–8078. 34 rooms with bath. Restaurant (reservations advised), pool, hot tub, tennis, croquet, horseback riding, bicycles, ice-skating, skiing, sleigh rides. B&B or MAP rates available. Closed Apr.–mid-May. AE, MC, V.*

LODGING

$$ **Horse and Hound Inn.** Off the beaten path yet convenient to the Can-
✳ non Mountain tram, this traditional inn is set on 8 acres surrounded by the White Mountain National Forest. Antiques and assorted collectibles offer guests a cheery atmosphere, and on the grounds are 10 kilometers (6 miles) of cross-country ski trails. ☎ *205 Wells Rd., Franconia 03580,* ☎ *603/823–5501. 10 rooms, 8 with bath; 2 suites. Restaurant, lounge, billiards. Closed Apr. and Nov. Full breakfast included. AE, D, DC, MC, V.*

Glen

DINING

$ **Margaritaville.** The taste of this authentic Mexican food is only enhanced by the tart, locally renowned drinks for which this restaurant is named. Guests enjoy outdoor dining on the patio in summer and the exceptional service of this family-run establishment. ✗ *Rte. 302,* ☎ *603/383–6556. MC, V.*

DINING AND LODGING

$–$$ **Bernerhof.** This Old World hotel is right at home in its Alpine setting. Rooms eschew the lace-and-doily decor of many Victorian inns, opting instead for such understated touches as hardwood floors with hooked rugs, antique reproductions, and large, plain windows. The fanciest four rooms have brass beds and spa-size bathtubs. One suite, on the third floor, even has a Finnish sauna. Stay three days, and you'll be served a champagne breakfast in bed. The chef describes his cuisine as a cross between Central European and new American. One side of the menu features such Swiss specialties as fondue, wiener schnitzel, and *delices de gruyère* (a blend of Swiss cheeses breaded and sautéed and served with a savory tomato sauce). The other side of the menu is a changing variety of classic French and new American dishes. The wine list favors French and Austrian labels. Ask about the Taste of the Mountains, a hands-on cooking school hosted by some of the region's top chefs. ☎ *Rte. 302, 03838,* ☎ *603/383–4414 or 800/548–8007,* FAX *603/383–0809. 9 rooms with bath. Restaurant (reservations advised), pub. Full breakfast included. AE, MC, V.*

$$–$$$ **Best Western Storybook Resort Inn.** On a hillside near Attitash, this
✳ family-owned, family-run motor inn is well suited to—what else?—families, particularly because of its large rooms. Copperfield's Restaurant has gingerbread, sticky buns, farmer's omelets, and a children's menu. ☎ *Box 129, Glen Junction 03838,* ☎ *603/383–6800 or 800/ 528–1234,* FAX *603/383–4678. 78 rooms with bath. Restaurant, indoor and outdoor pools, sauna. AE, DC, MC, V.*

Jackson

DINING AND LODGING

$$–$$$ **Inn at Thorn Hill.** This Victorian house, designed in 1895 by Stanford White, has frilly decor with polished dark woods, rose-motif papers, and plenty of lace, fringe, and knickknacks. Guests are just a few steps away from beautiful cross-country trails and the village itself. The specialty at dinner may be lobster pie with a brandy Newburg sauce, but that's not the only special thing on the menu. The four-course prix-fixe menu changes frequently and may include the *duck á deux* (a sautéed breast of duck with blackberry sauce and confit of duck leg) or a pounded tenderloin with apples, Calvados, cream, and Stilton cheese. Desserts include cappuccino crème caramel, dark-chocolate torte, and saffron-poached pears with raspberry coulis. The owners, from California, maintain an extensive wine list. ☎ *Thorn Hill Rd., 03846,* ☎ *603/383–4242 or 800/289–8990,* ℻ *603/383–8062. 20 rooms with bath. Restaurant (reservations required), pub, pool. MAP. AE, DC, MC, V. Closed Sun.–Thurs. in Apr.*

$$–$$$ **Christmas Farm Inn.** Despite its winter-inspired name, this 200-year-old village inn is an all-season retreat. Rooms in the main inn and the saltbox next door are all done with Laura Ashley prints. In the cottages, log cabin, and dairy barn, suites have beam ceilings and fireplaces and more rustic Colonial furnishings. These rooms are better suited to families. The restaurant's menu is mixed and varies with the seasons, but some standbys include vegetable-stuffed chicken, shrimp scampi, grilled salmon, and New York sirloin; the list of homemade soups and desserts varies nightly. The menu also includes "heart-healthy" options approved by the American Heart Association. ☎ *Box CC, Rte. 16B, 03846,* ☎ *603/383–4313 or 800/443–5837,* ℻ *603/383–6495. 38 rooms with bath, 5 with whirlpool tub. Restaurant (reservations advised), pub, pool, sauna, volleyball, recreation room, playground. MAP. AE, MC, V.*

$$ **Eagle Mountain House.** When this country estate, which dates from 1879, ❄ was restored and modernized in 1986, it became a showplace. Close to Wildcat Mountain ski area, the inn is now run by Colony Resorts. The public rooms are rustic-palatial, in keeping with the period of tycoon roughing-it; the bedrooms are large and furnished with period pieces. On a warm day, nurse a drink from a rocking chair on the wraparound deck. ☎ *Carter Notch Rd., Jackson 03846,* ☎ *603/383–9111 or 800/777–1700,* ℻ *603/383–0854. 92 rooms with bath, 20 are no-smoking. Restaurant, pool, saunas, health club. AE, D, DC, MC, V*

$–$$ **Wentworth.** This resort was built in 1869 as a wedding gift to General Marshall C. Wentworth from his future father-in-law. It still retains a Victorian look, although the new owner has added such European touches as French provincial antiques. All rooms have TVs and telephones; some have working fireplaces and whirlpool tubs, too. Although the dining room food is innovative—guests rave about the sautéed shrimp with a tequila lime sauce—take at least one snack in the lounge, where you can order raclette (melted cheese served with boiled potatoes, cornichons, pickles, pearl onions, and dark bread), and Swiss or chocolate fondue. ☎ *Rte. 16A, 03846,* ☎ *603/383–9700 or 800/637–0013,* ℻ *603/383–4265. 60 rooms with bath in summer, 40 in winter. Restaurant, lobby, pool, golf, tennis, ice-skating, cross-country skiing, sleigh rides. AE, D, DC, MC, V.*

$–$$ **Whitneys' Village Inn.** The Bowman family brings more than 30 years ❄ of innkeeping experience to this classic country inn at the base of Black Mountain. You'll find antiques in the living room, period pieces in the one-of-a-kind bedrooms, and suites that can take the bang of ski-week families. The windows of the dining room look out onto the slopes. ☎ *Box 822, Jackson 03846,* ☎ *603/383–8916 or 800/677–5737. 28 rooms with bath, 2 cottages. Restaurant, recreation room, pond. Rates are MAP or B&B. AE, D, MC, V.*

$–$$ Wildcat Inn & Tavern. After a day of skiing, collapse on a comfy sofa by the fire in this tavern, situated in the center of Jackson Village. Although only 12 rooms are available in this small 19th-century inn, it's a lodestone for skiers in nearby condos and bed-and-breakfasts. The fragrance of home-baking permeates into guest rooms, which are full of interesting furniture and knickknacks. There's often musical entertainment in the tavern, too. ☎ *Rte. 16A, Jackson 03846,* ☎ *603/383–4245, or 800/228–4245,* ☒ *603/383–6456. 12 rooms, 10 with bath. Restaurant. Full breakfast included. AE, DC, MC, V.*

LODGING

$$–$$$ Nordic Village. The light wood and white walls of these deluxe condos near Black Mountain are as Scandinavian as the snowy views. The ❄ Club House has a pool and spa, and there is a nightly bonfire at Nordic Falls. Fireplaces, full kitchens, and whirlpool tubs can be found in the larger units; some economy cottages have woodstoves and kitchenettes. ☎ *Rte. 16, Jackson 03846,* ☎ *603/383–9101 or 800/472–5207,* ☒ *603/383–9823. 140 condominiums. Indoor and outdoor pools, spa, steam room, ice-skating, sleigh rides. MC, V.*

$–$$ Inn at Jackson. This Victorian inn, built in 1902 from a design by Stanford White, has spacious rooms with oversize windows and an open, ❄ airy feel. Other than an imposing grand staircase in the front foyer, the house is unpretentious: The hardwood floors, braided rugs, smattering of antiques, and beautiful mountain views are sure to make you feel at home. The hearty breakfast, with homemade breads, coffeecakes, and an egg casserole or quiche, will fill you up for the entire day. ☎ *Thornhill Rd., 03846,* ☎ *603/383–4321 or 800/289–8600. 12 rooms with bath. Hot tub, cross-country skiing. AE, D, DC, MC, V.*

Lincoln

DINING AND LODGING

$$–$$$$ Mountain Club on Loon. This first-rate, slope-side resort hotel includes an assortment of accommodations, such as suites that sleep as many ❄ as eight; studios with Murphy beds; and 70 units with kitchens. Guest rooms are within walking distance of the lifts, and condominiums are both on-slope and nearby. There's a full range of activities offered to all guests, including live entertainment five nights a week in the lounge. Take Exit 32 from I–93 (Kancamagus Highway). ☎ *Rte. 112, Lincoln 03251,* ☎ *603/745–8111 or 800/433–3413,* ☒ *603/745–2317. 234 rooms with bath. Restaurant, lounge, indoor pool, sauna, fitness center, racquetball, squash. AE, D, MC, V.*

$$–$$$ Mill House Inn. This hotel on the western edge of the Kancamagus Highway offers country-inn style and free transportation to Loon Moun- ❄ tain during ski season. Nonskiers will have plenty to do, too: Shopping, a four-screen cinema, and the North Country Center for the Performing Arts are nearby. ☎ *Box 696, Lincoln 03251,* ☎ *603/745–6261 or 800/654–6183,* ☒ *603/745–6896. 72 rooms with bath, 24 suites. Restaurant, indoor and outdoor pools, sauna, tennis, exercise room, nightclub. AE, D, DC, MC, V.*

North Conway

DINING

$$ Scottish Lion. Although this restaurant-pub serves more than Scotch, it is its specialty—you can choose from 50 varieties. The tartan-carpeted dining rooms serve scones and Devonshire cream for breakfast, game and steak-and-mushroom pies for lunch and dinner. The "rumpldethump" potatoes (mashed potatoes mixed with cabbage and chives then baked au gratin) are deservedly famous in the region, and hot oat-cakes come with your meal. ✕ *Rte. 16,* ☎ *603/356–6381. Reservations advised. AE, D, DC, MC, V.*

DINING AND LODGING

$$–$$$$ **Red Jacket Mountain View Inn.** This motor inn–cum–resort has some of the amenities of a fine hotel: spacious bedrooms, indoor and out-door pools, a game room, and tennis courts. The cozy public rooms have deep chairs and plants, and the grounds are neatly landscaped. The manager, with 30-plus years' experience, runs a tight ship. ⊡ *Rte. 16, Box 2000, 03860,* ☎ *603/356–5411 or 800/752–2538,* ℻ *603/ 356–3842. 152 rooms with bath, 12 condo units. Restaurant, indoor and outdoor pools, saunas, tennis, recreation room, children's program in summer, playground. AE, MC, V.*

$$–$$$ **Hale's White Mountain Hotel and Resort.** The decor and room furnishings ❄ in this recently built resort have a Victorian flair. The hotel stands alone in a meadow, and the guest rooms offer spectacular mountain views. Proximity to the White Mountain National Forest and Echo Lake State Park makes guests feel farther away from civilization (and the nearby outlet malls) than they actually are. And the presence of a serene nine-hole golf course and 17 miles (30 kilometers) of cross-coun-try ski trails help, too. ⊡ *Box 1828, West Side Rd., 03860,* ☎ *and* ℻ *603/356–7100, or 800/533–6301. 80 rooms with bath, 11 suites. Restaurant, tavern, pool, golf, tennis, health club, hiking, cross-coun-try skiing. AE, D, MC, V.*

$$ **Eastern Slope Inn Resort and Conference Center.** Although this has been ❄ an operating inn for more than a century, restoration and refurbish-ing have updated its image and its facilities. The resort near Mt. Cran-more has the ambience of a historic site, and such modern amenities as an enclosed pool. Valley Square, the inn's restaurant, serves tradi-tional American fare in a glassed-in courtyard. There's also nightly en-tertainment. ⊡ *Main St., North Conway 03860,* ☎ *603/356–6321 or 800/258–4708,* ℻ *603/356–8732. 125 rooms with bath. Restaurant, pub, indoor pool, sauna, recreation room. AE, D, MC, V.*

$ **Cranmore Inn.** This authentic country inn, not a converted summer home or farmhouse, is at the foot of Mt. Cranmore. It opened in 1863, and the decor reflects this history with furnishings that date back to the mid-1800s. In summer local high school students serve the meals. ⊡ *Kearsarge St., 03860,* ☎ *603/356–5502 or 800/526–5502,* ℻ *603/356– 6052. 18 rooms with bath. Restaurant, pool. Full breakfast included. AE, MC, V.*

North Lincoln

LODGING

$$–$$$ **Indian Head Resort.** Views across the 180 acres of this resort motel near ❄ Cannon Mountain ski area are of Indian Head Rock, the Great Stone Face, and the Franconia Mountains. ⊡ *Rte. 3, take Exit 33 from I-93, then Rte. 3 north, North Lincoln 03251,* ☎ *603/745–8000 or 800/343– 8000,* ℻ *603/745–8414. 98 rooms with bath. Restaurant, indoor and outdoor pools, lake, sauna, tennis, fishing, ice-skating, recreation room. AE, D, DC, MC, V.*

Pittsburg

LODGING

$$ **The Glen.** This rustic lodge, with stick furniture, fieldstone, and pine, is on the First Connecticut Lake, surrounded by log cabins, seven of which are right on the water. The cabins are best for families and come equipped with efficiency kitchens and minirefrigerators—not that

you'll need either: The rates include meals in the lodge restaurant. ⊡ *Box 77, Rte. 3, 03592, ☎ 603/538-6500 or 800/445–4536. 8 rooms, 10 cabins, all with bath. Restaurant, dock. Rates are AP. No credit cards. Closed mid-Oct.–mid-May.*

Snowville

DINING AND LODGING

$$–$$$ **Snowvillage Inn.** The main gambrel-roof house began as a retreat built in 1916 by journalist Frank Simonds. The current owners, who bought the inn in 1986, appreciated the tome-jammed bookshelves and decided to keep the theme intact, naming the guest rooms after the likes of Faulkner, Hemingway, and Twain. Of course, the nicest of the rooms is a tribute to native son Robert Frost. Each of the two additional buildings—the carriage house and the chimney house—has a library, too. The innkeepers take guests on gourmet-picnic hikes up the mountains. The Austrian chef brings a touch of home to the cuisine here, as evidenced by the walnut beer bread and the Viennese beef tenderloin—mainstays of this five-course prix-fixe menu. Her assistant, however, is French, setting the stage for a little culinary dueling; for instance, dessert might force you to choose between apple strudel and French silk pie. ⊡ *Box 176, Stuart Rd., 03849, ☎ 603/447–4414 or 800/447–4345. 18 rooms with bath. Restaurant (reservations required), sauna, tennis, cross-country skiing. Full breakfast included; MAP available. AE, D, DC, MC, V. Closed Apr.*

Sugar Hill

DINING AND LODGING

$–$$ **Hilltop Inn.** Guests declare staying with innkeepers Mike and Meri Hern is just like staying at Grandma's house. The rooms are done in a quirky mix of antiques: handmade quilts, Victorian ceiling fans, piles of pillows, and big, fluffy towels. The library, upstairs, has books on every subject, and the TV room, downstairs, has hundreds of movies on tape. When the weather is nice, guests take morning coffee on one of the big porches and watch the sunset over cocktails or afternoon tea on the deck out back. Meri's cooking is so locally loved that she's opened a catering service. The inn serves dinner in the fall, but you'll be lucky to get a table. Even the locals fight for the chance to try Meri's specialty: duck glazed with a dazzling array of sauces such as poached pear, raspberry port, and curried apple-and-Vidalia-onion sauce. The inn serves a large country breakfast that includes homemade jams and pancakes made with homegrown berries, cheese soufflés, and locally smoked bacon or salmon. ⊡ *Rte. 117, Main St., 03585, ☎ 603/823–5695 or 800/ 770–5695; ℻ 603/823–5518. 5 rooms with bath, 1 suite. Restaurant (reservations required; open fall foliage season only), bar. Full breakfast included. D, MC, V. MAP available in fall.*

LODGING

$$–$$$ **Sugar Hill Inn.** The old carriage on the lawn and wicker chairs on the wraparound porch contribute to the Colonial charm of this converted 1789 farmhouse. Many rooms have hand-stenciled walls and contain antiques bought from nearby farms, then restored and refinished by the owners. Because the building has begun to tilt and sag over the years, not a single room is square or level, and many have rippled antique windows. Climb out of your four-poster, canopy, or brass bed, and set foot on braided rugs strategically placed to show off the pumpkin pine and northern-maple floorboards, some of which are as wide as 25 inches. Most rooms have a view of Franconia Notch. Afternoon tea includes scones and tea breads. The restaurant serves hearty New England fare that includes lamb and beef dishes, homemade chowders and soups (try the mushroom-dill soup), and delicious desserts. There are 10 rooms in the inn and six in three country cottages (some with fireplaces). ⚏ *Rte. 117, 03580, ☏ 603/823–5621 or 800/548–4748. 16 rooms with bath. Restaurant, pub, cross-country skiing. Full breakfast included; MAP available. MC, V. Closed Apr., Christmas wk.*

Waterville Valley

LODGING

$$$–$$$$ **Golden Eagle Lodge.** Waterville's premier lodging property is reminis-
❄   cent of the grand hotels of an earlier era. This complex, which opened in 1989, has a two-story lobby and a front-desk staff that provides all the services you'd find in a hotel. ⚏ *Snow's Brook Rd., Waterville Valley 03215, ☏ 603/236–4600 or 800/910–4499, ℻ 603/236–4947; 139 condominium suites. Kitchenettes, indoor pool, saunas, recreation room. AE, D, DC, MC, V.*

$$–$$$$ **Black Bear Lodge.** This all-suite hotel has one- and two-bedroom units with full kitchens; heated indoor and outdoor pools, a sauna, a steam room, and bus service to the slopes. Each unit in this family-oriented lodge is individually owned and decorated. Children's movies are shown every night in season. ⚏ *Village Rd. (Box 357), Waterville Valley 03215, ☏ 603/236–4501 or 800/468–2553, ℻ 603/236–4114; 107 suites. Indoor and outdoor pools, saunas, steam room, library. AE, D, DC, MC, V.*

$–$$$ **Snowy Owl Inn.** The fourth-floor bunk-bed lofts at this cozy, intimate
❄   inn are ideal for families; first-floor rooms are suitable for couples who want a quiet getaway. There is a three-story central fieldstone fireplace (one of seven fireplaces), a surrounding atrium supported by single-log posts, and lots of prints and watercolors of snowy owls. Four restaurants are within walking distance. ⚏ *Village Rd. (Box 407), Waterville Valley 03215, ☏ 603/236–8311 or 800/468–2553. 80 rooms with bath. Indoor pool, saunas. CP. AE, D, DC, MC, V.*

The Arts

Mt. Washington Valley Theater Company (Eastern Slope Playhouse, North Conway, ☏ 603/356–5776) has musicals and summer theater from July through September, as well as a local group called the Resort Players, who give pre- and post-season performances. **North Country Center for the Arts** (Mill at Loon Mountain, Lincoln, ☏ 603/745–6032) presents concerts, children's theater, and art exhibitions from July through September. At **Waterville Valley Music Festival** (Waterville Valley, ☏ 603/236–8371 or 800/468–2553), performers of every ilk of music, from folk to country to blues, play on the Concert Pavilion in the Town Square Saturday nights from July through Labor Day.

Nightlife

On Tuesday the tavern in the **New England Inn** (Intervale, ☏ 603/356–5541) hosts a high-quality open-mike session that the locals call "hoot night." **Red Parka Pub** (Glen, ☏ 603/383–4344) is a hangout for barbecue lovers. The crowd swells to capacity on the weekends. **Thunderbird Lounge** (Indian Head Resort, N. Lincoln, ☏ 603/745–8000) has nightly entertainment year-round. The **Shannon Door Pub** (Rte. 16, Jackson) is the place to enjoy a Greek salad, Guinness on draft, and the area's best British musicians. The **Shovel Handle Pub** in Whitneys' Village Inn (Jackson, ☏ 603/383–8916) is the après-ski bar adjacent to Black Mountain's slopes. **Hillwinds** (☏ 603/823–5551), on Main Street in Franconia, offers live entertainment weekends. Skiers love the **Granite Bar** at the **Mountain Club** at the Loon Mountain Resort (☏ 603/745–8111).

You can also dance at the **Loon Saloon** at the ski area. **Dickens** (☎ 603/745–2278), in the Village of Loon, has live musical entertainment. **Horsefeather's** (☎ 603/356–2687), on Main Street in North Conway, is also hopping on the weekends. The **Red Jacket Mountain View Inn** (☎ 603/356–5411) has weekend and holiday entertainment. In Glen, the **Bernerhof Inn** (☎ 603/383–4414) is the setting for an evening of fondue and soft music by the fireside. **Tuckerman's Lounge,** on Wildcat Mountain, is a good place to have a drink while looking over the ski photos and memorabilia on display. Waterville Valley has a number of popular lounges, taverns, and cafés. The **Comman Man** (☎ 603/236-8885), overlooking Corcoran's Pond, is known for a zesty cheese dip. Weekend and holiday entertainment can be found at **Legends 1291** (☎ 603/236–4678), Waterville's only year-round disco.

White Mountains Essentials

Getting Around

BY BUS

Concord Trailways (☎ 800/639–3317) stops in Chocorua, Conway, and Jackson. **Greyhound Lines** (☎ 800/231–2222) serves 37 New Hampshire towns.

BY CAR

Interstate 93 and Route 3 bisect the White Mountain National Forest, running north from Massachusetts to Quebec. To the east, Route 16 brings visitors north from the New Hampshire coast. The Kancamagus Highway (Route 112), the east–west thoroughfare through the White Mountain National Forest, is a scenic drive but is often impassable in winter. Route 302, a longer, more leisurely east–west path, connects Lincoln to North Conway.

BY PLANE

Berlin Airport (Milan, ☎ 603/449–7383) and the **Eastern Slope Regional Airport** (Fryeburg, ☎ 207/935–2800) both take charters and private planes.

Important Addresses and Numbers

EMERGENCIES

Memorial Hospital (Intervale Rd., North Conway, ☎ 603/356–5461).

VISITOR INFORMATION

Hours are generally weekdays 9–5. **Mt. Washington Valley Visitors Bureau** (Box 2300, North Conway 03860, ☎ 603/356–5701 or 800/367–3364). **White Mountain Attractions Association** (Box 10, North Woodstock 03262, ☎ 603/745–8720).

WESTERN AND CENTRAL NEW HAMPSHIRE

Here is the unspoiled heart of New Hampshire. While the beaches to the east attract sun worshipers, and the resort towns to the north keep the skiers and hikers beating a well-worn path up I–93, Western and Central New Hampshire has managed to keep the water slides and the outlet malls at bay. In the center of New Hampshire you'll see the pristine town green 50 times over. Here each village has its own historical society, a tiny museum filled with odd bits of historical memorabilia: a cup from which George Washington took tea, a piano that belonged to the Alcotts. The town of Fitzwilliam remembers Amos J. Parker. He was not a famous man, but a 19th-century lawyer whose belongings and papers survived him. His home has become a museum and a window into his era.

Beyond the museums and picture-perfect greens, this area offers the shining waters of Lake Sunapee and the looming presence of Mt. Monadnock, the second-most-climbed mountain in the world. When you're done climbing and swimming and visiting the past, look for the wares and small studios of area artists. The region has long been an informal artists' colony where people come to write, paint, and weave in solitude.

Exploring

Numbers in the margin correspond to points of interest on the Dartmouth–Lake Sunapee map.

From Concord, the journey to the Dartmouth–Lake Sunapee region can be an efficient 25-mile run on I–89 to the New London exit, or a more leisurely drive along scenic Route 4. Assuming the latter, you'll
1 want to stop in the small town of **Andover,** about 20 miles northwest of Concord, if only to visit the **Andover Historical Society Museum** (Potter Pl., ☎ 603/735–5950; ⊙ Sat. 10–3, Sun. 1–3), housed in a beautiful and ornamental mid-19th-century railway station. Museum exhibits include an original Western Union Telegraph office, a dugout canoe, and—on the tracks outside—an old caboose.

2 Follow Route 11 to Route 114 north and into **New London,** the home of Colby-Sawyer College (1837). The **Norsk Cross Country Ski Center** (Rte. 11, ☎ 603/526–4685) maintains several scenic cross-country ski trails, which are perfect for hiking in the warmer months. Be sure to visit the 10,000-year-old **Cricenti's Bog,** just off Business Route 11. A short trail, maintained by the local conservation commission, shows off the shaggy mosses and fragile ecosystem of this ancient pond.

3 In the distance you can see the sparkle of **Lake Sunapee.** Beyond it, Mt. Sunapee rises to an elevation of nearly 3,000 feet. Together they are the region's outdoor recreation center. **Mt. Sunapee State Park** (Rte. 103, Newbury, ☎ 603/763–2356) offers 130 acres of hiking and picnic areas along with a beach and bath house. You can rent canoes at the beach or take a narrated cruise on either the MV *Mt. Sunapee II* (☎ 603/763–4030) or the MV *Kearsarge* (☎ 603/763–5477). The park also operates a chairlift to the summit and hosts a barbecue picnic at the top. In winter the mountain becomes a downhill ski area and host to national ski competitions. In summer the park holds the League of New Hampshire Craftsmen's Fair, a Fourth of July flea market, the Antique and Classic Boat Parade, and the Gem and Mineral Festival. The **Lake Sunapee Association** (Box 400, Sunapee 03782, ☎ 603/763–2495) has information on local events.

4 Take the Lebanon exit from I–89 north to visit **Hanover** and the Dartmouth College campus. Eleazer Wheelock founded **Dartmouth** in 1769 to educate Native American youth. Daniel Webster graduated in 1801. Robert Frost spent part of a brooding freshman semester on this campus before giving up on college altogether. Today Dartmouth is the northernmost Ivy League school and the cultural center of the region. The buildings that cluster around the green include the Baker Memorial Library, which houses a number of literary treasures, including a collection of 17th-century editions of Shakespeare. If the towering arcade at the entrance to the **Hopkins Center** (☎ 603/646–2422) appears familiar, it's probably because it resembles the project that architect Wallace K. Harrison completed just after designing it: New York City's famed Metropolitan Opera House at Lincoln Center. In addition to the ex-

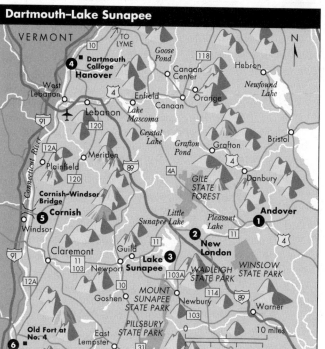

Dartmouth–Lake Sunapee

VERMONT
TO LYME
10
Goose Pond
118
Hebron
④ ■ **Dartmouth College**
Hanover
Canaan Center
Newfound Lake
West Lebanon
4
Enfield
Orange
Canaan
Bristol
91
Lebanon
Lake Mascoma
120
Crystal Lake
Grafton Pond
Grafton
4
12A
Meriden
89
Danbury
Plainfield
120
4A
GILE STATE FOREST
Cornish-Windsor Bridge
⑤ **Cornish**
Little Sunapee Lake
Pleasant Lake
Andover ①
Windsor
② **New London**
11
4
Claremont
Guild
11
② **New London**
WINSLOW STATE PARK
91
11 103
Newport
Lake Sunapee ③
103A
WADLEIGH STATE PARK
12A
10
Goshen
MOUNT SUNAPEE STATE PARK
Newbury
114
89
Warner
103
Old Fort at No. 4 ■
East Lempster
PILLSBURY STATE PARK
0   10 miles
⑥ ■ **Charlestown**
31
0   15 km
N

hibits on African, Asian, European, and American art, the **Hood Museum of Art** owns Picasso's Vollard etchings, Paul Revere's silver, and paintings by Winslow Homer. Rivaling the collection's force is the museum's architecture: a series of a austere redbrick buildings with copper roofs arranged around a small courtyard. Free guided tours are given on some weekend afternoons. *Wheelock St.,* ☎ *603/646–2808.* ☛ *Free.* ☺ *Tues.–Sat. 10–5 (Wed. until 9), Sun. noon–5.*

⑤ About 15 miles south on Route 12A you'll find the village of **Cornish,** best known today for its four covered bridges, one of which is the longest in the United States: The **Cornish-Windsor Bridge** was built in 1866 and rebuttressed in 1988–89. It spans the Connecticut River, connecting New Hampshire with Vermont. At the turn of the century Cornish was known primarily as the home of Winston Churchill, then the country's most popular novelist. His novel *Richard Carvell* sold more than a million copies. Churchill was such a celebrity that he hosted Teddy Roosevelt during the president's 1902 visit. At that time the town was an enclave of artistic talent. Painter Maxfield Parrish lived and worked here, and sculptor Augustus Saint-Gaudens (1848–1907) set up his studio and created the heroic bronzes for which he is known. Today the site of the **Saint-Gaudens National Historic Site,** Saint-Gaudens's house, studio, gallery, and 150 acres of gardens can now be toured. Scattered throughout are full-size replicas of the sculptor's work, as well as sketches and casting molds. Sunday afternoon at 2, you can sit on the lawn and enjoy chamber music. *Off Rte. 12A, Cornish,* ☎ *603/675–2175.* ☛ *$2 adults 17–62, free to all others.* ☺ *Memorial Day weekend–Oct., daily 8:30–4:30; grounds open until dusk.*

Follow Route 12A south until it merges with Routes 12/11, about 20 ⑥ miles, to find **Charlestown,** which boasts the state's largest historic district. Sixty-three homes of Federal, Greek Revival, and Gothic Revival architecture are clustered about the center of town; 10 of them pre-date 1800. Several merchants on Main Street distribute brochures that outline an interesting walking tour of the district. Just 1½ miles north of town, you'll find the **Fort at No. 4,** which in 1747 was an outpost on the lonely periphery of Colonial civilization. That year it withstood a massive attack of 400 French soldiers, which changed the course of New England history. Today it is the only living history museum from the era of the French and Indian War. Costumed interpreters cook dinner over an open hearth and demonstrate weaving, gardening, and candlemaking. In one building a blacksmith forges tools as he talks about the past. Each year the museum holds full reenactments of militia musters and battles from the French and Indian War–era. *Rte. 11W, Springfield Rd., Charlestown,* ☎ *603/826–5700.* ☛ *$6 adults, $4 children.* ☉ *Late May–mid-Oct., Wed.–Mon. 10–4.*

On a bright, breezy day you may want to detour to the **Morningside Flight Park** (Rte. 12/11, Charlestown, ☎ 603/542–4416), not necessarily to take hang-gliding lessons, although you could. Safer to watch the bright colors of the gliders as they swoop over the school's 450-foot peak.

Numbers in the margin correspond to points of interest on the Monadnock Region and Central New Hampshire map.

❼ Continue south along the Connecticut River on Route 12 to **Walpole** and yet another perfect town green. This one is surrounded by homes built about 1790, when the town constructed a canal around the Great Falls of the Connecticut River and brought commerce and wealth to the area. The town now boasts 3,200 inhabitants, more than a dozen of whom are millionaires. James Michener visited and wrote here, as did Louisa May Alcott, author of *Little Women.* The **Old Academy Museum** (Main St., ☎ 603/756–3449; ☉ Sun. 2–4) contains the original piano mentioned in that novel; it had been a gift to the Alcott sisters.

❽ Route 12 continues on to **Keene,** the largest city in the southwest corner, and the proud owner of the widest main street in America. On that tree-lined avenue is Keene State College, hub of the local arts community. Its **Arts Center on Brickyard Pond** (☎ 603/358–2168) has three theaters and eight art studios. The Thorne-Sagendorph Art Gallery houses George Ridci's *Landscape,* alongside traveling exhibits from museums around the country. Indoor and outdoor concerts are given here by nationally known rock and folk stars as well as local musicians and chamber groups. The **Putnam Art Lecture Hall** (☎ 603/358–2160) has a continuing art and international film series.

TIME OUT   Timoleans (25–27 Main St.) is a classic diner. You won't get a seat any time during the rush between noon and 1, but it's perfect for early and late lunches or the best pie in town.

From Keene, Route 101 leads east to Marlborough. At the junction of Route 124 you'll find the best used bookstore in the region, the **Homestead Bookshop** (☎ 603/876–4213), which carries an extraordinary collection of town histories, biographies, and cookbooks.

❾ Turn north off Route 101 for **Harrisville.** Founded in 1774 by Abel Twitchell, it's now a perfectly preserved mill town (Historic Harrisville, Inc., Church Hill, Harrisville 03450, ☎ 603/827–3722)—the Harris Mill, an old woolen mill, still stands in the heart of town. The combination of redbrick and blue sky reflecting off Harrisville Pond is worth at least one picture. **Harrisville Designs** (☎ 603/827–3996) operates out of a historic building and sells hand-spun and hand-dyed

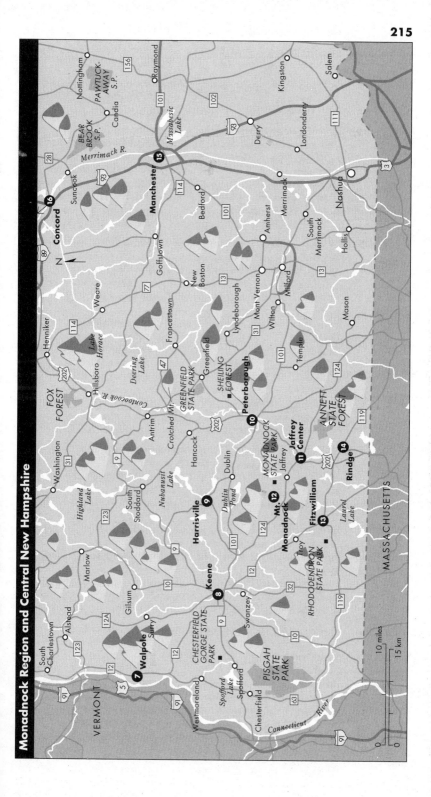

yarn sheared from local sheep, as well as looms for the serious weaver. The shop also teaches classes in knitting and weaving.

Beyond Harrisville is the town of Dublin, the highest town in the state, at an elevation of 1,493 feet. It is also the longtime home of *Yankee* magazine and the *Old Farmer's Almanac.*

⑩ Farther east, in **Peterborough,** you'll find the nation's first free public library, which opened here in 1833. The **MacDowell Colony** (100 High St., ☎ 603/924–3886 or 212/966–4860) was founded by the composer Edward MacDowell in 1907 as an artists' retreat. Willa Cather wrote part of *Death Comes for the Archbishop* here. Thornton Wilder was in residence when he wrote *Our Town*; Peterborough's resemblance to fictitious Grover's Corners is no coincidence. Artists reside here in solitude, so only a small portion of the colony is open to visitors.

TIME OUT   At **Twelve Pine** (1 Summer St., Peterborough, ☎ 603/924–6140), you can stock your picnic basket with chicken burritos—famous throughout the region—or one of the special pasta salads. They even sell leftovers out of the fridge for a reduced price. Don't expect to linger: There are no tables in this tiny place, just room enough for the line to form.

From Peterborough, drive south on Route 202 to Jaffrey and turn right ⑪ onto Route 124 into the historic village of **Jaffrey Center.** Novelist Willa Cather came to town in 1919 and stayed in the Shattuck Inn, which now stands empty on Old Meeting House Road. She pitched a tent not far from here in which she wrote several chapters of her signature work, *My Antonia.* She returned to Jaffrey nearly every summer thereafter until her death, and now she is buried here in the Old Burying Ground according to her last wishes. Nearby, the **Amos Fortune Forum** brings nationally known speakers to the 1773 meeting house on summer evenings.

⑫ The oft-quoted statistic about **Mt. Monadnock** is that it's the most climbed mountain in America—second in the world to Japan's Mt. Fuji. Whether this is true or not, locals agree that it's never lonely at the top. Some days more than 400 people crowd its bald peak. Monadnock rises to 3,165 feet, and on a clear day the hazy Boston skyline is visible from its summit. Five trailheads branch into more than two dozen trails of varying difficulty that wend their way to the top. Some are considerably shorter than others, but you should allow between three and four hours for any round-trip hike. A visitor center contains a small museum documenting the mountain's history with photos and memorabilia. **Monadnock State Park** (4 mi north of Jaffrey, off Rte. 124, ☎ 603/532–8862) maintains picnic grounds and some tent campsites and sells a trail map for $2.

A well-preserved historic district of Colonial and Federal houses has ⑬ made the town of **Fitzwilliam,** on Route 119, the subject of thousands of picture postcards—particularly views of its landscape in winter, when a fine white snow settles on the oval common. Town business is still conducted in the 1817 meeting house. The Historical Society maintains a museum and country store in the **Amos J. Blake House** (☾ Late May–mid-Oct., Sat. 10–4, Sun. 1–4). Blake's law office looks much as it did when he used it. The rest of the museum displays period antiques and artifacts.

Two and a half miles northwest of the common is the **Rhododendron State Park** (off Rte. 12), where more than 16 acres of wild rhododendrons burst into bloom in mid-July. This is the largest concentration of *Rhododendron maximum* north of the Alleghenies. Bring a picnic lunch and sit in a nearby pine grove or just follow the marked foot-paths through the flowers.

⑭ In the village of **Rindge,** 8 miles east of Fitzwilliam on Route 119, you can spend a quiet moment at the **Cathedral of the Pines,** an outdoor church and a memorial to the American women, both civilian and military, who sacrificed their lives in service to their country. The church offers an inspiring view of Mt. Monadnock and Mt. Kearsarge from its Altar of the Nation, which was composed of rock from every U.S. state and territory. All faiths hold services here, with organ meditations at midday, Monday through Thursday. The Memorial Bell Tower, with its carillon of international bells, is built of native stone; Norman Rockwell designed the bronze tablets over the four arches. Flower gardens, an indoor chapel, and a museum of military memorabilia share the hilltop. *Off Rte. 119, Rindge,* ☎ *603/899–3300.* ☉ *May–Oct., dawn–sunset.*

Route 202 leads back to Peterborough, where you can continue east on Route 101. You'll pass Temple Mountain, a wintertime cross-country and downhill ski area that's perfect for beginners, and **Miller State Park,** with an auto road that takes you almost 2,300 feet up Mt. Pack Monadnock. Farther east on Route 101 (past Milford), Amherst is known for both its town green and the dawn-to-dusk flea market held Sunday on the western outskirts of town. It operates April through October and attracts dealers and decorators from all over New England.

⑮ Farther along Route 101 is **Manchester,** New Hampshire's largest city, with just over 100,000 residents. The town grew around the power of the Amoskeag Falls on the Merrimack River, which fueled several small textile mills through the 1700s. By 1828, a group of investors from Boston had bought the rights to the river's water power and built on its eastern bank the **Amoskeag Textile Mills.** At its peak in 1906, the mills employed 17,000 people and churned out more than 4 million yards of cloth per week. They formed the entire economic base of Manchester, and when they closed in 1936, the town was devastated. As part of an economic recovery plan, the mill buildings have been converted into warehouses, classrooms, restaurants, and office space. You can wander among these huge blood-red buildings; contact the **Manchester Historic Association** (129 Amherst St., ☎ 603/622–7531) for a map.

The **Currier Gallery of Art,** in the Beaux Arts building downtown, has a permanent collection of paintings, sculpture, and decorative arts from the 13th through the 20th centuries. Don't miss the Zimmerman House, designed by Frank Lloyd Wright in 1950. A response to the Depression, Wright called this sparse, utterly functional living space "Usonian." It's one of only five Wright houses in the northeast and New England's only Wright-designed residence open to the public. *192 Orange St., Manchester 03104,* ☎ *603/669–6144.* ☛ *Gallery: $4 adults, $3 senior citizens; free Fri. 1–9. Zimmerman House: $6 adults, $4 senior citizens; reservations required.* ☉ *Mon., Wed., Thurs., Sat., Sun. 11–5; Fri. 11–9. Closed May 1995–Mar. 1996.*

⑯ Thirty miles north of Manchester is New Hampshire's capital, **Concord.** This quiet, conservative town (population 38,000) tends to the state's business but little else. The residents joke that the sidewalks roll up promptly at 6. Aside from shopping in the boutiques on Main Street, you may want to follow the **Coach and Eagle** walking trail through Concord's historic district. The tour includes the Greek Revival home that was the residence of Franklin Pierce (14 Penacook St., no ☎ ; ☉ Mid-June–Labor Day, weekdays 11–3; ☛ $2) until he moved to Washington to become our nation's 14th president. You can also walk through the gilt-dome **State**

House (107 N. Main St., 603/271–1110; ⊗ Weekdays 8–4:30), the oldest state house in which a legislature still meets. Get trail maps from the Chamber of Commerce (244 N. Main St.) or from stores along the marked trail. Visit the **New Hampshire Historical Society Museum** (30 Park St., ☏ 603/225–3381) to see an original Concord Coach. During the 19th century, when more than 3,000 of them were built in Concord, this was about as technologically perfect a vehicle as you could find—many say it's the coach that won the West.

The **Christa McAuliffe Planetarium,** one of the world's most advanced, was named for the teacher who was killed in the Challenger space-shuttle explosion in 1986. Shows on the solar system, constellations, and space exploration combine state-of-the-art computer graphics and sound equipment with views through the 40-foot dome telescope. Children especially love seeing the tornado tubes, magnetic marbles, and other hands-on exhibits. *3 Institute Dr., New Hampshire Technical Institute,* ☏ *603/271–7827.* ☛ *Exhibit free. Show admission: $6 adults, $3 senior citizens and children 3–17. Reservations advised for shows.* ⊗ *Tues.–Thurs. 9–4, Fri. 9–7, Sat. noon–5, Sun. noon–4. Call for show times.*

What to See and Do with Children

Christa McAuliffe Planetarium, Concord
Maple sugarhouses (*see* Off the Beaten Path, *below*)
Old Fort at No. 4, Charlestown

Off the Beaten Path

If you take I-89 from Concord to the Lake Sunapee region, a short detour is in order to **Rollins State Park** (off Rte. 103, Warner). Here a scenic auto road snakes nearly 3,000 feet up the southern slope of Mt. Kearsarge, where you can then tackle on foot the ½-mile trail to the summit. Along the way is the **Mount Kearsage Indian Museum,** a moving monument to Native American culture. You'll find incomparable artistry, including moose-hair embroidery, a tepee, quillwork, and basketry, and you'll learn of the bond between the region's Native American population and nature. Self-guided walks lead through gardens of vegetables and through "medicine woods" of herbs and healing plants. *Kearsage Mountain Rd., Warner,* ☏ *603/456–2600.* ☛ *$5 adults, $3 children 6–12.* ⊗ *May–mid-Dec., Mon.–Sat. 10–5, Sun. 1–5.*

Sugaring-Off

Around here, maple-sugar season is the first harbinger of spring, occurring about the first week in March. The days now are a bit warmer but the nights are still frigid; this is when a drive along maple-lined backroads reveals thousands of taps and buckets catching the fresh but labored flow of unrefined sap. Plumes of smoke rise from nearby sugarhouses—the residue of furiously boiling down this precious liquid. Many sugarhouses open to the public; after a short tour and demonstration, you can sample the syrup with traditional unsweetened doughnuts and maybe a pickle—or taste hot syrup over fresh snow, a favorite confection. Open to the public are **Bacon's Sugar House** (Dublin Rd., Jaffrey Center, ☏ 603/532–8836); **Bascom's** (Mt. Kingsbury, Rte. 123A, Alstead, ☏ 603/835–2230), which serves maple pecan pie and maple milkshakes; **Clark's Sugar House** (off Rte. 123A, Alstead, ☏ 603/835–6863); **Old Brick Sugar House** (Summit Rd., Keene, ☏ 603/352–6812); **Parker's Maple Barn** (Brookline Rd., Mason, ☏ 603/878–2308), where a restaurant serves a whole grain–pancake breakfast any time of day along with less maply items; and **Stuart & John's**

Sugar House & Pancake Restaurant (Rtes. 12 and 63, Westmoreland, ☎ 603/399–4486), which offers a tour and pancake breakfast. Always call ahead for hours and to see that the sap is running.

Shopping

You can lose yourself in the huge malls of Manchester and Concord or in the strip malls along Nashua's Route 3, but there's more colorful shopping in the downtown retail areas of Concord, Keene, Peterborough, and Hanover. Better yet, wander into one of the dozens of galleries and open studios marked along the roads by blue New Hampshire state signs. Summertime fairs, such as the **League of New Hampshire Craftsmen**'s, at Mt. Sunapee State Park, and **Hospital Day**, in New London, showcase some of the area's best juried arts and crafts.

Specialty Stores

ANTIQUES

People sometimes joke that New Hampshire's two cash crops are fudge and antiques. Particularly in the Monadnock region, dealers abound in barns and home stores that are strung along back roads and "open by chance or by appointment"; don't ignore the flea markets and yard sales rampant during the short summer—deals are just waiting to happen. Best antiquing concentrations are along Route 119, from Fitzwilliam to Hinsdale; Route 101, from Marlborough to Wilton; and the towns of Hopkinton, Hollis, and Amherst. A few good shops include **The Antique Shops** (Rte. 12, Westmoreland, ☎ 603/399–7039), where 40 dealers sell a little bit of everything. **Bell Hill Antiques** (Rte. 101 at Bell Hill Rd., Bedford, ☎ 603/472–5580) sells country furniture, glass, and china. **Fitzwilliam Antique Center** (Rtes. 12 and 119, Fitzwilliam, ☎ 603/585–9092) always has refinished cupboards in stock. The **New Hampshire Antiquarian Society** (Main St., Hopkinton, ☎ 603/746–3825) holds silent auctions. **Peterborough Antiques** (76 Grove St., Peterborough, ☎ 603/924–7297) sells English and Continental paintings, jewelry, and accessories.

CRAFTS

Artisan's Workshop (Edgewood Inn, Main St., New London, ☎ 603/526–4227) carries jewelry, hand-blown glass, and other local handcrafts. **Dorr Mill Store** (Rte. 11/103, Guild, ☎ 603/863–1197), the yarn and fabric center of the Sunapee area, draws droves of rug hookers, knitters, and quilters to browse the huge collection of fiber. The **Fiber Studio** (9 Foster Hill Rd., Henniker, ☎ 603/428–7830) sells beads, handspun natural-fiber yarns, spinning equipment, and looms. The **League of New Hampshire Craftsmen** (36 N. Main St., Concord, ☎ 603/228–8171) offers a vast array of juried crafts in many media. The owners of the **Mouse Menagerie of Fine Crafts** (W. Lebanon, ☎ 603/298–7090) have created a collector's series of toy mice in every profession and sport, but they also sell furniture, wind chimes, and hundreds of other gifts.

GALLERIES

North Gallery at Tewksbury's (Rte. 101 E, Peterborough, ☎ 603/924–3224) has a wide selection of thrown pots, sconces and candlestick holders, and woodworkings. **Partridge Replications** (83 Grove St., Peterborough, ☎ 603/924–3002; 53 S. Main, Hanover, ☎ 603/643–1660) specializes in reproductions of Colonial furniture and decorative accessories, including sconces, chandeliers, ironware, mirrors, and trivets. **Sharon Arts Center** (Rte. 123, Sharon, ☎ 603/924–7256) is not just a gallery of local pottery, fabric, and woodwork, but a learning center with classes on everything from photography to paper marbling.

JEWELRY

Goldsmith Paul Gross, of **Designer Gold** (3 Lebanon St., Hanover, ☎ 603/643–3864), designs settings for color gemstones and opals—all one-of-a-kind or limited-edition. He also carries some silver jewelry by other American artisans. **Mark Knipe Goldsmiths** (2 Capitol Plaza, Main St., Concord, ☎ 603/224–2920) will turn your antique stones into rings, earrings, and pendants.

SPORTING AND OUTDOORS EQUIPMENT

The corporate headquarters and retail outlet of **Eastern Mountain Sports** (Vose Farm Rd., Peterborough, ☎ 603/924–7231) not only sells everything from tents to skis to hiking boots, but also offers hiking and camping classes and gives kayaking and canoeing demonstrations.

Malls

Colony Mill Marketplace (222 West St., Keene, ☎ 603/357–1240) was an old mill building but has been converted into a shopping center of specialty stores and boutiques, including **Autumn Woods** (☎ 603/352–5023), which sells fine Shaker-style furniture and Colonial reproductions in birch, maple, and pine; **Country Artisans** (☎ 603/352–6980), which showcases the stoneware, textiles, prints, and glassware of regional artists; the **Toadstool Bookshop** (☎ 603/352–8815), which has a huge selection of children's books, and also carries good reading material on regional travel and history; and **Ye Goodie Shoppe** (☎ 603/352–0326), dating from 1931 and specializing in handmade chocolates and confections.

The **Powerhouse** (Rte. 12A, 1 mi north of Exit 20 off I–89, W. Lebanon, ☎ 603/298–5236), a onetime power station, comprises these three adjacent buildings of specialty stores, boutiques, and restaurants decorated with freestanding sculpture and picture-window views of the Mascoma River.

Steeplegate Mall (270 Loudon Rd., Concord, ☎ 603/224–1523), has more than 70 stores, including chain department stores and some smaller crafts shops.

The enormous **Mall of New Hampshire** (S. Willow St., Exit 1, ☎ 603/669–0433) has every conceivable store and is anchored by Sears, Filene's, and Lechmere.

Skiing

King Ridge

41 King Ridge Rd., New London 03257
☎ *603/526–6966; snow conditions, 800/343–1312*

They call it a summit village, which accurately—if a bit dramatically—describes the base facilities at King Ridge. The lodge and all attendant services are located at the top of the ski area, with the trails spinning off to points below. Skiers and family groups who come here make the adjustment quickly and appreciate the efficient and agreeable skiing.

DOWNHILL

Upside down it may be, but King Ridge's 850 vertical feet has the right kind of challenge for novices and intermediate skiers. Most of the terrain is for beginners, but several long intermediate runs are rewarding, and three advanced trails are fun, too. Two triple and one double chairlift and four surface lifts transport skiers. Lift-ticket prices are low.

OTHER ACTIVITIES
The nearby Racquet Club offers tennis, racquetball, volleyball, and an indoor golf simulator. The Hatter House restaurant and lounge is open daily. The family center has après-ski activities for kids only, with puppet shows, storytelling, and sing-alongs; the business center has office conveniences such as fax machines, computer access, and cellular-phone rentals.

CHILD CARE
The Children's Center takes children four months through six years old and offers "Playtime on Skis" lessons to ages four–six. All-day and half-day SKIwee lessons are available through the ski school for children 5–12.

Mt. Sunapee
Mt. Sunapee State Park, Rte. 103, Mt. Sunapee 03772
☎ *603/763–2356; snow conditions 603/763–4020; lodging, 603/763–2495 or 800/258–3530*

Without glitz or glamour, state-run Sunapee remains popular among locals and skiers from Boston, Hartford, and the coast for its low-key atmosphere and easy skiing. Two base lodges supply the essentials.

DOWNHILL
This mountain of 1,510 vertical feet, the highest in southern New Hampshire, has 19 miles of gentle-to-moderate terrain with a couple of pitches that could be called steep. A nice beginner's section is located beyond the base facilities, well away and well protected from other trails. Three triple and three double chairlifts and one surface lift transport skiers.

CHILD CARE
The Duckling Nursery takes children from 12 months through five years of age. Little Indians ski instruction gives ages three and four a taste of skiing, while SKIwee lessons are available for ages 5–12.

Pats Peak
Rte. 114, Henniker 03242
☎ *603/428–3245; snow conditions, 800/742–7287*

Near Boston and the coastal metropolitan region, Pats Peak is a feasible drive for families and is geared for such a clientele. Base facilities are rustic, and friendly personal attention is the rule.

DOWNHILL
Despite its size of only 710 vertical feet, with 19 trails and slopes, Pats Peak has something for everyone: New skiers are well served with a wide slope, chairlift, and several short trails; intermediates have wider trails from the top; and advanced skiers have a couple of real thrillers to choose from. One triple and two double chairlifts, two T-bars, and two surface lifts serve the runs.

CHILD CARE
The nursery takes children ages six months through five years. Special nursery ski programs for children ages 4–12 are offered on weekends and during vacations. All-day lessons for self-sufficient skiers ages 4–12 are scheduled throughout the season.

Other Sports

Biking
Eastern Mountain Sports (*see* Shopping, *above*) and the **Greater Keene Chamber of Commerce** (8 Central Sq., Keene 03431, ☎ 603/352–1303) have maps and information on local bike routes. For information on

organized bike rides in southern New Hampshire contact the **Granite State Wheelmen** (16 Clinton St., Salem, no ☎). **Monadnock Bicycle Touring** (Box 19, Keene Rd., Harrisville 03450, ☎ 603/827–3925) has inn-hopping tours of the region.

Camping

The following grounds are open mid-May–mid-October, unless noted otherwise. **Crow's Nest Campground** (Rte. 10, Newport 03773, ☎ 603/863–6170; ☉ Year-round), **Greenfield State Park** (Forest Rd., off Rte. 136, Greenfield 03047, ☎ 603/547–3497), **Monadnock State Park** (Rte. 124, Jaffrey 03452, ☎ 603/532–8862; ☉ Year-round), **Northstar Campground** (278 Coonbrook Rd., Newport 03773, ☎ 603/863–4001), **Otter Lake Camping Area** (Otterville Rd., New London 03257, ☎ 603/763–5600), **Rand's Pond Campground** (Brook Rd., Goshen 03752, ☎ 603/863–3350; ☉ Year-round), and **Surry Mt. Dam** (271 Rte. 12A, Surry 03431, ☎ 603/352–9770).

Canoeing

The Connecticut River is generally considered safe after June 15, but canoeists should always use caution. This river is not for beginners.

Hannah's Paddles, Inc. (15 Hannah Dustin Rd., Concord 03301, ☎ 603/753–6695; ☉ Daily June–Oct., weekends spring and fall) rents canoes for use on the Merrimack river. **Northstar Canoe Livery** (Rte. 12A, Balloch's Crossing, Cornish, ☎ 603/542–5802) rents canoes for half- or full-day trips on the Connecticut River. **Ledyard Canoe Club of Dartmouth** (Hanover 03755, ☎ 603/643–6709), on the Connecticut River, provides canoe and kayak rentals and classes.

Fishing

Lake Sunapee has brook and lake trout, salmon, smallmouth bass, and pickerel. Nearby **Pleasant Lake,** in Elkins, has salmon, brook trout, and bass. In **Lake Mascoma** you can fish for rainbow trout, pickerel, and horned pout.

In the Monadnock region there are more than 200 lakes and ponds, most of which offer good fishing. **Dublin Pond** (Dublin), **Gilmore Pond** (Jaffrey), **Nubanusit Lake** (Nelson), and **Granite Lake** (Stoddard) have several types of trout. You'll find rainbow trout, smallmouth and largemouth bass, and some northern pike in **Spoffard Lake** (Chesterfield). **Goose Pond** (West Canaan) has smallmouth bass and white perch. You can find rainbow and golden trout, pickerel, and horned pout in **Laurel Lake** (Fitzwilliam); and there are rainbow and brown trout in the **Ashuelot River.** For word on what's biting where, contact the **Department of Fish and Game** in Keene (☎ 603/352–9669).

Hiking

The region is rife with opportunity. Try the mile-long trail to the summit of **Mt. Kearsage** in Winslow State Park. Three trails wend to the summit of **Mt. Sunapee. Pillsbury State Park,** a pristine wilderness area in Washington, has a number of trails and rugged camping areas. You'll find a good beginner route, the Westridge Trail, on **Mt. Cardigan** (Orange), from which you can see Mt. Washington on a clear day. **Drummer Hill Preserve** (Keene), **Fox State Forest** (Hillsboro), **Horatio Colony Trust** (Keene), **Sheiling Forest** (Peterborough), and **Wapack Reservation** (Greenfield) all have trails. The **Harris Center for Conservation Education** (Hancock, ☎ 603/525–3394) sponsors guided walks.

State Parks

Mt. Sunapee State Park in Newbury has a tram up the mountain and is the site of a summer-long series of special events including the annual August Craftsmen's Fair. **Bear Den Geological Park** (Gilsum) is a 19th-century mining town surrounded by more than 50 abandoned mines; in **Curtiss Dogwood State Reservation** (Lyndeborough, off Rte. 31), namesake blossoms are out in early May; bring hiking boots, a mountain bike, a fishing pole, or skis to enjoy the 13,000 acres of **Pisgah State Park** (off Rte. 63 or Rte. 119), the largest wilderness area in the state.

Dining and Lodging

Chain hotels and motels dominate the lodging scene in Manchester and Concord and along major highways. But in the Monadnock region, dozens of colorful inns are tucked away in small towns and on back roads. There's a **lodging reservation service** in the Sunapee region (☎ 603/763–2495 or 800/258–3530).

Andover

LODGING

$ **English House Bed & Breakfast.** Afternoon tea is a must at this Edwardian inn. The British owners have furnished the large, sunny bedrooms with English and American antiques and watercolors by innkeeper Gillian Smith's mother and uncle, both well known in Britain. Smith offers occasional classes in jewelry making. The full English breakfast includes homemade yogurt. ⌂ *Main St., 03216,* ☎ *603/735–5987. 7 rooms with bath. Cross-country skiing. Full breakfast and afternoon tea included. MC, V.*

Bedford

DINING AND LODGING

$$$–$$$$ **Bedford Village Inn.** This luxurious Federal-style inn, just minutes from Manchester, was once a working farm and still shows horse-nuzzle marks on its old beams; gone, however, are the hayloft and the old milking room, which have been converted into lavish suites, complete with king-size beds, imported marble in the whirlpool baths, and three telephones. The other 12 rooms are equally sumptuous. The tavern has seven intimate dining rooms, each with the original wide pine floors and huge fireplaces. The menu, which often features such New England favorites as lobster and a cedar-planked Atlantic salmon with a chardonnay beurre blanc, changes every two weeks. ⌂ *2 Old Bedford Rd., 03110,* ☎ *603/472–2602 or 800/852–1166. 12 suites and 2 apartments. Restaurant (reservations advised), meeting rooms. AE, DC, MC, V.*

Bradford

DINING AND LODGING

$ **Bradford Inn.** This delightfully old-fashioned country inn in the village
❄ of Bradford has two common rooms and a popular restaurant, J. Albert's, which serves regional Eastern European fare. Rooms have details circa 1898, and there are family suites. Senior-citizen discounts and facilities for people with disabilities are available. ⌂ *11 W. Main St., Bradford 03221,* ☎ *603/938–5309 or 800/669–5309. 12 rooms with bath. Restaurant, lake. Full breakfast included. AE, D, DC, MC, V.*

Concord

DINING

$$–$$$ **Vercelli's.** If you can resist the homemade bread and olive butter (good luck), you might have room for one of the generous Italian entrées on this extensive menu. The many veal specialties are stellar, and the

seafood is exceptional, too. ✕ *11 Depot St.,* ☎ *603/228–3313. Reservations advised. MC, V.*

$$ Hermanos Cocina Mexicana. On the weekends the line to get in forms at 5 sharp; if you're not in it, don't bother. This restaurant's popularity has spawned a gift shop next door. The food is standard Mexican, raised to a higher level by fresh ingredients and the cook's ability to resist gloppy sauces. ✕ *6 Pleasant St. Ext.,* ☎ *603/224–5669. No reservations. MC, V.*

Cornish

LODGING

$$ Chase House Bed & Breakfast. This is the birthplace of Salmon P. Chase, who was Abraham Lincoln's secretary of the treasury, a chief justice of the United States, and a founder of the Republican Party. A few years ago it was restored to 19th-century elegance with Colonial furnishings and Waverly fabrics throughout. Ask for a room with a canopy bed or one with a view of the Connecticut River. The innkeepers will give you the history of the house and can point out all of the area's historical landmarks. Breakfast often includes pancakes made from an Amish friendship bread starter. ▥ *Rte. 12A (1.4 mi south of the Cornish-Windsor covered bridge), R.R. 2, Box 909, 03745,* ☎ *603/675–5391 or 800/401–9455,* 🖷 *603/675–5010. 7 rooms with bath. Boating. Full breakfast included. MC, V.*

Fitzwilliam

DINING AND LODGING

$ Fitzwilliam Inn. Vermont Transit buses from Boston's Logan Airport stop at the door, just as the stagecoach once did. Indoors, too, much remains as it was in 1796. Upstairs in the rooms the furniture is a hodgepodge of early and late hand-me-downs. The imperfections suggest that this is how inns really were in bygone times. Locals dally in the tavern, and the restaurant serves standard Yankee cooking spiced up with such innovations as pork medallions with a mustard cream sauce and jalapeño chutney chicken. In winter ask about the Sunday concert series and low mid-week room rates. ▥ *The Green, 03447,* ☎ *603/585–9000,* 🖷 *603/585–3495. 28 rooms, 15 with bath. Restaurant (reservations advised), bar, pool, cross-country skiing. AE, D, MC, V.*

LODGING

$ Amos Parker House. The garden of this old Colonial B&B is the most spectacular in town, complete with lily ponds, Oriental stone benches, and Dutch waterstones. Two rooms offer garden views, although any guest is welcome to sit on the deck and listen to the birds. Avid gardeners will want to visit, even if staying elsewhere. ▥ *Rte. 119, Box 202, 03447,* ☎ *603/585–6540. 4 rooms with bath. Full breakfast included. No credit cards.*

$ Hannah Davis House. This 1820 Federal house has, despite a full refurbishment and conversion into a B&B, lost none of its original elegance. The view of a nearby bog is marred only by the natural flaws in the antique windows. The original beehive oven still sits in the kitchen, and one suite has two Count Rumford fireplaces. The inn is just two buildings off the village green, and your host has the scoop on area antiquing. There's cable TV and a VCR in the common area. ▥ *186 Depot Rd., 03447,* ☎ *603/585–3344. 5 rooms with bath. Full breakfast included. MC, V.*

Francestown

DINING AND LODGING

$$–$$$ **Inn at Crotched Mountain.** This 1822 Colonial inn has nine fireplaces, four of which are in private rooms. The other five spread cheer among several common areas, which makes this a particularly romantic place to stay when the snow is falling on Crotched Mountain. Rooms are furnished with early Colonial reproductions. The chef splits the menu between such Eastern specialties as Indonesian charbroiled swordfish with a sauce of ginger, green pepper, onion, and lemon and more regional dishes such as cranberry-port pot roast. ▥ *Mountain Rd., 03043,* ☎ *603/588–6840. 13 rooms, 8 with bath. Restaurant (reservations accepted), bar, pool, tennis, cross-country skiing. Full breakfast included; MAP required weekends. No credit cards.*

Hancock

DINING AND LODGING

$$–$$$ **John Hancock Inn.** This Federal inn dates from 1789 and is the pride of the historically preserved town for which it's named. Common areas possess the warmth of a tavern, with fireplaces, big wing chairs, couches, dark-wood paneling, and murals. Rooms are done in the traditional Colonial style with high four-poster antique beds. One room features a pastoral mural painted by Rufus Porter in 1810; the work paid for a night's stay. The dining room serves unspectacular Yankee fare by candlelight; the rubbed natural woodwork gives an intimate feel. ▥ *Main St., 03447,* ☎ *603/525–3318 or 800/525–1789,* ℻ *603/525–9301. 11 rooms with bath. Restaurant, lounge. AE, D, MC, V.*

Hanover

DINING AND LODGING

$$$–$$$$ **Hanover Inn.** Owned and operated by Dartmouth College, this Georgian brick house rises four white-trimmed stories and is the oldest continuously operating business in New Hampshire. The building was converted to a tavern in 1780 and has been open ever since. A recent renovation created 16 rooms—done in Colonial reproductions, pastels, and Audubon prints—with large sitting areas. The highly acclaimed and very formal Daniel Webster Room serves such regional American dishes as soy-seared tuna steak with shrimp dumplings. The contemporary Ivy Grill offers a lighter menu. ▥ *The Green, Box 151, 03755,* ☎ *603/643–4300 or 800/443–7024,* ℻ *603/646–3744. 92 rooms with bath. 2 restaurants (reservations advised). AE, D, DC, MC, V.*

Henniker

DINING AND LODGING

$$ **Colby Hill Inn.** The cookie jar is always full in this Federal Colonial farmhouse. Guests are greeted warmly by a pair of Great Danes. There is no shortage of relaxing activities: You can curl up with a book by the parlor fireplace, stroll through the gardens and 5 acres of meadow, ice-skate out back in winter, or play badminton in summer. Rooms in the main house contain antiques, Colonial reproductions, and such frills as lace curtains and Laura Ashley prints. Carriage-house rooms are more austere, with white walls, exposed beams, and plain country furnishings. The innovative breakfast might include scrambled eggs and Boursin on a puff pastry or raspberry-stuffed French toast. The dining menu is excellent; try the chicken Colby Hill (breast of chicken stuffed with lobster, leeks, and Boursin cheese), the autumn venison, or the New England seafood pie. ▥ *The Oaks, 03242,* ☎ *603/428–3281 or 800/531–0330,* ℻ *603/428–9218. 16 rooms with bath. Dining room (closed Mon., Tues.), pool, ice-skating, recreation room. Full breakfast included. AE, D, DC, MC, V.*

LODGING

$$ **Meeting House Country Inn.** This quiet, cozy 200-year-old farmhouse,
✻ located conveniently at the base of Pats Peak, considers itself a lovers'
getaway. The old barn has become a restaurant that specializes in
leisurely, romantic dining; and guests enjoy breakfast in bed, which is
served in a picnic basket. ☎ *Rte. 114 (Flanders Rd.), Henniker 03242,*
☎ *603/428–3228. 6 rooms with bath. Restaurant, hot tub, sauna. Full
breakfast included. AE, D, MC, V.*

$ **Henniker House.** This vintage Victorian inn has fine views of the tum-
bling Contoocook River and serves lavish breakfasts in the inn's solarium:
soufflé roulade with béchamel sauce and toasted pine nuts; cottage-cheese
crepes with fresh strawberries and pecans; and a sumptuous sausage-
and-apple bake. ☎ *Box 191, 2 Ramsdell Rd., 03242,* ☎ *603/428–3198.
4 rooms, 3 with bath. Full breakfast included. MC, V.*

Keene

DINING

$–$$ **Henry David's.** The ambience is that of a greenhouse, especially upstairs, with hundreds of plants hanging from and perched upon the ex-
posed beams of this airy restaurant that was once a private home. Start
with the crab bisque or tomato cheddar soup. The house sandwiches,
though named for area towns and villages, are thinly veiled versions
of such popular standbys as Reubens and turkey clubs. A nice light
lunch or dinner can be made of the sweet pea spinach salad served with
a variety of breads. ✗ *81 Main St.,* ☎ *603/352–0608. Reservations
accepted for 5 or more. DC, MC, V.*

$–$$ **One Seventy Six Main.** Similar in quality to Henry David's, this restau-
rant distinguishes itself with a pub serving a vast selection of international beers. The menu features seafood, burgers, pasta, and a delightfully
spicy summer gazpacho. ✗ *176 Main St.,* ☎ *603/357–3100. AE, D,
MC, V.*

LODGING

$ **Carriage Barn Guest House.** The Main Street location across from Keene
State College puts major sights within walking distance. The house is
furnished with antiques and quilts, most of which were made locally;
the nightstands, for example, are fashioned out of antique desks from
a local school. In the warmer months, breakfast is served in a sum-
merhouse out under a willow tree. ☎ *358 Main St., 03431,* ☎ *603/357–
3812. 4 rooms with bath. CP. No credit cards.*

Milford

DINING

$$$ **Colonel Shepard House.** This Colonial house dates to 1757. Its four
dining rooms evoke romance and intimacy, with dark-wood wainscoting,
Oriental rugs, and candlelight flickering off the gilt-frame prints. The
meat-intensive menu features filet mignon, veal, and rack of lamb, com-
plemented by nightly seafood specials and an extensive wine list. At-
tentive service is only enhanced by the French chef who makes pan sauces
to order for each entrée. ✗ *29 Mt. Vernon St.,* ☎ *603/672–2527. Reser-
vations advised. AE, D, MC, V. No lunch. Closed Mon.*

New London

DINING AND LODGING

$$ **New London Inn.** This rambling 1792 country inn in the center of town
has two porches, with rocking chairs, overlooking Main Street. Rooms
are individually decorated with mostly Victorian pieces; those in the
front of the house overlook the pretty campus of Colby-Sawyer College. The owners' son runs the kitchen, and his nouvelle-inspired menu
is likely to start with such specials as homemade pierogies filled with

apples, smoked duck, and Gorgonzola, served on a bed of carmelized onions with crème fraîche, and such entrées as sautéed medallion of monkfish in a sauce of fennel, black olives, ginger, and vermouth. He also offers a wide selection of wines by the glass. ☎ *140 Main St., 03257,* ☎ *603/526–2791 or 800/526–2791,* ☎ *603/526–2749. 29 rooms with bath. Restaurant (reservations advised; no lunch; closed Sun., Mon. off-season). Full breakfast included. AE, MC, V.*

$ **Pleasant Lake Inn.** This quiet, family-run property is aptly named for
❄ its location and ambience. The herbs, preserves, and other yummy things found on the dining table were grown on the property; all the baked goods come from the inn's kitchen. The original farmhouse dates from 1790, and that early country look has been maintained with sparse furnishings and a fireplace. ☎ *125 Pleasant St., Box 1030, 03257,* ☎ *603/ 526–6271 or 800/626–4907. 11 rooms with bath. Dining room (guests only). Full breakfast included. MC, V.*

North Sutton

DINING AND LODGING

$$ **Follansbee Inn.** Built in 1840, this quintessential country inn on the
❄ shore of Lake Kezar is a perfect fit in the 19th-century village of North Sutton, about 4 miles south of New London. Common rooms and bedrooms alike are loaded with collectibles and antiques. You can ice-fish on the lake as well as ski across it; the King Ridge ski area is just a few miles away. ☎ *Rte. 114, 03260,* ☎ *603/927–4221 or 800/626–4221. 23 rooms, 11 with bath. Dining room (guests only), skating, cross-country skiing, tobogganing. Full breakfast included. MC, V.*

Peterborough

DINING

$$$ **Boilerhouse Restaurant.** A mid-19th-century woolen mill has been converted into offices, shops, a café, and this upscale restaurant, which manages a diverse menu that includes everything from venison to pasta. Dinner entrées include gravlax of Norwegian salmon (cured on the premises with salt, sugar, dill, and vodka, then served with Bermuda onions, capers, and caviar) or veal with forest mushrooms in a brandy-Madeira cream sauce. Popular lunch entrées are tricolor tortellini with red pepper, and the lemon chicken with pine nuts and capers. A dish of homemade ice cream tops things off nicely. ✗ *Rte. 202 S,* ☎ *603/ 924–9486. Reservations advised. D, MC, V.*

$–$$ **Latacarta.** Put a New Age restaurant in an old movie theater and you get the essence of Peterborough. The low-fat, low-cholesterol menu, which changes daily, features foods from a variety of cultures. Salt-free and reduced-calorie dishes are available on request. You won't believe that the incredible desserts—Indian pudding, pear crisp—are all sugar-free. ✗ *6 School St.,* ☎ *603/924–6878. Reservations advised. AE, MC, V. Closed Mon.*

Plainfield

LODGING

$$–$$$ **Home Hill Country Inn.** This restored 1800 mansion set back from the river on 25 acres of meadow and woods is a tranquil place. The chef-owner, from Brittany, has given the inn a French influence with 19th-century patrician antiques and collectibles. A suite in the guest house is a romantic hideaway. The dining room serves classic and nouvelle French cuisine. ☎ *River Rd., 03781,* ☎ *603/675–6165. 7 rooms with bath, 2 suites. Pool, 6-hole golf course, tennis, cross-country skiing. CP. MC, V.*

Temple
DINING AND LODGING

$ **Birchwood Inn.** Thoreau slept here, probably on his way to climb Monadnock or to visit Jaffrey or Peterborough. In 1825 Rufus Porter painted the mural in the dining room. Country furniture and handmade quilts outfit the bedrooms, as they did in 1775 when the house was new and no one dreamed it would someday be listed in the National Register of Historic Places. In the dining room, she-crab soup and roast duckling are two Saturday-night specials, and if you're really lucky you might find cream-cheese pecan pie or one of the fresh fruit cobblers on the blackboard dessert menu. Everything is cooked to order, so allow time for lingering. ☎ *Rte. 45, 03084, ☎ 603/878–3285. 7 rooms, 5 with bath. Restaurant (reservations required; BYOB; no lunch, closed Sun., Mon.), piano. Full breakfast included. No credit cards.*

Troy
DINING AND LODGING

$$ **Inn at East Hill Farm.** At this 1830 farmhouse inn, children are not only allowed, they are expected. In fact, if you don't have kids, you may be happier elsewhere. Children collect the eggs for the next day's breakfast—they milk the cows and feed the animals, too. Later they participate in the likes of arts and crafts, storytelling, hiking, and games. Three meals are included in the room rate, all served family-style. The innkeepers schedule weekly sleigh rides or hay rides, and can whip up a picnic lunch for families who want to spend the day away. Almost anything you want in an easygoing family vacation is available here, including baby-sitting. ☎ *Monadnock St., 03465, ☎ 603/242–6495 or 800/242–6495, FAX 603/242–7709. 42 rooms with bath. Restaurant, indoor pool, 2 outdoor pools, sauna, tennis, horseback riding, boating, waterskiing, fishing. AP required. D, MC, V.*

West Chesterfield
DINING AND LODGING

$$$ **Chesterfield Inn.** The inn sits on a rise above Route 9, the main Brattleboro–Keene road, surrounded by gardens. The rooms, which are quite spacious, are tastefully decorated with armoires, fine antiques, and period-style fabrics, but they also smack of luxury with air-conditioning, refrigerators, and telephones in the bathroom. The dining room entrance leads through the kitchen, allowing a sneak preview of what's to come. Favorites include country pâté and duck with mango chutney. ☎ *Rte. 9, 03466, ☎ 603/256–3211 or 800/365–5515, FAX 603/256–6131. 11 rooms with bath, 2 suites. Restaurant (reservations advised). Full breakfast included. AE, D, DC, MC, V.*

Wilton
DINING

$$ **Ram in the Thicket.** The first course of this inviting prix-fixe menu might be artichoke hearts and mushrooms in brie served warm over French bread or perhaps a kalamata-olive paste on polenta—the choices change monthly but are always delicious. Do try the filet mignon—which is prepared to order—the rack of lamb, or the pork tenderloin. The late 19th-century house has a screened-in porch that's perfect for summer dining. ✗ *Off Rte. 101, ½ mi from Wilton, ☎ 603/654–6440. Reservations advised. AE. Closed Mon., Tues. No lunch.*

The Arts

The **Arts Center at Brickyard Pond** (Keene, ☎ 603/358–2168) offers year-round performances in music, theater, and dance. **Claremont Opera House** (Claremont, ☎ 603/542–4433) is a beautifully restored

19th-century opera house with plays and musicals from September through May. **Hopkins Center** (Dartmouth College, Hanover, ☎ 603/646–2422) has a 900-seat theater for film and music, a 400-seat theater for plays, and a black-box theater for new plays and the Dartmouth Symphony Orchestra. Each summer, the Big Apple Circus performs here.

Music

Monadnock Music (Peterborough, ☎ 603/924–7610) produces a summer series of concerts from mid-July to late August, with solo recitals, chamber music, and orchestra and opera performances by renowned musicians. Concerts usually take place evenings at 8 and Sunday at 4; many are free. The **Temple Town Band** (☎ 603/878–2829), founded in 1799 and believed to be the oldest band in the nation, and the **Apple Hill Chamber Players** (E. Sullivan, ☎ 603/847–3371) also produce summer concert series.

Theater

American Stage Festival (Rte. 13 N, Milford, ☎ 603/673–4005) is the state's largest professional theater. The season runs from early June through Labor Day and includes five Broadway plays and one new work, as well as a children's theater series. The **New London Barn Playhouse** (☎ 603/526–6570), a converted barn on Main Street, has been putting on nonequity Broadway-style and children's plays every summer since 1933. The **Palace Theatre** (80 Hanover St., Manchester, ☎ 603/668–5588) is the state's performing arts center—home to the state symphony and opera and the New Hampshire Philharmonic. It also hosts national tours and musical acts. The **Peterborough Players** (Stearns Farm, Middle Hancock Rd., Peterborough, ☎ 603/924–7585) have been taking summer stock theater to a new level for more than 60 seasons. The plays are held in a converted barn (now fully air-conditioned).

Nightlife

The **Colonial Theater** (95 Main St., Keene, ☎ 603/352–2033) opened in 1924 as a vaudeville stage. It still hosts some folk and jazz concerts and has the largest movie screen in town **Del Rossi's Trattoria** (Rtes. 137 and 101, Dublin, ☎ 603/563–7195) brings big names in jazz, bluegrass, and blues to the Monadnock region Friday and Saturday nights. Come early and dine on homemade pasta in this unpretentious Italian restaurant (reservations advised). **Folkway** (85 Grove St., Peterborough, ☎ 603/924–7484), a restaurant and coffeehouse, has become a New England institution, with such artists as the Story, Greg Brown, Trout Fishing in America, and dozens of local musicians. The best seats are saved for those who have dinner, too (reservations advised). The crafts shop, upstairs, has a great selection of folk tapes and CDs, as well as the work of local artisans and weavers. **Rynborn** (Main St., Antrim, ☎ 603/588–6162) has Chicago blues on Saturday night, although the room is too small for dancing. The restaurant upstairs offers good food before the show. **Peter Christian's Tavern** (39 S. Main St., Hanover, ☎ 603/643–2345) has live folk and jazz performances Tuesday and Thursday evenings. The **Moving Company Dance Center** (76 Railroad, Keene, ☎ 603/357–2100) holds theme dances on Friday and Saturday nights, which range from swing to line dancing to Latin ballroom.

Western and Central New Hampshire Essentials

Getting Around

BY BUS
Concord Trailways (☎ 800/639–3317) runs from Concord to Berlin and from Littleton to Boston. **Advance Transit** (☎ 802/295–1824) services towns in the upper valley.

BY CAR
Most people who travel up from Massachusetts do so on I–93, which passes through Manchester and Concord before cutting a path through the White Mountains. Interstate 89 connects Concord to the Merrimack Valley and continues on to Vermont. Interstate 91 follows the Vermont border and the Connecticut River. On the New Hampshire side, routes 12 and 12A are picturesque but slower back roads. route 4 crosses the region, winding between Lebanon and the seacoast. Farther south, Route 101 connects Keene and Manchester, then continues to the seacoast.

Important Addresses and Numbers

EMERGENCIES
Dartmouth Hitchcock Medical Center (1 Medical Ctr. Dr., Lebanon, ☎ 603/650–5000). **Cheshire Medical Center** (580 Court St., Keene, ☎ 603/352–4111). **Monadnock Community Hospital** (452 Old Street Rd., Peterborough, ☎ 603/924–7191). **Elliot Hospital** (1 Elliot Way, Manchester, ☎ 603/669–5300 or 800/235–5468). **Concord Hospital** (250 Pleasant St., Concord, ☎ 603/225–2711). **Nashua Memorial Hospital** (8 Prospect St., Nashua, ☎ 603/883–5521).

Monadnock Mutual Aid (☎ 603/352–1100) responds to any emergency, from a medical problem to a car fire.

VISITOR INFORMATION
Hours are generally weekdays 9 to 5. **Concord Chamber of Commerce** (244 N. Main St., Concord 03301, ☎ 603/224–2508). **Hanover Chamber of Commerce** (Box A–105, Hanover 03755, ☎ 603/643–3115). **Lake Sunapee Business Association** (Box 400, Sunapee 03782, ☎ 603/763–2495 or, in New England, 800/258–3530). **Manchester Chamber of Commerce** (889 Elm St., Manchester 03101, ☎ 603/666–6600). **Monadnock Travel Council** (48 Central Sq., Keene 03431, ☎ 603/352–1303). **Peterborough Chamber of Commerce** (Box 401, Peterborough 03458, ☎ 603/924–7234). **Southern New Hampshire Visitor & Convention Bureau** (Box 115, Windham 03087, ☎ 800/932–4282).

NEW HAMPSHIRE ESSENTIALS

Arriving and Departing

By Bus
Greyhound (☎ 800/231–2222) and its subsidiary **Vermont Transit** (☎ 603/228–3300 or 800/451–3292) link the cities of New Hampshire with major cities in the eastern United States. **Peter Pan Bus Lines** (☎ 800/237–8747) also serves the state.

By Car
Interstate 93 is the principal north–south route through Manchester, Concord, and central New Hampshire. To the west, I–91 traces the Vermont–New Hampshire border. To the east, I–95, which is a toll road, passes through the coastal area of southern New Hampshire on its way

from Massachusetts to Maine. I–89 travels from Concord to Montpelier and Burlington, Vermont.

By Plane

Manchester Airport (☎ 603/624–6556), the state's largest, has scheduled flights by USAir, Delta, Continental, Northwest Airlink, United, and TWA. **Keene Airport**'s (☎ 800/272–5488) Colgan Air offers flights to Rutland, Vermont, and Newark, New Jersey. **Lebanon Municipal Airport** (☎ 603/298–8878), near Dartmouth College, is served by Delta Business Express and USAir. **Pease International Tradeport** (☎ 603/433–6088), near Portsmouth, is served by Delta Business Express.

Getting Around

By Bus

Coast (Durham, ☎ 603/862–2328), **C&J** (☎ 603/742–5111), **Concord Trailways** (☎ 800/639–3317), and **Vermont Transit** (☎ 603/228–3300 or 800/451–3292) provide bus service among the state's cities and towns.

By Car

The official state map, available free from the Office of Travel and Tourism Development (*see* Important Addresses and Numbers, *below*), has directories for each of the tourist areas and is useful for navigating the state's major roads.

By Plane

Small local airports that handle charters and private planes are **Berlin Airport** (☎ 603/449–7383) in Milan, **Concord Airport** (☎ 603/224–4033), **Jaffrey Municipal Airport** (☎ 603/532–7763), **Laconia Airport** (☎ 603/524–5003), **Nashua Municipal Airport** (☎ 603/882–0661), and **Sky Haven Airport** (☎ 603/332–0005) in Rochester.

Guided Tours

Bike Tours

Bike & Hike New Hampshire's Lakes (☎ 603/968–3775), **Bike the Whites** (☎ 800/933–3902), **Great Outdoors Hiking & Biking Tours** (☎ 603/356–3271 or 800/525–9100), **Monadnock Bicycle Touring** (Box 19, Harrisville 03450, ☎ 603/827–3925), **New England Hiking Holidays** (☎ 603/356–9696 or 800/869–0949), and **Sunapee Inns Hike & Bike Tours** (☎ 800/662–6005) organize bike tours.

Skiing

Scandinavian settlers who came to New Hampshire's high, handsome, rugged peaks in the late 1800s brought their skis with them. Skiing got its modern start in the Granite State in the 1920s, with the cutting of trails on Cannon Mountain.

Today there are 28 ski areas in New Hampshire, ranging from the old, established slopes (Cannon, Cranmore, Wildcat) to the most contemporary (Attitash, Loon, Waterville Valley). Whatever the age of the area, traditional activities—carnivals, races, ski instruction, family services—are important aspects of the skiing experience. On the slopes, skiers encounter some of the toughest runs in the country alongside some of the gentlest, and the middle range is a wide one.

The New Hampshire ski areas participate in a number of promotional packages allowing a sampling of different resorts. There's Ski 93 (referring to resorts along I–93), Ski New Hampshire, Ski the Mt. Washington Valley, and more.

Dining

New Hampshire's visitors need not live on boiled dinners alone. The state is home to some of the best seafood in the country, and not just lobster, but everything from salmon pie to steamed mussels, fried clams to seared tuna steak. Each region has its share of country French dining rooms and nouvelle American kitchens, but the best advice is to eat where the locals do. That can be anywhere from a local greasy-spoon diner to an out-of-the-way inn whose chef builds everything—including the home-churned butter—from scratch. And while it's still in vogue to stop by country stores for fudge and penny candy, roadside farmstands and small gourmet groceries—stocking the likes of cranberry chutnies and hot pepper jellies—are growing in popularity.

CATEGORY	COST*
$$$$	over $35
$$$	$25–$35
$$	$15–$25
$	under $15

*per person for a three-course meal, excluding drinks, service, and 8% meals tax

Lodging

New Hampshire has long been a mecca for summer vacationers. In the mid-19th century, wealthy Bostonians would pack up and move to their grand summer homes in the countryside for two- or three-month stretches. Today many of these homes have been restored and converted into country inns, offering the truest local experience. An occupational hazard of innkeepers is that they invariably know, and feel compelled to tell you, where to find the best off-the-beaten-track restaurant, secluded hiking trail, and heretofore undiscovered antiques shop. Inns vary greatly in size and feel. The smallest have only a couple of rooms; typically, they're done in period style. The largest let more than 30 rooms and offer private baths, fireplaces, even hot tubs. A few of the grand old resorts still stand, with their world-class cooking staffs and their tradition of top-notch service. And for those who prefer cable TV to precious antiques, the hotel chains are well represented in the larger cities and along major highways.

CATEGORY	COST*
$$$$	over $190
$$$	$145–$190
$$	$100–$145
$	under $100

*All prices are for a standard double room during peak season, with no meals unless noted, and excluding service charge and 8% occupancy tax.

Important Addresses and Numbers

Visitor Information

New Hampshire Office of Travel and Tourism Development (Box 1856, Concord 03302, ☎ 603/271–2343). **Events, foliage, and ski conditions** (☎ 800/258–3608 or 800/262–6660). **New Hampshire State Council on the Arts** (40 N. Main St., Concord 03301, ☎ 603/271–2789).

New Hampshire Campground Owners Association (Box 320, Twin Mountain 03595, ☎ 800/822–6764) will send you a list of all private, state, and national-forest campgrounds.

INDEX

Fodor's Travel Publications

Available at bookstores everywhere, or call 1–800–533–6478, 24 hours a day.

Gold Guides

U.S.

Alaska

Arizona

Boston

California

Cape Cod, Martha's Vineyard, Nantucket

The Carolinas & the Georgia Coast

Chicago

Colorado

Florida

Hawaii

Las Vegas, Reno, Tahoe

Los Angeles

Maine, Vermont, New Hampshire

Maui

Miami & the Keys

New England

New Orleans

New York City

Pacific North Coast

Philadelphia & the Pennsylvania Dutch Country

The Rockies

San Diego

San Francisco

Santa Fe, Taos, Albuquerque

Seattle & Vancouver

The South

U.S. & British Virgin Islands

USA

Virginia & Maryland

Waikiki

Washington, D.C.

Foreign

Australia & New Zealand

Austria

The Bahamas

Bermuda

Budapest

Canada

Cancún, Cozumel, Yucatán Peninsula

Caribbean

China

Costa Rica, Belize, Guatemala

Cuba

The Czech Republic & Slovakia

Eastern Europe

Egypt

Europe

Florence, Tuscany & Umbria

France

Germany

Great Britain

Greece

Hong Kong

India

Ireland

Israel

Italy

Japan

Kenya & Tanzania

Korea

London

Madrid & Barcelona

Mexico

Montréal & Québec City

Moscow, St. Petersburg, Kiev

The Netherlands, Belgium & Luxembourg

New Zealand

Norway

Nova Scotia, New Brunswick, Prince Edward Island

Paris

Portugal

Provence & the Riviera

Scandinavia

Scotland

Singapore

South Africa

South America

Southeast Asia

Spain

Sweden

Switzerland

Thailand

Tokyo

Toronto

Turkey

Vienna & the Danube

Fodor's Special-Interest Guides

Branson

Caribbean Ports of Call

The Complete Guide to America's National Parks

Condé Nast Traveler Caribbean Resort and Cruise Ship Finder

Cruises and Ports of Call

Fodor's London Companion

Gay USA

France by Train

Halliday's New England Food Explorer

Healthy Escapes

Italy by Train

Kodak Guide to Shooting Great Travel Pictures

Shadow Traffic's New York Shortcuts and Traffic Tips

Sunday in New York

Sunday in San Francisco

Walt Disney World, Universal Studios and Orlando

Walt Disney World for Adults

Where Should We Take the Kids? California

Where Should We Take the Kids? Family Adventures

Where Should We Take the Kids? Northeast